The Warren Court

ABC-CLIO SUPREME COURT HANDBOOKS

Peter G. Renstrom, Series Editor

ABC-CLIO SUPREME COURT HANDBOOKS

The Warren Court

Justices, Rulings, and Legacy

Melvin I. Urofsky

Virginia Commonwealth University

A B C   C L I O

Santa Barbara, California • Denver, Colorado • Oxford, England

Library of Congress Cataloging-in-Publication Data

Urofsky, Melvin I.
    The Warren court : justices, rulings, and legacy / Melvin I. Urofsky.
        p. cm. — (ABC-CLIO Supreme Court handbooks)
    Includes bibliographical references and index.
    ISBN 1-57607-160-X (hard : acid-free paper) — ISBN 1-57607-593-1 (e-book : acid-free paper)
    1. United States. Supreme Court—History—20th century. 2. Warren,
Earl 1891–1974. 3. Constitutional history—United States. I. Title.
II. Series.
  KF8742 .U764 2001
  347.73'26—dc21   2001-000011

07 06 05 04 03 02 01   10 9 8 7 6 5 4 3 2 1

ABC-CLIO, Inc.
130 Cremona Drive, P.O. Box 1911
Santa Barbara, California 93116-1911

This book is printed on acid-free paper ∞ .
Manufactured in the United States of America

For Emma Beatrice Urofsky
Like her grandmother, an ever-changing delight

Contents

Series Foreword

T here is an extensive literature on the U.S. Supreme Court, but it contains discussion familiar largely to the academic community and the legal profession. The ABC-CLIO Supreme Court series is designed to have value to the academic and legal communities also, but each volume is intended as well for the general reader who does not possess an extensive background on the Court or American constitutional law. The series is intended to effectively represent each of fourteen periods in the history of the Supreme Court with each of these fourteen eras defined by the chief justice beginning with John Jay in 1789. Each Court confronted constitutional and statutory questions that were of major importance to and influenced by the historical period. The Court's decisions were also influenced by the values of each of the individual justices sitting at the time. The issues, the historical period, the justices, and the Supreme Court's decisions in the most significant cases will be examined in the volumes of this series.

ABC-CLIO's Supreme Court series provides scholarly examinations of the Court as it functioned in different historical periods and with different justices. Each volume contains information necessary to understand each particular Court and an interpretative analysis by the author of each Court's record and legacy. In addition to representing the major decisions of each Court, institutional linkages are examined as well—the political connections among the Court, Congress, and the president. These relationships are important for several reasons. Although the Court retains some institutional autonomy, all the Court's justices are selected by a process that involves the other two branches. Many of the significant decisions of the Court involve the review of actions of Congress or the president. In addition, the Court frequently depends on the other two branches to secure compliance with its rulings.

The authors of the volumes in the ABC-CLIO series were selected with great care. Each author has worked extensively with the Court, the period, and the personalities about which he or she has written. ABC-CLIO wanted each of the volumes to examine several common themes, and each author agreed to work within certain guidelines. Each author was free, however, to develop the content of each volume, and many of the volumes advance new or distinctive conclusions about the Court under examination.

Each volume contains four substantive chapters. The first chapter will introduce the Court and the historical period in which it served. The second chapter will examine each of the justices who sat on the particular Court. The third chapter will represent the most significant decisions rendered by the particular Court. Among other things, the impact of the historical period and the value orientations of the individual justices will be developed. A fourth and final chapter will address the impact of each particular Court on American constitutional law—its doctrinal legacy.

Each volume will contain several features designed to make the volume more valuable to those whose previous exposure to the Supreme Court and American constitutional law is limited. Each volume will have a reference section that will contain brief entries on some of the people, statutes, events, and concepts introduced in the four substantive chapters. Entries in this section are arranged alphabetically. Each volume will also contain a glossary of selected legal terms used in the text. Following each of the four chapters, a list of sources used in the chapter and suggestions for further reading will appear. Each volume will also have a comprehensive annotated bibliography. A listing of Internet sources is presented at the end of the bibliography. Finally, there will be a comprehensive subject index and a list of cases (with citation numbers) discussed in each volume. ABC-CLIO is delighted with the quality of scholarship represented in each volume and is proud to offer this series to the reading public.

Permit me to conclude with a personal note. This project has been an extraordinarily rewarding undertaking for me as series editor. Misgivings about serving in this capacity were plentiful at the outset of the project. After tending to some administrative business pertaining to the series, securing authors for each volume was the first major task. I developed a list of possible authors after reviewing previous work and obtaining valuable counsel from several recognized experts in American constitutional history. In virtually every instance, the first person on my list agreed to participate in the project. The high quality of the series was assured and enhanced as each author signed on. I could not have been more pleased. My interactions with each author have been most pleasant, and the excellence of their work will be immediately apparent to the reader. I sincerely thank each author.

Finally, a word about ABC-CLIO and its staff. ABC-CLIO was enthusiastic about the project from the beginning and has done everything necessary to make this series successful. I am very appreciative of the level of support I have received from ABC-CLIO. Alicia Merritt, senior acquisitions editor, deserves special recognition. She has held my hand throughout the project. She has facilitated making this project a reality in every conceivable way. She has encouraged me from the beginning, provided invaluable counsel, and given me latitude to operate as I wished while keeping me on track at the same time. This project would not have gotten off the ground without Alicia, and I cannot thank her enough.

—Peter G. Renstrom

Preface

When I received an invitation to write about the Warren Court, it appealed to me for several reasons, chief among them that a great deal of new research has appeared within the last tenyears, and I wanted to see how much this would affect my earlier interpretation of the Court's work. Also, given the format of this series, I would have the opportunity to evaluate the legacy left by Earl Warren and his associates.

All history is interpretive. Once you get past the "fact" that John F. Kennedy took the oath of office as president on January 20, 1961, or that Dwight Eisenhower nominated Earl Warren to be chief justice on September 30, 1953, then we have to interpret what happened next, either in the Kennedy administration or during Warren's tenure in the center chair. Interpretation is, however, subjective, and no matter how careful one is with historical facts, we see them in the light of our own experiences, biases, and interests. This is not a matter of "liberal" or "conservative," whatever those terms may mean, but our view of the role of the Supreme Court in American society, our notions of what courts can and cannot do, our beliefs in how a democratic society works.

More than most courts the so-called "Warren Court" arouses fierce debate on this issue. One never hears impassioned comments on the Court during Fred Vinson's tenure, and, with the exception of *Roe v. Wade* (1973), most people view the work of the Burger Court with a yawn of disdain. But more than three decades after Warren resigned from the Court, we are still debating the work that he and his brethren did.

Go into any constitutional law course in any American university, and the centerpiece cases will be those of the Warren Court: *Brown v. Board of Education* (1954) ending state-sponsored school segregation; *Engel v. Vitale* (1962) banning mandatory prayers from the schools; *Gideon v. Wainwright* (1963) guaranteeing the right to counsel; *Reynolds v. Sims* (1964) establishing the one-person, one-vote rule; *New York Times v. Sullivan* (1965), freeing newspapers from the threat of libel for investigative reporting; *Griswold v. Connecticut* (1965) establishing a right to privacy; *Miranda v. Arizona* (1966) setting out the famous rule to protect persons accused of a crime; *Brandenburg v. Ohio* (1969) interring the use of seditious libel to chill free speech; and the list goes on. This is an enormous legacy, all the more amazing in that not a single one of these decisions has been overruled or even seriously mitigated.

The reader of this volume should know that I favor the Warren Court's commitment to what has been called a jurisprudence of a living Constitution, i.e., one that is interpreted and reinterpreted so as to make that eighteenth-century document applicable to the conditions we face today. I believe that if the adherents of so-called "original intent" had to live with the fruits of a strict application of their doctrine they would soon be very uncomfortable. People, nations, and institutions change over time, and it is part of the great genius of the American Constitution that its Framers made it flexible enough to adapt to changing circumstances.

But my judicial hero is not Earl Warren, but Louis Dembitz Brandeis, whom many scholars see as the great twentieth-century voice of judicial restraint. How can I square my approval of judicial activism by the Warren Court and Brandeis's call for judicial restraint? The answer is easy. Although Brandeis fought against use of the Fourteenth Amendment's Due Process Clause by conservative judges to void reform legislation, he shared the belief articulated by Harlan Fiske Stone that Courts had a special role to play in the protection of individual liberties. The Warren Court did show judicial restraint when it came to all matters not affecting civil rights and civil liberties, but it played what I believe to be an appropriate role for courts in our American system—the special guardian of the people's liberties.

Laura Kalman has suggested that many of us now teaching in universities and law schools were caught up, either ourselves or by our teachers, in the Warren Court's commitment to democracy and justice, and that we see the Warren Court as the norm, that is, we believe this is how the Court should act. This is only partially true. Just as the conservative justices of the 1920s and 1930s overstepped their bounds in a frenzied effort to protect property, so it is possible for a liberal court to overstep its bounds as well. As I hope to show in the pages that follow, most of the time the Court acted appropriately, and if it struck out in new directions, there was legitimate ground for it to do so. But sometimes it went too far, and the work of the Burger Court in part consisted of correcting those excesses.

All in all, however, I think it fair to say that even if they stretched the bounds of judicial precedent, the justices of the Warren Court asked the right questions: Should people be discriminated against because of the color of their skins? Should the state be examining the marital bedchamber for signs of contraceptives? Should people accused of crimes be informed of their rights? And in these and many other areas, I think the Warren Court gave the American people the right answers.

This is not, however, a book of apologetics about the Warren Court. My interpretation is admittedly subjective, but it is also informed by my training in both history and law, and I hope that this training will be as evident as my sympathy toward many of the Court's decisions. The verdict, as always, is in the hands of the reader.

Finally, I would like to thank Peter Renstrom for inviting me to write this volume in the series, and I want to thank Alicia Merritt and Melanie Stafford of ABC-CLIO for their help; it has truly been a pleasure to work with them.

The book is dedicated to my granddaughter Emma, with the hope that she will not only enjoy but continue the Warren Court's fight for democracy, justice, and individual liberties.

Melvin I. Urofsky

The Warren Court

PART ONE

Justices, Rulings, and Legacy

The Warren Court and the Period

I f one is to understand the Warren Court properly, then one has to look at the two decades preceding Earl Warren's nomination to the bench. During that era events both political and jurisprudential laid the foundation on which the Warren Court built its home. Politically, we need to look at the struggle between Franklin Roosevelt's New Deal and the Court in the mid-1930s, the civil rights movement that gained steam after World War II, and the Red Scare that culminated in McCarthyism.

Jurisprudentially, the Court's agenda changed sharply beginning in the 1930s. Prior to that time, questions of economic rights dominated each term's docket; afterward issues of individual liberties took more and more of the Court's time. As a result, the doctrine of substantive due process, which conservatives had relied on since the 1890s to strike down reform legislation, fell into disuse. A key event here is the famous fourth footnote in Justice Harlan Fiske Stone's opinion in an otherwise minor case, *United States v. Carolene Products Co.* (1938). Most important is the debate over incorporation, that is, the application to the states of the liberties guaranteed in the Bill of Rights through the Fourteenth Amendment's due process clause. Once we examine these issues, then it will be possible to understand the issues and decisions of the Warren Court.

The Roosevelt Era

The administration of Franklin Roosevelt, which took office in March 1933, faced the greatest domestic crisis in the nation's history since the Civil War. Between 1929 and 1932 industrial production dropped more than half, while industrial construction fell from $949 million to a scant $74 million. Steel plants, the backbone of an industrial economy, operated at 12 percent of capacity, and the stock market average, which had stood at 452 on September 3, 1929, bottomed out at 52 in July 1932. But vast human suffering marked the real tragedy of the Great Depression: thirteen million people unemployed; two million homeless and riding the country in boxcars; people living in tarpapered shacks dubbed "Hoovervilles"; and families fighting outside the back doors of restaurants for scraps of garbage. "The country needs," declared the Democratic presidential candidate in 1932, "and, unless I mistake its temper, the country demands bold, persistent experimentation" (Leuchtenburg 1963, 9).

Roosevelt and his advisors recognized that the old dogmas no longer held true. Government could no longer stand by idly waiting for the business cycle to restore an equilibrium—if, in fact, it ever would. In one area after another they proposed, and Congress quickly passed, legislation dealing with banking, agriculture, labor, industry, conservation, and a host of other topics. It is not necessary to go into the details of the legislation; the important thing is how the Court dealt with these measures.

The enormous mass of legislation churned out in the first hundred days of the New Deal rested on constitutional bases as questionable as some of the economic theories that animated those statutes. Moreover, they had been drafted for the most part by enthusiastic, but inexperienced, young lawyers under impossible time constraints—Roosevelt had given the committee that drew up the National Industrial Recovery Act just one week to overhaul the nation's business structure, for example. In general, the drafters relied for constitutional authorization on the relatively permissive mandates of the commerce clause and the taxing power, with the emergency powers thrown in to bolster their case. When they did not quite know how to specify what they wanted, they indicated a general goal and delegated authority to the president to work out the particulars. New Deal planners often ignored both traditional constitutional limits as well as the division of powers between state and national governments in a federal system. The states, in their view, had already shown their inability to deal with a nationwide crisis, so the federal government should assume full powers.

Even if there had been no conservative bloc on the Supreme Court, the sloppy legislative draftsmanship would inevitably have caused the administration trouble with the judiciary. The cavalier attitude of many New Dealers toward constitutional considerations bothered all the members of the Court, as did the administration's seeming indifference to basic constitutional doctrine. Even the liberal bloc of Louis D. Brandeis, Harlan Fiske Stone, and Benjamin N. Cardozo found some New Deal measures personally distasteful. The conservatives—James C. McReynolds, Pierce Butler, Willis Van Devanter, and George Sutherland—despised the New Deal program as anti-American and socialistic and condemned it out of hand as unconstitutional. The so-called Four Horsemen could usually garner the fifth vote they needed from the two men in the middle, Chief Justice Charles Evans Hughes and Associate Justice Owen J. Roberts.

New Dealers had hoped that before the courts heard challenges, their programs would be so well entrenched as to withstand judicial hostility. In fact, when the Court began to hear cases involving federal legislation in December 1934, the administration quickly paid the costs of sloppy procedures, poor draftsmanship, and inadequate counsel. The two cases that stand out challenged the New Deal head-on, and seemingly implied that there could be no constitutional basis for reform.

The Schechter brothers operated a kosher poultry business in Brooklyn, and the government charged them with violating the live poultry code provisions on wages, hours, and fair trade requirements of the National Industrial Recovery Act, the omnibus bill designed to revivify the nation's economy. The government prepared an elaborate exhibit to show the interstate implications of the Schechter plant, but as one of the Justice Department officials later conceded, "no amount of economic research to unearth judicially noticeable matter could . . . show in a convincing manner that these practices in New York substantially affected the interstate poultry market" (Irons 1982, 91).

On "Black Monday," May 27, 1935, the Supreme Court unanimously struck down the National Industrial Recovery Act in *Schechter v. United States*. Although the Court as a matter of jurisprudential practice normally tries to decide cases on as narrow a basis as possible, Chief Justice Hughes posed three major questions in *Schechter* and proceeded to answer them all: Did the economic crisis create extraordinary governmental powers? Had the Congress lawfully delegated power to the president? Did the act exceed the government's authority under the commerce clause? This radical departure from the conservative procedures of the Court convinced many observers that not only Hughes, but the entire bench, wanted to make sure that after the Court had killed it, the National Industrial Recovery Act would stay dead.

The delegation problem, if that had been the only difficulty with the statute, could easily have been remedied. The ruling that emergencies did not create new powers might have cramped the administration somewhat but would still have been acceptable if the Court had at least conceded the government's power to regulate these industries. But Hughes—joined by all his colleagues—in answering the third question took an extremely restrictive a view of commerce. Hughes revived the old distinction between the direct and indirect effects of local activity on interstate commerce; he declared that only those intrastate activities that directly affected interstate commerce fell within the reach of the federal government's powers. The Schechter brothers' business had no direct effect—and in fact very little indirect effect—on interstate commerce and therefore could not be regulated by Congress.

In contrast to the National Industrial Recovery Act, the Agricultural Adjustment Act (AAA) did seem to work. Although it often suffered from the excessive enthusiasms of some administrators, the AAA began the necessary task of limiting production in order to raise the prices farmers received for their crops. During Roosevelt's first term, farmers' gross income rose more than 50 percent and rural debts fell sharply—although the drought of 1934 to 1935 may deserve as much credit as the government for limiting production. Congress also acted after the *Schechter* decision to relieve the farm program of those problems of delegation that had plagued the industrial program. But New Dealers still worried that a restrictive view of interstate commerce, such as Hughes had explicated, would invalidate agricultural legislation, and their fears came true in January 1936, when, by a six to three vote in *United States v. Butler*, the Court struck down the New Deal farm program.

The AAA processing tax provided the funds to underwrite crop subsidies and soil restrictions, and the drafters had felt confident that in the taxing power at least they had a recognized federal power. But officials of the Hoosac Mills Corporation attacked the levy, which they characterized as an integral part of an unconstitutional plan to control agricultural production. The government challenged their right to sue, because several cases—especially *Frothingham v. Mellon* (1923)—had held that taxpayers had no standing to question in court how the federal government spent its tax revenues. But the conservatives on the bench brushed this defense aside. The plaintiffs had not challenged just the tax and its uses, but the whole plan of which the tax, according to Justice Roberts, "is a mere incident of such regulation."

Roberts's majority opinion is the most tortured and confusing of all the Court's New Deal decisions. The tax, Roberts held, like the one in the Child Labor Act, could not be considered a true tax, for none of the proceeds went into the general coffers; instead, the tax purchased compliance with a program that went beyond the legitimate bounds of congressional power. Because of its local nature, agriculture could only be regulated by the state, and even if the sum of many local conditions had created a national problem, this still did not permit Congress to "ignore constitutional limitations" imposed by the Tenth Amendment.

Lest he be accused of substituting his own judgment of what constituted the general welfare in places of congressional discretion, Roberts explained how the Court operated. It did no more than lay the challenged statute next to the Constitution, and see if the former squares with the latter. This so-called T-square rule, if true, would represent judicial decision making at its most mechanistic; but as the Legal Realists and common sense indicate, judges rarely hear cases amenable to such a simplistic determination. Judges do read their biases into law; they do invade the legislative realm of policy making; and no better example can be found than in Roberts's *Butler* opinion.

The ruling brought forth strong protests from within and outside the Court. Justice Stone, considered the most knowledgeable person on the high bench regarding taxation, dissented sharply from what he considered Roberts's myopic view of the taxing power. Joined by Brandeis and Cardozo, Stone pointed out that unlike the child labor tax, which admittedly had been regulatory, the processing tax did no more than raise revenue; the regulatory part of the farm program came through appropriations. He also attacked Roberts's "tortured construction of the Constitution," and the majority's resort to *argumentum ad horrendum*, its claim that if this terrible program were approved, then Congress would attempt to regulate all areas of the nation's economic life. Finally, he cut through the hypocrisy of Roberts's denial that judges interposed their own views and attacked the notion that courts should sit in judgment of the legislative wisdom.

By 1936 the Court stood at the head of conservative protest against the New Deal. Nearly all the major parts of the so-called First New Deal, such as the National Industrial Recovery Act and the Agricultural Adjustment Act, had been struck down. The core bloc of McReynolds, Sutherland, Butler, and Van Devanter, often joined by Roberts, had made clear their objections to the extension of federal authority into areas they considered either the exclusive domain of the states or beyond the reach of either federal or state government. Even some conservative politicians felt the Court had gone too far; after the Court struck down a New York minimum wage law, for example, Herbert Hoover complained that the Court had taken away powers from the states that they legitimately had.

By early 1937 the stage had been set for the most serious constitutional crisis since the Civil War. The Supreme Court had opposed presidents before, as in Marshall's confrontation with Jefferson, and had in turn been challenged, as in Jackson's day. But never had the Court apparently set out to destroy an entire legislative program agreed on by both the executive and legislative branches. And, if the election results meant anything, never had the Court set itself up so completely against the will of the people. With the Depression still raging and Franklin Roosevelt promising action, Americans did not ask whether the president would challenge the Court, but when and how he would do so.

Two weeks after his inauguration, the president dropped a bombshell on the country in a message to Congress calling for the reform of the federal judiciary. In his February 5, 1937, message to Congress, Roosevelt claimed that a shortage of personnel had led to congested dockets in the federal courts, with the judges being unable to handle the case load expeditiously. The Supreme Court, for example, had denied 87 percent of petitions for writs of certiorari in a single year without citing its reasons. The problem could be attributed in part to "the capacity of the judges themselves," and the delicate question of aged or infirm judges could not be ignored. To remedy the situation and revitalize the courts, Roosevelt proposed that when a federal judge who had at least ten years' service on the bench waited more than six months past his seventieth birthday to resign or retire, the president could add a new judge to that particular court. In total, he could appoint no more than six justices to the Supreme Court and forty-four to the lower benches. The whole plan, according to Roosevelt, would serve the higher principle of efficient and effective administration of justice. Only a few days later in a "Fireside Chat" over the radio did Roosevelt admit that "we cannot yield our constitutional destiny to the personal judgment of a few men who, fearful of the future, would deny us the necessary means of dealing with the present" (Buhite and Levy 1992, 93).

For once, Roosevelt's famed political sagacity had deserted him, and he now appeared too clever for his own good. Opponents had little difficulty showing that what the president really wanted was to pack the courts—especially the high Court—

so as to get majorities friendly to New Deal measures. The sophistic allusion to 87 percent of petitions denied fooled no one; the president, and certainly his legal advisers, knew that the Court routinely dismissed such a large proportion because the petitions either were frivolous, had no merit, or raised no federal question. The age argument made no sense either; the oldest member of the Court, Louis Brandeis, had been consistently sympathetic to the New Deal, and although one might argue with the logic of the Four Horsemen, no one could deny that they carried their share of the Court's work. The age issue, in fact, offended many older senators. Carter Glass, then seventy-nine years old, pointed out that Littleton had been seventy-eight when he wrote his great treatise on property, and Coke had been eighty-one when he produced his most enduring commentaries on the laws of England. Roosevelt's secrecy also disturbed many of his supporters. He had neither mentioned court reform during the campaign nor consulted key members of Congress ahead of time; even within the cabinet only Homer Cummings had known about it. A mediocre attorney general, Cummings still thought in the political terms of the Democratic national chairman he had once been.

The political fight over the measure turned into the bitterest domestic battle of Roosevelt's twelve years in office, and provided a rallying point for all the different factions opposed to the New Deal. But it also served a useful purpose in triggering public debate over the role of the judiciary in the governmental system and its relationship to the public and responsibilities in the light of a national emergency. As had happened earlier during the Progressive Era, critics loosed a barrage of books and articles claiming that the Founding Fathers had never intended the Supreme Court to have the power of judicial review. Although that argument still reappears occasionally, it had already become a sterile debate by the time of the court fight. For over a century and a half the Court had gained power and respect as an institution to enforce constitutional limitations. By 1935 the majority of the American people expected the Court to act as a brake on social experimentation.

Brakes, however, can slow a vehicle down or make it stop completely. Unpopular decisions can be tolerated if the public views the Court as moving along in the same general direction as the other branches of government. However, the four conservatives on the Court in the mid-1930s did not want to just slow down the New Deal and deflect it from excesses (as liberals did in the *Schechter* decision), but to stop it altogether. McReynolds, Butler, Sutherland, and Van Devanter considered the New Deal completely wrong—its legislative program outside the narrow limits of federal power that they believed the Constitution allowed. They risked the considerable reserve of authority and legitimacy that the Court had built up over a century and a half and assumed that the public would applaud their efforts to turn back government from the positive steps Roosevelt had proposed toward the essentially negative government that Calvin Coolidge and Herbert Hoover had advocated.

Fortunately for the Court, however, the reservoir of respect it had built up protected it not only from irresponsibility from within, but also from political frustration from without. The court measure bogged down in the Senate; Majority Leader Joe Robinson of Arkansas, to whom Roosevelt had promised the next seat on the Court, thought he could get the president an immediate expansion of the bench to eleven if Roosevelt abandoned the rest of the plan, but the president refused to budge. Chief Justice Hughes, with the concurrence of Justices Van Devanter and Brandeis, publicly rebutted Roosevelt's charges of inefficiency. In a letter to Senator Burton K. Wheeler of Montana, a leading opponent of the president's plan, Hughes pointed out that the Court had just heard arguments on cases it had accepted for review barely a month earlier. An increase in justices, he asserted, instead of making the Court more efficient, would only cause delays because of "more judges to hear, more judges to confer, more judges to discuss, more judges to be convinced and to decide" (Leuchtenburg 1995, 140–141).

The death blow to the court-packing plan came in a series of decisions the Court handed down beginning in March 1937. Both Hughes and Roberts, each of whom had frequently given the conservative bloc its majority, now joined with Brandeis, Stone, and Cardozo to validate a string of state and federal measures.

On March 29, by a five-to-four vote, the Court sustained a Washington State minimum wage law in *West Coast Hotel Co. v. Parrish*. Roberts, who had written the decision invalidating a similar New York law a year earlier in *Morehead v. New York ex rel. Tipaldo* (1936), now joined the liberals in Chief Justice Hughes's opinion that *Adkins v. Children's Hospital* had been wrong and should be overruled. Hughes dismissed the relevance of the *Morehead* case by asserting that the Court had not reexamined the constitutionality of minimum wage legislation at that time because it had not been asked to do so. Sutherland, perhaps aware that the tide had turned against the conservatives, used his dissent to lash out against what he saw as the theory that the Constitution's meaning changed depending on current economic conditions.

West Coast Hotel Co. v. Parrish helped pull the Court back to the path it had followed prior to 1935 in sustaining state economic regulations under the broad rubric of the police power. That same day, March 29, 1937, the Court approved three federal statutes, each similar to one struck down a few years earlier. *Wright v. Vinton Branch* sanctioned a federal plan for farm debtor relief. Collective bargaining, the same issue that the Court had condemned in the *Carter v. Carter Coal Co.* (1936) case, now won the stamp of constitutionality in *Virginia Railway v. System Federation No. 40*. Finally, the Court approved a penalty tax on firearms, designed to help law enforcement officials, in *Sonzinsky v. United States*. This last case greatly encouraged reformers, for the majority had in essence validated the use of the taxing power for regulatory purposes in direct opposition to the Roberts decision in *Butler*.

Roosevelt later claimed that he had lost the battle but won the war, and to some degree this was true. The same month that he lost the battle, he made his first appointment to the Supreme Court, after Willis Van Devanter took advantage of the new law allowing judges to retire at full pay. The president named to the Court Senator Hugo L. Black of Alabama, a man despised by Southern conservatives for his populist liberalism. Black's nomination generated an ugly controversy when the press learned that he had once been a member of the Ku Klux Klan, but his later championing of civil liberties and civil rights more than confirmed the fact that he was neither a racist nor a bigot. Other changes soon followed. In January 1938 Justice Sutherland resigned, and Solicitor General Stanley F. Reed ascended the bench. When Benjamin Cardozo died toward the end of the year, the president nominated his friend, informal adviser, and the leader of the neo-Brandeisians, Harvard law professor Felix Frankfurter to the "scholar's seat." Within a week after Frankfurter took the oath of office in February 1939, Louis Brandeis finally acknowledged the toll of years and retired after twenty-three terms on the Court, to be succeeded by William O. Douglas, chairman of the Securities and Exchange Commission and former professor at the Yale Law School. Pierce Butler died in November, and Frank Murphy, the former governor of Michigan and then attorney general, took his place. Then, in February 1941, James C. McReynolds, the last of the Four Horsemen, resigned, and Roosevelt named Attorney General Robert H. Jackson, whose economic views diametrically opposed those of McReynolds.

Finally, in June, Chief Justice Charles Evans Hughes stepped down, and Roosevelt elevated Harlan Fiske Stone, a Republican, to the center chair. To replace him, the president chose Senator James Byrnes, but a little over a year later, Byrnes resigned to become Roosevelt's special assistant in the prosecution of the war. To take Byrnes's place, Roosevelt made his last appointment, Wiley Rutledge of Iowa, in February 1943. Thus, the only justice whom Roosevelt did not replace was Owen J. Roberts, who did not resign until after Roosevelt's death in 1945. But those who claimed that Roosevelt had replaced an independent judiciary with a rubber stamp misunderstood the character of the men he had appointed, as well as the institutional integrity of the Court itself. Frankfurter, Douglas, Jackson, and Black did not fit any cookie-cutter mold; they differed, sometimes bitterly, among themselves on a number of issues. They all agreed, however, on the need to preserve the independence and integrity of the Court from political interference. Roosevelt had appointed men who he believed shared his own expansive view of what powers the Constitution allocated to government, as he had every right to do.

But the issues that had been so important between 1933 and 1937 quickly faded from view. The Court's docket, which had been overwhelmingly concerned with questions of economic rights and regulation of labor and markets, quickly assumed new priorities: the protection of individual liberties. The Roosevelt Court, and in fact all Courts until that headed by Chief Justice William H. Rehnquist in the 1990s, assumed that as a matter of course Congress had broad authority under the commerce clause to regulate industry and labor. In a 1942 decision, *Wickard v. Filburn,* Justice Robert H. Jackson seemingly gave the legislature almost unlimited power to regulate all economic matters, no matter how local in nature. All that a legislature needed to do was provide a rational basis for its policy; the courts would not second-guess Congress or state legislatures on their judgment as to the wisdom of such policies.

The conservatives on the Court had used the doctrine of substantive due process ever since the 1890s to defeat reform legislation, whether of the type to regulate business or to protect labor. Under this doctrine, the due process clauses of the Fifth and Fourteenth Amendments placed severe limits on both the national and state governments. Due process referred not only to procedural matters in litigation and criminal prosecution, but, according to the conservatives, it also protected a body of basic rights, especially the ownership and untrammeled use of private property. Because of the use to which it had been put by these justices, substantive due process fell into disrepute after 1937 and would not be revived until the Warren Court realized that it could be used effectively to protect individual liberties, especially the rights of privacy and personal autonomy.

World War II

World War II completed the work of the New Deal insofar as economic recovery was concerned. Once idle factories now worked round the clock to produce tanks, guns, uniforms, and the other paraphernalia of war. Unemployment lines disappeared as able-bodied young men went into the armed services, and older men—as well as many women of all ages—reported to work in the factories. When the war ended, the prosperity continued, and one might have thought that America in the late 1940s and early 1950s would have been a happy and secure place in which to live. But all was not perfect.

African Americans had been and remained the most persecuted group in America. New Deal programs had benefited them to some degree, and the war had opened up new vistas to many others, but for the vast majority of blacks the United States in 1945 was no Garden of Eden. In the South a pervasive system of apartheid had been implemented following Reconstruction, rigidly separating blacks and whites and consigning the former slaves and their descendants to a markedly inferior position. Black children attended substandard and segregated schools and, compared to their white counterparts, few of them went much further than grade school. In stores and factories blacks held the most menial and low-paying jobs, while hundreds of thousands lived in impoverished conditions on small farms that they often rented at usurious rates from white owners.

Legal segregation did not exist in Northern states, and African Americans living above the Mason-Dixon line did enjoy some privileges denied to their Southern brethren. They could vote and in some cities enjoyed a fair amount of political power because of their numbers. They did not attend legally segregated schools, although de facto residential segregation in many areas led to the same results—whites in better schools and blacks in poorer ones. But the system at least allowed black children to go to high school and even to college, and much of what there was of a black middle class could be found in the Northern cities.

By statistical standards, the lot of black Americans certainly improved during and after the war. The number of Negroes, as they were then called, in manufacturing jobs shot up from 500,000 to 1.2 million during the war. In 1944 for the first time a black reporter was admitted to a presidential press conference, and three years later blacks gained access to the Senate press gallery. The National Association for the Advancement of Colored People (NAACP) had begun its legal campaign against legally sanctioned racial prejudice and had begun to win some notable victories. In 1944 the Supreme Court in *Smith v. Allwright* outlawed the white primary, a device that had enabled Southern states to exclude blacks from the only election that really counted. Two years later the Court outlawed racial segregation on interstate carriers in *Morgan v. Virginia*. Branch Rickey of the Brooklyn Dodgers signed a young black ballplayer named Jackie Robinson to a minor league contract, and in 1947 he became the first Negro to play in the major leagues.

These steps forward were merely symptoms of a growing mood in the black community. After a war fought against the racism of the Third Reich in Germany, people of color in the United States came to believe that they, too, should be treated as full and equal citizens of the republic. The great landmark decision in *Brown v. Board of Education* in 1954 did not trigger a civil rights movement, but rather resulted from one that had been growing for years.

As early as 1941, A. Philip Randolph, head of the all-Negro sleeping-car porters' union, had threatened to lead a march on Washington if the federal government did not do something to end the discrimination in the armed forces and in the distribution of federal contracts. To prevent the march Franklin Roosevelt issued an executive order against such practices and also set up a Fair Employment Practices Commission (FEPC) to ensure its enforcement. In fact, the order was widely ignored, but black people took notice. Instead of quietly submitting to discrimination, if they stood up and protested they would be heard, and if they protested long enough and loudly enough, something might happen. During the war years membership in the NAACP, the most important civil rights organization, increased from 50,000 to 450,000.

Activists began pushing for greater civil rights on a number of fronts. Perhaps nothing affronted the black community more than the discrimination its men faced in the armed forces. Although only 10 percent of the population, blacks made up 16 percent of those who served in the war, more than a million between 1942 and 1945. And they confronted discrimination at every turn. The navy took blacks only for menial positions, such as mess attendants. The army segregated Negroes in training camps and units, assumed that blacks were poor fighters and hesitated to send them into combat, and refused to train blacks as officers. But manpower shortages forced the army to use black units in combat where, of course, they behaved and fought as well as white troops. Beyond that, it instilled a new militancy that would not go away after the war.

President Harry S. Truman, beset by a multitude of crises after taking office, put up no protest when Congress killed the wartime FEPC. Later on, however, he asked Congress to create a permanent FEPC, and in December 1946 he appointed a distinguished panel to serve as the President's Commission on Civil Rights to recommend "more adequate means and procedures for the protection of the civil rights of the people of the United States" (*New York Times*, 6 Dec. 1946). The commission's report, "To Secure These Rights," issued in October 1947, defined the nation's civil rights agenda for the next generation. The commission noted the many restrictions on blacks, and urged that each person, regardless of race, color, creed, or national origin, should have access to equal opportunity in securing education, decent housing, and jobs. Among its proposals, the commission suggested antilynching and antipoll tax laws, a permanent FEPC, and the strengthening of the civil rights division of the Justice Department.

In a courageous act the president sent a special message to Congress on February 2, 1948, calling for prompt implementation of the commission's recommendations. The Southern delegations promptly blocked any action by threatening to filibuster. Unable to secure civil rights legislation from Congress, Truman moved ahead by using his executive authority. He bolstered the civil rights section of the Justice Department and directed it to assist private litigants in civil rights cases. He appointed William Hastie, the first black judge of a federal appeals court, and named several African Americans to high-ranking positions in the administration. Most important, by executive orders later in the year, the president abolished segregation in the armed forces and ordered full racial integration in the services.

The achievements of the Truman administration fell far short of the promises. While Southern control of key congressional committees blocked legislative action, the president never made civil rights a top priority of his administration. Aware that he had limited political capital, Truman chose not to expend it on an issue the outcome of which remained uncertain. Nonetheless, black Americans had gotten the attention of the nation's political leaders; not until they learned to exert political force of their own would they be able to move civil rights to the top of the country's agenda.

Despite the accomplishments of black soldiers and Truman's call for civil rights for all, white Southerners were not prepared to grant blacks even a semblance of racial equality, and in the years after the war racial hostilities sharpened perceptively in the South where, despite massive migrations to the North, more than two-thirds of all American Negroes still lived in the late 1940s. Just about everything remained seg-regated—schools, train stations, parks, libraries, hospitals, and drinking fountains.

With this attitude the South dug in its heels against the new black militancy. Black veterans came home and tried to vote and ran into both legal and physical opposition. Whites in 1946 killed three black men, and two of their wives, who sought to vote in Georgia. Negroes who had risked their lives for their country now wanted to take advantage of the G.I. Bill of Rights and tried to enroll in state-supported colleges and universities, only to be told that no blacks would be accepted. Despite the opposition they met and the physical danger that always lurked just beneath the sur-face, African Americans refused to give up, and in the years after the war increased their struggle against Jim Crow. Although the numbers seemed small in comparison to the great civil rights campaigns of the 1960s, blacks in the late 1940s tried to reg-ister to vote, to join unions, to go to schools. Moreover, these years also saw the cre-ation of or the strengthening of local institutions—especially churches and all-black colleges—to support the campaign.

Nor was the protest confined to the South. Blacks living in the North may not have faced the legal restrictions of Jim Crow, but they hardly counted themselves as fully equal citizens. As early as 1943, the Congress of Racial Equality (CORE) led sit-ins against Chicago restaurants that refused service to blacks. Because blacks could vote in the North, legislatures in eleven states and twenty-eight cities created state and local FEPCs between 1945 and 1951, and eighteen states enacted laws prohibit-ing discrimination in public accommodations. In 1948 the Supreme Court, in *Shelley v. Kraemer*, ruled that racially restrictive housing covenants could not be enforced in courts. While conditions still remained barely tolerable for most black Americans, a growing sense of frustration as well as a demand for change marked the decade after the war and set the stage for the *Brown* decision.

The Post–World War Era

Postwar eras are often marked by conservatism, as turmoil gives way to a desire for what Warren Harding called "normalcy." After twelve years of upheaval, of depres-sion followed by a world conflict, it would not have been surprising to find the Amer-ican people seeking respite from turbulence. In 1946 the American people elected a Republican Congress for the first time in sixteen years. Not only did conservatives tried to undo parts of the New Deal, they also ushered in the largest "red scare" in American history in an effort to root out alleged security risks in the government. The Red Scare of the late 1940s and early 1950s subverted civil liberties, destroyed the reputation of many innocent persons, and gave congressional investigations a bad name that lasted for years.

In January 1945 Representative John Rankin of Mississippi—racist, anti-Semitic, conservative, and bitterly anti-Roosevelt—secured House approval for the creation of a permanent Committee on Un-American Activities. When the Republicans took over the House two years later, J. Parnell Thomas became the committee's chairman, and he used the committee as a bludgeon against the Truman administration in the committee's quest to expose alleged communists and communist sympathizers in the government. Before long the committee had expanded its search into labor unions, colleges and universities, and even Hollywood. Any group, in fact, that committee members or staff suspected of being too liberal became a target.

Communism certainly posed a danger to the United States, as one could plainly see in the arrests and trials of Julius and Ethel Rosenberg, Judith Coplin, Klaus Fuchs, and others as spies. But with the exception of Alger Hiss (who was convicted for perjury, not spying), the committee contributed nothing to the exposure of espionage or subversion. The FBI—not the committee—uncovered the major postwar spy rings. The committee, however, kept repeating undocumented charges that communists had infiltrated government and society and demanded that the president "do something."

Harry Truman tried to act sensibly. He had access to FBI reports that the Communist Party of the United States had been largely discredited. It had fewer than 20,000 members, many of whom might have been better described as inactive sympathizers. But common sense and caution merely infuriated the witch hunters. When the president named a Temporary Commission on Employee Loyalty in November 1946, conservatives attacked it as a cover-up of previous sins and also an admission that there were communists in the government—otherwise why establish a commission?

Four months later, in response to this pressure, Truman issued Executive Order 9835, instituting the Federal Loyalty and Security Program. Under it the attorney general was to compile a list of subversive organizations, defined as "totalitarian, Fascist, Communist or subversive . . . or approving the commission of acts of force or violence to deny to others their constitutional rights." Membership in any group on the attorney general's list by itself constituted "reasonable doubt" as to an employee's loyalty and could be grounds for dismissal. The massive investigation of federal workers that followed included the collection of a great deal of unverified information from numerous sources, which could be the basis for dismissal as a security risk. In the end, the attorney general's office named eighty-two organizations, and although the list carried a disclaimer that the government of the United States did not believe in "guilt by association," right-wing groups and private employers often considered membership in any one of the proscribed organizations as evidence of disloyalty. The House Un-American Activities Committee condemned the attorney general's list as wholly inadequate; it issued its own report, naming 624 organizations that were allegedly communistic or dedicated to the overthrow of the government.

Truman's loyalty program paid little attention to civil liberties. The very word "loyalty" was problematic, encouraging zealots to bring charges on the flimsiest of evidence, as well as allowing people with grudges to file unfounded charges. While employees had a right to hear the charges against them, they did not have a right to confront their accusers, even at public hearings to determine guilt or innocence. So-called evidence produced by the FBI and other sources often amounted to little more than a file full of rumors and innuendo that the loyalty boards read but that remained closed to the accused. Many so-called subversives had done nothing more than belong to one or more left-leaning or even just liberal organizations named by Red hunters as communist.

Despite its abuses, the presidential security program never deteriorated to the mudslinging that characterized the congressional hearings. Between 1947 and 1951 the Civil Service Commission, charged with conducting the initial probes under rules of basic fairness, gave more than three million federal employees a clean bill of health. Some 14,000 "doubtful" cases went to the FBI. Of these, 2,000 persons left government service, although the evidence indicates that few of the resignations resulted from the investigation. All told, the FBI recommended that only 212 people be discharged as possible security risks, hardly the numbers expected in a bureaucracy allegedly "honeycombed" by subversives.

To demonstrate its opposition to communism, the administration did prosecute twelve leaders of the American Communist Party under the Smith Act of 1940. The statute made it a crime to teach or advocate the overthrow of the government by force, or to belong to a group advocating such overthrow; it thus departed drastically from the classical civil liberties position of proscribing only those words or actions presenting a "clear and present danger" to society. Before 1948 the government had invoked the Smith Act only twice, once against a Trotskyite faction of a Teamsters Union local in Minnesota, and once against a group of thirty-one alleged Fascists. But as early as 1945 the FBI had begun compiling information on the Communist Party; its dossier reached over 1,800 pages within two years. Under pressure from the House Un-American Activities Committee, Attorney General Tom Clark finally initiated prosecution. In July 1948 a federal grand jury returned indictments against twelve national leaders, and the nine-month trial—the "Battle of Foley Square"—began in January 1949. The often contentious trial ended with the conviction of all the defendants, who immediately launched a series of appeals.

The twelve defendants claimed that the government had not proved that either their words or deeds met the "clear and present danger" test. They had good reason to believe that they could win on this argument because the Supreme Court had used it frequently in the 1940s to strike down a variety of restrictions on various forms of speech. There had, however, been growing criticism of that standard from a number of sources. Strict advocates of free speech protested the "balancing" of speech against other, and supposedly lesser, values. Some critics believed that the test restricted the government too much and prevented it from taking the necessary measures to protect against subversion. A middle position condemned "clear and present danger" as oversimplified, because the whole problem of freedom and order required the consideration of many other variables.

The Supreme Court had entered the postwar era with relatively little speech clause jurisprudence, aside from the "clear and present danger" test developed by Holmes and Brandeis in the 1920s. (The full implications of Brandeis's opinion in *Whitney v. California* [1927] would not be recognized and developed until the Warren era.) But Holmes's famous aphorism about falsely shouting fire in a theater is not a very useful analytical tool to determine when a danger is real, and if real, when it is proximate, and if proximate, whether it is of the magnitude that justifies state intervention.

Justices Black and Douglas had become increasingly unhappy with the test, especially as applied by the conservative majority after the war. Douglas believed that, had Holmes and Brandeis had the opportunity to develop their ideas more fully in additional cases, they would have abandoned the "clear and present danger" test in favor of free and unrestricted speech in all but the most dire emergencies. Black began developing a new jurisprudence that viewed the First Amendment, especially the speech clause, as occupying a "preferred" position among constitutionally protected rights. He and Douglas also argued for an "absolutist" interpretation of the First Amendment's prohibitions against the abridgment of speech. In their view the First Amendment barred all forms of governmental restrictions on speech, and no place existed in the regime of the First Amendment for any "clear and present danger" test.

For Frankfurter the balancing implicit in the "clear and present danger" test fitted perfectly with his conception of the judicial function. Even while recognizing that a conservative majority might read their own views into the test, he believed that by applying rigorous tools of analysis and clearheadedly evaluating the circumstances, judges could determine when a danger existed and when it did not. By this view, explicating First Amendment issues did not differ at all from explicating commerce clause questions. In a letter to Stanley Reed, Frankfurter complained about the Black position: "When one talks about 'preferred,' or 'preferred position,' one means preference of one thing over another. Please tell me what kind of sense it makes that one provision of the Constitution is to be 'preferred' over another. . . . The correlative of 'preference' is 'subordination,' and I know of no calculus to determine when one provision of the Constitution must yield to another, nor do I know any reason for doing so" (Urofsky 1991, 109).

The two opposing views clashed in *Dennis v. United States* (1951), in which twelve leaders of the Communist Party of the United States had been indicted under the 1940 Smith Act for conspiring to teach and advocate the overthrow of the government. A majority of the justices sustained the convictions, as Chief Justice Fred M. Vinson declared that there is no "right" to rebellion where means for peaceful and orderly change exist. "We reject any principle of governmental helplessness in the face of preparation for revolution. No one could conceive that it is not within the power of Congress to prohibit acts intended to overthrow the Government by force and violence" (*Dennis v. United States* [1951], 501). As for the Smith Act's alleged infringement of speech, Vinson noted that the law aimed to outlaw "advocacy, not discussion." The "clear and present danger" test, according to the chief justice, obviously did not mean "that before the Government may act, it must wait until the putsch is about to be executed, the plans have been laid and the signal is awaited" (*Dennis v. United States* [1951], 509).

Both Hugo Black and William Douglas dissented. Black reasserted his belief in the preferred position of First Amendment rights and recalled Brandeis's earlier warning of the difficulty in determining the limits of free speech when popular emotions run high. Douglas, who in later opinions would frequently criticize the *Dennis* decision, pointed out that the Smith Act required the element of intent; one not only had to say something, but had to believe it as well, so that "the crime then depends not on what is taught but on who the teacher is. That is to make freedom of speech turn not on what is said but on the intent with which it is said" (*Dennis v. United States* [1951], 583).

The *Dennis* decision came at the height of the anticommunist sentiment sweeping the nation, and it immediately ran into criticism from civil libertarians and legal scholars. The "clear and present danger" test assumed that only speech or related action that posed an immediate danger could be limited, and that speech that sought to bring change at some unspecified future time remained fully protected. *Dennis* removed this temporal element, so that the government could now reach not only an actual effort to overthrow, but a conspiracy to do so, or even advocacy of such a conspiracy, an act twice removed from actual danger. Moreover, in *Dennis* the Court made no distinctions between theoretical and concrete advocacy.

Vinson's opinion is so strained and illogical because he worked very hard to prove something impossible to prove—namely, that thinking about ideas, or even thinking about teaching and discussing ideas, without anything else, without any overt action, constitutes a clear and present danger to the state. To do this he had to read evil intent into the record, a notion that Holmes and Brandeis had specifically disavowed. The illogic of the majority opinion marked a low point in the Court's Cold War record, and even the majority members realized they would have to rethink the issue. This they would do in the Warren era.

The worst aspect of the Red Scare, and the greatest abuse of power, involved the activities of the Republican senator from Wisconsin, Joseph R. McCarthy. "McCarthyism," as *Washington Post* cartoonist Herbert Block labeled the phenomenon of undocumented defamation of character, soon affected nearly every aspect of national life. The junior senator knew how to exploit the media with his constant accusations of treason in high places and his tirades against "State Department perverts," the "bright young men who are born with silver spoons in their mouths," and who now were "selling the Nation out."

The Republican victory in 1952 made McCarthy chairman of the Senate Committee on Government Operations, and he used the forum as a bludgeon against various foreign affairs agencies. For a while he seemed undefeatable, and those who opposed him wound up labeled as traitors or worse. Men and women appeared before his committee to answer charges of disloyalty, without any opportunity to know who had accused them or the basis of the charges. Those who dared to invoke their rights, such as refusing to answer under the Fifth Amendment's protection against possible self-incrimination, found themselves accused by McCarthy as traitors.

Because congressmen and senators are immune from criminal and civil liability for anything they say in the course of their duties, people smeared by McCarthy had no legal redress against him. He cannily refused to be specific when outside the capital, and although his daily accusations grabbed the headlines, his victims' denials invariably wound up on the back pages. The turning point came when the courageous newscaster Edward R. Murrow exposed McCarthy's tactics on his widely viewed television show, *See It Now.*

Soon afterward, the senator overreached himself. Failing to get preferential treatment from the army for a young protege, G. David Schine, McCarthy decided to investigate the armed services for alleged communist influences. The televised portion of the "Army-McCarthy hearings" ran from April 22 to June 17, 1954. For the first time, instead of hearing McCarthy's accusations on the evening news or reading about them in the morning paper, Americans saw the man in action; it proved a revelation. His bullying, his disdain for procedural fairness, and the obvious falseness of his accusations all left a sour taste. The Democratic victory in that fall's election deprived him of the committee chairmanship, but even his Republican colleagues had finally grown weary of his indiscriminate attacks. On December 2, 1954, by a vote of sixty-seven to twenty-two, the Senate condemned him for affronting the dignity of the chamber. As much as anything that event marked the end of the Red Scare.

But the Warren Court had to labor under the shadow of the Red Scare, especially in its early years. It would decide a number of cases relating to various internal security programs, and most important, it would have to establish guidelines regarding the meaning of the First Amendment protection of speech, guidelines severely strained during the postwar years of hysteria.

The Black-Frankfurter Debate

The great expansion of civil liberties that is often identified with the Warren Court actually began much earlier. Litigation involving individual rights had been coming to the Supreme Court with greater frequency ever since World War I. During the supposedly reactionary 1920s, the Taft Court had begun the process of incorporation, by which the protections of the first eight amendments had been applied to the states through the due process clause of the Fourteenth Amendment.

In 1925 the Court, almost in passing, noted that the First Amendment's protection of free speech applied to the states as well as to the federal government; a few years later, it also held the press clause to apply. The question then arose as to whether incorporation meant that all of the guaranties in the first eight amendments applied to the states, or only some. Benjamin Nathan Cardozo, the shy, retiring successor to the flamboyant Holmes, held the same commitment to freedom, but also believed in the necessity of drawing boundaries. A blanket application of the Bill of Rights would undermine an important aspect of federalism and deprive the nation of diversity and the states of their opportunity to experiment. In late 1937 Cardozo delivered the majority opinion in *Palko v. Connecticut*, and in doing so defined much of the judicial debate for the next generation.

Palko involved a relatively limited question: did the Fourteenth Amendment incorporate the guarantee against double jeopardy in the Fifth Amendment and apply it to the states? Cardozo said that it did not, for the Fourteenth Amendment did not automatically subsume the entire Bill of Rights. This meant that it incorporated some rights, but which ones? Cardozo included all the protections of the First Amendment, for freedom of thought and speech "is the matrix, the indispensable condition, for nearly every other form of [freedom]" (*Palko v. Connecticut* [1937], 325). But as for the Second through Eighth Amendments, the Court should apply only those that are "of the very essence of a scheme of ordered liberty" and "so rooted in the traditions and conscience of our people as to be ranked as fundamental" (*Palko v. Connecticut* [1937], 327). One test would be whether a violation of such a right would be "so acute and so shocking that our polity will not bear it" (*Palko v. Connecticut* [1937], 328).

This doctrine of "selective incorporation" lodged enormous power and discretion in the courts. Nothing in the Constitution provided guidance; rather judges had to modernize the Bill of Rights and decide which parts applied to the states based on their views (guided at least in part by history and precedent) of what constituted a "fundamental" right. *Palko* made it possible to expand constitutional safeguards without amendment, but it required the justices to develop some hierarchy of values.

The first step came in a non–civil liberties case, *United States v. Carolene Products Company* (1938), dealing with government regulation of so-called filled milk, that is, milk to which nondairy additives had been added. In upholding the law Justice Harlan Fiske Stone added what is certainly the most famous footnote in American constitutional history. Stone suggested that while the courts should defer to legislatures in economic matters, it should impose a higher standard of review in areas of civil liberties and civil rights. Practically unnoticed at the time, the *Carolene Products* footnote would play an important role in Warren Court jurisprudence. Footnote 4 referred to "insular minorities" as needing special protection by the courts, as well as a higher standard of review when dealing with questions of rights. The Warren Court put flesh on this skeleton, in effect making African Americans special wards of the judiciary and also articulating the higher standards of review that would apply when citizens challenged government statutes on free speech and other rights grounds.

Hugo Black had just joined the Court when the *Palko* decision came down and at first he subscribed to it. But he grew increasingly uncomfortable with the philosophy and method of selective incorporation and the great power it lodged in the courts. Black's intuitive commitment to civil liberties derived from his populist background, which often led him to ignore precedent and listen to his own instincts for fair play and justice. Over the next decade he mulled over this problem, attempting to find a solution other than Cardozo's selective approach.

During these years he and Felix Frankfurter (who subscribed to the Cardozo approach) engaged in an ongoing debate over the meaning of the Fourteenth Amendment. Black's reading of history led him to believe that the framers of the amendment, especially Senator John A. Bingham, had intended to apply all of the Bill of Rights protections to the states. Frankfurter's equally detailed reading of history led him to the opposite conclusion, and he doubted whether the states would have ratified the Fourteenth Amendment if, in fact, it did subject them to such restrictions. Due process required no more, Frankfurter believed, than that the Court impose standards of procedural fairness on state criminal procedures.

As early as 1939 Frankfurter had responded to comments Black made in conference about the applicability of the Fourteenth Amendment to state action. Black had evidently said that he thought the Bill of Rights had been intended to apply to the states from the start, and that the Marshall Court had been wrong in ruling that it did not. Frankfurter said he could understand that position, but disagreed with it. "What I am unable to appreciate is what are the criteria of selection," he said, "which applies and which does not apply" (Urofsky 1991, 95). This, of course, was exactly the question with which Black would wrestle for almost a decade.

The debate almost came to a head in 1942 in *Betts v. Brady*, in which a majority of the Court held that the Sixth Amendment right to counsel did not apply to the states. In conference Black argued passionately that Betts was "entitled to a lawyer from the history of the Fourteenth Amendment," which had been "intended to make applicable to the States the Bill of Rights." He brought up his own experience as a trial lawyer, and asked his colleagues how many of them thought that a layman could adequately plan a defense, summon witnesses, and conduct a trial against a trained prosecutor. "If I am to pass on what is fair and right," he declared, "I will say it makes me vomit to think men go to prison for a long time" because they had no benefit of counsel (Yarbrough 1988, 87).

Frankfurter responded just as heatedly and claimed that if the Court interpreted the Fourteenth Amendment to apply all of the Bill of Rights to the states, it would destroy the federal system and "uproot all the structure of the states." About a year later, Frankfurter sent Black a lengthy letter trying to get him to be more explicit in his evidence for interpreting the Fourteenth Amendment to mean total incorporation. "Believe me," Frankfurter wrote, "nothing is farther from my purpose than contention. I am merely trying to get light on a subject which has absorbed as much thought and energy of my mature life as anything that has concerned me" (Urofsky 1991, 95). One can, I think, take Frankfurter seriously here, even if one can discern some hyperbole. He had given much thought to the meaning of the due process clause, and he did believe that, at a minimum, it required the states to provide procedural fairness in criminal trials.

But here Frankfurter and the other members of the Court ran into a jurisprudential conundrum. As Mark Silverstein has pointed out, Frankfurter boxed himself into a jurisprudential contradiction almost from the time he came onto the Court. On the one hand, he continued to oppose judicial subjectivity, by which judges could interpret a statute or constitution to meet their own prejudices. He also opposed absolute standards as a means of controlling subjectivity, because he believed that judges needed some flexibility in interpreting the law. Frankfurter had as a paradigm the scientific expert, who would be able to reach a proper conclusion through correct reasoning. Theoretically, such an enlightened judge would be free from overt subjectivity as well as rigid dogma. Judges could enforce principles, but they would reach those principles in a disinterested, scientific manner. Although nominally not a Legal Realist, Frankfurter had shared the Realists' perception that individual traits predisposed judges toward particular, subjective ends. He knew that could not be changed, yet he resisted imposing external standards to limit judicial discretion. Judges had to choose, Frankfurter believed, but they had to choose in an enlightened manner.

Black not only opposed judicial subjectivity, but he also condemned leaving judges free to choose from among competing alternatives. He distrusted so-called experts, and reposing constitutional choices in their hands smacked too much of an elitism—the few choosing the right course for the many—that offended his populist sensibilities. He proposed instead the imposition of absolutes through a literal reading of the Constitution. But in narrowing the scope of judicial discretion, Black made the Court the prime vehicle for guaranteeing the values of those absolutes, thus increasing the power of judges.

Black grew increasingly uncomfortable with the philosophy and method of selective incorporation and the great power it lodged in the courts. Over the next few years he thought about this problem endlessly, and finally reached his solution in 1946.

By then Black identified the heart of his differences with Frankfurter as centering on the great discretion that the Frankfurter-Cardozo approach vested in the

Court. If judges could strike down state laws that failed to meet "civilized standards," then the courts had reverted to a "natural law concept whereby the supreme constitutional law becomes this Court's view of 'civilization' at a given moment" (Urofsky 1991, 96). This philosophy, he declared, made everything else in the Constitution "mere surplusage," and allowed the Court to reject all of the provisions of the Bill of Rights and substitute its own idea for what legislatures could or could not do. Black, however, still had difficulty articulating the standards he would apply.

The answer for Black came in a California murder case. Admiral Dewey Adamson (his real name) was a poor, illiterate black man who had twice served time for robbery. He had, however, been out of prison for seventeen years when police arrested him for the murder of an elderly white widow. The only evidence linking Adamson to the crime consisted of six fingerprints on a door leading to the garbage container in the woman's kitchen that police identified as his. On the advice of his attorney, a veteran of the Los Angeles criminal courts, Adamson did not take the stand in his own defense. Had he done so, the prosecutor could have brought up Adamson's previous record and that would have resulted in a sure conviction. But the prosecutor, as he was allowed to do under California law, pointed out to the jury Adamson's failure to testify, and claimed that this surely proved his guilt. If he had been innocent, the prosecutor declared, it would have taken fifty horses to keep him off the stand. The jury convicted Adamson, and his lawyer on appeal challenged the California statute as violating the Fourteenth Amendment. Allowing comment on the failure to testify was equivalent to forcing a defendant to take the stand; both violated due process.

In conference Frankfurter convinced a majority of his colleagues that the issue had already been decided, and correctly. In *Twining v. New Jersey* (1908) the Court had ruled that a state law permitting comment on a defendant's refusal to testify did not violate procedural fairness. Justice Reed, assigned the opinion, conceded that such behavior by the prosecutor in a federal proceeding would be unacceptable and a violation of the Fifth Amendment. But it was "settled law" that the self-incrimination law did not apply to the states; it was not "a right of national citizenship, [n]or . . . a personal privilege or immunity secured by the Federal Constitution as one of the rights of man that are listed in the Bill of Rights" (*Adamson v. California* [1947], 50–51). In short, it was not one of the fundamental principles inherent in "the concept of ordered liberty" test of *Palko*. "For a state to require testimony from an accused," Reed concluded, "is not necessarily a breach of a state's obligation to give a fair trial" (*Adamson v. California* [1947], 54).

Black dissented and set forth his belief in the "total incorporation" of the first eight amendments by the Fourteenth. He would consider it the most important opinion of his career. "There I laid it all out. . . . I didn't write until I came to the complete conclusion that I was reasonably sure of myself and my research. It was my work from beginning to end" (Newman 1994, 352). Just as the Bill of Rights applied objective standards to the behavior of the federal government, so the application of the first eight amendments to the states would provide equally ascertainable criteria by which to judge state action. In a lengthy appendix he presented the historical evidence he had assembled to support this position, an essay that most scholars find less than convincing. As might be expected from a former senator, Black relied entirely on the congressional history of the Fourteenth Amendment, the account of what Congress did in drafting it. But amending the Constitution requires ratification by the states, and Black neglected to look at the debates there, nor did he look at the abolitionist antecedents of the amendment. As Roger Newman notes, "Black's was an advocate's history: he proved too much and ignored or swept away all doubtful evidence" (Newman 1994, 352).

What is most interesting in Black's rationale is that in many ways it resembled Frankfurter's own views on limiting judicial power. Black rejected Cardozo's criteria as too vague, because phrases like "civilized decency" and "fundamental liberty and justice" could be interpreted by judges to mean many things. This "natural law" theory of the Constitution "degrade[s] the constitutional safeguards of the Bill of Rights and simultaneously appropriate[s] for this Court a broad power which we are not authorized by the Constitution to exercise" (*Adamson v. California* [1947], 68, 70). The only way to avoid this abuse of judicial power would be to carry out the original intent of the framers of the Fourteenth Amendment and apply all the protections of the Bill of Rights to the states.

Douglas joined Black's opinion, but Murphy filed a separate dissent in which he attempted to combine elements of both the Frankfurter and Black approaches. He had found Black's essay "exciting reading," but "I think you go out of your way—as you always do—to strike down natural law" (Fine 1984, 503). Murphy wanted to incorporate all of the Bill of Rights, as Black proposed, but he objected to what he saw as the rigidity in Black's approach. There were times when one had to be flexible, when a strict reading of the first eight amendments would not suffice to provide justice. In those instances Frankfurter's use of due process would allow judges to secure justice. Murphy's reading of Black's opinion was not that wrong. Although Black would later adopt some of Frankfurter's views regarding due process as fundamental fairness, at the time of the *Adamson* case he told a group of clerks with whom he was having lunch that the due process clauses of the Fifth and Fourteenth Amendments had "no meaning, except that of emphasis" (Fine 1984, 503).

Black had his clerk, Louis Oberdorfer, deliver the first draft to Frankfurter, who on reading it flung it on his desk and declared "At Yale they call this scholarship?" Oberdorfer, a recent Yale Law School graduate, picked up the pages and excused himself. To his own clerk, Frankfurter fumed that "Hugo is trying to change the world and misreading history in the attempt, just making things up out of whole cloth" (Newman 1994, 354). Frankfurter, who had originally written a brief concurrence, now set to work to respond to Black, and the results must surely rank as one of his most forceful and important opinions. In probably no other statement, either for the Court or in dissent, do we get such a clear exposition of Frankfurter's philosophy of judging, one that scholars have termed "process jurisprudence." Relying on his own historical research, Frankfurter denied that the framers of the Fourteenth Amendment had intended to subsume all of the Bill of Rights. Frankfurter also responded to what he took as the most serious of Black's charges, that the vague criteria of *Palko* left judges too much discretion, and protection of rights relied on the mercy of individual subjectivity. The real issue, he declared,

> is not whether an infraction of one of the specific provisions of the first eight Amendments is disclosed by the record. The relevant question is whether the criminal proceedings which resulted in conviction deprived the accused of the due process of law. Judicial review of that guaranty of the Fourteenth Amendment inescapably imposes upon this Court an exercise of judgment upon the whole course of the proceedings in order to ascertain whether they offend those canons of decency and fairness which express the notions of justice of English-speaking peoples even toward those charged with the most heinous offenses. These standards of justice are not authoritatively formulated anywhere as though they were prescriptions in a pharmacopoeia. But neither does the application of the Due Process Clause imply that judges are wholly at large. The judicial judgment in applying the Due Process Clause must move within the limits of accepted notions of justice and is not to be based upon the idiosyncrasies of a merely personal judgment. The fact that judges among themselves may differ whether in a particular case a trial offends accepted notions of justice is not disproof that general rather than idiosyncratic standards are applied. An important safeguard against such merely individual judgment is an alert deference to the judgment of the State court under review (*Adamson v. California* [1947], 68, 70).

Frankfurter portrayed judging as a process removed from the fray of daily pressures. Protected in their sanctum, justices may engage in that process of discovery that will yield the right answer—not an objective, eternally fixed answer, but the right answer for the time. Frankfurter did not espouse a moral relativism, but believed that judges in their decisions should reflect the advances that society has made, so that the due process clause does not mean fairness in terms of 1868, but fairness today. Courts thus help keep the Constitution contemporary, but they must do so cautiously, always following strict intellectual processes and always deferring to those who are in the thick of the battle—the state courts and legislatures—who must in turn be left free to reform their procedures according to their standards of fairness. As Frankfurter noted in another case:

> [D]ue process of law requires an evaluation based on a disinterested inquiry pursued in the spirit of science, on a balanced order of facts exactly and fairly stated, on the detached consideration of conflicting claims, on a judgment not ad hoc and episodic but duly mindful of reconciling the needs both of continuity and change in a progressive society (*Rochin v. California* [1952], 172).

Thus, if the judge adheres to certain methods and standards, it does not matter what the result is in a particular case, because the process will assure ultimate fairness across the spectrum of cases. "Whatever shortcut to relief may be had in a particular case," Frankfurter wrote a year after *Adamson*, "it is calculated to beget misunderstanding and friction and to that extent detracts from those imponderables which are the ultimate reliance of a civilized system of law" (*Uveges v. Pennsylvania* [1948], 449–450). The *process* and not a particular *result* is the desideratum of judging.

The great appeal of process jurisprudence is that it attempts to remove idiosyncrasy and individuality from judicial decision making and replace them with objectivity and consistency. Public faith in the judicial process is enhanced if the public believes that judges are acting fairly and adhering to a common set of methods and principles in all cases, regardless of the results in specific instances. During the Warren years Frankfurter grew increasing uncomfortable as Warren in effect abandoned process for result; the new chief wanted to see justice done and believed that while process was not unimportant, it should not be allowed to stand in the way of protecting individual liberties and minorities.

Conclusion

This, then, is the background, the context, in which we can try to understand the Warren Court. Without taking any credit away from Earl Warren and his colleagues, they did not write on a blank slate. They casually ignored nearly all questions of economic regulation because that issue, as far as they were concerned, had been settled once and for all by the constitutional crisis of 1937. They avoided, for the same reason, using the powerful constitutional tool of substantive due process, because it had been discredited by the conservatives in the 1930s. They struck down school segregation and other forms of racial discrimination against a backdrop of a growing civil rights movement and redefined the meaning of free speech after witnessing firsthand the ravages of the postwar Red Scare. Although they would raise constitutional protections of individual liberties to new heights, they did not have to scale those heights unaided. The Court's agenda had become more involved with issues of civil liberties and civil rights since the late 1930s, and there had been an active and fruitful dialogue on the nature of incorporation of rights since the *Palko* decision in 1938. The building material was there. Now let us look at the men who took that material and the house they built.

References

Buhite, Russell, and David Levy. 1992. *FDR's Fireside Chats.* Norman: University of Oklahoma Press.

Fine, Sidney. 1984. *Frank Murphy: The Washington Years.* Ann Arbor: University of Michigan Press.

Irons, Peter. 1982. *The New Deal Lawyers.* Princeton, NJ: Princeton University Press.

Leuchtenburg, William E. 1963. *Franklin D. Roosevelt and the New Deal.* New York: Harper and Row.

———. 1995. *The Supreme Court Reborn: The Constitutional Revolution in the Age of Roosevelt.* New York: Oxford University Press.

Newman, Roger K. 1994. *Hugo Black: A Biography.* New York: Pantheon.

Urofsky, Melvin I. 1991. *Felix Frankfurter: Judicial Restraint and Individual Liberties.* Boston, MA: Twayne.

Yarbrough, Tinsley E. 1988. *Mr. Justice Black and His Critics.* Durham, NC: Duke University Press.

2

The Justices

Seventeen men served on what we call the Warren Court. One of them, Hugo L. Black, had been appointed in 1937, and would serve until 1971; another, Byron White, appointed in 1962, would remain on the bench until 1993. In terms of jurisprudence, some of the associate justices—"side judges" as Oliver Wendell Holmes called them—would have a greater jurisprudential impact than the chief, but there can be little doubt that Earl Warren dominated the Court from the time he took his seat in 1953 until his retirement in 1969.

The chief justice occupies the center seat on the Court and, while his or her vote is no greater than that of his or her colleagues, the chief presides over oral argument as well as the conferences at which the justices decide cases. The chief justice also controls the procedural aspects of the Court's work, such as the assignment of opinions, and oversees the Court's support staff, such as the clerks and marshals. A strong chief justice—such as John Marshall, William Howard Taft, or Charles Evans Hughes—can have a major impact on the Court's work, not only defining its agenda but influencing the general jurisprudential direction that the Court takes. A weak chief—such as Harlan Fiske Stone or Frederick M. Vinson—can often find himself or herself stymied by strong colleagues and end up doing little more than presiding over a judicial battlefield. Earl Warren clearly deserves to be ranked among the strong chief justices.

The associate justices are here presented in the order of their appointment because that order greatly affected the decisions of the Warren Court. In 1953, when Warren came to the Court, the conservatives led by Felix Frankfurter and Robert Jackson held a majority of the votes. While they opposed racial discrimination, they held aloft the banner of "judicial restraint" and firmly opposed the judicial expansion of rights that would be the great legacy of the Warren Court. Gradually, however, more liberal men made their way into the Marble Palace. The original cadre of Hugo Black and William O. Douglas found allies in Warren and William Brennan, but not until Arthur Goldberg took Frankfurter's place in 1962 did the liberal activists have the consistent five votes they needed. When we talk about "the Warren Court" in terms of its great achievements, with the exception of the desegregation cases, all of those decisions took place between 1962 and 1969.

The Warren Court from 1953 to 1954: (left to right, front row) Felix Frankfurter, Hugo L. Black, Earl Warren, Stanley F. Reed, and William O. Douglas; (left to right, back row) Tom C. Clark, Robert H. Jackson, Harold H. Burton, and Sherman Minton. (Fabian Bachrach, Collection of the Supreme Court of the United States)

The Warren Court from 1957 to 1958: (left to right, front row) William O. Douglas, Hugo L. Black, Earl Warren, Felix Frankfurter, and Harold H. Burton; (left to right, back row) William J. Brennan, Tom C. Clark, John M. Harlan, and Charles E. Whittaker. (Harris & Ewing, Collection of the Supreme Court of the United States)

The Warren Court from 1962 to 1965: (left to right, front row) Tom C. Clark, Hugo L. Black, Earl Warren, William O. Douglas, and John M. Harlan; (left to right, back row) Byron R. White, William J. Brennan, Potter Stewart Jr., and Arthur J. Goldberg. (Harris & Ewing, Collection of the Supreme Court of the United States)

The Warren Court from 1967 to 1969: (left to right, front row) John M. Harlan, Hugo L. Black, Earl Warren, William O. Douglas, and William J. Brennan; (left to right, back row) Abe Fortas, Potter Stewart Jr., Byron R. White, and Thurgood Marshall. (Harris & Ewing, Collection of the Supreme Court of the United States)

A good way to understand this is to take a look at the composition of the Court at four different times—1953, when Warren came to the Court; 1956, by which time Brennan and Harlan had been appointed; 1962, when Frankfurter left; and 1969, Warren's last term:

> 1953: Liberals—Warren, Black, Douglas;
>   Conservatives—Reed, Frankfurter, Jackson, Burton, Clark, Minton
> 1956: Liberals—Warren, Black, Douglas, Brennan;
>   Conservatives—Reed, Frankfurter, Burton, Clark, Harlan
> 1962: Liberals—Warren, Black, Douglas, Brennan, Goldberg;
>   Conservatives—Clark, Harlan, Stewart, White
> 1969: Liberals—Warren, Black, Douglas, Brennan, Fortas, Marshall;
>   Conservatives—Harlan, Stewart, White

The Superchief and His Associates

Earl Warren

Earl Warren (1891–1974) grew up in Bakersfield, California, where his father worked as a railroad car repairman for the Southern Pacific Railroad. At the turn of century Bakersfield still had a rough, semifrontier atmosphere, and in his memoir Warren recounted that he had witnessed "crime and vice of all kinds countenanced by a corrupt government" (Warren 1977, 31). Summer work on the railroad gave him knowledge about working people and problems, as well as a familiarity with the pervasive anti-Asian racism so common on the West Coast. Perhaps the most indelible impression of Warren's youth was the great and corrupting power exercised by the Southern Pacific in local politics, and the total lack of compassion the corporation displayed towards its employees. "I knew of men who were fired for even considering a suit against the railroad for the injuries they sustained," he wrote. "There was no compensation for them, and they went through life as cripples" (Warren 1977, 31). These were lessons that would shape his entire career.

Warren attended the University of California at Berkeley and its law school, Boalt Hall, served briefly in the army during World War I, and then joined the district attorney's office in Alameda County for what he thought would be a short stint. But he stayed for eighteen years, thirteen of them as district attorney. During this phase of his career Warren proved to be an effective, tough prosecutor, but he also showed himself sensitive to the rights of accused persons and fought to set up a public defender's office for indigents. A 1931 survey listed Warren as the best district attorney in the United States, a fact often ignored by critics who would call Chief Justice

Earl Warren (Harris & Ewing, Collection of the Supreme Court of the United States)

Warren "soft" on criminals. This experience proved valuable when the Warren Court began its so-called due process revolution dealing with the rights of the accused. Only Hugo Black besides Warren had had any experience in criminal law before going on the bench; these two, far more than their colleagues, understood how the criminal justice system in the United States actually operated.

In 1938 Warren ran successfully for attorney general of California, a post he held until 1942. During his one term Warren modernized the office and implemented a number of reforms, but he is remembered primarily for his outspoken demands that Japanese and Japanese-Americans be evacuated from the West Coast. Throughout his life Warren maintained that at the time it seemed the right and necessary thing to do. Not until the posthumous publication of his memoirs did he acknowledge that it had been an error. It is also ironic in light of his later reputation as a champion of civil liberties that as attorney general, Warren opposed the appointment of Berkeley law professor Max Radin to the California supreme court, engaging in the sort of red-baiting that he would later come to despise.

The popular Warren easily won election as governor of California in 1942 and would twice be reelected. It seemed to many people that Warren was headed for national office, and in 1948 he ran as the Republican vice presidential candidate with Thomas E. Dewey. Four years later he played a key role at the Republican national convention in securing Dwight D. Eisenhower's nomination. For that Eisenhower promised him the first available appointment to the Supreme Court. Warren had, in fact, already accepted Eisenhower's offer to become solicitor general (a tried and proven path to the high court) when Chief Justice Fred Vinson unexpectedly died on September 8, 1953. Although Eisenhower seemed reluctant to name Warren to head the Court, the Californian pointedly reminded Attorney General Herbert Brownell of Ike's promise. With Congress out of session at the time, the president named Warren to a recess appointment at the end of September; the Senate confirmed his appointment the following March.

Legal historians have ranked Warren as one of the great chief justices in the Court's history; some have even compared him to John Marshall, the "Great Chief Justice." William Brennan called him the "Superchief," and for William O. Douglas, he was always *the* chief." But this evaluation rests primarily on Warren's superb political skills, which enabled him to lead the Court during a time of tremendous social and political controversy. Scholars, however, have struggled with Warren's written opinions in an effort to piece out a coherent judicial philosophy, some sort of jurisprudential compass by which one might get a clear set of bearings. Warren never considered himself a great jurist, nor have scholars of the Court; to his detractors he was and remains a results-oriented judge, one who voted his personal preferences instead of following the Constitution.

One of his biographers and a former clerk, G. Edward White, has argued that there is a coherence in Warren's judicial writings. Warren, according to White, "equated judicial lawmaking with neither the dictates of reason . . . nor the demands imposed by an institutional theory of the judge's role, nor the alleged 'command' of the constitutional text, but rather with his own reconstruction of the ethical structure of the Constitution" (White 1982, 358). One might liken this approach to the two differing strands of the Old Testament, the priestly and the prophetic. The priests in the name of God laid down strict rules, which they demanded that the people of Israel follow literally, whatever the consequences. The prophets, on the other hand, looked for the larger ethical values. "Do good; seek justice; correct oppression," thundered Isaiah (Isaiah 1:17) and, while not ignoring the priestly rules, placed them in a decidedly secondary position behind ethical principles.

Not everyone agrees with this analysis. While the "ethicist" approach certainly helps to explain results in particular cases, it does not necessarily capture fully the reasoning in others. Quite often Warren's writings were stolid and doctrinally underdeveloped. In some cases, such as *Brown v. Board of Education* (1954) or *Miranda v. Arizona* (1966), he relied on statistical data or social science findings without adequate explanation of how this nonlegal material linked to and supported the constitutional result. Fortunately, he had the assistance of some of the finest legal minds ever to sit on the Court, and once Warren determined which way he wanted to go, he could turn to Black or Douglas or especially to William Brennan to devise the appropriate judicial rationale.

Hugo Lafayette Black

To the right of the chief justice sits the senior associate justice, and throughout Warren's tenure Hugo Lafayette Black (1886–1971) occupied that chair. Black had grown up in rural Alabama, graduated first in his University of Alabama Law School class, and after practicing a few years in his native Ashland, moved to Birmingham in 1907. To supplement his income Black served as a part-time municipal judge and then for three years as Jefferson County prosecuting attorney. In his most famous case, he investigated and prosecuted several police officers for beating and forcing confessions from black defendants.

In his private practice Black tried hundreds of cases and honed his considerable talents as a debater and orator, skills that led to his election as a United States senator in 1926. In 1932 he won a second term and became a staunch defender of Franklin Roosevelt's New Deal, a position that put him at odds with his more conservative Southern colleagues. Black espoused a view that the federal government had sufficient authority under the commerce clause to enact legislation necessary to deal with the Great Depression, and that Congress could in fact regulate any activity that directly or indirectly affected the national economy. With this power, the courts could not interfere.

Hugo Lafayette Black (Harris & Ewing, Collection of the Supreme Court of the United States)

Black joined the Court amid a cloud of controversy. At the time many people believed that Roosevelt had named Black as a reward for the Alabaman's support of the court-packing plan. The populist Black antagonized many conservative senators, and Roosevelt knew that no matter what its members thought of him, the Senate would not reject one of its own, even one whom many believed lacked the credentials for the job. Robert Jackson later recalled: "I had been rather amused at the President's maneuver, which enabled him to get even with the court and with the Senate, which had beat his [court] plan, at the same time. He knew well enough that the Senate could not reject the nomination because of senatorial courtesy. He knew perfectly well it would go against their grain to confirm. He knew it would not be welcomed by the court" (Urofsky 1997, 15–16). Then shortly after he had been sworn in, it was revealed that Black had once belonged to the Ku Klux Klan. It was hardly an auspicious start to a judicial career.

Black had some difficulty adjusting to the Court, but despite questions raised about his ability, he soon adapted to the demands of the office. Moreover, Black came to the Court with a fairly well-developed judicial philosophy that included a clear reading of the constitutional text, limited judicial discretion, the protection of individual rights, and broad powers for the government to address a wide range of economic and social problems. Someone once commented that Black's lasting influence on the Court grew out of his willingness to "reinvent the wheel." Like his friend and colleague William O. Douglas, Black had little use for precedent, especially if he thought the case erroneously decided.

At the center of Black's philosophy stood a populist belief in the Constitution as an infallible guide. He opposed judicial subjectivity; the Constitution did not empower judges to select from competing alternatives. He distrusted so-called experts, and leaving either legislative or judicial decision making in their hands smacked too much of elitism. Instead, he relied on the absolutes he found through a literal reading of the Constitution. This narrowed the scope of judicial discretion, but it reinforced the role of the courts as the prime vehicle for guaranteeing the values of those absolutes.

Although the seeds of a fully developed philosophy can be found in Black's early opinions, not until the late 1940s did he articulate what came to be his bedrock principles, namely that the Fourteenth Amendment's due process clause incorporated all of the protections of the Bill of Rights against the states, and that the First Amendment, which protected speech and press, enjoyed a preferred position among constitutional values. Prior to Warren's appointment Black could never garner majority support for this philosophy, but the new chief almost immediately signed on to Black's views, and within a few years this liberal, activist jurisprudence would be embraced by a solid majority on the bench.

A good part of Black's effectiveness derived from the considerable political skills he possessed and had honed in his two terms in the Senate. More than any other justice of his time, Black proselytized, "working" the other justices as he had once worked his senatorial colleagues. Black once told a story that explained a good deal of his effectiveness. Black talked about an unnamed senator who, when he wanted to accomplish something, would introduce two bills—the one he wanted passed and another that made the first one seem conservative. Robert Jackson somewhat disdainfully noted that these methods might be suitable for a legislative body where one deals with adversaries, but not in a court of law where the members supposedly are colleagues. Nonetheless, Black's political prowess, like that of Warren, made him an extremely effective champion of his views.

In later years Black seemed to grow more conservative, and his long-time companion in arms, William O. Douglas, complained that Black had left him. This is only partially true. In his devotion to expanding the Bill of Rights to the states Black remained firm, but his devotion to textual literalism made him strongly opposed to the idea of a "living Constitution" championed by Warren and the other liberals. In the last years of the Warren era Black grew disillusioned with what he saw as the free-wheeling interpretive style of his colleagues, and he strongly denounced their efforts to bring the Constitution into harmony with the times. This could sometimes lead him into an absurd position, as can be seen in the 1967 wire-tapping case, *Katz v. United States.*

The eight-man majority held that attaching a microphone to a public telephone booth did in fact violate the Fourth Amendment, which in Justice Stewart's memorable phrase protects people, not things. Black's lone dissent was rigidly literal, and concluded that such a device was no better than eavesdropping, but certainly not outlawed by the Fourth Amendment. Similarly, his dissent in the great privacy case of the Warren Court, *Griswold v. Connecticut* (1965), also displayed a formal literalism almost devoid of reality.

Stanley Forman Reed

During Warren's first four terms, Stanley Forman Reed (1884–1980) sat on his immediate left as the second most senior justice. A friendly man who lived to be ninety-five, he told Potter Stewart that he would not want to live his life over again, as "it could not possibly be as good the second time" (Urofsky, ed. 1994, 367). Born in 1884, Reed had gone to the Yale Law School, and then built up a thriving practice in Maysville, Kentucky, where he also dabbled in state politics and helped manage his friend Fred Vinson's congressional campaigns. In 1929 he moved to Washington when Herbert Hoover named him counsel to the Federal Farm Board, a position he retained in the Roosevelt administration. Reed's geniality, as well as his passionate belief in the desirability of the federal government playing a major role in the nation's social and economic life, soon caught the attention of the president, who named him solicitor

Stanley Forman Reed (Harris & Ewing, Collection of the Supreme Court of the United States)

general. His performance in that role was lackluster at best, but in early 1938 Roosevelt named Reed to replace George Sutherland on the bench.

Once on the Court Reed, in the recollections of his clerk John Sapienza, "was friendly with everyone. He didn't even exchange any nasty words with McReynolds, and he was on good terms with Frankfurter, with Black, with Butler. . . . He never engaged in any feuds with anybody. He never had an unkind word to say about anybody" (Sapienza n.d., n.p.). William O. Douglas, who personally liked the gentle, courtly Reed, nonetheless termed him a reactionary. Reed tended to be a follower rather than a leader, and he could usually be counted upon to vote with Felix Frankfurter and the conservative wing of the Court.

Reed tended to defer to Congress, and a determination of what Congress had intended often proved dispositive for him, whether the issue was of constitutional, statutory, or administrative interpretation. He stood willing to grant Congress the full range of powers under the commerce clause, but had less faith in state and local government and little interest in civil liberties or civil rights; he was the last of the nine justices to sign onto Warren's opinion in *Brown* striking down school segregation. The one area that did arouse his concern was the First Amendment, and during his tenure he voted often, but not in every case, to broaden First Amendment rights. On the whole, his record is marked by inconsistency, a not unfamiliar characteristic of many New Dealers.

Felix Frankfurter

Next in seniority and the leader of the conservative bloc was Felix Frankfurter (1882–1965), appointed to succeed Benjamin Nathan Cardozo in 1938 amid high hopes that he would become the intellectual leader of the Court. Solicitor General Robert H. Jackson claimed that only Frankfurter had the legal resources "to face Chief Justice Hughes in conference and hold his own in discussion" (Gerhart 1958, 166). Upon news of Frankfurter's nomination, New Dealers had gathered in the office of Secretary of the Interior Harold Ickes to celebrate, and all those present heartily agreed with Ickes's judgment of the nomination as "the most significant and worthwhile thing the President has done" (Ickes 1954, 2:552). There is, unfortunately, no way one can predict whether an appointee will be great or mediocre once on the bench, and Frankfurter ranks as one of the great disappointments in modern times.

Born in Vienna, Frankfurter emigrated to the United States as a child. His innate brilliance had shone first at the City College of New York and then at the Harvard Law School. Upon graduation, he briefly joined a Wall Street firm, but soon fled to work with U.S. Attorney Henry L. Stimson; he then followed Stimson into the Roosevelt and Taft administrations. Short, exuberant, a brilliant conversationalist and an inveterate idol worshipper, Frankfurter soon became the center of a group of young bureaucrats

Felix Frankfurter (Harris & Ewing, Collection of the Supreme Court of the United States)

and writers who shared quarters on 19th Street, a place they dubbed the "House of Truth." There Gutzom Borgum sketched his proposed presidential monument, Herbert Croly and Walter Lippmann planned the *New Republic* and expounded on contemporary problems, and Oliver Wendell Holmes and Louis Brandeis were frequent visitors.

Frankfurter and Holmes fell under each other's spell; the younger man adored Holmes, and the sentiment was reciprocated. When Frankfurter accepted a position at the Harvard Law School after World War I, he took responsibility for choosing Holmes's clerks. Holmes appealed to Frankfurter for a number of reasons, but from a jurisprudential point of view, Holmes held high the banner of judicial restraint, a banner that Frankfurter in his own time would also carry. Frankfurter later wrote: "You must bear in mind that the great influences of my formative years were Dean Ames and Harry Stimson; later Holmes and to some, but less extent, Brandeis. . . . They all converged toward making me feel deeply that it makes all the difference in the world whether you put truth in the first place or the second" (Urofsky 1997, 20).

Despite this comment, in many ways the relationship with Brandeis proved more decisive. In Frankfurter, Brandeis found a surrogate to carry on his reform work; he urged Frankfurter to take the professorship at Harvard, and he provided a financial subsidy to enable Frankfurter, who lacked an independent income, to devote himself to reform efforts. During the 1920s Frankfurter, through his defense of Sacco and Vanzetti and his writings for the *New Republic*, became a leading reformer in his own right, a man Brandeis called "the most useful lawyer in the United States" (Urofsky 1997, 20). Frankfurter's influence also was spread by his students. A brilliant teacher, he trained a whole generation of lawyers in administrative law, and when the Great Depression came and government burgeoned under the New Deal, Frankfurter became a one-man placement agency, staffing one federal office after another with his former students. He also exerted a quiet but effective influence on several New Deal policies, not only through his many contacts with leading administration figures, but with President Roosevelt as well. The two men had known each other since World War I, and during the 1930s Frankfurter was a frequent guest at the White House.

Frankfurter, like Black, went onto the Court with a well-developed judicial philosophy, but one far different from the Alabaman's. Both men believed in judicial restraint, but Frankfurter took what Black considered a much too subjective approach, leaving too great a power in the hands of judges to "interpret" constitutional injunctions. Most importantly, however, Black drew a sharp distinction between economic legislation and restrictions on individual liberties, with judges carrying a special obligation to protect the latter; Frankfurter considered all legislation equal, and demanded that judges defer to the legislative will unless they found a clear-cut constitutional prohibition. The debate between these two views would fragment the Court during the chief justiceships of Harlan Fiske Stone and Fred M. Vinson, and make it one of the most contentious in history.

Frankfurter, according to Richard Kluger, "was reportedly outraged that Eisenhower would name a mere politician to lead the Court" (Kluger 1976, 664). But to a friend Frankfurter apparently rejoiced in the nomination of Earl Warren to be chief justice. The California governor, he said, "brings to his work that largeness of experience and breadth of outlook which may well make him a very good Chief Justice provided he has some other qualities which, from what I have seen, I believe he has" (Urofsky 1991b, 136).

For Frankfurter, who never seemed to learn, Warren provided still another "student," one more opportunity to teach someone the "right" way to be a judge. He began preparing memoranda and reading lists for Warren, attempting to overwhelm him by both his learning and his helpfulness. Gerald Gunther, whom Frankfurter had indirectly arranged to be Warren's clerk, recalled that the chief had asked Frankfurter if he could recommend some reference he could consult on a relatively minor point of jurisdiction. A half-hour later Frankfurter's clerk wheeled a library cart into Warren's chambers loaded with volumes that could clear up the point.

Frankfurter and Warren got off to a good start, however, because they both agreed on the proper strategy for dealing with the segregation cases. According to one Warren biographer, Frankfurter may have suggested the strategy, and then relied on Warren's political skills to pull it through. Warren at first seemed a most promising prospect, but Frankfurter misinterpreted the Californian's caution in taking over the chief's role as eagerness to be tutored by Frankfurter. When Warren asked Frankfurter a due process question, Frankfurter quickly sent him a copy of every opinion he had written in the previous fifteen years on the subject, and rejoiced when he received a note from Warren later that summer saying that he was reading through them. In the next two terms, Warren sought Frankfurter's advice on a number of subjects, and Frankfurter responded not only with what had been asked, but offers of further assistance as well as effusive praise for some of Warren's opinions and speeches before bar groups.

But as Warren began to feel more comfortable in his role, he found that he not only needed Frankfurter's advice less, but he also began to resent the patronizing tone. Here comparison with Black is instructive. Warren had had little time to prepare for his new role when named to the Court, but had been urged by the attorney general to hasten to Washington in time for the new session, as the Court faced many difficult questions. Not wishing to embarrass either himself or the Court, Warren asked Black, as the senior justice, to preside at the conference until Warren could acclimate himself. Black accepted the invitation, and during the few months that he led the conference discussions he never once tried to "teach" Warren what had to be done. When Warren felt ready, he took over the reins and Black just as easily slid back into his old role, confident that in time he and Warren would work well together.

By the summer of 1955 Warren could no longer be considered a neophyte, and he chafed under the constant barrage of suggestions and reading material that came down from Frankfurter's chambers. More important, Warren had begun to enunciate his own activist view of the Court, and an analysis of his voting patterns indicate a definite shift toward Black and Douglas, a shift soon accentuated by the arrival of William Brennan in 1956. By the end of the 1956 term, Frankfurter had lumped the chief with the "hard-core liberal wing" of the Court, whose "common denominator is a self-willed self-righteous power-lust." Warren, along with Black and Douglas, he told Learned Hand, desired "to join Thomas Paine and T. Jefferson in the Valhalla of 'liberty' and in the meantime to have the avant-garde of the Yale Law School . . . praise them!" (Urofsky 1991b, 136). Conditions deteriorated during the late fifties, as the Court began to take on a more activist coloration, and Warren's patience, if there had been any left with Frankfurter, snapped with the Little Rock decision, *Cooper v. Aaron* (1958).

William Orville Douglas

When Louis D. Brandeis retired in February 1939, Franklin Roosevelt named William Orville Douglas (1898–1980) to take his place. A true product of the Pacific Northwest, Douglas had grown up in Yakima, Washington, where as a child he contracted infantile paralysis. Gradually, he regained limited use of his legs, but was still a sickly child at the time of his father's death. He later wrote that in the middle of the funeral he stopped crying only after he looked up and saw Mount Adams in the distance. "Adams stood cool and calm, unperturbed . . . Adams suddenly seemed to be a friend. Adams subtly became a force for me to tie to, a symbol of stability of strength" (Douglas 1974, 13).

Between the strong will of his mother and his own self-determination, Douglas overcame his physical disabilities. He started to hike in the mountains, an experience that not only built up his strength but turned into a lifelong devotion to the environment. The drive to build himself physically carried over into other areas of his life. The Yakima High School yearbook of 1916 noted that its valedictorian that year had been "born for success."

After graduation from Whitman College, Douglas headed east in the summer of 1922 with $75 in his pocket to attend Columbia Law School. Douglas entered Columbia at a time when its faculty had just begun to explore new areas of legal research that would eventually lead to the "Legal Realism" movement. The Realists believed that to understand the law and the behavior of legal institutions, one had to look at individual behavior and use the social sciences to find the real causes of particular actions. Douglas became a devoted adherent to this new philosophy, and after a miserable two years working in a Wall Street law firm, he returned to Columbia as a teacher in 1927. Within a year, however, he resigned to accept a position at the Yale Law School, which under

William Orville Douglas (Harris & Ewing, Collection of the Supreme Court of the United States)

the leadership of its brilliant young dean, Robert M. Hutchins, quickly became the center of Legal Realism, and Douglas one of its star exponents.

His tenure at Yale may have been the most peaceful in his life, but beneath a surface tranquility he remained restless, especially when he looked to Washington and saw the dynamic activities going on under the New Deal umbrella. In 1934 Douglas secured an assignment from the newly created Securities and Exchange Commission (SEC) to study protective committees, the agency stockholders use during bankruptcy reorganization to protect their interests. He began commuting between New Haven and Washington, and soon came to the attention of the SEC chair, Joseph P. Kennedy, who arranged for the then thirty-seven-year-old Douglas to be named to the Commission in 1935. Two years later, President Roosevelt named Douglas chair of the SEC.

During these years in Washington Douglas became part of Franklin D. Roosevelt's inner circle, often joining the weekly poker games at the White House. There was a great deal of speculation that the bright, handsome westerner might have a future in politics. In fact, Douglas had already tired of the game and wanted to return to Yale. When a messenger interrupted a golf game on March 19, 1939, to tell Douglas that the president wanted to see him at the White House, Douglas almost did not go, because he fully expected that Roosevelt was going to ask him to take over the troubled Federal Communications Commission. But after teasing him for a few minutes, Roosevelt offered Douglas the seat on the Supreme Court vacated by Louis D. Brandeis a month earlier.

Although Douglas always claimed the offer came as a surprise, in fact he had had his friends busily at work promoting his name for the opening. Following the bruising court battle of 1937, Roosevelt wanted to make sure that his appointees would support his program, and in Douglas he had a confirmed New Deal liberal, someone who could mix it up with the conservatives, a quick mind, a westerner, and a loyal personal friend.

Douglas, the youngest person ever appointed to the Supreme Court, would establish a record of longevity for service before illness forced him to retire in late 1975. Moreover, no other justice ever engaged in so extensive and public a nonjudicial life. Douglas always claimed that the work of the Court never took more than three or four days a week; he read petitions rapidly, rarely agonized over decisions, could get to the heart of an issue instantly, and wrote his opinions quickly. A clerk related the story of Douglas leaving the bench after an oral argument, predicting the exact vote of the Court on the case, what the major points would be in the majority opinion, and what he would say in dissent. This left him time for other activities, such as travel, lecturing, writing, climbing mountains, and, as some critics claimed, getting into trouble.

Douglas and Felix Frankfurter had been friends—and friendly rivals—from their days as law school professors, and the younger Douglas had often looked to the more established Frankfurter for advice. Jurisprudentially, the two seemed to share the same basic values, but the shifting agenda of the Court soon highlighted the fact that on the crucial issues to confront the judiciary in the 1940s and 1950s they differed significantly. During the first years of the Stone regime Douglas allied himself with Black, but eventually proved far more willing and activist than his friend. As much, and perhaps even more than Warren, Douglas believed in a living Constitution.

Douglas has come in for a great deal of criticism for his results-oriented jurisprudence. He has been accused of deciding cases based on his political views, and of failing to develop a coherent, acceptable legal analysis in his decisions so that scholars and other judges could draw a useful pattern from his opinions. G. Edward White, in particular, has attacked Douglas for rejecting what White calls the two "principal twentieth-century devices designed to constrain subjective judicial lawmaking: fidelity to constitutional text or doctrine, and institutional deference" (White 1988b, 18). In other words, Douglas was unwilling to show proper respect for the constitutional opinions of Congress and the executive, and he refused to engage in the analysis of text that Frankfurter espoused. But Douglas, as even White has to admit, always asked the right question and came up with the right answer.

The best way to understand Douglas is to see him as a common-law judge, one who, when faced with new circumstances, tried to work out a legal solution that captured the spirit of the law rather than adhered to its literal niceties. To give one example, when critics charged that one of his wire-tapping decisions did not conform to the intent of the Framers, Douglas shot back, "What did the Framers know about wire-tapping? They didn't even have telephones!" Rather Douglas, like Brandeis before him, believed that the Fourth Amendment was meant to protect privacy and that in an age of telephones that meant adapting the old law to new circumstances.

A good example of Douglas asking the right question came in *Frank v. Maryland* (1959), one of the lesser-known Warren Court decisions. The Court faced the question of whether city health inspectors could enter premises without a search warrant. Nearly everyone on the bench thought of it as a simple question because the Fourth Amendment had previously been limited to criminal situations. Felix Frankfurter, who considered the Fourth Amendment his private preserve, received the assignment to write the majority opinion. Frankfurter wrote his typical law review article, buttressing it with copious references to prior rulings to prove that the warrant clause did not apply to civil searches.

Douglas disagreed, and requested his clerk, Charles Miller, to start researching a dissent. Miller retrieved a multitude of books from the Court's library and pored through numerous cases; he was unable, however, to find support for Douglas's dissent. An angry and frustrated Douglas told Miller to "bring in all the books you got, and let me see what I can do." Douglas stayed in his office for three days, working at the materials Miller had collected. At the end of the time he had scratched out ten pages that, according to Miller, "bowled me over. It was the most persuasive thing I had seen in my life" (Urofsky 1991c, 151).

Douglas circulated the draft, and three justices—Warren, Black, and Brennan—immediately switched their vote. Charles Evans Whittaker almost joined in as well, but after intense lobbying by Frankfurter, remained with the majority in a one-paragraph concurrence. Eight years later, the Court overruled the Frankfurter opinion and in two cases, *Camara v. Municipal Court* and *See v. Seattle*, adopted the Douglas view that a search conducted by the government—either by the criminal division or by civil officials—is still a search and subject to Fourth Amendment protections. Frankfurter's formalistic analysis led to a bad result. Douglas's unconventional analysis asked the right question—should there be any difference between a civil search and a criminal search if both are conducted by the government—and came up with the right answer. It is this ability to ask the right question that, more than anything, marks Douglas's jurisprudence.

Robert Houghwout Jackson

Robert Houghwout Jackson (1892–1954) was the last of the Roosevelt appointees to sit with Warren, although he was in ill health by then and died a few months after the Court handed down its decision in *Brown v. Board of Education*. Jackson is one of the least-known men to have served on the high Court, despite the fact that he had a notable career and a facile pen and he helped to create the modern doctrinal rules for judicial review of economic regulations in *Wickard v. Filburn* (1942).

Born on a western Pennsylvania farm, Jackson was self-educated; he briefly attended Albany Law School but then qualified for the bar by reading as an apprentice in a lawyer's office, the last Supreme Court justice to do so. He established a thriving practice in western New York and, as a fourth-generation Democrat, became active in state politics and an advisor to then governor Franklin Roosevelt. After Roosevelt entered the White House in 1933 he brought Jackson to Washington, where the New York lawyer advanced from general counsel at the Bureau of Internal Revenue to solicitor general to attorney general. Jackson later described his tenure as solicitor general as the happiest part of his life, and he won high marks for his role as the government's chief litigator; Louis Brandeis once commented that Jackson should be named solicitor general for life.

Many people considered Jackson a possible presidential candidate in 1940 until Roosevelt announced his intention to run for a third term. The president had promised Jackson a seat on the Supreme Court when he asked him to become attorney general; the next vacancy, however, resulted from the resignation of Chief Justice Charles Evans Hughes, and Roosevelt felt he had to promote Republican Harlan Fiske Stone from associate to chief justice so as to show bipartisanship as the war approached. A loyal

Robert Houghwout Jackson (Harris & Ewing, Collection of the Supreme Court of the United States)

supporter of the president, Jackson agreed, but it appears that Roosevelt may have promised Jackson that he would elevate him to the center chair upon Stone's departure from the Court. Both men assumed that Stone, who was sixty-nine when appointed chief, would probably not stay on the bench more than another year or two, and that would leave Jackson, then only fifty, a fair amount of time to lead the high Court.

Had Jackson been chief justice he might have been happier on the bench, but his activist nature chafed at the restrictions of judicial propriety. During the war he felt cut off from the great events going on around him; he remarked that on the Monday following the Japanese attack on Pearl Harbor the Court heard arguments about the taxability of greens fees! While he—like Frankfurter and Douglas—continued secretly to advise Roosevelt, he wanted to do more. Thus, he had leaped at the opportunity when President Harry S. Truman asked him to head the American prosecutorial team at the Nuremberg trial of Nazi war criminals.

Although Jackson tended to join Frankfurter on many issues, he could not be considered a predictable vote for the conservative bloc. He parted from Frankfurter, for example, in the second flag salute case, *West Virginia State Board of Education v. Barnette* (1943). His decision in *Wickard v. Filburn* (1942) is a ringing endorsement of an all-encompassing congressional power over commerce, yet he took a far more restricted view of presidential power during the Korean War in the steel seizure case, *Youngstown Sheet & Tube Co. v. Sawyer* (1952). Some of his opinions seem quirky—for example, his dissent in *Beauharnais v. Illinois* (1952), in which he endorsed the idea of treating racist speech as group libel, yet argued that the defendant had a right to a jury trial to prove the truth of the libel.

The three most junior members of the Court that Warren took over in 1953 had all been appointed by Harry Truman, and none of them could be considered "distinguished jurists." Hugo Black once told a nephew that "Truman's appointees were mediocre at best. We didn't get the best people," a sentiment William O. Douglas shared (Newman 1994, 419). When a vacancy occurred shortly after Truman entered the White House, political prudence dictated that he extend an olive branch to the Republicans by naming one of their own to the Court.

Harold Hitz Burton

Harold Hitz Burton (1888–1964), a moderate Republican senator from Ohio, fit the bill perfectly. Burton had spent his early years in Switzerland, where his ailing mother was being treated. After her death he returned to the United States and compiled an excellent record at both Bowdoin College and the Harvard Law School, from which he graduated in 1912. He then practiced law, first in Cleveland and then in Salt Lake City. After distinguished army service in France and Belgium during World War I, he returned to Cleveland and resumed his law practice.

Harold Hitz Burton (Harris & Ewing, Collection of the Supreme Court of the United States)

The affable Burton soon entered politics and, after holding a number of local offices, was elected to the Senate as a Republican in 1940. Burton was never a party ideologue, and in the Senate he broke with traditional Republican isolationists to favor an active American role in shaping the postwar world. His road to the Court also included service on Harry Truman's wartime defense procurement oversight committee, and he became one of the more adept members of the upper house in tax matters.

Burton came in for some heavy criticism, much of it unfounded, during his first years on the bench. In terms of the Court's output, he was never a prolific opinion writer, which led some columnists to charge that he shirked his judicial obligations. In June 1947 Drew Pearson, in his national column, not only attacked Burton for his "meager" productivity but also characterized him as an inveterate partygoer and implied that his social life interfered with his Court duties.

Felix Frankfurter, who detested Pearson, immediately came to Burton's defense, as did William O. Douglas at the other end of the jurisprudential spectrum. In his memoirs, Douglas called Burton "as conscientious a man as ever sat on the Court, God-fearing, and painfully slow in his work. He spent night after night, way after midnight, in his office." Hugo Black acknowledged that Burton had been slow when he first came on the Court, but soon he could "discuss cases in conference with considerable clarity due I think to the fact that he studies and understands the points raised" (Urofsky 1997, 152–153).

Evaluations of Burton as a judge have varied. His biographer, Mary Frances Berry, noted that Burton's overriding trait appears to have been judicial restraint. His background gave him a "generally conservative mindset," but his conscientiousness made him a "lawyer's judge" (Berry 1978, 231). Other scholars have given him high marks for seeing both sides of an argument, but agree that the one characteristic that stood out in his jurisprudential career was judicial restraint.

It is difficult to chart a consistent path through Burton's opinions; they run the gamut from liberal to conservative. He may not have been a results-oriented jurist, but it seems clear that he voted his beliefs as much as anything, as can be seen in his dissent in *Louisiana ex rel. Francis v. Resweber* (1947), in which he objected to the state's efforts to electrocute a black man a second time after the first effort had failed to kill him. He had a pragmatic mind, one that did not always tend toward jurisprudential consistency. But on a bench riven by factionalism, Burton proved a point of calm and stability, liked and respected by all his colleagues.

Tom Campbell Clark

When the liberal Frank Murphy died in the summer of 1949, Truman named Tom Campbell Clark (1899–1977) to replace him. Later on Truman reportedly said "Tom Clark was my biggest mistake. . . . He was no damn good as Attorney General, and on

Tom Campbell Clark (Harris & Ewing, Collection of the Supreme Court of the United States)

the Supreme Court . . . he has been even worse. He hasn't made one right decision I can think of" (Miller 1974, 225–226). Given Truman's warmth toward Clark during his years in the White House and after, it is hard to reconcile this statement with anything other than pique at Clark's vote against presidential seizure of the steel mills during the Korean conflict.

Born in Dallas, Texas, Clark practiced law there after service in the army during World War I. Though successful, Clark was restless in private practice and in 1937 he eagerly accepted an offer to join the Justice Department. He started as an assistant in the war risk litigation section, and his ability quickly moved him up. Following Pearl Harbor, Roosevelt named him civilian coordinator of the Western Defense Command, in which role he handled all the legal aspects of the Japanese relocation. After that he took over the war frauds unit in Justice, and worked closely with Harry Truman's Senate committee. When Truman became president he named Clark attorney general.

Clark's record as head of the Justice Department reflects the different aspects of the man. He energetically enforced antitrust laws and proved friendly to the emerging civil rights movement. He pressured the FBI to investigate lynchings and called on Congress to make lynching a federal crime. While advocating fairness in criminal procedure, Clark was also a Cold Warrior and personally authorized prosecution of the top leaders of the Communist Party. According to one scholar, Truman appointed Clark at the urging of Chief Justice Fred Vinson, a close friend of the president; Vinson wanted a colleague who would support his views.

In his first few years on the bench, Clark did in fact become an ally of Vinson, especially in civil liberties cases. Clark rejected civil liberties claims 75 percent of the time, a little below Vinson's rate of 83 percent, and he was a strong supporter of the government position in the Cold War cases that came before the high Court. But Clark was not a red-baiter, and over the years he moved away from the conservative wing of the Court. William O. Douglas praised Clark in his memoirs. Clark, he said, unlike the other Truman appointees, "was different in the sense that he changed. He had the indispensable capacity to develop so that with the passage of time he grew in stature and expanded his dimensions" (Douglas 1981, 245).

Sherman Minton

Truman's last appointment to the Court was another good friend, Sherman Minton (1890–1965) of Indiana. According to Douglas, "Shay" Minton, then a member of the Court of Appeals for the Seventh Circuit, had flown to Washington upon hearing of Wiley Rutledge's death and gone to the White House to see his old buddy. The following conversation then reportedly took place:

Sherman Minton (Harris & Ewing, Collection of the Supreme Court of the United States)

"What can I do for you, Shay?"

"Harry, I want you to put me on the Supreme Court to fill that vacancy."

"Shay, I'll do just that." (Douglas 1981, 245)

Whether this conversation actually took place is difficult to determine, since Minton had a reputation as a great storyteller. But the record is clear on the enormous friendship between Minton and Truman, and the president considered this appointment his best. Years later Harry Truman wrote that there "never was a finer man or an abler public servant than the Honorable Sherman Minton" (Rudko 1988, 111).

Born in Indiana, Minton had excelled in academics as well as sports. While in the army in France during World War I he had found time to study law at the Sorbonne; after the war he finished his law study, set up a practice in New Albany, Indiana, and began dabbling in Democratic politics. This led to his appointment to the Indiana Public Service Commission, where he soon achieved a reputation as a champion of the consumer and the nemesis of the utilities. In 1934 he successfully ran for the United States Senate on the slogan "You can't offer a hungry man the Constitution."

In the Senate Minton proved a staunch supporter of the Roosevelt administration, and wholeheartedly endorsed the president's court reform plan in 1937; he also became a close friend of another first-term senator, Harry Truman of Missouri. In 1940 Minton lost his bid for reelection when Indiana went solidly for another native son, Wendell Willkie, whose coattails swept a number of Republican candidates into office. But Roosevelt rewarded Minton for his past loyalty by naming him to the Seventh Circuit.

Once on the high Court Minton, more than any of the other Truman appointees, committed himself to the philosophy of judicial restraint, and proved to be a natural ally of Felix Frankfurter, although in many instances Frankfurter's willingness to look beyond formalistic application of precedent led him to disagree with Minton. His beliefs grew out of his political experience in Indiana and in the Senate during the Depression, and especially from his reaction to the conservative justices who had sought to block New Deal measures. He firmly believed that, barring a specific constitutional prohibition, the legislature had almost unlimited powers and should not be second-guessed by the courts. While in the Senate Minton had introduced a measure that would have required the vote of seven justices to declare a federal statute unconstitutional.

Minton was well aware of the internecine feuding that had taken place on the high Court, and wanted no part of it. He believed that whenever possible the Court should act as a unified deliberative body and that an opinion should reflect the judgment of the Court—not of an individual justice. As a result he proved amenable to altering passages of his opinions to garner support and eschewed what had become the common practice of writing concurring opinions, because he believed they confused the public about what the Court had in fact decided. He wrote only three concurrences in his seven years on the bench. When writing for the majority, Minton attempted to lay out the line of decision as neatly as possible and ignored opposing arguments. One does not find in any of Minton's writings the jurisprudential musings that Frankfurter loved.

The one exception to Minton's deference to the other branches of government involved race relations, and from the start he showed himself an ardent opponent of any form of government-sponsored racial discrimination. He considered the landmark decision of *Brown v. Board of Education* (1954) to be the most important case in which he participated. When ill health forced him to retire after only seven years on the bench, he noted presciently that "there will be more interest in who will succeed me than in my passing" (Urofsky, ed. 1994, 325).

John Marshall Harlan

Following his appointment of Warren, Eisenhower next named the highly respected Wall Street lawyer John Marshall Harlan (1899–1971) to the high Court. His grandfather, also named John Marshall Harlan, had been the sole dissenter in *Plessy v. Ferguson* (1896), the case that had established the "separate but equal" doctrine. Harlan's appointment replaced one moderate conservative (Jackson) with another, and for the years he and Frankfurter served together, they constituted the core of the opposition to Warren, Black, and Douglas. Harlan was anything but a stodgy reactionary, however, and had none of the acerbity that so poisoned Frankfurter's relations with his colleagues.

Harlan had studied at Princeton, been a Rhodes scholar at Balliol College, Oxford, where he began the study of law, and then completed his legal education at the New York Law School. Following graduation Harlan began a career that involved not only an extensive and varied practice with the Wall Street firm of Root, Clark, Buckner & Howland, but public service as well. When the senior partner, Emory Buckner, was appointed U.S. attorney for the Southern District of New York in 1925, Harlan became his assistant. In 1931 he became a partner in the firm, and after Buckner's death in 1941 became its leading trial lawyer. During World War II Harlan headed the operational analysis section of the Eighth Air Force, which analyzed and advised on bombing operations. For his work he received the United States Legion of Merit and the Croix de Guerre of Belgium and France.

On his return to civilian life Harlan again mixed a varied private practice, which included several arguments before the Supreme Court, and public service. From 1951 to 1953 he acted as chief counsel to the New York State Crime Commission, and in January 1954 President Eisenhower named him to the Court of Appeals for the Second Circuit. He sat on that bench less than a year before going to Washington.

John Marshall Harlan (Harris & Ewing, Collection of the Supreme Court of the United States)

The patrician Harlan brought great learning and high legal skills to the Court and quickly earned a reputation as a "lawyer's judge," one whose opinions spoke not only to the theoretical concerns of academics but also to the practical issues that lawyers, prosecutors, and others needed to know and understand. Numerous clerks reported that a Harlan opinion also received great respect and a careful reading in the other eight chambers, even if one stood on the opposite side of the argument. William O. Douglas learned this lesson in a case in which he had written for the majority. Late on Friday afternoon Harlan circulated his dissent. Douglas's clerk wanted to know if the justice was going to read the dissent, and Douglas, eager to get away for the weekend, in essence said, "Why bother? The vote has been taken." On Monday morning Douglas returned to discover that Harlan's draft had won over a majority of the Court to his view. Norman Dorsen declared that Harlan's opinions "have not been exceeded in professional competence by any Supreme Court Justice since Brandeis" (Urofsky 1991a, 12).

After Frankfurter's retirement in 1962, Harlan became the conservative conscience of an ever more activist Court. His conservatism, however, was a far cry from that of the Truman appointees and certainly from that of the Four Horsemen—George Sutherland, Pierce Butler, Willis Van Devanter, and James McReynolds—who had so bitterly fought the New Deal in the 1930s. Harlan respected precedent but did not make of it an icon; to overturn a precedent, however, he demanded that a strong case should be made. Like Brandeis, he did not believe that every wrong could be righted by the Court and that under a federal system there had to be great flexibility and diversity accorded to the states. He could not accept Black's blanket application of the Bill of Rights to the states and, like Frankfurter, would sustain a state criminal procedure if it passed a "fundamental fairness" standard. Harlan's conservatism had a Burkean flavor to it as well as a sensitivity to individual rights, particularly those protected under the First Amendment. He would devise the method by which the Warren Court managed to extricate itself from the Cold War speech rulings of the Vinson era.

Throughout his tenure, Harlan provided a form of resistance to the dominant liberal motifs of the Warren Court, but did it in a way that was intelligent, determined, and above all—principled. But as his former clerk, Norman Dorsen noted, it would be a mistake to view Harlan solely in this conservative light. To a large degree he concurred in the liberal activism of the Court, picking his way carefully and above all seeking to be true to his core judicial values—federalism and proceduralism, both directed to keeping the delicate balance of state-federal relations in good working order. His view of federalism is best summarized in a dissenting opinion by Justice Stephen Field in *Baltimore & Ohio Railroad v. Baugh* (1893), which Harlan often quoted:

> The Constitution of the United States . . . recognizes and preserves the autonomy
> and independence of the States. . . . Supervision over either legislative or judicial

action of the States is in no case permissible except as to matters by the Constitution specifically authorized or delegated to the United States. (p. 401)

Harlan viewed federalism as essential to preserving pluralism and local experimentation. No other political system, he declared, "could have afforded so much scope to the varied interests and aspirations of a dynamic people representing such divergencies of ethnic and cultural backgrounds" and still "unify them into a nation" (Urofsky, ed. 1994, 216).

His dedication to proceduralism was equally firm. By proceduralism Harlan meant not only the rules that govern trials and appeals, but also issues that determine when the judicial power will be exercised. Harlan tried to occupy a centrist position, but on a court that became more and more activist during the Warren years, this often made him appear to be a doctrinaire conservative, which he was not. Neither was he a civil libertarian in the mold of a Black, Douglas, or Brennan, even though his overall voting record shows a strong concern for such rights.

William Joseph Brennan, Jr.

The nomination of William Joseph Brennan, Jr. (1906–1997) in 1956 dramatically shifted the balance of the Court toward a more liberal activism. Supposedly, Eisenhower had wanted to name a Catholic and a Democrat just prior to the 1956 election, and his attorney general, Herbert Brownell, had recently met and been impressed with Brennan, then a member of the New Jersey Supreme Court.

A 1931 graduate of the Harvard Law School (where he had been a student of Frankfurter), Brennan had joined one of New Jersey's leading law firms and soon became a specialist on the management side in the fledgling field of labor law. His credibility was based, at least in part, on the memory of his late father's popularity as a union leader whose reputation had helped him to win election as Newark's commissioner of public safety. In fifteen years of private practice before and after World War II, Brennan demonstrated his considerable skills as an advocate and trial lawyer, as a legal tactician and draftsman, and as a conciliator who could get along with all parties in a dispute. These qualities would prove invaluable in his tenure on the nation's high Court.

After the war Brennan became active with a group of young lawyers who were pressing for reform of the state judicial system, and in 1947 New Jersey adopted a new constitution that included a restructured court system. Two years later Brennan was appointed to the new superior court by a Republican governor. From there Brennan was quickly promoted to the appellate bench and in 1952 to the state supreme court, where his mentor, Arthur Vanderbilt, a nationally prominent legal figure with whom Brennan had worked in the reform drive, was the chief justice.

William Joseph Brennan, Jr. (Ken Heinen, Collection of the Supreme Court of the United States)

Soon after the president sent Brennan's name to the Senate, Justice Douglas put his law clerk, William Cohen, to work reading Brennan's state court opinions to see if they could get a measure of how the new man would vote. Cohen concluded that one could not predict Brennan's future behavior on the basis of his writings. Eisenhower had clearly expected that Brennan would be a conservative, but Brennan's friends in New Jersey and other local legal observers knew he was unmistakably liberal. It took little time for Brennan to align himself with Warren, Black, and Douglas, and the latter wrote enthusiastically that the new justice "is a wonderful person and a grand human being. He has courage and independence. He is imbued with the libertarian philosophy and I would be willing to give odds that he will leave as fine a record on this Court as Holmes, Hughes, Murphy or any of the greats" (Urofsky 1991a, 13).

Brennan eventually emerged as a dominant member of the Warren Court and as one of the great consensus builders in the Court's history. He developed a special relationship with Earl Warren, which gave him added leverage in determining the direction of the Court. In the 1960s the regular conference of all the justices would invariably be preceded by a private meeting between Warren and Brennan to plan strategy. Brennan—no mean political strategist himself—admired Warren's skills in this area, and served him as a judicial technician, providing the jurisprudential points needed to advance their point of view.

Brennan's influence, however, derived not from his judicial skills that, while impressive, were not overwhelming. Instead, much of it grew out of his personality, his friendliness, his political instincts, and above all, from his uncanny ability to define a liberal consensus that could bring in centrists and sometimes even conservatives. Brennan would massage an opinion to cut away the sharp jurisprudential edges and thus make it palatable to those who would never have accepted the results if stated as Black or Douglas would have done. Brennan could get on well with his colleagues and understood that a vote against him in one case never precluded a future vote for his position in another. During the Warren years Brennan's influence on the Court was often underestimated, because the liberal activists seemed so dominant, and he stood in the shadow of Warren, Black, and Douglas. When Warren Burger became chief justice in 1969, and even into the Rehnquist era, Bill Brennan kept building consensus and winning over majorities.

Brennan's priorities in terms of individual rights emerged fairly quickly and clearly. The Bill of Rights, he believed, gives to every person enormous protection against the state. People cannot be stopped from expressing their views, from petitioning the government, and from exercising the full range of those liberties that Americans hold dear. The government, on the other hand, must always be kept in check, and the judiciary must assure that there is no established church, no infringement on the rights of persons accused of crimes, and above all, no interference with individual privacy and personal autonomy. While he agreed with Black's views on the total incorporation of the Bill of Rights against the states and the preferred position of the First Amendment, he went further than Black and, like Douglas, was willing to read into that document implied rights regarding privacy and autonomy. Brennan was the judicial activist par excellence of the twentieth century, and the leading proponent of the philosophy of a "living Constitution," one whose provisions must not be interpreted literally or restricted by the understandings of the past, but by the conditions of the present.

The year Brennan joined the Court also marked the term Warren broke away from Felix Frankfurter's efforts to corral him for the conservative camp. As a result, the liberal wing now had four firm votes—the chief, Black, Douglas, and Brennan:—and depending on the issue, could often pick up the fifth vote necessary for a majority. One could not say that the balance had swung over from conservatism to liberalism, from judicial restrain to judicial activism, as Frankfurter and Harlan still exerted considerable influence. But one could say that with Brennan's appointment, the pendulum had started to swing and had reached a middle position that could swing one way or the other depending on the issue.

Charles Evans Whittaker

Of the five appointments Dwight Eisenhower made, Charles Evans Whittaker (1901–1973) was the least distinguished; historian Bernard Schwarz suggests that "he may have been the worst Justice of the [twentieth] century" (Schwartz 1983, 216). A farm boy who had quit high school at sixteen, Whittaker had never gone to college and had attended an unaccredited law school at night. He worked hard, however, and became a fairly prosperous lawyer and an active Republican in Missouri. Eisenhower named him to the federal district court in 1954, elevated him to the Eighth Circuit two years later, and then appointed him to the Supreme Court in 1957 when Stanley Reed retired.

Whittaker tried hard, but he was in over his head. He lacked intellectual capacity and could not make up his mind. In a Fourth Amendment case (*Frank v. Maryland* [1959]), Douglas had circulated a draft dissent that drew three votes away from what had been an eight-to-one decision assigned to Frankfurter. Whittaker was reportedly wavering, and Frankfurter, furious at the possibility of losing his majority, hounded him mercilessly. Finally, Whittaker fled from Washington to the country for the weekend, taking his clerk with him, and declared he would announce his decision when he returned on Monday. After three days of agonizing he stayed with Frankfurter, but entered a one-paragraph concurrence that made no sense.

In his memoirs Douglas described Whittaker as "an affable companion" with extremely reactionary ideas who had trouble making up his mind and writing an

Charles Evans Whittaker (Abdon Daoud Ackad, Collection of the Supreme Court of the United States)

opinion (Douglas 1981, 250). In one case, *Meyers v. United States* (1960), Whittaker had been assigned the opinion for the Court, and could not write anything. He turned to Douglas for help, and Douglas, who had dissented, wound up writing both the majority and minority opinions. Although Douglas derived some malicious pleasure from recalling this episode, he and his wife, Mercedes, went out of their way to help Whittaker when the strain began to take its toll. They convinced him to seek medical help and provided some badly needed emotional support when he resigned from the Court in 1962.

Potter Stewart

Eisenhower's last appointment, Potter Stewart (1915–1985) to replace Harold Burton in 1959, proved one of the most able and interesting men on the bench. At age forty-four, he was the second youngest person to be appointed in a century and gave off an air of vigor and youth that at times seemed almost out of place on the bench. Stewart loved being a judge and once remarked that it involved "all the fun of practicing law without the bother of clients" (Woodward and Armstrong 1979, 10).

Prior to ascending the bench, Stewart's life read like that of many upper-middle-class, white, male success stories. Educated at Hotchkiss, Yale, and Cambridge, he served in the navy in World War II, worked in a leading midwestern law firm, and, like his father before him, joined the Republican Party in Cincinnati, where he rose to a position of judicial eminence. In 1954 Eisenhower named him to the Sixth Circuit, and then four years later tapped him for the high Court.

Although Douglas offhandedly characterized Stewart as a conservative, labels such as liberal, conservative, or activist are nearly meaningless when applied to this man. Stewart himself said that he had enough trouble trying to figure out what these terms meant in the political world and that they had no meaning at all on the bench. To Stewart, such labels suggested a judge who acted upon his own economic, political, social, or religious values. In contrast, Stewart asked repeatedly that he be thought of as simply a good lawyer. His justice-as-lawyer role model suggested a jurist capable of applying objective legal reasoning to questions before the Court, uninfluenced by his own values. In his twenty-three years on the Court, Stewart managed to elude the pigeonholes.

Although he dissented from many of the Warren Court's more activist decisions in the 1960s, Stewart had little in common with Frankfurter, or even Harlan. One of his law clerks, Ellen Borgerson, described him as the quintessential common-law judge, and that may be the best clue to understanding his jurisprudence.

Although common-law judges are nominally bound by stare decisis (rulings in prior cases), they also have the obligation of squaring the legal rules of the past with current needs and conditions, fulfilling Holmes's famous aphorism that "the life of the

Potter Stewart (Harris & Ewing, Collection of the Supreme Court of the United States)

law has not been logic; it has been experience. The felt necessities of the time . . . have had a good deal more to do than the syllogism in determining the rules by which men should be governed" (Holmes 1881, 5). Stewart could parse past cases with the best of his colleagues, but he had a keen sensitivity to how law would actually work in the real world and of the danger of erecting inflexible and irrelevant rules. He felt bad that many people would remember him only for his comment in a 1964 case (*Jacobellis v. Ohio*) that he would not attempt to define pornography, "But I know it when I see it."

This common-sensical approach reflected Stewart's pragmatic view of life, and it led him to examine each case not only on its legal merits but also in terms of how the rule would work in the real world. He was never as results oriented as Douglas or Brennan, but in his own way Stewart sought the right solution, the workable solution, and then could weave the legal ropes to support it. If one tries to analyze his opinions over twenty-three terms from a strictly jurisprudential context, one might conclude that Stewart lacked any doctrinal consistency at all. His decisions make far more sense if we view them in terms of a somewhat conservative, but certainly not hidebound, common-law judge trying to figure out what rules will do the least harm to past decisions and still keep the law flexible and in tune with modern needs.

Byron Raymond White

With the accession of John Kennedy to the White House, one might have expected that his appointments would give the four activists a consistent fifth vote. That is, in fact, what happened, but not with Kennedy's first appointment, Byron Raymond White (b. 1917), who brought an impressive list of firsts with him to the Court—first former All-American back, first former professional football player, and first former Supreme Court clerk to become a member of the Court. White had impressed Kennedy with his personal courage as deputy attorney general in handling the Freedom Riders' protest in Alabama in the spring of 1961. Aside from civil rights, however, White tended to be pragmatic and during the Warren years could not be counted as firmly anchored in any particular doctrinal grouping. He seemed to grow more conservative with the years, however, and after the Nixon appointees joined the bench in the early seventies, White appeared to have found his jurisprudential home with Burger and Rehnquist. But a close examination of White's jurisprudence shows a consistent philosophy.

As an attorney in private practice in Colorado in the 1950s, White seemed to his partners to be an effective problem solver, and he adhered to this pragmatism in joining the Kennedy administration. He devised much of the civil rights strategy of the administration, convincing Attorney General Robert Kennedy as well as the president

Byron Raymond White (Joseph Bailey, National Geographic, Collection of the Supreme Court of the United States)

that the only proper course for the Justice Department to take was one that could be defended in court, and thus would not be seen by the Southern states as a vendetta.

When White went onto the bench, he did not lose his attachment to civil rights and always stood against any form of state-sponsored discrimination. But in later years, when the agenda had changed to questions of affirmative action and race-determined districting, he did not find these new solutions attractive in either a pragmatic or a constitutional sense.

White shared the Justice Department's view of rights of the accused, namely, minimal constitutional standards had to be maintained, but in a battle against criminals, law enforcement officials needed every legitimate edge they could get, and he refused to sign on to Warren's efforts to expand the rights of those accused of crimes. As to freedom of expression, White certainly believed in the First Amendment, but like others in the government thought that protesters were not entitled to the type of protection that Black and Douglas were willing to give them. Similarly, White did not see the state as the enemy, and did not share the view of the liberals that the Court served as the last protector of individual freedom against the state.

Those who claimed that White abandoned the liberals and became more conservative as the years went by missed the fact that Kennedy liberalism—of which White stood as a prime exemplar—never shared the same values as the liberal wing of the Warren Court. Like Stewart, White retained an independence that often surprised those who took his vote for granted.

Arthur Joseph Goldberg

The appointment of Arthur Joseph Goldberg (1908–1990) finally gave the liberals a solid fifth vote, and there is a certain irony that the very activist Goldberg replaced this century's chief exponent of judicial restraint, Felix Frankfurter. The youngest of eleven children of an immigrant fruit peddler, Goldberg had worked his way through North-western Law School, graduating first in his class. He then developed a highly successful labor practice, became counsel to the AFL-CIO, and then Kennedy's secretary of labor. The politically sensitive president knew that Jewish groups would want one of their own to replace Frankfurter, and he was not about to disappoint them.

Goldberg differed from Frankfurter in almost all ways. He got along well with the brethren, championed an activist role for the Court, and was not afraid to take on new issues. The new justice easily articulated the differences between himself and his predecessor. Frankfurter, he said, "always was fearful that the Court would injure itself [by taking controversial issues]. . . . Well, it's not the function of a Supreme Court Justice to worry about the Court injuring itself. It's the sworn duty of a Supreme Court Justice to do justice under law and apply the Constitution" (Schwartz 1983, 448). His good friend, Bill Douglas, could not have said it better.

Arthur Joseph Goldberg (Harris & Ewing, Collection of the Supreme Court of the United States)

The years 1962 to 1969 were the heyday of Warren activism. The liberal bloc not only had five sure votes on most issues, but could often count on one or more of the moderate conservatives to join them. Tom Clark seemed to grow more susceptible to Warren's influence as the years went by. Harlan remained closest to the Frankfurter view of judicial restraint, but without the inflexibility that had isolated Frankfurter in his last years on the Court. Stewart and White, while they frequently disagreed with the liberals, found many occasions when they could vote with the majority. The only problem, from the liberal point of view, seemed to be Black's growing conservatism after 1964, but even that did not diminish the liberal strength significantly.

Goldberg did not stay on the Court very long; after the rough and tumble of labor law and Democratic politics, he found the marble temple somewhat quiet. There is a difference of opinion whether Goldberg wanted to leave the Court, or whether he just could not resist Lyndon Johnson's arm twisting, but in 1965 he agreed to take over the thankless job of American ambassador to the United Nations.

Abe Fortas

When Lyndon Johnson named his good friend Abe Fortas (1910–1982) to the Court in 1965, it began one of the more tragic stories involving the Court in this century. Johnson practically had to beat Fortas over the head to join the Court. An insider among insiders in Washington, he had been Bill Douglas's student at Yale and then a protégé during the New Deal. Fortas personified those New Dealers who had come to Washington to do good, and then stayed on to do well. He was a senior partner in the quintessential Washington law firm of Arnold, Fortas & Porter, had a very lucrative law practice, and was a close personal friend of Lyndon Johnson and other Capitol Hill powerhouses. When Johnson became president he continued to rely on Fortas's judgment, and Fortas was among those who always had direct access to the Oval Office. Yet Fortas had also found time to do public interest work as well and had been the counsel for Clarence Earl Gideon in the landmark case that established a right to counsel in all felony cases, *Gideon v. Wainwright* (1963). He and his wife, Carolyn Aggar, enjoyed an opulent life style, and she opposed the appointment because of the enormous salary reduction involved. It might have been better for all concerned if the president had just left Goldberg on the bench and kept Fortas at his side.

Yet there is no doubt that Fortas had one of the best legal minds of any member of the Court this century, and many compared him to the greatest legal craftsman ever to sit on the high court, Louis Brandeis, in terms of legal skill. John Harlan, the "lawyer's judge" on the bench, admired the quality of Fortas's work. Like his former teacher and close friend, Bill Douglas, Fortas was an activist; he had all of Goldberg's proclivities, but far more skill as a judge. He might have made a great justice, perhaps even a great chief justice, but his inability to remove himself as an advisor to Johnson ultimately led to his downfall.

Abe Fortas (Harris & Ewing, Collection of the Supreme Court of the United States)

Thurgood Marshall

Johnson made his second appointment in 1967. Thurgood Marshall (1908–1993) became the last member of the Warren Court and the first black appointed to the nation's highest court. Douglas, in his memoirs, stated baldly that Johnson named Marshall "simply because he was black, and in the 1960s that was enough" (Douglas 1981, 251). No one, certainly, represented the African American legal struggle for equal rights as did Marshall. The grandson of a slave and the son of a railroad steward, he had been the chief strategist for the NAACP in its long campaign leading up to *Brown v. Board of Education* in 1954, and one of the most successful attorneys ever to appear before the Court.

The successful litigator, however, turned into a mediocre judge. John Kennedy had named Marshall in 1961 to the important Court of Appeals for the Second Circuit, and at least some of his colleagues there questioned his judgment and judicial ability. He left the bench in 1965 to become solicitor general, a job in which he could fully exercise the skills he had honed over many years. Then Johnson named him to the high Court in 1967, where he quickly became a vote without an identifiable voice. He supported the activists down the line, but never developed any identifiable jurisprudential philosophy he could call his own. A decade later, when only he and Brennan remained from the liberal bloc, the joke among law clerks was that Burger might have the center chair, but Brennan had two seats.

This is unfair in many ways. Like most new justices, he was assigned few important decisions in his first terms, and by the time he found his voice, the composition of the Court had changed; over his tenure it would move consistently to the right. Marshall had been, and would always be, a voice for minority rights, and thanks to his own knowledge of how blacks had been treated by the criminal justice system, he became one of the strongest advocates of rights for the accused. He also articulated a firm belief that capital punishment violated the Eighth Amendment ban against cruel and unusual punishment, especially as it was imposed far more frequently against blacks than against white defendants convicted of similar crimes. Had he been appointed to the Court ten years earlier, Marshall might have been a key player among the activists; that moment, however, passed him by before he could get used to the Marble Temple.

Conclusion

These, then are the men who made up the Warren Court. Some, like Black and Frankfurter, are among the Court's greatest jurists, and the debate in which they engaged over the reach of the Bill of Rights became a critical part of the Court's agenda in the

Thurgood Marshall (Joseph Lavenburg, National Geographic Society, Collection of the Supreme Court of the United States)

last half of the twentieth century. Others, like Douglas and Brennan, towered over most of the other hundred-plus men and women who have sat on the high Court. But from all of the available evidence, as well as the testimony of many of the justices themselves, there is no question that this was the Warren Court. Earl Warren may not have been the greatest intellectual ever to occupy the center chair, but he had the political skills to rank him among the great chief justices. He set the agenda of the Court and led the activist bloc in his goal to breathe more democracy into a living Constitution.

References

Berry, Mary Frances. 1978. *Stability, Security, and Continuity: Mr. Justice Burton and Decision-Making in the Supreme Court, 1945–1958.* Westport, CT: Greenwood Press.

Douglas, William O. 1974. *Go East, Young Man.* New York: Random House.

————. 1981. *The Court Years: The Autobiography of William O. Douglas.* New York: Random House.

Gerhart, Eugene. 1958. *America's Advocate: Robert H. Jackson.* Indianapolis, IN: Bobbs-Merrill.

Ickes, Harold L. 1954. *The Secret Diaries of Harold L. Ickes.* New York: Simon & Schuster.

Holmes, Oliver Wendell, Jr. 1881. *The Common Law.* Boston, MA: Little, Brown.

Kluger, Richard. 1976. *Simple Justice.* New York: Knopf.

Miller, Merle. 1974. *Plain Speaking: An Oral History of Harry S. Truman.* New York: Berkeley Books.

Newman, Roger K. 1994. *Hugo Black: A Biography.* New York: Pantheon.

Rudko, Frances Howell. 1988. *The Truman Court: A Study in Judicial Restraint.* Westport, CT: Greenwood.

Sapienza, John. n.d. "Addendum to Stanley Reed Oral History Memoir." New York: Columbia University Library.

Schwartz, Bernard. 1983. *Super Chief: Earl Warren and His Supreme Court.* New York: New York University Press.

Urofsky, Melvin I. 1991a. *Continuity and Change: The Supreme Court and Individual Liberties, 1913–1986.* Belmont, CA: Wadsworth.

————. 1991b. *Felix Frankfurter: Judicial Restraint and Individual Liberties.* Boston, MA: Twayne.

————. 1991c. "William O. Douglas as a Common Law Judge." *Duke Law Journal* 41: 133.

————. 1997. *Division and Discord: The Supreme Court under Stone and Vinson, 1941–1953.* Columbia, SC: University of South Carolina Press.

Urofsky, Melvin I., ed. 1994. *The Supreme Court Justices: A Biographical Dictionary.* New York: Garland.

Warren, Earl. 1977. *The Memoirs of Earl Warren.* Garden City, NJ: Doubleday.

White, G. Edward. 1982. *Earl Warren: A Public Life.* New York: Oxford University Press.

White, G. Edward. 1988a. *The American Judicial Tradition.* New York: Oxford Uniiversity Press.

———. 1988b. "The Anti-Judge: William O. Douglas and the Ambiguities of Individuality." *Virginia Law Review* 74:17.

Woodward, Bob, and Scott Armstrong. 1979. *The Brethren.* New York: Simon & Schuster.

The Decisions

In the sixteen years we define as the Warren era, the Supreme Court revolution-
ized American constitutional law. In some instances, it built upon a string of decisions that were leading up to a particular doctrinal change; in others, the justices
created policy with little or no precedent. In all of these cases, however, we can see
two main themes at work—justice and democracy.

The Court eventually departed from the principles enunciated by Felix Frankfurter, who believed that limits on the Court's powers and jurisdiction meant that
some wrongs did not have a judicial solution, and that deference should be paid in
almost every instance to the legislative will. Rather, Earl Warren—backed initially by
Hugo Black and William O. Douglas, and then later by William Brennan, Arthur Goldberg, and Abe Fortas—saw the Constitution as guaranteeing to every American equal
justice before the law. This meant that if a wrong existed, then so did a judicial remedy. As we look at the Warren Court's decisions in the area of criminal procedure, we
can see that a desire for justice runs like a leitmotif from *Gideon v. Wainwright*
through *Miranda v. Arizona*.

The second theme is that of democracy, and this desire to further the participa-
tory nature of the American polity can best be seen in the decisions on free speech
and apportionment. Here again the Warren Court had some limited guidance from
past decisions, but no set of cases in the nation's history so affected the political
process as those requiring that states reapportion their legislatures on a one-person,
one-vote basis.

Behind the specific issues of justice and democracy lay a basic question of how
the Court should interpret the Constitution. Ever since the founding of the Republic
there had been a division between the followers of Thomas Jefferson and those of
Alexander Hamilton. Jefferson believed in a narrow construction; the federal government enjoyed only those powers specifically delegated to it in the Constitution, and
nothing more. Hamilton had taken the position that the Constitution gave the national
government all powers except those specifically denied to it. Hamilton's theory, especially as expounded by Chief Justice John Marshall, had seemingly won out over the
Jeffersonian view. But even the Hamilton/Marshall doctrine recognized that the gov-

ernment created under the Constitution was a government of limited authority, and that view was also part of the constitutional legacy with which courts continue to wrestle.

Specifically, how much leeway does the Constitution grant to the branches of the government to deal with changing issues. Is the Constitution to be interpreted as society stood in 1789, when the states ratified the Constitution, or in 1868, when they ratified the Fourteenth Amendment, or is it to be a "living Constitution," continuously adapted to meet changing social, economic, and political conditions? If the former, then the constraints are apparent, because we must deal with rights as they were conceived—or even existed—in times past. On the other hand, who is to interpret what a "living Constitution" means? John Marshall had claimed in *Marbury v. Madison* (1803) that it was clearly the function of the courts to interpret the laws, and he thus made the Supreme Court the supreme arbiter of what the Constitution has meant for the past two centuries. Under Earl Warren, the Court took it upon itself to interpret a Constitution written in 1789, but applicable to the middle of the twentieth century.

Questions both of justice and democracy were waiting on the Court's docket when Earl Warren arrived from California. While, had he followed Frankfurter's advice, he might have avoided some of the issues—or at least deferred them—Warren's own sense of moral imperatives demanded that he act. And he did.

The Equal Protection of the Law

The most pressing issue confronting the Supreme Court in the fall of 1953 involved a challenge to the decades-old practice by Southern states of segregating schoolchildren on the basis of race. The National Association for the Advancement of Colored People (NAACP), through its Legal Defense Fund, had been slowly eroding the basis of "separate but equal" and now asked the Court to overthrow that doctrine completely.

Section 1 of the Fourteenth Amendment provides that no state shall "deny to any person within its jurisdiction the equal protection of the laws." In its first interpretation of that clause, the Supreme Court indicated that it applied only to racial concerns. "We doubt very much," said Justice Miller in the *Slaughterhouse Cases* (1873), "whether any action of a State not directed by way of discrimination against the Negroes as a class, or on account of their race, will ever be held to come within the purview of this provision" (16 Wall. 36, 81). However, in the decades that followed, the Court approved a variety of state measures designed to segregate the former slaves, so that the equal protection clause became in effect a dead letter. In the 1920s, Justice Holmes referred to it as "the usual last resort of constitutional arguments" (*Buck v. Bell* [1927]).

The Warren Court revived equal protection in the most significant cases of this century, those calling for the desegregation of schools and other public facilities.

Although most of the Warren Court's equal protection cases dealt with race, there are some tantalizing hints that the justices might have been willing to extend equal protection analysis to other groups. It would be the Burger Court, however, that actually dealt with nonracial issues.

Whether one sees the desegregation decisions as radical is a matter of judgment; for blacks and other supporters of civil rights, *Brown v. Board of Education* (1954) and its progeny finally corrected seven decades of constitutional error and secured the reading of the equal protection clause that its Framers had intended. Critics of the Court, however, have seen these same cases as judicial policy making of the worst sort, grounded only in the predilections of the justices and not in the Constitution itself.

The Road to *Brown*

Before looking at the Warren Court's desegregation decisions, one has to note—at least briefly—prior decisions in the area of race. A strong case can be made that *Brown* merely carried forward a line of reasoning that had been building within the Court for nearly two decades.

Following the Civil War the Court initially saw the due process and equal protection clauses of the Fourteenth Amendment solely in the light of protecting the freedmen from discrimination by the states. When Congress, however, tried to pass legislation to protect the freedmen's rights, the Court took an extremely cramped view of the enforcement provisions of the Thirteenth and Fourteenth Amendments, and in the *Civil Rights Cases* (1883), denied Congress any affirmative powers to prevent discrimination. Only if a state restricted black peoples' rights could Congress act to remedy the injustice. Moreover, Justice Bradley held that if a state by inaction tolerated discrimination—such as exclusion from hotels, restaurants, and clubs—Congress lacked authority to interfere. By this one decision, the Court nullified nearly all congressional power under the Reconstruction Amendments to protect the freedmen and left their fate to the states.

By the time of the segregation cases in the 1890s, both the Court and Congress had essentially washed their hands of the racial problem. In the best known of these cases, *Plessy v. Ferguson* (1896), Justice Henry Billings Brown held that distinctions based on race ran afoul of neither the Thirteenth nor Fourteenth Amendments. In the nature of things, he declared, the Fourteenth Amendment "could not have been intended to abolish distinctions based upon color, or to enforce social, as distinguished from political, equality, or a commingling of the two races unsatisfactory to either" (*Plessy v. Ferguson* [1896], 544). Although nowhere in the opinion can the phrase "separate but equal" be found, the Court's ruling approved racial segregation, provided the law did not make facilities for blacks inferior to those for whites.

Between 1900 and 1920 Jim Crow—the legal and systematic segregation of the races—triumphed throughout the former slave states. Signs marked "Whites Only" and "Colored" showed up everywhere, and hundreds of laws appeared on the statute books establishing and enforcing segregation. The statutes themselves, however, are not a fair index of the extent of racial discrimination; the laws set minimal standards, and in practice segregation normally went beyond what the laws required. Institutionalized segregation bred hatred and distrust between whites and blacks, and fostered deeply ingrained attitudes that would not easily be changed after 1954.

Beginning in 1914, however, the Court slowly but surely began to unravel the fabric of discrimination it had helped weave in the latter nineteenth century. In the landmark case of *Buchanan v. Warley* (1917), the Court unanimously struck down residential segregation ordinances as violating the Fourteenth Amendment's protection of property rights on the basis of color.

The Court did not hear another major race case until 1938. By then the Southern states had for many years ignored the "equal" part of the *Plessy* formula, and were shocked when in *Missouri ex rel. Gaines v. Canada* (1938), Chief Justice Charles Evans Hughes insisted that if the South wanted to maintain segregation, it had to provide truly equal facilities. That same year, in the otherwise insignificant case of *United States v. Carolene Products Co.*, Justice Harlan Fiske Stone wrote what is undoubtedly the most famous footnote in American constitutional history. While describing the deference the courts should pay to legislative policy decisions and the simple "rational basis" test that would be applied to economic legislation, Stone inserted a footnote indicating that the Court would apply a higher standard of scrutiny when legislation affected rights protected by the Constitution, threatened the integrity of the political process, or affected "discrete and insular minorities." This idea of a stricter standard became the basis for subsequent equal protection analysis, and played a significant role in the Warren Court's desegregation and apportionment decisions.

The war and Hitler's racist persecution of the Jews, leading to the slaughter of six million innocent people, made many Americans extremely uncomfortable with segregation, which bore a striking resemblance to the Nazi program. This unease in the late 1940s and early 1950s, along with legal challenges to segregation coordinated by the NAACP's Legal Defense Fund, led to a serious reconsideration of the *Plessy* doctrine. When Oklahoma refused to admit Ada Sipuel to the state's only law school, the Court in *Sipuel v. Oklahoma State Board of Regents* (1948) unanimously ordered the state to provide her with a legal education "in conformity with the equal protection clause of the Fourteenth Amendment and to provide it as soon as it does for applicants of any other group." A few years later the Court came down even harder on Oklahoma when, after reluctantly admitting a sixty-eight-year-old black man to the University of Oklahoma's graduate school, it required him to sit in the corridors outside the classrooms or in separate, roped-off areas. Chief Justice Fred Vinson spoke for a unanimous Court in *McLaurin v. Oklahoma State Regents for Higher Education* (1950), holding that such rules violated the equal protection clause.

In *Shelley v. Kraemer* (1948), the Court also struck down state enforcement of restrictive covenants, a device adopted in many areas following the 1917 invalidation of segregated zoning. Although the courts had long held that the Fourteenth Amendment did not reach private discrimination, if private individuals utilized state courts to enforce the restrictive covenants, then state action existed that violated the Equal Protection Clause. But the Court had so far not indicated any willingness to question the basic premise of "separate but equal," nor had the NAACP directly attacked the doctrine. Thurgood Marshall and his colleagues at the Legal Defense Fund kept attacking the failure of Southern states to provide equal facilities, and in doing so established a basis for the ultimate argument that separate accommodations could never be equal.

The Court hinted that it might be willing to consider that argument in its ruling in *Sweatt v. Painter* (1950). After the University of Texas refused to admit a black man into its law school, a lower court had ordered the state to provide a law school for blacks. The hastily created, makeshift law school certainly did not measure up to the prestigious white school in Austin, and if nothing else, the justices knew what made a good law school. For a unanimous Court, Chief Justice Vinson ordered Heman Sweatt admitted to the University of Texas Law School, the first time the Court had ever ordered a black student admitted to a previously all-white institution. For many observers, the Court's opinion marked the end of *Plessy*; for Thurgood Marshall, the opinion was "replete with road markings telling us where to go next" (Tushnet 1984, 135).

The NAACP now altered its strategy to launch a direct attack on segregation. In the 1952 term of the Court, it brought up challenges to various state segregation statutes in Delaware, Virginia, South Carolina, and Kansas, as well as the District of Columbia. The justices heard the cases that fall, but—unable to reach agreement— they asked counsel to reargue the cases the following term. Specifically, they wanted both sides to discuss whether Congress in proposing, and the states in adopting, the Fourteenth Amendment, had intended to ban racial segregation in schools. For the first time in more than fifty years, the Court would examine the root premise of the *Plessy* decision. One month before the Court convened for the October 1953 term, Fred Vinson died unexpectedly of a heart attack. To replace him, President Eisenhower named the popular Republican governor of California, Earl Warren. When Warren arrived in Washington to take up the center chair, he found the school cases at the top of the Court's agenda.

Brown v. Board of Education (1954)

The story of *Brown* is by now very familiar, but one needs to look at the decision in terms of its alleged radical departure from precedent, the basis it provided for future equal protection jurisprudence, and the guiding principles of the Warren Court: democracy, justice, and a living Constitution. The decision itself is deceptively simple; the Court, after all, had few cases to which it could refer for guidance, and while they led away from *Plessy,* none had directly rejected the underlying premise of "separate but equal." The Court, as an amicus brief from the Justice Department pointed out, had several options. It could avoid overruling *Plessy* by the simple expedient of finding the colored schools unequal, and then ordering either integration or another remedy. It could meet the issue head-on and condemn segregation as violating equal protection, but determine the particular remedy at a later date and then leave its implementation to the lower courts. Or, of course, it could affirm segregation, as former Solicitor General John W. Davis, representing South Carolina, proposed in oral argument in December: "To every principle comes a moment of repose when it has been so often announced, so confidently relied upon, so long continued, that it passes the limits of judicial discretion and disturbance" (Kluger 1976, 671).

But could the Warren Court have reaffirmed *Plessy*? After a series of cases in which the judiciary had chipped away at the notion of "separate but equal," after the president of the United States had ordered the desegregation of the armed forces, and after granting certiorari in the five school cases, could the Court really have simply said that the Constitution permitted racial segregation? It would have set the civil rights movement back a generation, or worse it might have led to the type of widespread violence that it took to end apartheid in South Africa. But even if the Court had been predisposed to overrule *Plessy,* how it could be done remained a puzzle.

Up until recently, scholars believed that the Court in Vinson's last term stood deeply divided over whether to reverse *Plessy.* Supposedly Black, Douglas, Burton, and Minton wanted to overrule *Plessy* outright, while Vinson, Reed, and Clark believed segregation constitutional. Frankfurter and Jackson opposed racial discrimination, but questioned whether the Court had the power to interfere in what had traditionally been a local matter. Recent scholarship, as well as common sense, tells us that the supposed divisions on the bench in 1952 could not have been concrete, because, with the exception of one person, the Court that handed down the unanimous decision in *Brown* in 1954 was the same court that first heard the five cases in 1952. It now appears that once Vinson died, Stanley Reed was the only justice who supported segregation and believed it constitutional.

When the justices met in conference after oral argument, Earl Warren announced that he considered racial segregation not only unconstitutional but immoral as well. He did not ask for a vote, but said that the brethren would discuss the matter until a consensus emerged. Warren then took it upon himself to draft an opinion, and imposed severe security arrangements so that knowledge of the decision would not leak out. The chief justice met with all of the members of the Court individually, cementing the support of those who backed him, and gradually overcoming the objections of those, like Frankfurter and Jackson, who opposed segregation but worried about the Court's power. Finally, only Stanley Reed remained, and when Warren confronted him on what he would do, Reed agreed to go along with the others. Warren now had what he had all along believed would be necessary, a unanimous Court, one he had forged based on his view of segregation as immoral and using his formidable political skills in building a coalition.

The Court, speaking through the chief justice, announced its decision at 12:51 P.M. on Monday, May 17, 1954. The history of the Fourteenth Amendment and its relation to education, which the Court had asked both sides to argue, had been "inconclusive," because public education in the South in 1868 had been so primitive that no one had bothered to think about it. There may, in fact, have been more guidance in history than Warren admitted, but the Court was examining the problem in the middle of the twentieth century. In words that perfectly captured the idea of a living Constitution, the Chief Justice noted that "in approaching this problem, we cannot turn the clock back to 1868 when the Amendment was adopted, or even to 1896 when *Plessy v. Ferguson* was written" (492). In 1954 public education played a far more central role in the nation's life than it had at the end of the Civil War.

Warren had read through two-thirds of the eleven-page opinion when he finally reached the crucial issue: "Does segregation of children in public schools solely on the basis of race . . . deprive the children of the minority group of equal educational opportunities?" Pausing for a moment, Warren then reaffirmed the eloquent dissent of the first Justice Harlan in *Plessy*, that separate could never be equal. To segregate black schoolchildren

> from others of similar age and qualifications solely because of their race generates a feeling of inferiority as to their status in the community that may affect their hearts and minds in a way unlikely ever to be undone. . . . Segregation with the sanction of law, therefore, has a tendency to retard the educational and mental development of Negro children. (494)

As a result, Warren concluded, "in the field of public education the doctrine of 'separate but equal' has no place. Separate educational facilities are inherently unequal." (494)

The last paragraph of the opinion reflected Warren's famed political skill. Noting the wide applicability of the decisions and the complexity of deriving an appropriate solution, he invited the parties to return to the Court that fall to assist the Court in fashioning a proper remedy. The phrase "wide applicability" indicated that legal segregation, either North or South, in rural or urban areas, would henceforth be unconstitutional. The reference to complexity signaled the South that the justices recognized the emotional and political distress that the decision would cause, and the delay in implementation would allow the states to accustom themselves and their citizens to the necessity for change. By inviting the parties to help fashion the remedy, the Court hoped that the Jim Crow states would cooperate in order to avoid potentially harsher solutions. Finally, Warren had framed the opinion to apply to only one area, the segregation by race of children in primary and secondary schools, a group most likely to win public sympathy as victims of racism. The Court did not even mention the many other facets of Jim Crow, and, while one could hardly expect segregation to be struck down in one area and not in others, for the moment at least, the Court concerned itself only with education.

Is the *Brown* decision radical? Does it represent naked judicial policy making? Is it grounded in the rule of law? How one answers these questions depends in large measure on how one views racial segregation. If it offended one, if one believed that in a democratic society people should not be penalized and treated as inferiors because of the accident of skin color, then the Court's decision represented nothing more than "simple justice," and freed not only black persons, but the white South and the Court itself from the weight of history. If one believed segregation to be not only constitutional but morally and socially right, then *Brown* was a disaster, pure and simple. We need not go into either of these arguments because, nearly a half-century after the decision, an overwhelming body of public opinion opposes legal discrimination based on race. Moreover, without *Brown*, it is unlikely that Congress or the Southern states would have voluntarily done away with racial segregation.

The question remains, however, whether the decision is good jurisprudence, and that is a matter separate from either politics or morality. Ideally, one can agree with Blackstone that law represents what is right and good, but we know that often law is not a choice between good and evil, but between two competing goods or the lesser of two evils. Law is valued in society because it provides stability, anchoring society with a set of knowable rules so that people can act accordingly. If these rules are wrong, then it is up to the legislature to change them; that is a policy decision, reposed by the Constitution in the Congress. When courts make policy, even "good" policy, there is a danger of upsetting the delicate constitutional balance of powers.

Much may be said for this reasoning, and people who by no stretch of the imagination can be described as racist have been uncomfortable with the *Brown* decision because it seems to rely less on legal reasoning than on moral intuition, less on legal precedent than on questionable social science findings. If one goes back to the conclusion in *Brown* quoted above, one finds a powerful assertion that segregation is harmful to children. The basis for this claim cannot be found in law reports; that segregation damages schoolchildren, wrote Warren, "is amply supported by modern authority" (494). At this point the chief justice inserted the famous—or infamous—

Footnote 11, citing, among others, Kenneth B. Clark's controversial study of children's reactions to dolls. Black children between the ages of six and nine attending segregated schools had been shown drawings of otherwise identical black and white dolls. When asked to select the "nice" doll, a majority had chosen the white doll, which Clark claimed showed that school segregation implanted in blacks a negative image of themselves at an early age.

This is, of course, a simplified view of Clark's study, but one has to recall the limited ability of social scientists to measure the effect of discrimination in the 1940s and 1950s. There has been an ongoing debate as to the accuracy of social science studies and whether courts should rely on them in reaching legal decisions. One can hardly quibble with law professor Edmund Cahn's assertion that "I would not have the constitutional rights of Negroes—or of any other Americans—rest on such flimsy foundation as some of the scientific demonstrations in these [trial] records" (Cahn 1955, 157). To Cahn and others, one did not need questionable studies to see the obvious; the sources in Footnote 11 did not strengthen the decision, but in fact gave critics an opening to attack it without invoking a straightforward racism.

For some, the Court had turned "over the making of law to social science opinion and the writers of books on psychology" (Urofsky 1991, 202). Former associate justice and then governor of South Carolina James F. Byrnes and Mississippi senator James O. Eastland attacked the social science sources as communist inspired. The Georgia attorney general zeroed in on the citation of Gunnar Myrdal's classic study of racism, *An American Dilemma* (1944). The black radical W. E. B. DuBois had been one of Myrdal's teachers, he claimed, and DuBois had "sent a message of condolence on the death of Stalin" (202). And, of course, the South had produced dozens of social scientists of its own over the decades, men untainted by foreign ideologies, who had supposedly proved conclusively the inferiority of the Negro.

A more serious attack came from someone who not only opposed segregation, but had been an active foe of racial discrimination and had advised the NAACP on several cases, including *Brown*. Columbia Professor Herbert Wechsler, one of the leading exponents of "process" jurisprudence, did not object to the fact that the high Court had departed from precedent, nor to the fact that it insisted on viewing the Fourteenth Amendment in the light of current conditions rather than those that governed at the time of its adoption. Rather, the justices had reached the conclusion that separate schools, because "inherently unequal," were therefore unconstitutional. But how did they get there? What reasoning, what rules of constitutional interpretation, had the Court used to get from A (separate schools) to B (are inherently unequal) to C (and therefore unconstitutional)? Would all laws that segregated one group from another (such as men from women) be unconstitutional? Would all conditions that created inequality (such as poverty) be subject to constitutional remedy? The Court had failed, Wechsler claimed, to ground its conclusions in "neutral principles." Decisions must rest "on reasons with respect to all the issues in the case . . . that in their generality and neutrality transcend any immediate result that is involved" (Wechsler 1959, 1). Only if society could see that such far-reaching decisions as *Brown* had, in fact, been reached through a rational and explainable method of legal reasoning would society be willing to accept the changes imposed by those decisions. The integrity of the judicial process outweighed any particular results.

Is process, or "neutral principles," enough? Is justice or society served if the courts only concern themselves with neutral principles? What about right results? For many, the "rightness" of *Brown* was sufficient. Professor Edward Beiser defended *Brown* as properly decided "because racial segregation was a grievous evil. Were this not so, the Supreme Court's decision would have been unjustified" (Wilkinson 1979, 35). Professor Paul Bender agreed that *Brown* had not been "tightly reasoned," but so what? The opinion had been "right," and if the Court had waited until it could write an "'airtight opinion' . . . it would have sadly failed the country and the Constitution" (35).

This debate between process and result is neither new nor concluded. Throughout the Warren era critics of particular decisions claimed that the Court had abandoned its responsibility to judicial process, and had exercised raw, unprincipled power. Certainly society has a right to expect that its judiciary, constitutionally protected and insulated from the tides of emotionalism and politics, will act in a principled manner and that there will be articulable standards by which to judge decisions. At the same time, society also expects its law to be morally acceptable, and in America particularly, people look to the courts to correct many perceived societal wrongs. Centuries ago, when the law proved so rigid that people often saw it as immoral, English kings established and then expanded the powers of the chancellor, the "keeper of the king's conscience," so that justice could be served by equity in those instances when law proved inadequate. Over the centuries the common law responded to changing social conditions and, when necessary, common-law judges struck out in new directions, despite the contrary holdings of previous decisions. In the United States, the Constitution wiped out the barriers between law and equity, and, if one accepts the premise that racial segregation is harmful and unfair, not just in broad terms, but within the type of equality guaranteed under the Constitution, then Chief Justice Warren's opinion, while admittedly weak in legal reasoning, is nonetheless a powerful statement of the moral grandeur of the law. Whatever its flaws, according to J. Harvie Wilkinson, now a federal circuit judge, *Brown* "was humane, among the most humane moments in all our history. It was, with the pardonable exception of a footnote, a great political achievement, both in its uniting of the Court and in the steady way it addressed the nation" (39).

While the Court considered the five cases, Justice Frankfurter asked his law clerk, Alexander Bickel, to research what the framers of the Fourteenth Amendment had in mind in regard to racial segregation. After looking at a wide variety of sources, Bickel concluded that the framers had no specific intent to do away with racially segregated schools. Strict adherence to the original intent of the Fourteenth Amendment, therefore, would prevent the Court from using the equal protection clause to end segregation. But Bickel, later to be one of the most astute commentators on the Court and the Constitution, argued that the conclusion based on history should not end the search for meaning of what the clause means today. The Framers had written in general terms, and so later generations should not be bound by how that generation would have applied the language in particular cases. The meaning of "equal protection of the law" can only depend how those words are applied in changing historical circumstances. This notion of changing circumstances, essential to the notion of a living Constitution, wound its way into Warren's opinion, where he declared that "in approaching this problem, we cannot turn the clock back to 1868 when the Amendment was adopted, or even to 1896 when *Plessy v. Ferguson* was written" (492).

Brown is the most famous example of the Warren Court's adherence to a living Constitution, and the notion that the judiciary had a special role to play in this process. According to legal scholar John Hart Ely, there is a direct connection between Stone's *Carolene Products* note and the desegregation decision. Stone had referred to the need for especially close constitutional scrutiny of laws aimed at "discrete and insular minorities." The Warren Court recognized not only the need for representation of minorities in the political process, but also that effective representation required that all people be guaranteed dignity. Democracy demanded that the equal protection clause protect those whom the majority abused.

Historian Morton Horowitz suggests that we ask whether the *Brown* decision was consistent with democracy. Clearly the Court intended to protect the rights of blacks—the clearest example in our history of a "discrete and insular minority"—from the tyranny of the white majority. But a crucial aspect of democracy is majority rule, and many scholars have attacked what they condemn as the countermajoritarian tendencies of the Warren Court, because it thwarts the democratic process.

But one could argue that slavery is incompatible with democracy, a truism that it took a civil war to confirm. If practices that discriminate against minorities—such as racial segregation—are similarly incompatible with democracy, then when a court strikes down such laws it is, in effect, acting not in opposition to, but in support of, basic democratic values. One of the great accomplishments of the Warren Court is that it redefined democracy from simply a question of majority rule to a process by which all voices in a polity are heard, in which minorities are not powerless and despised, and in which differences, especially in matters of speech and religion, are prized rather than scorned.

Bolling v. Sharpe (1954)

Usually lost in the attention paid to *Brown* is that one of the five segregation cases applied not to the states but to the federal government. *Bolling v. Sharpe* posed the same legal issue as did *Brown*, but in the context of the federal government and the schools in the District of Columbia. This change in context may not have mattered much in terms of justice to individual people of color; segregation harmed those affected whether they went to school in Mississippi or Washington, D.C. But it meant a great deal in terms of constitutional argument; there is no equal protection clause applicable to the federal government.

The lack of an appropriate text did not stop Warren, because as he wrote, "[i]t would be unthinkable that the same Constitution would impose a lesser duty on the Federal government" (*Bolling v. Sharpe* [1954], 500). The Court could hardly hold that segregation in the South violated the Constitution and then leave Congress free to operate the only legally segregated schools in the country. But even if, as Warren put it, such an option would be "unthinkable," on what grounds could the Court rationalize its decision; some textual basis had to be found.

Warren called the due process clause of the Fifth Amendment into play, a clause that does apply to the federal government and is matched by identical language in the Fourteenth Amendment clause applicable to the states. The due process clause, Warren wrote, stems from "our American ideal of fairness," and so does the equal protection clause. While the two are clearly not interchangeable, neither are they mutually exclusive, and both could therefore be called upon to delegitimize discrimination. Because segregation in public education "is not reasonably related to any proper governmental objective," the chief justice concluded, it is an arbitrary deprivation of liberty (500).

In some ways, *Bolling* is a far stronger constitutional opinion than *Brown*. It did not rest on questionable social science data, or even on an innate sense of fairness, or that historical circumstances had changed. The analysis that government lacked a proper objective had been part of due process analysis for several decades. Where *Brown* invalidated segregation because it generated feelings of inferiority among black children, *Bolling* found that it could not be justified by any reason. Warren said explicitly in the District of Columbia case what he had been only able to intimate in *Brown*, that keeping any group of citizens and their children in an inferior position could never be a legitimate objective of American government. But, as he also knew, it would be the *Brown* decision, applicable to all of the Southern and border states, and not *Bolling*, that would be read and reprinted and discussed.

The Failure of *Brown II*

While one can lavish praise on *Brown*, the Court's ruling the following year in *Brown II* on how desegregation should take place disappointed nearly everyone. Warren had assumed that during the year's grace period the Southern states would come to accept the Court's decision, and the initial reaction to *Brown* in the South had seemed fairly moderate. The governor of Virginia, Thomas Stanley, called for "cool heads, calm study, and sound judgment" (Urofsky 1991, 203–204). The respected *Louisville* (Kentucky) *Courier-Journal* assured its readers that "the end of the world has not come for the South or for the nation. The Supreme Court's ruling is not itself a revolution. It is rather acceptance of a process that has been going on a long time" (203–204). The editors endorsed the Court's example of moderation, advice akin to that of the *Atlanta Constitution*, which called on Georgians "to think clearly" (203–204).

Some Southern communities did not wait for the Court to hand down its implementation decree, but began desegregating their schools by the time the new academic year began in September 1954. Baltimore adopted a "freedom of choice" plan, which enabled 3,000 young blacks to attend previously all-white schools that fall. Louisville changed over its school system within a semester, while St. Louis initiated a two-year conversion plan. Counties in West Virginia, junior colleges in Texas, and public schools in Washington, D.C., and Wilmington, Delaware, all enrolled blacks in previously segregated schools. But the vast majority of Southern school districts remained segregated, waiting to see what the Court would require.

The justices heard arguments on proposed remedies that winter and again in April 1955. Aside from the controversial nature of the problem itself, the Court also had to decide whether to abandon in this instance its traditional policy of ruling only on the case before it. Normally, if someone raises a valid claim that his or her constitutional rights have been violated, the decree provides relief only for the petitioner; other persons suffering from the same infringement do not immediately benefit from the decision. Lower courts then take notice of the ruling, and apply it prospectively to future petitioners raising the same issue. In the school cases, however, this would have meant that every black child wishing to attend a previously all-white school would have had to seek a court order to enjoy the same rights as Linda Brown now enjoyed in Topeka. Determined states and localities could tie up the desegregation process for years by litigating every single black child's efforts to secure a desegregated education.

Moreover, the Court usually takes little notice of practical problems in implementation. If a constitutional right exists, it has to be available to the citizenry, regardless of institutional dislocations. But circumstances across the South and in the border states varied enormously, and the Court recognized that in some schools desegregation would mean a few blacks sitting in predominantly white classrooms, and in other schools just the opposite—and this made a difference.

How long should the South have? Too precipitate an order could trigger wide-scale resistance, even violence. On the other hand, every day that black children remained in segregated, and therefore inferior classrooms, they suffered deprivation of their constitutional rights.

The NAACP pushed for full integration, while Southern states urged the Court to face the "reality" of racial differences. Virginia offered statistical proof of the inferiority of blacks, while a poll in Florida showed that only one police officer in seven would enforce attendance at racially mixed schools. The federal government urged a middle position between "integration now" and "segregation forever."

On May 31, 1955, Chief Justice Warren, again for a unanimous Court, read the seven-paragraph implementing decision. *Brown II* called for the end of segregation everywhere, but recognized that different localities would face different problems. Local school districts must "make a prompt and reasonable start toward full compliance." Oversight would be lodged in the federal district courts, whose judges would exercise the "practical flexibility" traditionally associated with equity. Delay and noncompliance should not be contemplated, and desegregation of the nation's public schools should proceed "with all deliberate speed."

The Court did not fix a date for the end of segregation, nor even require, as the Justice Department had suggested, that the initial plans be filed within ninety days. The decision, in fact, gave the South far more than it had expected. Segregationists believed that implementation could be postponed indefinitely, because assignment of primary responsibility to the local federal courts meant that Southerners would decide what had to be done. Lieutenant Governor Ernest Vandiver of Georgia rejoiced when he heard the news. District judges, he declared, "are steeped in the same traditions that I am. . . . A 'reasonable time' can be construed as one year or two hundred. . . . Thank God we've got good Federal judges" (Woodward 1974, 153).

As it turned out, federal judges in the South made it quite clear that they took their oaths to support the Constitution seriously. By January 1956, decisions had been rendered in nineteen cases, and in every one district judges had reaffirmed the Supreme Court's holding that segregation denied equal protection of the laws. Then the South dug in its heels; it would be another decade before the former slave states finally bowed to the *Brown* rulings, and another decade after that before one could claim that legally enforced segregation had ended.

Why the delay? Why did the Court, after the magisterial moral statement of the first *Brown* case, back off so dramatically in *Brown II?* The phrase, "all deliberate speed," seemed to invite delay, and Southern states did all they could to evade the rulings, from dragging out litigation to imposing alleged health and welfare criteria, to actually closing schools in some areas. "There is not one way, but many," John Temple Graves of Alabama proclaimed. "The South proposes to use all of them that make for resistance. The decision tortured the Constitution—the South will torture the decision" (Woodward 1974, 159).

As has often been noted, the Supreme Court has the power neither of sword nor purse, and can rely for obedience to its decisions only on the moral authority it commands, or on the aid of Congress and the president. In the years immediately following the two *Brown* decisions, the South refused to recognize any moral authority in the Court, and neither the White House nor Congress appeared very willing to sign on to the decision. Dwight Eisenhower lamented the appointment of Warren as "the biggest damn fool mistake I ever made," and denounced the decision as setting back racial progress in the South by fifteen years (Weaver 1967, 18). Yet Eisenhower refused to use the moral authority of the presidency to lead the South away from intransigence. When officials at the University of Alabama defied a court order to admit a black student, the president refused to intervene, and the University remained segregated another seven years.

In his behalf it should be noted that Eisenhower had personally signed off on Attorney General Herbert Brownell's decision that the United States had to participate in the argument in *Brown* and that it had to oppose *Plessy*. Eisenhower made four more appointments to the high court, and made no effort to select someone who might oppose implementing the decision. Moreover, he did not wait until *Brown II* to order the District of Columbia Board of Commissioners to set an example of peaceful desegregation. And when Arkansas officials defied the federal courts, a reluctant chief executive finally acted.

Little Rock and *Cooper v. Aaron* (1958)

In the fall of 1957 the Little Rock, Arkansas, school board agreed to a court order to admit nine black students to Central High School. Governor Orville Faubus, previously considered a moderate, called out the state militia to block the students from enrolling. He then withdrew the militia following another court order, but when mobs attacked black students trying to attend Central, he recalled the guard. In essence, the governor of a state was using the state militia to block enforcement of a federal court order, and Eisenhower could no longer sit back and watch federal authority flouted. He ordered a thousand paratroopers into Little Rock and federalized 10,000 Arkansas guardsmen to maintain order and protect the black students.

The Court, which had been silent on school desegregation since *Brown II*, now spoke out in a case arising out of the Little Rock turmoil, *Cooper v. Aaron* (1958). The justices not only reaffirmed the *Brown* ruling, but in an unusual opinion signed by each of them, reasserted the Court's authority as the ultimate interpreter of the Constitution, the position first enunciated by Chief Justice John Marshall in *Marbury v. Madison* in 1803.

Arkansas officials claimed they were not "bound" by the original *Brown* ruling because the state had not been a party to those suits. The later lower-court decision, which Faubus had tried to evade, had ordered the Little Rock school board to desegregate, and the high Court could have contented itself with a sharp reminder that states have no power to nullify federal court orders. But the nine justices went on to affirm

that the federal judiciary is supreme in the exposition of the law of the Constitution. . . . It follows that the interpretation of the Fourteenth Amendment enunciated by this Court in the *Brown* case is the supreme law of the land, and Art. VI of the Constitution makes it of binding effect on the States "any Thing in the Constitution or Laws of any State to the Contrary notwithstanding." Every state legislator and executive and judicial officer is solemnly committed by oath . . . "to support this Constitution." (*Cooper v. Aaron* [1958], 18)

Some discussion has ensued as to whether the Warren Court merely reiterated Marshall's dictum in *Marbury* or went beyond it to assert an exclusive power that had not been claimed before. The debate over the Court's power has been going on practically from the time the Court began to hear cases in 1790, and is not likely to end as long as Americans insist on litigating every major public policy question. It is equally clear that while federal, state, and local officials are theoretically bound to obey the Constitution, unless there is a final arbiter of what that Constitution means we will have a legal morass that will undermine social stability. Once the Court had declared that the equal protection clause forbade segregation, it had little choice but to invalidate any and all state and local interpretations to the contrary.

A good part of the problem, though, derived from the Court's miscalculation in *Brown II*. In trying to accommodate the South in the hope that reason would prevail, the Court gave segregationists an opening they aggressively exploited. And so long as neither the executive nor legislative branches would support the moral authority of the Court, it could do very little. Beginning with the Little Rock decision, however, the pendulum began to swing the other way.

First the justices began to state openly that the phrase "all deliberate speed" did not mean indefinite delay. "There has been entirely too much deliberation," declared Justice Hugo Black of Alabama, "and not enough speed" (*Griffin v. Prince Edward County School Board* [1964]). The growing impatience of the Court resulted, at least in part, from recognition of its own prior miscalculations, and the mounting criticism it faced both in academic and civil rights circles. *Brown II*, designed to allow the better elements in the South to work out a peaceful solution, wound up permitting the most bigoted and violent segments of society to prevail.

Yet the very disgust generated by racist elements in the deep South finally moved the executive and legislative branches, as well as public opinion, to back the Court's ruling that segregation had to be ended. Congress passed the first civil rights law since Reconstruction in 1957. Although it had limited scope, it set the stage for further legislation that would eventually bring to bear the full power of the federal government to protect the civil rights of minority groups. While Dwight Eisenhower never showed much enthusiasm for the cause, the Kennedy and Johnson administrations put civil rights near the top of their domestic agendas. Despite continued violence in the South and grandstand defiances by Ross Barnett of Mississippi and George Wallace of Alabama, there could be no mistaking the trend. The 1963 March on Washington and Lyndon Johnson's eloquent promise that "we shall overcome" set the civil rights agenda for the 1960s. And with that shift, the Court resumed its role as the chief exponent of constitutionally protected rights.

The Court Picks Up the Tempo

After remaining largely silent in the late 1950s, the Court began accepting more segregation cases, and in one unanimous ruling after another added to the growing national consensus that the time had come to act. It not only reaffirmed the basic premise that segregation violated the Fourteenth Amendment, but addressed itself to specifics.

In *Goss v. Board of Education* (1963), the Court struck down a transfer plan that would have allowed white students to reestablish one-race schools. The following year, the justices attacked massive resistance in *Griffin v. Prince Edward County School Board.* They told school officials in Prince Edward County, Virginia, to reopen the public schools that had been closed for five years to evade desegregation. Justice Black also warned the South to stop its delaying tactics; ten years had been long enough for Southerners to reconcile themselves to *Brown.*

In 1968 the Court decided its last "easy" school desegregation case, one in which the justices took a significant new step in interpreting the constitutional mandate. *Green v. County School Board* involved a "freedom of choice" plan that supposedly allowed students of either race to attend the school of their choice. Local officials in predominantly rural New Kent County, Virginia, defended the plan as a good faith effort to comply with Brown, but critics charged that it discouraged blacks from attending white schools, and had little overall effect. After three years, not one white child had chosen to attend a formerly black school, and 85 percent of the black students still went to all-black schools. Nor should New Kent be considered an aberration. Fourteen years after *Brown*, segregated schools continued to be the rule in most of the country, North and South. Nearly a half-century after *Brown*, even in the absence of state sanctions, de facto segregation in schools and housing is prevalent throughout the nation.

Speaking for the Court, Justice Brennan declared that henceforth results, not good intentions, would be the mark of an acceptable plan, and the Court took the unusual step of indicating specific proposals that would be acceptable, such as dividing the county geographically, with all students living in each half attending the schools in that half.

Green was "easy" in the sense that it marked the last case in which black students had been segregated on the basis of law or of easily perceived racial discrimination. The "freedom of choice" plan that had been struck down in this case, and that lower courts overturned in similar situations, had been patently designed to avoid the *Brown* mandate. The case also marked the end of what might be called the first phase of school desegregation, in which the Court, following its initial pronouncements, showed a willingness to allow the states and localities to work things out, to accept tokens of good faith in the hope that a gradualist approach would, in the end, work.

No doubt a gradualist approach had been necessary, despite the fact that the *Brown II* formula of "all deliberate speed" proved a failure, because of a lingering sense that if the Court—without the support of the other branches of government—had pushed for greater desegregation sooner, the reaction might have been even bloodier and more violent. The Court could, however, have provided greater leadership; it could have, as the Justice Department had urged, required school districts to submit plans with specific timetables. It could have taken more cases on appeal to give the lower courts and the nation more guidance. From *Brown* to *Griffin* the Court said practically nothing. After setting in motion one of the great social upheavals of the century, the Court retreated into silence. Given the deep-seated prejudice in the South, perhaps little more could have been expected.

Expanding the Meaning of Equal Protection

Even if the rate of progress in desegregating schools seemed glacially slow, in other areas the Court's pronouncements had a significant impact. Even while NAACP lawyers continued their attacks on segregation in public schools, they picked up on the unavoidable logic of *Brown:* If separating persons in school on the basis of race violated the equal protection clause, then so did racial segregation elsewhere in public life. Civil rights litigants initiated a flurry of lawsuits aimed at racial segregation in public facilities.

The Southern-born historian C. Vann Woodward noted that "something very much like a panic seized the South toward the beginning of 1956, a panic bred of insecurity and fear" (Woodward 1974, 154). No doubt the Montgomery bus boycott that began in December 1955 contributed to this malaise, as well as the fact that some of the border states had begun desegregating their schools. But as much as anything it was the realization that *Brown* not only impacted on schools; the rationale applied to every other facet of segregated society as well. *Brown* was not about education, or at least not just about education; it was about race, and the Supreme Court had put into effect a judicial juggernaut to dismantle apartheid.

Typically, a local federal judge would rule that the old *Plessy* doctrine of "separate but equal" no longer applied after *Brown*, and that segregation in a particular public facility violated the Fourteenth Amendment. An appeal to the Supreme Court invariably resulted in a *per curiam* (unattributed opinion of the whole court) affirmation of the lower court ruling. In those few cases in which district judges sustained segregation, the high Court remanded with directions to proceed in a manner "not inconsistent with *Brown.*" These brief one- and two-sentence rulings ended decades of segregation on public beaches, buses, golf courses, and in parks. In *Johnson v. Virginia* (1963), the Court reversed a contempt conviction imposed upon a black man for refusing to move to a section of the courtroom reserved for blacks. "Such a conviction cannot stand, for it is no longer open to question that a State may not constitutionally require segregation of public facilities."

A more complicated issue faced the Court in the question of segregation in private facilities. Ever since the *Civil Rights Cases* in 1883, private discrimination had been considered beyond the reach of the Fourteenth Amendment. In *Shelley v. Kraemer* (1948), the Vinson Court had ruled that state enforcement of private restrictive covenants was in effect state action, and therefore prohibited. Using this idea of state action, the Warren Court struck down exclusion of blacks from a private theater located in a state park, from private restaurants in a courthouse, and from a municipally owned and operated parking garage. In modern times there is very little private business that cannot be made to appear to have some real or imagined nexus to state authority, but as Justice Clark warned, the state action doctrine did have limits. The state, he said, had to be involved to some significant extent, and over the next two decades a number of cases would test what constituted a "significant extent."

The Court also struck down a series of state laws that regulated private conduct on the basis of race. Nearly all Southern states, for example, had antimiscegenation laws on the books, some of them dating back to colonial times, that prohibited sexual relations, marriage, or cohabitation between members of different races. In *Pace v. Alabama* (1883), the Court had sustained a state law imposing higher penalties upon partners in interracial fornication than those of the same race, on the grounds that the higher penalty applied equally to members of both races. At first the Court had avoided taking cases challenging the antimiscegenation laws, because the justices recognized that interracial sexual relations remained one of the great fears in the South. In *McLaughlin v. Florida* (1964), however, the Court invalidated a Florida criminal statute prohibiting cohabitation by interracial married couples as a violation of the equal protection clause. As Justice Stewart noted in his concurrence, "it is simply not possible for a state law to be valid under our Constitution which makes the criminality of an act depend upon the race of the actor."

Challenges to laws prohibiting interracial marriages had come to the high Court in 1955 and 1956, but the justices had hidden behind technicalities to avoid deciding the question. A dozen years after *Brown*, however, sixteen states still had such laws on their statute books, and after the Florida case the Court could evade the issue no longer. In *Loving v. Virginia* (1967), Chief Justice Warren spoke for a unanimous Court in invalidating the antimiscegenation laws. "Restricting the freedom to marry solely because of racial classification," he declared, "violates the central meaning of the Equal Protection Clause."

To nearly everyone's surprise, there was almost no public backlash to the *Loving* decision. Civil rights proponents had feared that the school cases would bring to the fore all the repressed fears associated with interracial sex, an issue that had always been a major part of race relations in the United States. White slaveholders, of course, had often abused their female slaves, and some scholars believe that guilt over that history, as well as fear that black men would retaliate by attacking white women, accounted for the brutal way in which the white South treated black men accused of making sexual advances to white women. Black men convicted of rape received harsher prison sentences, and were put to death more often, than white men convicted of similar crimes.

Some members of the Warren Court suggested that there ought to be a per se rule invalidating any legislative distinctions based on racial classification, but a majority of the Court never went that far. Rather, the Warren Court expanded on the suggestion Justice Stone had put forward in his *Carolene Products* footnote that certain categories required closer scrutiny by the courts. In all cases involving racial classification, the Court since *Brown* has applied a "strict scrutiny" standard, in which the state has the heavy burden of proving that a compelling governmental interest requires such classification. It is a difficult standard to meet, but in a few instances states have been able to show a legitimate, nondiscriminatory reason. In *Tancil v. Woods* (1964), the Court upheld a requirement that divorce decrees indicate the race of the parties for record-keeping purposes, and in *Lee v. Washington* (1968), it allowed prison authorities "acting in good faith, and in particularized circumstances," to take racial hostility into account to maintain order and, if necessary, to separate black and white prisoners.

Demonstrations, Sit-Ins, and Public Accommodation Cases

The segregation, state action, and racial classification cases proved fairly easy for the Court once it had adopted the general rule of *Brown*. But in the early sixties a series of cases broke the unanimity that otherwise governed the Warren Court's handling of civil rights cases. How far could demonstrations protesting racial segregation go before they ran up against the state's legitimate need to maintain order?

In 1961 African American students in Columbia, South Carolina, and Baton Rouge, Louisiana, marched downtown in orderly fashion, carrying placards protesting segregation and singing "The Star Spangled Banner." In doing so they attracted large crowds of white onlookers before the police ordered the demonstrators to disband and arrested the leaders. In *Edwards v. South Carolina* (1963), the Court unanimously reversed their convictions for breach of the peace, declaring that "the circumstances of this case reflect an exercise of these basic constitutional rights in their most pristine and classic form."

Two years later, however, in dealing with much larger demonstrations in *Cox v. Louisiana*, Justice Goldberg, certainly one of the most liberal members of the bench, stated that the case did not involve speech "in its pristine form but conduct of a totally different character," and he proceeded to detail some of the dangers of "mob rule." Although the Court again reversed the convictions based on *Edwards*, it is clear that the path of civil disobedience triggered by *Brown* had begun to worry several members of the Court. This can best be seen in the sit-in cases.

In February 1960 four neatly dressed students from the all-black Agricultural and Technical College in Greensboro, North Carolina, sat down at the segregated lunch counter in Woolworth's and asked for a cup of coffee. When they were refused service, they remained in their seats until arrested. Black youths quickly took up the sit-in technique, and by the end of the year had desegregated lunch counters in 126 cities. They then adapted this new weapon to protest other areas of discrimination, and the public began reading about "wade-ins" at public pools and "kneel-ins" at churches.

Prior to passage of the 1964 Civil Rights Act restaurants had been considered private and, in the absence of a state law requiring segregation, had been considered free to choose whom they wished to serve or not serve. A protester sitting in at a segregated lunch counter or restaurant violated the owner's property rights, and could be arrested for trespass. Although a majority of the Court obviously sympathized with the activist students, they could not agree on a rule to cover the situation.

Justice Douglas alone seemed willing to eliminate totally the distinction between state action and private discrimination, but others on the Court believed that in a free society, one had to tolerate some forms of private discrimination. Under the First Amendment people have the right of free association, which means they can choose not to associate with certain groups. Private clubs, therefore, can elect to keep out Jews, blacks, women, or any other group that a majority of the members finds distasteful. The only constitutional bar prevented the use of state resources to enforce that discrimination.

Douglas won more support when he suggested that restaurants and hotels not be seen as purely private property, but as a type of public activity, a property "affected with a public interest," and therefore subject to legal prohibitions against discrimination. Under common law, for example, common carriers had to offer their services on a nondiscriminatory basis. If the Court had wanted to remain doctrinally consistent, it might have expanded the state action doctrine. In *Shelley v. Kraemer* the Court had refused to allow state power to enforce private housing restrictions; why not bar the use of trespass to enforce discriminatory practices?

The Court began hearing the sit-in cases as Congress debated the bill that would become the 1964 Civil Rights Act, and a majority of the justices wanted to avoid making a doctrinal decision until after the measure passed. In most of the cases, the Court seized upon technical reasons to set aside the sit-in convictions without citing *Shelley*, a sign that the justices felt state action had to be more than just even-handed enforcement of private property rights. In only one case did six of the justices reach the broader issue, and then they divided evenly. *Bell v. Maryland* (1964) arose from the convictions of civil rights protesters under Maryland's criminal trespass law. After their conviction, the state had passed a public accommodations law forbidding restaurants and hotels from refusing service on the basis of race. Justice Brennan then vacated the conviction, and remanded for further consideration by the state court in consideration of the new law, an easy way to avoid a doctrinal decision.

Justice Douglas concurred in the result, but entered a lengthy opinion joined by Goldberg and Warren. He believed the discrimination to be unlawful even in the absence of a civil rights statute. He argued that restaurants constituted businesses affected with public interest, and therefore came within the *Shelley* doctrine. Douglas reached back into the common law, which, he claimed, guaranteed nondiscriminatory access to public accommodations. Goldberg and Warren were even willing to read the equal protection clause to bar discrimination in private facilities. Though one could find some historical justification for these arguments, the three justices ignored the view held by most jurists and scholars that this issue had, in fact, never been settled, and would not be until Congress spoke. They also ignored the fact that if their view reflected settled law, why hadn't anyone put forward such an argument in the century following the Civil War?

Justice Black, joined by Harlan and White, took just the opposite view, and argued that the Fourteenth Amendment did not prohibit property owners from discriminating as to whom they would allow on their property. Bigots as well as saints had the right to call upon the state to protect their legitimate property rights. Black's dissent had originally been the majority opinion, but Brennan was determined not to let that opinion come down while Congress debated the civil rights bill. Moreover, when a state passes a so-called intervening measure that moots a case, the Court normally sends it back for a rehearing, but Brennan wanted the convictions reversed. In the struggle, Brennan proved himself more than a match for Black, who for nearly three decades had been the Court's preeminent behind-the-scenes strategist. Brennan managed both to delay the announcement of the opinion and to win over Justices Clark and Stewart away from the Black position.

Nonetheless, *Bell* is the only case in which the Court fully rehearsed the constitutional arguments surrounding the sit-in demonstrations, and it takes up 120 pages of the *United States Reports*. What is particularly interesting is that Douglas and Black both cited the same historical sources, often even the same passages, to support their completely contradictory conclusions.

As the justices wrestled with the sit-in cases, Congress debated civil rights legislation. President Kennedy had proposed legislation that would, in effect, have adopted Justice Douglas's reasoning and precluded discrimination in public accommodations. The bill stalled under Southern pressure, but following Kennedy's assassination, Lyndon Johnson declared passage of the measure a top priority as well as a tribute to the fallen Kennedy. Under heavy pressure from the White House as well as civil rights groups, Congress enacted the 1964 Civil Rights Act. Within six months a unanimous Court had upheld the key provisions of the bill, the Title II restrictions against discrimination in public accommodations.

In *Heart of Atlanta Motel v. United States* (1964), the Court sustained the powers of Congress under the commerce clause, as well as the equal protection clause, to declare racial discrimination a burden on interstate commerce. Seventy-five percent of the motel's guests came from out of state, and its business therefore clearly came within the reach of congressional power to regulate interstate commerce. In the companion case, *Katzenbach v. McClung*, the Court, also unanimously, upheld the law as it applied to restaurants. With these cases, the Court could note that Congress and the executive had finally taken the path it had blazed a dozen years earlier in *Brown*. For the first time, all three branches stood agreed that the Fourteenth Amendment not only banned racial discrimination, but that it also gave the federal government extensive affirmative powers to protect the civil rights of its minority citizens.

Ironically, after the passage of the 1964 law in another demonstration case, *Adderley v. Florida* (1966), Justice Black managed to put together a five-to-four majority that in essence held that trespass trumps the First Amendment. Local police arrested thirty-two Florida A & M students on charges of trespass with a malicious or mischievous intent for peacefully picketing outside the county jail, where other students were being held after having been arrested the day before for protesting segregation.

Black saw the protest as nothing other than trespass, and he saw no difference between public and private property. Once the sheriff had told the demonstrators to leave, they should have left. The jail and its surrounding grounds could under no stretch of the imagination be considered a public forum. The case is typical of Black's growing conservatism in his later years, and the fear of the mob that had been announced in *Cox* managed to win a majority in *Adderley*.

William O. Douglas wrote one of his best opinions for the dissenters. The case was not just about civil rights, but about the ability of the poor as well as the rich to try to influence public opinion and gain the government's attention. "Those who do not control television and radio, those who cannot advertise in newspapers or circulate elaborate pamphlets have only a more limited type of access to public officials" (*Adderley v. Florida* [1966]). He argued that turning the students' protest into trespass does violence to the First Amendment, although he agreed that not all demonstrations are protected by the Constitution. But this was a jail, the students were orderly, and there was clearly no threat of a riot. Warren, Brennan, and Fortas agreed with Douglas, but Black had Reed, Harlan, Stewart, and White, the conservative bloc with which Douglas normally disagreed, and they were delighted to go with Black.

Voting Rights

The Fifteenth Amendment had prohibited the denial of suffrage on account of race, but Southern states had worked out a variety of stratagems to deny blacks an effective franchise. In Alabama, for example, Negroes made up about half the population, but only 1 percent of the registered voters. To protest that situation, Martin Luther King Jr. organized a march from Selma to the state capitol in Montgomery in March 1965. Governor George Wallace forbade the march, and when King went ahead, state troopers attacked unarmed men, women, and children using bullwhips, clubs, and tear gas as television broadcast the sickening spectacle to the nation and to the world. President Johnson immediately federalized the Alabama national guard to protect the demonstrators, and then asked Congress for legislation to guard the right to vote against the ingenious devices employed by Southern officials.

The 1965 Voting Rights Act authorized the attorney general to send federal registrars into any county that he suspected of discrimination, in particular those counties where 50 percent or more of the voting age population had failed to register. Local voting regulations and procedures could be suspended, as could literacy tests and any other devices used to prevent otherwise eligible persons from exercising their right to vote. The attorney general, Nicholas Katzenbach, soon afterwards issued a proclamation identifying Alabama, Alaska, Georgia, Louisiana, Mississippi, South Carolina, Virginia, thirty-four counties in North Carolina, and isolated counties in Arizona, Hawaii, and Idaho as meeting the statutory criteria. For the first time, federal law would be used to protect the integrity of registration and voting processes in the South, and unlike the first Reconstruction, all three branches of the federal government now stood united in their determination to protect black voting rights.

Southern states quickly challenged the Voting Rights Act, and to expedite the matter so that another election would not go by with blacks still disenfranchised, the Court heard *South Carolina v. Katzenbach* (1966) on the basis of its original jurisdiction, instead of waiting for the appeals process to send the issue to it. Whatever technical difficulties may have existed, the justices wanted to settle the constitutionality of this law as quickly as possible. After watching the Southern states flout the desegregation ruling for more than a decade, they wanted to hand down their opinion so a sympathetic administration could enforce the law.

South Carolina's long and convoluted brief boiled down to three major challenges. First, the state claimed that Section 2 of the Fifteenth Amendment spoke only in general terms; specific remedies to voting rights violations belonged to the judiciary and not to the legislature. Second, the formula for determining which parts of the country fell within the act's coverage violated the constitutional guarantee that all states be treated equally. Finally, a provision barring court review of administrative findings constituted a bill of attainder and infringed on the separation of powers.

A nearly unanimous Court (Justice Black dissented on a minor point), speaking through the chief justice, dismissed all of the state's challenges in upholding the law. Reciting a long line of cases reaching back to the Marshall era, Warren held that Congress could choose from a full range of means in carrying out a legitimate end. Congress had studied the problem at length, and had noted information supplied by both the Justice Department and the Civil Rights Commission. It could therefore rationally decide that resources and remedies should be targeted toward those areas in which one found the greatest discrimination. In the specific remedies, Warren concluded, Congress had chosen "appropriate means of combatting the evil" (*South Carolina v. Katzenbach* [1966]).

The unanimity of *Heart of Atlanta* and *Katzenbach v. McClung* did not surprise most observers, but the general consensus of the justices was unusually high. In the 1963 term Brennan agreed with the majority 96 percent of the time, Warren 93 percent, Goldberg, Douglas, and White over 85 percent, Black, Clark, and Stewart over 83 percent. Even Justice Harlan, who by now constituted the conservative bloc, still agreed with his brethren in two out of three cases.

Shortly after *Katzenbach*, the Court overturned the use of poll taxes in state elections in *Harper v. Virginia Board of Elections* (1966). The Twenty-fourth Amendment, ratified in January 1964, had abolished the poll tax in federal elections, and Justice Douglas, for a six-to-three Court, invoked the equal protection clause to inter the state tax as well. Douglas's opinion utilized two different equal protection analyses, "fundamental interests" and "suspect classification." The Constitution, he conceded, nowhere specifically mentioned a right to vote in state elections, but voting constituted such a basic right of free citizens that any effort to restrict it ran into a strong presumption of unconstitutionality. To limit it on the basis of wealth, moreover, created a classification that could not withstand equal protection analysis. "Wealth, like race, creed, or color, is not germane to one's ability to participate intelligently in the electoral process. Lines drawn on the basis of wealth or property, like those of race, are traditionally disfavored" (*South Carolina v. Katzenbach* [1966], 668). Douglas had argued that the meaning of the equal protection clause "is not shackled to the political theory of a particular era. . . . Notions of what constitute equal treatment for purposes of the Equal Protection Clause do change" (669).

Douglas's opinion is one of his boldest—as well as one of the most activist—of the Warren Court era, and it brought forth impassioned dissents from Black and Harlan (joined by Stewart). While Black stood willing to expand the reach of the Bill of Rights through the Fourteenth Amendment, both he and Harlan took a fairly conservative approach in requiring some textual basis for establishing a constitutionally protected right. They attacked the majority opinion as akin to earlier courts' use of due process to strike down economic legislation that the justices had not liked, and they also objected to the notion of a living Constitution, the idea that the meaning of the Constitution changed over time.

"I did not join the opinion of the Court in *Brown* on any theory that segregation . . . denied equal protection in 1954 but did not similarly deny it in 1896," Black wrote. "I thought when *Brown* was written, and I think now, that Mr. Justice Harlan was correct in 1896 when he dissented from *Plessy v. Ferguson*" (*South Carolina v. Katzen-*

bach [1966], 677 n.7). For Black, the Constitution did not change with the years. But Douglas had also cited the "one person, one vote" decision in the apportionment cases (discussed below) for his argument that the meaning of equal protection changes over time. It is hard to see how he could have denied Douglas's assertion that the original understanding of the Fourteenth Amendment did not require that both houses of a state legislature be apportioned by population. That conclusion could only have been reached because ideas about equality and democracy had changed over time.

To conservatives, this argument smacked of heresy, for in their eyes it deprived the Constitution of fixed meaning, and left it subject to the passing whims of changing judicial personnel. Equal protection, due process, all had to mean something, and that meaning had to be stable so that people could rely on it. But a fixed and rigid interpretation, as Douglas recognized, would be just as bad, because it would preclude the Constitution from ever having a contemporary meaning.

Poverty as a Suspect Classification

Douglas seemed willing to open up the range of suspect classifications to include wealth, an approach that horrified conservatives and appalled many constitutional scholars. There is a significant difference between a constitutional promise of equal treatment before the law and a promise of full economic, as well as political and legal, equality. One can find a textual basis in the Constitution to prohibit classification by race or religion, but it would be stretching the common sense of the document to suggest that it seeks to abolish economic inequity.

Efforts to bring wealth (or more accurately, poverty) in as a suspect classification have been raised periodically, but with very limited success. The Court has held that the absence of money cannot be used to deny a basic right. In *Griffin v. Illinois* (1956), for example, the Court ruled that a state had to provide a trial transcript to an indigent appealing a criminal conviction, because the inability to pay for a transcript would deny the defendant any appeal. A few years later in *Douglas v. California* (1963), the Court held that a state could not deny an indigent counsel on appeal, and at the end of the Warren era the Court struck down durational residence requirements for welfare payments as violating equal protection. Comments in Justice Brennan's opinion in this case prompted much speculation regarding the future of fundamental interest analysis. If one adopted the view, as Brennan implied, of food, housing, and education as fundamental in establishing a decent life, then could one utilize the equal protection clause to force government to provide those items to all, or institute a wide-ranging redistribution of wealth? How did one determine what constituted fundamental interests? Who made the determination?

In this area, at least, the Warren Court left a legacy of ambivalence, with advocates of the poor arguing for the inclusion of poverty as a suspect classification. In fact, the Warren Court itself only applied this fundamental interest analysis to voting, criminal appeals, and interstate travel. Douglas in *Harper* and Brennan in *Shapiro v. Thompson* (1969) suggested that this analysis could be taken much further, but how far it could have gone is questionable. Douglas and Brennan put forward a very open-ended view, one amenable to reinterpretation in the light of changing social standards. But do courts have the institutional competence to force the type of legislation that a judicial attack on poverty would have necessitated? And the sparse comments in both cases hardly qualify as a full-blown doctrinal explication of why poverty could or should be attacked through use of the equal protection clause.

What Douglas, Brennan, and Warren were trying to do is make more meaningful the promises of American democracy. A debate had been ongoing for much of the twentieth century over what democracy meant, and what it required. For some people political equality is all that matters; give people equal access to the ballot box and everything else will take care of itself. Others believe that there can be no effective political equality without a corresponding social and economic equality. People who are poor or illiterate or ill informed cannot use their vote as effectively as the rich, educated, and informed citizen. Those who are poor will rarely have the leisure time to engage in politics; only the rich man or woman will be able to run for public office. If campaigns get more expensive, as they have over the past few decades, this will, it is claimed, magnify the influence of big donors and drown out the voices of the middle and lower classes.

Members of the Warren Court understood this, but they differed significantly on just how far the judiciary should go in trying to level the political playing field. Even if one conceded that society could not have true political equality amidst significant economic disparities, could or should the courts intervene? Whether out of ideological commitment or merely recognizing the inherent difficulties, a majority of the Court did not want to get involved in those questions. But when it came to ensuring political equality, the justices were not only more willing, but also proved to be extremely effective.

The Reapportionment Cases

After his retirement, someone asked Earl Warren what had been the most important decision he had written. To the audience's surprise, he did not answer *Brown,* but instead said the reapportionment cases. No other set of cases, not even those involving racial discrimination, so captured the democratic idealism of the Warren Court.

Douglas's suggestions in *Harper* regarding poverty never developed into a mature doctrinal statement, but his comments on fundamental interests became a standard form of equal protection analysis. For the Warren Court, as for so many of its predecessors, the right to vote constituted the basic interest, because without it a citizenry could neither control its government, nor act to redress grievances. Given this view, as well as the Court's acknowledged activism, its decisions in the apportionment cases should have come as no surprise. Yet in a way that did not apply to any other group of decisions, including the desegregation cases, the apportionment rulings constituted perhaps the most radical of all the Warren Court's actions.

The Constitution assigns to each state two senators and a number of representatives proportional to its population, but does not specify how these seats are to be allocated within each state. James Madison had implied that the arrangement should be equitable, and many states had constitutional provisions designed to ensure at least a rough equality between congressional districts as well as among the seats in the state assemblies. During the 1950s, in fact, three-fifths of all the states reapportioned one or both of their legislative chambers.

Twelve states, however, had not redrawn their district lines for more than thirty years, despite major population shifts. Tennessee and Alabama had not redrawn their lines since 1901, and Delaware since 1897. Within some states discrepancies of enormous magnitude existed; in Vermont, for example, the most populous assembly district had 33,000 persons, and the smallest had 238, yet each had one seat. Distortions also appeared in many state senates, which often followed geographical boundaries. In eleven state senates a voting majority could be elected by less than one fifth of the population. In California, where 11 percent of the voters could elect a majority of the state senate, the senatorial district comprising Los Angeles had six million people, while a more sparsely populated district had only 14,000. In all of the states that had not reapportioned, as well as in many that had reapportioned but not along strict demographic criteria, the results magnified the power of the older rural areas, while undervaluing the ballot of the new urban and suburban districts. Needless to say, the rural minorities who controlled the state houses had no incentive to reform, as that would have dissipated their power.

Prior to the Warren era the Supreme Court had steadfastly refused to accept cases challenging state apportionment formulas. The Court described the issue as "nonjusticiable," that is, it either did not appear amenable to judicial resolution, or it involved an issue so political in nature that the judiciary should not interfere. The "political question doctrine" was first enunciated by Chief Justice Roger Brooke Taney in *Luther v. Borden* (1849), a case that grew out of the political revolt in Rhode Island known as the Dorr Rebellion. Essentially, two rationales exist for a court to invoke this doctrine; one is that responsibility is clearly and textually committed to either another branch of the federal government or to the states, and the other is that the court cannot fashion a judicially manageable solution.

The first constitutional attack against malapportionment arose under the guarantee clause of the Constitution (Art. IV, Sec. 4) which states: "The United States shall guarantee to every State a Republican Form of Government." For the most part, the Supreme Court over the decades had refused to assign any greater meaning to that clause other than that the federal government would protect states against foreign invasion or domestic rebellion. Challengers of congressional districting in Illinois claimed that districts had to be approximately equal in population in order not to violate the Constitution. In *Colgrove v. Green* (1946), Justice Frankfurter, speaking for only a plurality of the seven justices who heard the case, declared that

> the petitioners ask of this Court what is beyond its competence to grant. . . . Effective working of our government revealed this issue to be of a peculiarly political nature and therefore not meet for judicial determination. This controversy concerns matters that bring courts into immediate and active relations with party contests. From the determination of such issues this Court has traditionally remained aloof. It is hostile to a democratic system to involve the judiciary in the politics of the people. Due regard for the Constitution as a viable system precludes judicial correction. Authority for dealing with such problems resides elsewhere. The short of it is that the Constitution has conferred upon Congress exclusive authority to secure fair representation by the States in the popular [House]. Courts ought not to enter this political thicket. (*Colgrove v. Green* [1946])

Frankfurter spoke only for himself, Reed, and Burton, and got a plurality when Justice Rutledge concurred in the result. But three members of the Court, Black, Douglas, and Murphy, dissented, believing that the complaint did, in fact, present a justiciable case and controversy. Four years later in *South v. Peters* (1950) the Vinson Court again refused to enter the "political thicket," turning aside a challenge to Georgia's county unit system, which heavily weighted the electoral process in favor of rural areas.

Ironically, the first hint of change came in an opinion written by Frankfurter, who nonetheless continued to insist that courts should stay out of this political morass. In 1960 the high Court struck down a flagrant gerrymandering scheme in Tuskegee, Alabama, that effectively disenfranchised nearly all of the city's blacks. Frankfurter's opinion in *Gomillion v. Lightfoot* relied entirely on the Fifteenth Amendment, and he carefully avoided any intimation that the ruling might apply to other districting imbalances. Whatever Frankfurter's intentions, reformers believed they now had a foot in the courthouse door; two years later, over Frankfurter's objections, the Court accepted a suit brought by urban voters in Tennessee, where there had been no redistricting in sixty years.

Baker v. Carr, handed down late in 1962, took the Court away from the position Frankfurter had so vigorously defended in *Colgrove.* In one of his best and most scholarly opinions, Justice Brennan spoke for a six-to-two majority that issues such as alleged malapportionment could be litigated in federal court. He prescribed no particular solution, but sent the case back to district court for a full hearing; the high

Court would not deal with a remedy until the matter had been fully litigated and a final decree entered.

Brennan's opinion did not flatly reject the political question doctrine; it had often served the Court well as a safety valve, allowing the justices to evade, when they chose, issues the decision of which—one way or the other—might damage the Court. Nor did he challenge the traditional interpretation of the guarantee clause, which had very little precedential value in this case. Rather, he noted (correctly) that even in *Colgrove* a majority of the Court had thought the issue justiciable, and in *Gomillion*, it had specifically asserted judicial power to remedy the problem. Brennan justified his conclusion by drawing a distinction between recognized political questions, in which the Constitution demonstrably assigned responsibility to another branch of government, and apportionment, which he claimed could be resolved through "judicially discoverable and manageable standards." Malapportionment, he believed, violated the equal protection clause.

Despite strenuous and predictable dissents from Justices Harlan and Frankfurter, both of whom urged judicial restraint and deference to the political process, it is easy to see why the majority of the Court agreed to consider the apportionment cases. Frankfurter's dissent, as a matter of fact, gives us a clear understanding of exactly what the majority had in mind. He accused the majority of risking the Court's prestige in an area that should be left to the political process. "In a democratic society like ours, relief must come through an aroused popular conscience that sears the conscience of the people's representatives" (*Baker v. Carr* [1962], 270). While Harlan thought the system might be better, he found nothing in the Constitution to prevent a state "acting not irrationally, from choosing any electoral structure it thinks best suited to the interests, tempers and customs of the people" (*Baker v. Carr* [1962], 334).

Both men ignored the heart of the issue—the political process had been stymied and perverted, so that the majority of the people could not adopt that system "best suited" to their needs because an entrenched minority blocked any and all change. The Court on a number of occasions had declared that not all issues could be resolved through litigation, and that in questions of public policy change would have to come through the political process and not through the courts. In those cases, however, there had always been an assumption that the process would be amenable to majoritarian decision making, that all voters would have a say in the matter.

One month after delivering his dissent Frankfurter suffered a stroke, and soon afterwards retired. The appointment of Arthur Goldberg to take his place greatly distressed Frankfurter, as he realized that the liberals now held the balance of power on the bench. The Court had, in fact, been moving away from Frankfurter's philosophy of judicial restraint as witnessed by its decision in *Baker v. Carr*. The reapportionment cases, coming so soon after Frankfurter's departure, provide the clearest example of the great sea change that took place in the Warren Court. In 1953 when Warren joined the Court, only Black and Douglas stood out against Frankfurter's philosophy. Warren gave them a third vote, and Brennan a fourth. While the chief justice could almost always get unanimity on racial cases, the liberals lacked a consistent fifth vote. Goldberg gave them that vote, as did his successor Abe Fortas.

The reapportionment cases are key to understanding the Warren Court's commitment to democracy. Its members placed a high value on the integrity of the political process, because for all the debate about judicial activism and policy making, the Court always looked to that process to resolve most of the public questions of the day. The whole rationale for judicial restraint and deference to the legislative will had been based on the belief that the legislature truly and accurately reflected the will of the people. For the majority of the Warren Court, depriving a person of the full value of his or her ballot deprived that individual of the equal protection of the law, whether that deprivation came about because of race, poverty, or residence in an urban area.

"People, not land or trees or pastures, vote."

Despite the dire warnings that the Court would do immeasurable harm to itself through entanglement in the "political thicket," in the end the Court found not only a clear standard, but one that quickly won the support of a majority of Americans. Following *Baker v. Carr*, the Court handed down decisions invalidating the Georgia county unit system as well as the state's congressional districting plan.

Gray v. Sanders (1963) technically dealt with voting rights rather than apportionment, but given the gist of *Baker*, it was an easy case. Attorney General Robert F. Kennedy chose it as his maiden appearance in any court and argued the United States' amicus position against the Georgia unit system. Kennedy had memorized the facts of the case well, but most important, in his argument he uttered the words "one man, one vote" that would give the Court the key to overcoming Frankfurter's claim that there could be no judicially manageable relief. Justice Douglas applied an equal protection analysis, and then borrowing from Kennedy's phrase, articulated the formula that not only provided judicial guidance but also caught the popular imagination—"one person, one vote." Who could object to assuring every person that his or her vote counted equally with those of others? Support of the formula equated with support of democracy and the Constitution; opposition seemed undemocratic and petty.

Although Douglas did not dwell on the matter, his opinion implicitly dismissed original intent as irrelevant in this case. His history was evolutionary, not static, and as a result needed a Constitution that could also live and change with the times. Moreover, Douglas in large measure ignored the constitutional text and appealed to the ideas of democracy as set forth in the Declaration of Independence and the Gettysburg Address. In essence, he suggested, the living Constitution embraced far more than its basic text.

Following *Baker* many legislatures had voluntarily redistricted one or both of their legislative chambers, but they did not know exactly what criteria the Court would apply to measure the fairness of their plans. In some states rural minorities blocked any effort at reform, and in Colorado the electorate, by a two-to-one margin, approved a plan that apportioned the lower house on a population basis, but gave rural areas additional, although not controlling, weight in the upper house. In states where reapportionment had occurred, as well as in states where it had been blocked, reformers launched dozens of suits seeking redress under the equal protection clause.

In June 1964 Chief Justice Warren handed down the Court's decision in six representative cases. The leading suit, *Reynolds v. Sims*, attacked malapportionment of the Alabama legislature, which, despite a constitutional requirement for representation based on population and a decennial reapportionment, remained based on the 1900 census. Lower courts had found that this scheme, as well as two proposed "reforms," violated the equal protection clause, and had ordered a temporary reapportionment plan that combined features from the new proposals. Both sides in the lower court case then appealed. Warren built upon the analyses in the two Georgia cases, and adopted Douglas's "one man, one vote" formulation as the constitutional standard. The chief justice dismissed all formulas that attempted to weigh certain factors:

> To the extent that a citizen's right to vote is debased, he is that much less a citizen. The weight of a citizen's vote cannot be made to depend on where he lives. . . . A citizen, a qualified voter, is no more nor no less so because he lives in the city or on the farm. This is the clear and strong command of our Constitution's Equal Protection Clause. (*Lucas v. Forty-Fourth General Assembly of Colorado* [1964], 567, 568)

In the Colorado case, *Lucas v. Forty-Fourth General Assembly*, the state contended that a majority of its voters, by a two-to-one margin, had voluntarily diluted their voting power to protect the rural minority. Warren rejected the argument out of hand; the Court dealt here not with the rights of minorities but with the rights of individuals. "It is a precept of American law," he declared, "that certain rights exist which a citizen cannot trade, barter, or even give away" (*Lucas v. Fourty-Fourth General Assembly of Colorado* [1964], 736–737). An individual's constitutional rights could not be infringed because a majority of the people voted to do so.

With Frankfurter now gone from the bench, only Justice Harlan remained to object to the apportionment decisions. The majority opinion, he charged, rested on bad history and bad law, and ignored the special qualities of a pluralist federal system. Harlan would have allowed apportionment formulas to take into account such factors as history, economics, geography, urban-rural balance, theories of bicameralism, and majoritarian preferences of particular schemes. To this the chief justice responded that "neither history alone, nor economics or other sorts of group interests are permissible factors in attempting to justify disparities. . . . Citizens, not history or economic interests, cast votes. People, not land or trees or pastures vote" (*Reynolds v. Sims* [1964], 579–580).

At Justice Douglas's urging, the Court handed down its decisions in the six cases at the end of the term in June rather than holding them up until the fall, so that reapportionment could take place before the November elections. This time the Court did not repeat the mistake it had made in *Brown II;* there was no talk of "all deliberate speed" or any other phrase that might be countenanced as inviting delay. The Court clearly indicated that it expected rapid compliance, and urged that unless the district courts, which would have primary responsibility for evaluating new plans, found some compelling reason to the contrary, they should allow no more state elections to be held under invalidated plans.

Despite the uproar from rural-dominated legislatures and their allies in Congress that greeted these decisions, the opposition soon faded as new legislatures, elected under court-ordered plans, took control of the state houses. Moreover, influential citizen groups such as the League of Women Voters endorsed *Reynolds* and the "one person, one vote" concept, and conducted educational campaigns to explain the rulings. And once implemented, reapportionment faced little opposition as formerly dominant minorities could no longer block the majority will. No state, once reapportioned, sought to revive the old system.

Although the "one person, one vote" rule provided a clear and judicially manageable standard, some questions did remain, such as the level of exactitude, as well as the reach of the decision. In *Swann v. Adams* (1967), the Court invalidated a Florida plan that had only minor aberrations from the formula. Justice White agreed that the Constitution did not require absolute precision, but in this case the statute had failed to provide adequate justification for certain important deviations. As with all equal protection cases, the Court would employ a strict standard of scrutiny, so that states would have to show a compelling reason for any significant deviation. The following year in *Avery v. Midland County*, the Court brought city and county governments under the "one person, one vote" rule; remaining questions, and there were many, would be decided by the Burger Court.

Reapportionment and Democracy

The apportionment cases seemed a fitting climax to the Warren Court's so-called equal protection revolution. What had been the "last resort of constitutional arguments" had become, in a little over a dozen years, a powerful tool to protect the civil rights and liberties of individuals. In some ways the apportionment cases constitute the most "radical" decisions. Unlike the desegregation cases, in which the Court had chipped away at the "separate but equal" doctrine for many years, apportionment had been a stranger in the courts. Conservatives later seized Frankfurter's argument in *Colgrove* as the proper standard for judicial restraint, yet that argument had never enjoyed support from a majority of his colleagues. Four of the seven justices who heard the case thought it justiciable, but they lacked any idea of how to develop a clear and manageable judicial standard.

By the time the Court agreed on the justiciability of apportionment in *Baker v. Carr* in 1962, it had had the experience of the desegregation cases, and had learned several valuable lessons. First, the political process cannot always be relied upon to remedy even a clear violation of constitutionally protected rights. Second, if courts intervene to protect such rights, then they must act boldly and set out clear rules. Third, new standards must be implemented without delay. The apportionment decisions showed the wisdom of these lessons; despite some vocal opposition from rural groups who would now lose power, the country quickly accepted the rationale of the decisions and the rightness of the solution.

One could also portray the apportionment decisions as quite conservative. Opponents of judicial activism always justify their call for deference to the legislative will on grounds that elected assemblies represent the will of the people, in whom sovereignty ultimately resides. If one is to take that argument seriously, then it seems absolutely necessary that the legislatures actually and fairly represent the people. If they do not, if a rural minority blocks the will of an urban majority, if older areas have greater voting strength than newer and more populated districts, then the legislatures do not represent the will of the people. In this sense, the Warren Court fostered greater democracy; it made it possible for the majority to gain control of the political process.

A more complex question involves the nature of federalism and the role of minorities in a pluralist society. The Court, in the speech and religion cases to which we now turn, declared that the majority cannot silence a minority. It also recognized "suspect" classifications, such as race and religion, that trigger strict scrutiny under equal protection analysis. Furthermore, the Constitution, in setting up a federal system, did not establish equality as the criteria. All states, from the largest to the smallest, have two senators, and if one applied the Court's calculus to this system, it would certainly fail under the "one person, one vote" rule. But it is constitutionally mandated, and if the federal system allows such disparities and the use of criteria other than population, then why shouldn't the states also be allowed to set up smaller versions of a federal system, with some counties, no matter how small, assured of the same number of representatives as larger counties in order to protect their rights?

It is a logical argument, but the Court's response is equally logical. The Constitution does not recognize any unit smaller than a state, and from the beginning courts have held that local governments are merely administrative units of the state. Fights for local control of schools, taxes, and other functions clearly show that states are the locus of sovereignty for such matters. One does not find a state constitution that says "We the counties of this state, in order to form a more perfect state . . ." The states and their internal arrangements, therefore, are different from the federal government and its relations with the states.

Finally, should courts be agents of social and political change? Where is the mandate to overturn the majority's desire for segregated schools or legislatures that favor certain areas? Opponents of judicial activism say that courts should not be involved, that social and political change are evolutionary processes that can only be derailed by precipitate action. The answer, Court defenders would say, is in the Constitution. Of what value are guarantees of free speech, due process, or the equal protection of the laws if they can be limited by majority whim? What value is the Constitution itself unless it is obeyed?

The First Amendment: The Speech Clause

Earl Warren arrived in a nation's capitol in the grip of a red scare, this one fueled by the junior senator from Wisconsin, Joseph McCarthy. In the late 1940s and early 1950s the Supreme Court had apparently been gripped by the same antiradical hysteria, and as a result had given ground in its quarter-century drive to erect strict protections around the First Amendment. Warren did not share his predecessor's anticommunist hysteria, and by 1954 the worst aspects of McCarthyism seemed to be in retreat. Speech inhibited by fear had no place in a democratic regime, nor did efforts to try to control what people read or saw. In its speech cases the Court received—and deserves—high marks for finally achieving the protection of speech at the level that Brandeis and Holmes had demanded. In other areas, however, the Court left its successor a convoluted set of half rules on what constitutional protection nonpolitical speech enjoys.

The hallmark of a free society is the ability of its citizens to express their opinions, on any number of topics and in a variety of ways, without fear of punishment by the state. Freedom of expression is the core value of democracy, the right valued above all others, or as Justice Cardozo phrased it, "the indispensable condition of nearly every other form of freedom" (*Palko v. Connecticut* [1937], 327). Although speech cases arising under the First Amendment are a relatively recent development, free expression issues have become a significant part of the Court's business.

For absolutists like Justices Black and Douglas, the clear wording of the First Amendment—"Congress shall make no law . . . abridging the freedom of speech, or of the press"—allowed only one interpretation. Neither Congress, nor by incorporation the states, could in any way limit individual expression. For them the First Amendment rights constituted the cornerstone of American liberty, and occupied a "preferred" position in the hierarchy of protected rights. Other members of the Court, even while conceding the importance of speech, never accepted the Black/Douglas view of a constitutionally protected right to unlimited speech. The Court has thus wrestled with a number of issues, such as what constitutes speech, what restraints may be imposed in balancing freedom against order, and whether certain types of speech are more "valuable" and therefore deserving of special attention. Before examining specific issues, it may help to look briefly at some historical and philosophical developments that underlie modern notions of free speech.

Free Speech and Society

When Sir William Blackstone wrote his *Commentaries* in the latter eighteenth century, he defined freedom of speech as the lack of prior restraint, that is, government could not prevent someone from saying or publishing what he or she believed, although such freedom did not extend to "blasphemous, immoral, treasonable, schismatical, seditious or scandalous" speech, and a speaker could be punished afterwards for having uttered or printed forbidden speech. The English, like the ancient Greeks, established legal restrictions on three types of speech—sedition, defamation, and blasphemy, each of which they called "libels." Of these, the most politically important was seditious libel, because ruling elites believed that any criticism of government or its officials, even if true, subverted public order by undermining confidence in the government. The provocation itself, not the falsity of the charge, invited the punishment.

During the seventeenth and eighteenth centuries, the Crown prosecuted hundreds of cases of seditious libel, and often imposed Draconian penalties. When William Twyn published a book supporting the right of revolution, he was convicted of sedition and of "imagining the death of the king," and the court sentenced him to be hanged, emasculated, disemboweled, quartered, and beheaded. Given the possibility of such punishment after publication, the lack of prior restraint meant little, and English writers for the most part imposed a rigid self-censorship to avoid such penalties.

English common law carried over to America, but there seems to have been a great discrepancy between theory and practice in the colonies. Assemblies passed a number of statutes regulating speech, but neither royal governors nor local courts seemed to have enforced them with any degree of regularity or stringency. Then in the important case of John Peter Zenger, the colonists established truth as a defense to charges of seditious libel. One could still be charged if one criticized government officials, but now a defendant could present evidence of the truth of his or her statements, and it would be up to the jury to determine their validity. Despite the infamy heaped upon the 1798 Sedition Act and its use by the Adams Administration against Republican critics, the statute did embody truth as a defense.

The Sedition Act raises the question of what the Framers of the First Amendment intended, and there is no clear answer. James Madison and his colleagues in that first Congress knew their British history, in which the most prominent restrictions on speech had been licensing of printers and prosecution for seditious libel. Although licensing had been abandoned in England in 1694, it is possible that the Framers wanted to make sure that it would not be resurrected in America. However, when Madison penned the Virginia Resolution against the 1798 Sedition Act, he paid relatively little attention to the First Amendment and based his opposition on states' rights grounds. Following Jefferson's election Congress allowed the Sedition Act to expire, and with the exception of a few Civil War regulations, did not attempt to limit speech or press again until World War I. It is with the cases arising out of the Espionage Act of 1917 and the Sedition Act of 1918 that the debate, both within the Court and out, really began over the meaning of free speech.

Zechariah Chafee Jr., a professor at the Harvard Law School and the scion of an old Rhode Island family, entered the lists in the wake of the World War I sedition prosecutions. In his influential book, *Free Speech in the United States*, first published in 1920, he argued that the Framers had more in mind than merely prohibiting licensing; instead, they "intended to wipe out the common law of sedition and make further prosecutions for criticism of the government, without any incitement to lawbreaking, forever impossible" (Chafee 1941, 21). For Chafee, free speech served two purposes, individual interest (persons speaking on matters that are crucial to their own beliefs and desires), and social interest (matters that citizens must understand so that democratic government can function). The latter interest is by far the more important, and can only be achieved by full and free discussion. Chafee criticized Holmes's "clear and present danger" test in *Schenck v. United States* because it failed to differentiate degrees of danger; for Chafee, speech could be limited only "when the interest in public safety is really endangered" (Chafee 1941, 21). While the defendants in *Schenck* may have posed a distant, abstract threat to society, no real danger existed. The value of free and unfettered speech to the democratic workings of society far outweighed the minor inconvenience that the Schencks of the world posed.

While Chafee argued for nearly unlimited speech in the political arena, he did not suggest expanding the meaning of the First Amendment in regard to nonpolitical speech, such as the profane, the indecent, or the insulting. Such speech contributed nothing to the analysis of ideas and the search for truth, and could be restricted in order to serve the greater social values of "order, morality, the training of the young, and the peace of mind of those who see and hear" (Chafee 1941, 50). The Supreme Court unanimously endorsed Chafee's view of the social uselessness and lack of First Amendment protection for obscenity, libel, and so-called fighting words in *Chaplinsky v. New Hampshire* (1942).

One of the most influential theorists of free speech in this century happened to have been a man who taught Chafee when the latter was an undergraduate. Alexander Meiklejohn went even farther than his former pupil in postulating an absolute protection for political speech, which he saw as essential to self-government. Meiklejohn used the analogy of a New England town meeting where the voters are made wise by means of vigorous debate. In such a situation, he argued, it is not necessary that each person be heard, but that "everything worth saying shall be said" (Meiklejohn 1960, 28). Although there may be procedural rules to allow for orderly debate, there must be no fetters on ideas. "The freedom of ideas shall not be abridged" (28).

The protection of congressional speech in the Constitution (Art. I, Sec. 6) is designed to allow just that type of robust, unfettered discussion, and according to Meiklejohn, it is as essential for the people to enjoy that protection as congresspersons and senators, for both are engaged in the business of developing public policy. Where Chafee drew a limit on political speech when it created a real and imminent danger, Meiklejohn seemed to believe it totally untouchable, "beyond the reach of legislative limitation, beyond even the due process of law. . . . Congress has no negative powers whatever" (37).

Private speech, on the other hand, defined primarily as not involving political matters, enjoys only a limited protection. Chafee criticized Meiklejohn on this bifurcation between public and private speech, asserting that no historical evidence supports the view that the founders had any such distinction in mind. Moreover, the line is not always sharp, and what may strike one person as "public" may seem "private" to another. Would a novel, for example, be considered a private expression if it dealt fictionally with important social matters? For Chafee, it would be far better to exclude clearly useless speech, and to protect all other expression, be it private or public.

The problem of line drawing, or balancing, led Yale law professor Thomas I. Emerson to attempt a systematic exploration of free speech, in which he proposed the "expression/action" theory, a criterion reminiscent of the belief/action dichotomy utilized by the Court in religion cases. For Emerson, freedom of expression is absolute, no matter what form it takes. People can express their views either through traditional speech or writing, or by other means, such as music and art. Moreover, the right of free expression includes the right to hear the opinion of others, the right to inquire freely, and the right to associate with others of similar view. The benefits of this libertarian policy, Emerson argued, are individual self-fulfillment, discovering truth, democratic decision making, and the achievement of a more stable community.

Emerson drew the line between the expression of ideas, no matter what form they take, and their manifestation as action, which may be controlled by other constitutional requirements. The problem, as he himself recognized, is that the distinction between expression and action is not always clear, especially in areas that Chafee delineated as outside the reach of First Amendment protection—obscenity, libel, and provocation. While Emerson's scheme is more systematic than that of Chafee or Meiklejohn, and provides judges with greater guidance in determining what is protected and what is not, in the end it too requires judges to make balancing decisions.

All of the distinctions—political/nonpolitical, public/private, expression/action —give members of the Court rational and systematic criteria by which to strike a balance between freedom of speech and social order. But they require balancing through subjective evaluation because the lines are rarely clear cut, and as all of the philosophers conceded, there are community concerns, such as the need to maintain peace and social order, that must also be considered.

Justices Black and Douglas opposed balancing and adopted an absolutist position—the First Amendment allowed no abridgements of speech. Even the "clear and present danger" test failed their standards because it involved balancing, and could therefore be used to punish advocacy of unpopular ideas. For Douglas, advocacy even for the purpose of incitement fell within the ambit of constitutional protection, and he declared he could see "no place in the regime of the First Amendment for any 'clear and present danger' test" (*Brandenburg v. Ohio* [1969]) The only time speech could be in any way restricted was when it involved, as he put it, "speech brigaded with action," and then the state could regulate the action that posed a threat to public order or safety (*Brandenburg v. Ohio* [1969]).

Despite powerful advocacy of their position, Black and Douglas could never win over a majority away from balancing tests. Over the years the Court adopted different strategies in trying to strike an appropriate balance. In some areas it attempted to establish definitional categories to include or exclude certain types of speech. It adopted absolute prohibitions against particular types of regulation. It subjected all regulation of speech and press to "strict scrutiny," in which the burden of proof falls upon the state to show that it has compelling interests to justify limitations on speech. While members of the Court disagreed among themselves on strategies and philosophic rationales, all of them agreed that protected free expression is one of the greatest liberties incorporated in our constitutional system.

The Red Scare

In the year that Earl Warren took the center chair, the country remained gripped in anticommunist hysteria, and security-related speech cases came before the Court throughout Warren's tenure. The worst aspects of the Red Scare manifested themselves most sharply in the demagoguery of Wisconsin Senator Joseph McCarthy, who exploited the fear of foreign ideologies that had played a major role in American politics since the Depression era. That fear had found legislative expression in 1940, shortly after the fall of France, when Congress had passed an Alien Registration Act, commonly called the Smith Act. Its sedition sections specifically aimed to muzzle and punish anyone who attempted to create disloyalty in the military, advocated the forceful overthrow of the government, or conspired with other people to violate any portion of the act. Punishment ranged from a fine of up to $10,000 and/or ten years in jail, later increased to $20,000 and/or twenty years in jail.

During the war the government had invoked the Smith Act only twice, but the most notorious prosecution came in 1948 when the Justice Department secured indictments against Eugene Dennis and ten other members of the American Communist Party Central Committee. In a trial that lasted six months and at times seemed a mockery of justice, all the defendants were convicted for advocating the forceful overthrow of the government and conspiring with others to spread this doctrine. The court of appeals upheld the conviction, and in *Dennis v. United States* (1951), the Supreme Court, by a six-to-two vote, affirmed the convictions. The majority opinion, written by Chief Justice Vinson, seemed to ignore two decades of history in which the Court had expanded the concept of protected speech, and took the very restrictive view that even if the words did not present a clear and present danger, they nonetheless represented a "bad tendency" that could prove subversive of the social order.

Two Truman appointees, Tom Clark and Sherman Minton, were conservatives who had little understanding of free speech issues. They easily fell under the guidance of Felix Frankfurter, whose passion for judicial restraint led to the conclusion that almost any form of repression could be upheld and justified in the name of national security. Frankfurter himself had no use for McCarthy, and in the 1920s had taken a courageous stance in favor of Sacco and Vanzetti. But his belief in judicial restraint became perverted to the point that in many instances he abdicated his judicial responsibility.

Justices Black and Douglas dissented, in tones reminiscent of Holmes and Brandeis in the twenties. Both men articulated a belief in the nearly unfettered right of free expression under the First Amendment. Black claimed that the Smith Act conspiracy section violated constitutional bans against prior restraint, but that even if one believed that advocacy of the Communist Party line might be dangerous, proof had never been introduced to show that it posed any clear and present danger to the government. Justice Douglas pointed out that the defendants were being punished for the "crime" of meeting together for the purpose of teaching themselves and others the doctrines of Marx and Lenin. Because in another setting this might be perfectly appropriate, their crime had to consist in their purpose for learning this information, and the First Amendment did not allow Congress to punish people for what they thought.

Whatever philosophical test one wished to apply—Chafee's, Meiklejohn's, or Emerson's—there seemed little justification for such a drastic restriction on speech, and *Dennis* has not stood the test of time. About the only justification one can find for *Dennis* and other Vinson Court security decisions is that the majority had been caught up in the hysteria of the times. The historian John P. Frank charged that "the McCarthy-McCarran era could scarcely roll the repression along fast enough to keep pace with the Vinson Court's approval of it" (Frank 1961, 252), while another historian, Paul L. Murphy, termed the Vinson majority "pusillanimous" (Murphy 1972, 301) in its failure to protect free speech against congressional witch hunting.

As the Red Scare slowly receded following the exposure of McCarthy in the army hearings and the Senate's censure of him, and with the addition of Earl Warren, William Brennan, and John Marshall Harlan to the Court, a majority of the bench now stood ready to take a different tack on sedition trials. The three newcomers did not subscribe to the Black/Douglas view, which would have thrown out any conviction resulting from a state effort to restrict speech, but neither would they go along with the timidity disguised as restraint that Frankfurter preached. Rather, they applied the same techniques used in the desegregation cases—vigorous statutory interpretation in which the words of the law could be used to achieve the ideals of the First Amendment, or as Paul Murphy phrased it, "By steering a middle course between the preferred freedoms activism of Black and Douglas and the self-restraint of Frankfurter, [the Warren Court] accomplished many of the goals of the former through the techniques of the latter" (Murphy 1972, 320). Much of the credit goes to the political astuteness of Earl Warren, the lawyerly skills of John Harlan, and the genius and passionate devotion to the First Amendment of William Brennan.

Thus, in three 1955 cases challenging the investigating authority of congressional committees in general and the techniques of the House Un-American Activities Committee (HUAC) in particular—*Quinn v. United States, Emspak v. United States,* and *Bart v. United States*—Chief Justice Warren acknowledged the right of Congress to investigate as part of the legislative process. However, even this power had limits and could not be used to pry into "private affairs unrelated to a valid legislative purpose" (*Quinn v. United States* [1955]), 161). The following term, in *Pennsylvania v. Nelson* (1956), the Court struck a major blow against state versions of the HUAC by ruling that in the Smith Act the federal government had preempted the field of subversive control, thus in one swoop invalidating all or part of sedition statutes in forty states. Over the next few years the Court kept chipping away at the problem, finding one technicality after another to invalidate congressional contempt citations or actions of the Subversive Activities Control Board.

During these years the Justice Department, following its victory in *Dennis,* had invoked the Smith Act against a number of lower-echelon Communist Party officials, and in 1957 the Court heard the appeal of Oleta Yates and thirteen other "leaders" of the movement. With *Dennis* so recently decided and Cold War fears still rampant, the Court no doubt believed it would have been impolitic to have summarily overturned that ruling. So Justice Harlan, speaking for the majority, danced around *Dennis* and took a narrow view of the meaning of "organize" and "advocate." As First Amendment scholar Harry Kalven put it, "a more unlikely 'great' precedent [than *Yates v. United States*] would be hard to imagine; at first acquaintance it seems a sort of *Finnegans Wake* of impossibly nice distinctions" (Kalven 1988, 211).

Harlan ruled that the lower court had erred in accepting the government's overly broad meaning of the term "organize," and that in fact the statute of limitations had run on any organizational crime. The Court also struck an important note in rejecting the government's claim that the Smith Act applied especially to the Communist Party; rules regarding speech, Harlan declared, must be general rules, and must apply equally to all groups. In what we would term an "Emersonian" opinion, Harlan limited the applicability of *Dennis* to acts rather than speech. The Smith Act, he explained, proscribed advocacy "to do something, now or in the future, rather than merely to *believe* in something" (*Yates v. United States* [1957], 325).

It is true that, as Justice Clark noted in his dissent, the *Yates* group could hardly be distinguished from the *Dennis* defendants; they "served in the same army and were engaged in the same mission" (*Yates v. United States* [1957], 345). But it is unlikely that the Court that decided *Yates* would have decided *Dennis* as the Vinson Court had done. While precedents are limiting, the Court in these cases showed itself responsive (in *Dennis* perhaps overresponsive) to popular sentiment. In the earlier case a court influenced by Cold War hysteria had affirmed the conviction of communist leaders for advocating the overthrow of the government, although no proof existed that they had done more than engage in radical rhetoric; in the latter case, with the public climate changing against red-baiting, the court renewed an earlier commitment to rational and close examination of limits on speech.

That same day, June 17, 1957—known to some critics as "Red Monday"—the Court handed down three other decisions indicating that, as far as it was concerned, the Cold War would no longer have the chilling effect on civil liberties that had existed during the McCarthy era. In *Watkins v. United States* and *Sweezy v. New Hampshire*, it put an end to some of the arbitrary abuses of the legislative investigating power by committees looking into subversion, and in *Service v. Dulles* the justices overturned a dismissal finding, leading to the firing of an employee, in an infamous loyalty security case. Even though the Court had begun to look more critically at restrictions based on the need to combat subversion, it had not yet articulated a major doctrinal shift that would weight the First Amendment's protection of free expression more heavily than society's need to maintain order.

Chief Justice Warren's opinion in *Watkins* marked the first time that the Court had interfered with the investigative powers of a congressional committee, but never before had a congressional committee so abused its authority as had the House Un-American Activities Committee. In the 150 years between 1792 and 1942, all congressional committees had issued only 108 contempt citations, or about one every seventeen months. Between 1945 and 1947, the HUAC issued 135 contempt citations against people unwilling to testify about their past or about people they had known in their past.

Warren's challenge to this witch hunting constituted a politically dangerous move. The Court was under attack by Southerners, then mounting "massive resistance" to the desegregation cases, and those leading the anticommunist hysterics charged that the Court had come under the influence of the Kremlin. The rabidly right-wing John Birch Society plastered the country with billboards and bumper stickers demanding "Impeach Earl Warren!" But Warren, if nothing else, was politically astute.

Like Harlan's decision in *Yates*, Warren's opinion in *Watkins* was based on narrow technical grounds. He did not deny Congress broad authority to investigate communist subversion. Rather, he said, there was no clear authorization by the House of Representatives to the HUAC to conduct this particular investigation. "There is no congressional power," he wrote, "to expose for the sake of exposure" (*Yates v. United States* [1957], 200). While it was still theoretically possible for the House to authorize every future HUAC investigation, the *Watkins* decision required every member of the House or Senate for the first time to take personal responsibility for outrages committed by the HUAC and the McCarthy committee. A month after the senator from Wisconsin had died, Warren sensed that the country was getting fed up with witch hunting and wanted to return to a more normal and a quieter life.

Although Harlan's opinion in *Yates* curtailed Smith Act prosecutions, the Court later upheld that part of the law that made membership in any organization advocating the overthrow of the government by force or violence a felony in *Scales v. United States* (1961). Yet on the same day in a companion case—*Noto v. United States*—Harlan invalidated just such a conviction on the grounds that the evidentiary test had not been met; the prosecution had failed to prove that the Communist Party actually advocated forceful or violent overthrow of the government.

A similar pattern of seeming to uphold the power to restrict speech, while in fact strictly limiting the use of that power, can be seen in the Court's handling of McCarran Act cases. Congress passed the Subversive Activities Control Law, commonly known as the McCarran Act, in the spring of 1950, and through a series of highly complex procedures tried to force the Communist Party to register as a subversive organization. Had the party agreed to do so, of course, it would have forfeited nearly all the rights that nonviolent political groups enjoy in the United States. President Truman had vetoed the measure, calling it "the greatest danger to freedom of speech, press, and assembly since the Sedition Act of 1798" (Urofsky 1991, 75), but Congress, fearful of being considered "soft" on communism in an election year, overrode the veto by large margins in both houses.

In the first case testing the law, *Communist Party v. Subversive Activities Control Board* (1961), the Court sustained the registration provisions by a five-to-four vote, with Justice Frankfurter denying that the First Amendment prevented Congress from requiring membership lists of organizations "substantially dominated or controlled by that foreign power controlling the world Communist movement" (*Communist Party v. Subversive Activities Control Board* [1961]). But if the Court, albeit by a hair-thin margin, had affirmed the power in general, it then proceeded to make the exercise of that power impossible. It set aside convictions of communists refusing to register on grounds that the Subversive Activities Control Board's orders were so worded as to constitute a violation of the Fifth Amendment's right against self-incrimination in *Albertson v. Subversive Activities Control Board* (1965). It also overturned the provisions denying passports to communists and prohibiting them from working in defense facilities as overly broad and vague in *Aptheker v. Secretary of State* (1964).

Burying Seditious Libel

The Court finally reached the position it had been searching for regarding "subversive speech" in the final term of the Warren Court. In a *per curiam* decision, it did away with the last vestiges of seditious libel in *Brandenberg v. Ohio* (1969). The issue in Brandenburg, as it had been in all these cases, was the problem of regulating speech that carries the risk of moving the audience to forbidden action—whether it be directed against one individual (a speaker urging the lynching of a prisoner in a local jail) or against the state (advocacy of rebellion). Long ago Oliver Wendell Holmes had noted that all ideas are incitement to action, and no doubt fringe groups as well as mainstream bodies hope that their words will move their listeners to particular actions—whether it be casting a vote in an election, or joining the revolution.

In *Schenck v. United States* (1919) the Court held that the First Amendment did not protect general advocacy of violence; starting with their dissent in *Abrams v. United States* that same year, Holmes and Brandeis set out the argument that radical speech could be curtailed only by showing that it would provoke an imminent danger. During the early 1940s, this "clear and present danger" test, as articulated by Holmes and Brandeis, seemed to have gained ascent, and was used to protect dissident speech in several cases. Then in *Dennis*, the Court seemingly reformulated it to make it an even more stringent limitation on speech, one that penalized thought as well. Between *Dennis* and *Brandenburg*, however, the country rid itself of the McCarthy mentality, and the Court itself engaged in an active examination of just what freedom of expression meant. The central meaning of the First Amendment, the Court agreed, was a core of free speech without which democracy cannot function.

In *Brandenburg* the Court articulated what Justice Harlan had intimated in *Yates*, that only "incitement to imminent lawless action" can justify restriction of free speech. The Ku Klux Klan had held a rally near Cincinnati, and invited a local television station to cover the event. About a dozen members of the Klan, garbed in white sheets and hoods, with some carrying arms, had burned a cross in an open field. Their leader then proceeded to mumble several antiblack and anti-Semitic remarks, called for the expulsion of blacks and Jews from the country, and declared that the Klan would resort to violent action if Congress and the Supreme Court did not stop denying true Americans their country. Brandenburg had been arrested and convicted under the Ohio Criminal Syndicalism statute, fined $1,000, and sentenced to one to ten years in prison.

The Ohio law dated back to 1919, and in 1927, over a strenuous protest by Holmes and Brandeis, the Court had upheld a similar statute in *Whitney v. California*. The Court now validated Brandeis's eloquent opinion calling for full and unfettered speech, and enunciated the rule that "the constitutional guarantees of free speech and free press do not permit a State to forbid or proscribe advocacy of the use of force or of law violation except where such advocacy is directed to inciting or producing imminent lawless action and is likely to incite or produce such action" (*Brandenburg v. Ohio* [1969], 447).

Brandenburg remains the clearest statement of the Warren Court's understanding of the First Amendment's protection of political ideas. It concedes that if speech can incite imminent unlawful action, it may be restricted, but the burden of proof in all speech cases rests on the state to show that action will result, rather than on the defendant to show that it will not. It does, of course, as do all First Amendment cases, retain an element of judicial balancing, a fact that upsets some who would prefer a completely objective test. In constitutional law, however, there are few completely objective rules; the judicial process is at heart a balancing of rights and interests, and all of the speech cases from 1919 on involved the same process. A clear line runs from Holmes's classic dissent in *Abrams* through Brandeis's concurrence in *Whitney* to *Brandenburg*. The Court was slowly expanding the meaning of First Amendment rights. Although the extent of First Amendment protection had never before been stated quite so broadly, the Warren Court in fact did no more than develop the precedents it had inherited. *Dennis*, although it cast such a huge shadow in the 1950s, may better be seen as an aberration, the last gasp of the older restrictive view of speech set forth in *Schenck* and the majority opinion in *Whitney*. The Warren Court recognized this and had moved quickly to disencumber itself of the *Dennis* ruling; when viewed in the fifty-year history of speech cases, there is little doubt as to the wisdom of that decision.

Freedom of Association

One area of First Amendment jurisprudence that reflected the Court's thinking in both the civil rights and subversive cases is that of freedom of association. The First Amendment does not specifically name such a right, but the courts have interpreted the "right of the people peaceably to assemble" to mean that they have a right to associate with others of like mind. The most important Warren Court case in this area resulted from an attack on the National Association for the Advancement of Colored People (NAACP).

Because school boards never voluntarily desegregated, the NAACP had to file countless lawsuits, and Southern states realized that if they could disable the organization, they could stop, or at the very least slow down, the already torpid pace of desegregation. The strategy was to demand that the NAACP publish its membership lists, and then rely on White Citizens Councils and other groups to visit economic recrimination on the members. But the lawlessness of Mississippi and other Deep South states appalled moderates as well as liberals.

In 1956 the attorney general of Alabama, John Patterson, went into state court and claimed that the NAACP had violated state law by doing business without registering. The judge did not want to hear from the NAACP, enjoined it without a hearing, and declared, "I intend to deal the NAACP a mortal blow from which they shall never recover" (Powe 2000, 165). The NAACP would gladly have registered, but the judge would not allow it to do so; instead he ordered it to produce its records, including its membership list. When the organization refused, the judge imposed a $10,000 fine, increased it to $100,000 after five days, and continued the injunction. The NAACP tried to appeal to the Alabama Supreme Court, but—in a scenario out of Kafka—the court found one rule after another that made it impossible to file the appeal. The injunction stayed in effect, although the NAACP had never had a hearing on whether it had ever done anything illegal.

The NAACP now went to the U.S. Supreme Court, although its grounds to do so were far from clear. The high Court does not review cases when state law governs, unless there is a clear constitutional violation, and the state law here merely required the NAACP to register. Moreover, a 1928 decision had held that a state could require the Ku Klux Klan to turn over its membership lists, and the Red Scare cases had made Communist Party lists public. But the out-and-out lawlessness of Alabama officials, especially the judges, could not be ignored. In *NAACP v. Alabama* (1958), Justice Harlan stated that it was "beyond debate that the freedom to engage in association for the advancement of beliefs and ideas is an inseparable aspect of the 'liberty' assured by the Due Process Clause" (*NAACP v. Alabama* [1958], 460). The state could prevail in compelling disclosure of membership only if it had a compelling interest, which it did not. The Alabama Supreme Court refused to accept this reversal, and the NAACP had to go back to the U.S. Supreme Court three more times before an angry Court finally managed to make its will felt.

In *Bates v. Little Rock* (1960), the Court overturned the conviction of Arkansas NAACP leader Daisy Bates for refusing to turn over that state's membership lists, but when some states began questioning whether there was communist influence in the NAACP, the Court, still blinded by the Red Scare, allowed the states to go fishing. In *Gibson v. Florida Legislative Investigating Committee* (1963), the Court let stand the conviction of a Florida civil rights leader for refusing to provide membership lists to a committee supposedly investigating communist influence. For Potter Stewart, who cast the decisive vote, there was a significant difference between communists and civil rights leaders, and the state had a legitimate interest in ferreting out the former. That in doing so they could also identify the latter seemed to make little difference to him. The Court, when it heard *Keyishian v. Board of Regents* (1967), seemed to recognize this, and struck down a New York state law requiring public employees to sign an affidavit that they did not belong to the Communist Party.

Obscenity

In a 1942 decision, *Chaplinsky v. New Hampshire*, the Court had stated explicitly that First Amendment protection did not cover obscene or libelous speech, a judgment that reflected not only contemporary thinking but historic legal tradition as well. The origin of obscene libel in English law dates to the medieval ecclesiastical courts, which until the early eighteenth century heard all cases involving charges of lewdness, profanity, heresy, and blasphemy. In 1708 the Queen's Bench dismissed a secular indictment against James Read for publishing *The Fifteen Plagues of a Maid-enhead*, noting that while a "crime that shakes religion" was indictable, writing an obscene book was not, "but punishable only in the Spiritual Court." Less than twenty years later, however, secular authorities indicted Edmund Curll for publishing *Venus in the Cloister, or the Nun in Her Smock*, a "dialogue" about lesbian love in a convent. Although the Court had the Read case as a precedent, it abandoned it, found Curll guilty, and obscene libel entered the common law.

Originally, obscenity cases involved heresy, blasphemy, and antireligious tracts as much as sexually explicit material, but by the latter nineteenth century obscene libel prosecutions dealt almost entirely with sexually oriented literature. Parliament passed several anti-obscenity acts, including one designed to keep French postcards out of the country. In 1857 it adopted Lord Campbell's Act, which empowered magistrates to seize books and prints that they considered obscene. In the initial case tried under Lord Campbell's Act, *Regina v. Hicklin* (1868), we get our first judicial test for determining whether a particular work is obscene. Lord Chief Justice Cockburn declared that obscenity could be determined on the basis of certain passages that would have the tendency "to deprave and corrupt those whose minds are open to such immoral influences and into whose hands a publication of this sort may fall." In other words, the test was based on the effect the most explicit sexual passages would have on those particularly susceptible (such as children and young adults), and not on the work as a whole.

The *Hicklin* test became the standard in the United States as well as in England, and most people assumed that government could ban material it deemed obscene under the police power. As a result, the Post Office compiled an ongoing list of allegedly obscene literature that could neither be imported into the United States nor handled by the mails. Unfortunately, new forms of literature often shocked the postal inspectors, who consigned works such as James Joyce's *Ulysses* to that list. In a famous 1933 case involving that book, federal judge John M. Woolsey relied on the testimony of literary experts to sustain the artistic value of the Joyce novel, and ruled it was not obscene. Woolsey's decision, however, still accepted the premise that obscene materials did not enjoy First Amendment protection, an assumption reinforced by Justice Murphy in his 1942 *Chaplinsky* opinion.

That case, however, did not involve obscenity, and the Court dealt with the substantive issues only tangentially over the next fifteen years. It ducked the issue in *Doubleday & Co. v. New York* (1948), when by a four-to-four vote it affirmed, without opinion, a state court conviction for the publication of Edmund Wilson's *Memoirs of Hecate County*. Aside from procedural issues, the Court may have been troubled by the prospect of having to review every work alleged to be obscene. State and lower federal courts did, however, begin to hear more censorship cases, and articles on the subject proliferated in the law journals. Meanwhile, local censors went after such works as James T. Farrell's *Studs Lonigan* trilogy, William Faulkner's *Sanctuary*, and Erskine Caldwell's *God's Little Acre*.

In 1956 the Warren Court faced the issue of censorship directly in *Butler v. Michigan*, in which it overturned a state statute making it a crime to "publish materials tending to the corruption of the morals of youth." The Court interpreted the statute to mean that the general adult public could not buy a book that state authorities considered unsuitable for impressionable children. A unanimous bench, speaking through Justice Frankfurter, held that the statute violated the First Amendment by arbitrarily curtailing "one of those liberties of the individual . . . that history has attested as the indispensable conditions for the maintenance and progress of a free society" (*Butler v. Michigan* 1956, 383–384). The decision, however, still excluded obscene works from First Amendment protection; it merely said that material judged unsuited for children could not on that criterion alone be labeled obscene. Otherwise, the law would "reduce the adult population of Michigan to reading only what is fit for children" (*Butler v. Michigan* 1956, 384).

The Court confronted the issue directly later that year in *Roth v. United States*. Samuel Roth, at the time one of the nation's leading distributors of sexually oriented material, had been convicted of mailing obscene publications in violation of federal law. At his trial Roth claimed that the statute unconstitutionally restricted freedom of speech and press. The trial court denied the claim, as did the court of appeals, which noted that Supreme Court precedent clearly excluded obscene works from constitutional protection. In a concurring opinion, however, Judge Jerome Frank explored the legal and philosophical considerations of censorship, and suggested that only material that posed a clear and present danger of inducing serious antisocial behavior should be proscribed.

Judge Frank's comments directly addressed the dilemma faced by the high Court. Over nearly five decades, both liberals and conservatives on the Court had utilized the "clear and present danger" test for evaluating restrictions on speech. To uphold the federal and state obscenity laws, which obviously restricted speech, the Court would have to point to some clear danger presented by dirty books. But what would that danger be? Putting aside the problem of the children's audience, the alleged evils of obscenity, according to one of the leading scholars of the First Amendment, Harry Kalven, are:

> (i) The material will move the audience to anti-social sexual action; (ii) the material will offend the sensibilities of many in the audience; (iii) the material will advocate or endorse improper doctrines of sexual behavior; and (iv) the material will inflame the imagination and excite, albeit privately, a sexual response from the body.
>
> On analysis, these purported evils quickly reduce to a single one. The first, although still voiced by occasional politicians and "decency" lobbies, lacks scientific support. The second may pose a problem for captive audiences, but obscenity regulations have been largely aimed at willing, indeed all too willing, audiences. The third, thematic obscenity, falls within the consensus regarding false doctrine; unsound ideas about sex, like unsound ideas about anything else, present an evil which we agree not to use the law to reduce. (Kalven 1988, 33–34)

This left the Court faced with upholding a restriction on speech because it possibly posed a "clear and present danger" of exciting the sexual fantasies of adults!

Speaking through Justice Brennan, the Court evaded the dilemma by reverting to the *Chaplinsky* dicta that obscenity is not covered by the First Amendment. But there had been too many lower federal and state court cases, too many questions raised about how one determined if a work was indeed obscene. Even granting that the state had the power to regulate or ban obscene materials, did the judges have any constitutionally acceptable criteria with which to validate or void these determinations. Brennan recognized that unless the Court could fashion a judicially manageable definition of obscenity, *Roth* would be only the first of a flood of cases. And so he tried.

"All ideas having even the slightest redeeming social importance—unorthodox ideas, controversial ideas, even ideas hateful to the prevailing climate of opinion—have the full protection" (*Roth v. United States* [1957], 484) of the First Amendment; but obscenity did not. In the first major reformulation since *Hicklin* of what constituted obscenity, Brennan established the new test: "Whether to the average person, applying contemporary community standards, the dominant theme of the material taken as a whole appeals to prurient interest" (*Roth v. United States* [1957], 489).

There is no question that the *Roth* test, which reflected four decades of growing liberalism and sophistication in American case law, is an improvement over *Hicklin*. It takes the work as a whole, rather than the most salacious parts; it applies to the average adult, not the susceptible child; it utilizes overall community standards, not those of the self-styled keepers of purity; and it asks whether the theme of the entire work appeals to prurient interests. It is, however, still censorship; it still requires judges and juries to make subjective judgments; and by conceding that work with "even the slightest redeeming social importance," no matter how sexually explicit or disturbing, is entitled to First Amendment protection, it issued an open invitation to every smut peddler to show that he or she dealt, no matter how marginally, with matters of social import. By shifting the focus of obscenity litigation away from the substantive issue of First Amendment coverage, from the question of whether state interests justified restraint, to one of definition, the Court sank into a morass from which it spent the next twenty years trying to extricate itself. In the following decade the Court heard thirteen more obscenity cases, in which the justices handed down fifty-five separate opinions. Shortly after his retirement, Chief Justice Warren characterized obscenity as the Court's "most difficult area" (Urofsky 1991, 80).

The majority opinion in *Roth* expanded the two-tier strategy that had first appeared in *Chaplinsky*. On one level can be found "important" speech, which can be regulated only if the state can show that the utterance will pose a "clear and present danger" to social order, the standard test used in the seditious libel cases. On another level is speech that is deemed unimportant and lacking in social utility, and this type of speech may be regulated. Obscenity can, by this strategy, be regulated not because it is dangerous but because it is worthless. By declaring obscenity in the second category, Justice Brennan did not have to confront the harder questions involved.

The dissenters in *Roth* did try, at least to some extent, to deal with the broader issue of whether the Constitution permitted regulation, and if so, under what conditions. Justice Harlan objected to the broad definition sketched in by Brennan, which he warned would undermine the "tight reins which state and federal courts should hold upon the enforcement of obscenity statutes" (*Roth v. United States* [1957], 496). Second, he opposed lumping state and federal statutes together; he believed that the states, reflecting local community standards, had the power under the constitution to control obscene materials, while the First Amendment denied a similar power to the national government.

Justice Douglas, joined by Justice Black, entered a short opinion reaffirming their belief in the absolute nature of the First Amendment's prohibition, which "was designed to preclude courts as well as legislatures from weighing the values of speech" (*Roth v. United States* [1957], 514). Neither the states nor the federal government may control expression under the guise of protecting morality. As for the "community conscience" standard, he pointedly asked whether such a standard would be constitutionally acceptable "if religion, economics, politics or philosophy were involved. How does it become a constitutional standard when literature treating with sex is concerned?" (*Roth v. United States* [1957], 512). The Brennan opinion evaded these issues not by explanation but by assertion, and failed to provide a rationale for why the state should be allowed to exercise censorship. The Douglas/Black view may have been simplistic, but it had the virtue of consistency, and had it been followed the Court might have avoided decades of frustration.

The Growing Morass

One year later the New York Board of Regents withheld an exhibition license for the motion picture version of D. H. Lawrence's novel, *Lady Chatterly's Lover*. The Regents acted under a 1954 statute that defined an immoral film as one "which portrays acts of sexual immorality, perversion or lewdness, or which expressly or impliedly presents such acts as desirable, acceptable or proper patterns of behavior." Chief Judge Conway of the New York Court of Appeals upheld the Regents, on the ground that the film depicted adultery as "proper behavior," and therefore fit the definition of the statute. But he did more than that; he tried to frame a rational constitutional standard to determine when sexually explicit films fell within the ambit of obscenity regulation.

The Supreme Court reversed in *Kingsley International Pictures Corp. v. Regents* (1959). It did so on precisely the grounds set out by the New York court, but without any effort to establish judicially manageable standards. According to Justice Stewart, the Regents had prevented exhibition of the film because it advocated an unpopular idea, that adultery might be proper behavior, and thus "the state, quite simply, has struck at the very heart of constitutionally protected liberty" (*Kingsley International Pictures Corp. v. Regents* [1959]). Why the advocacy of adultery is protected, while other materials are not, is never explored in Stewart's opinion, and invites the suggestion that all one has to do is present pornographic material in a matter that implies some sort of advocacy and one can draw the constitutional mantle around the smut and its peddler. Does the literature deal with perverse sexual practices in an explicit manner? Yes it does, but is it explicit in order to make a point about how such behavior may at times be proper? That is an idea, and therefore, protected.

Kingsley Pictures opened the floodgates, and during the remaining decade of the Warren Court the justices struggled valiantly to deal with the issue. It would take far too much time to examine each case in depth, but a brief summary of the major ones will illustrate the problems faced by the Court.

In *Manual Enterprises v. Day* (1962), the Court continued its trend toward defining obscenity in terms of hard-core erotica. The Post Office had excluded from the mails three magazines catering to homosexuals and featuring pictures of nude men. Justice Harlan had the onerous job of writing the Court's opinion, and he added the criterion of "patent offensiveness" to the *Roth* test of "prurient interest." Harlan, like Brennan, evaded the substantive issue while attempting to develop a clear test in an area that had become anything but clear. And, as had become the norm, the Court handed down multiple opinions.

The task of finding a workable definition returned to Justice Brennan in the next two cases. In *Jacobellis v. Ohio* (1964), the Court overturned the conviction of an Ohio theater owner for showing the French film, *Les Amants* (The Lovers). Brennan expanded the *Roth* test of "contemporary community standards" to mean national rather than local standards; otherwise, "the constitutional limits of free expression in the Nation would vary with state lines" (*Jacobellis v. Ohio* [1964], 194–195). Moreover, Brennan made explicit what had been implicit in his *Roth* opinion, that the phrase "utterly without social importance" was part of the constitutional test.

Jacobellis is perhaps best remembered for Justice Stewart's concurring opinion, in which he pointed out that the Court's opinions since 1957 had pointed in the direction of a "hard-core only" test for obscene materials. As he noted, however, a definition of hard-core obscenity had evaded the Court, and would probably continue to do so:

> I shall not today attempt to define the kinds of material I understand to be embraced within that short-hand definition; and perhaps I could never succeed in intelligibly doing so. But I know it when I see it and the motion picture involved in this case is not that. (*Jacobellis v. Ohio* [1964], 197)

Although Stewart later complained that people remembered only his "I know it when I see it" test, in fact he had put his finger directly on the central problem of the obscenity issue. He knew what offended him, and this picture did not; it obviously had offended others. Obscenity, like beauty, is in the eye of the beholder, and so long as we have an open, tolerant, and pluralistic society, one will find an enormous range of opinion on the nature of sexually oriented material. Nonetheless, the Court continued doggedly to seek a workable definition.

Two years later the Court, again speaking through Justice Brennan, narrowed the requirements even further in *Memoirs v. Massachusetts* (1966). The state had attempted to suppress sale of a book that had been the subject of one of the first American obscenity cases in 1821, John Cleland's *Memoirs of a Woman of Pleasure*, popularly known as *Fanny Hill*. In overturning the state decision, Brennan elaborated the obscenity test as first enunciated in *Roth* and now refined by nearly a decade's experience:

> Three elements must coalesce: it must be established that (a) the dominant theme of the material taken as a whole appeals to a prurient interest in sex; (b) the material is patently offensive because it affronts contemporary community standards relating to the description or representation of sexual matters; and (c) the material is utterly without redeeming social value. (*Memoirs v. Massachusetts* [1966], 418)

The new tripartite test hardly commanded the full allegiance of the brethren. Only Chief Justice Warren and Justice Fortas joined Brennan's opinion, the former somewhat reluctantly. Justices Stewart, Black, and Douglas concurred in the result, but not the reasoning; Stewart would have cut through the morass and stated simply that only hard-core pornography remained outside First Amendment protection, while Black and Douglas remained consistent in their opposition to any form of censorship. Among the dissenters, Justice Harlan, as he had in *Roth,* would have left control of obscenity to state discretion; Justice White would have eliminated social value from Brennan's test, a point elaborated upon by Justice Clark.

If the majority had hoped to clarify the issue, it muddied the waters even more in two other opinions handed down the same day, in which the Court affirmed obscenity convictions. *Mishkin v. New York* (1966) involved sadomasochistic materials, and was the easier case because of the particularly brutal and revolting contents of the magazine. The publisher, however, took the interesting approach in defense that the contents did not appeal to prurient interest because they did not appeal to the average person's normal definition of sexual relations! The Court dismissed this bit of sophistry, and declared that the test would apply to the audience to which the magazines deliberately aimed.

The other case, *Ginzburg v. United States*, involved a glossy, sophisticated magazine, *Eros*, that featured highly erotic articles and pictures. Whether it met the tripartite test is unclear, because the case centered on the prosecution's claim that the material had been promoted and marketed to appeal to the lascivious. The Court upheld the conviction, and thus added the feature of "pandering" to the obscenity morass.

The decision is troubling and confusing, because there is a strong argument that the defendant had been denied due process; as the dissenters pointed out, the Court had rewritten the law so that it sustained Ginzburg's conviction on a different theory (pandering) than that under which he had originally been tried (distributing obscene materials). Moreover, "pandering" is perhaps an even more obscure term than "obscene," and calls into question all sorts of subjective judgments. It has been suggested that the Court, concerned at the time by charges that it was "soft" on criminals and was fostering moral permissiveness by its obscenity decisions, wanted to show that convictions could be secured against pornographers.

These three cases—*Memoirs, Mishkin,* and *Ginzburg*—reflect the ambivalence that marked the Warren Court's efforts to deal with obscenity and to determine how much freedom of expression is protected when it deals primarily with sexually oriented material. As Justice Black noted in dissent in *Ginzburg*, there had been fourteen separate opinions handed down that day in the three cases, and "no person, not even the most learned judge much less a layman, is capable of knowing in advance of ultimate decision in his particular case by this Court whether certain material comes within the area of 'obscenity'" (*Memoirs v. Massachusetts* [1966], 480–481).

Following these three cases, the Court seemed to abandon its effort to articulate a definition of obscenity, and finally began to look at what it should have examined in the first place, whether sufficient state interests existed to regulate such material, and if so, under what rationale. In 1967, the Court in *per curiam* decisions reversed several obscenity convictions. The accompanying brief opinion noted that the seven justices who constituted the majority for reversal held four different theories to justify their views. But as the memorandum in *Redrup v. New York* (1967) noted, in none of the cases

> was there a claim that the statute in question reflected a specific and limited state concern for juveniles. . . . In none was there any suggestion of an assault upon individual privacy by publication in a manner so obtrusive as to make it impossible for an unwilling audience to avoid exposure to it. And in none was there evidence of the sort of "pandering" which the Court found significant in *Ginzburg v. United States* (771).

The Court does not even mention the tripartite *Roth-Memoirs* test; in fact, it hardly mentions obscenity per se. Rather, it asks whether there have been intrusions into certain accepted areas where the state police power is acknowledged—protection of children, of captive audiences, and prevention of pandering. The Court had finally gotten around to asking the right questions; the terseness of the *Redrup* memorandum, however, indicated that the Court had a long ways to go until it would find the right answers.

The following year the Court upheld a New York statute that forbade the sale to minors of material deemed to be obscene to them. As Justice Brennan explained in *Ginsberg v. New York* (1968), the courts had traditionally left the care of children to their parents, and so if parents wanted their children to read some of these materials, they could buy them for them. But the state also had a traditional interest in protecting the welfare of its minor citizens, and under its police power may pass legislation to that effect. (Protection of children had been acknowledged in the *Redrup* memorandum as a justifiable grounds for regulation.) Because obscenity still remained unprotected speech, Brennan invoked the two-tier strategy and asked: Did New York have a reasonable basis to conclude that children might suffer some harm from exposure to pornography? If the legislature believed this so, then the courts would not question the wisdom of that decision.

The Court in some ways adopted a two-tiered approach, because nearly all of the major philosophers of free expression, from John Stuart Mill through Chafee, Meiklejohn, and Emerson had dealt with political, as opposed to artistic, expression. The great dissenting opinions of Learned Hand, Oliver Wendell Holmes, and Louis D. Brandeis had similarly focused on the importance of robust political speech. Artistic expression just cannot be judged within those boundaries, and is moreover a highly personal experience. Critics at one time considered Marcel Duchamps's "Nude Descending a Staircase," James Joyce's *Ulysses,* and Igor Stravinsky's "La Sacré du Printemps" as obscene; even today there are persons who object to Mark Twain's *Huckleberry Finn.* Justice Stewart's comment well summed up the Court's problem in its definitional approach, in that it tried to establish objective criteria for a subjective topic. Only when they began to explore what might be considered the artistic parallel to the "clear and present danger" test—the balance of state against individual interests—did the justices finally begin to make sense.

In its last term, the Court took another step in trying to define the legitimate interests of the state. In its final case dealing with obscenity—*Stanley v. Georgia*—the Warren Court unanimously held that the mere possession of obscene material for private viewing in one's home could not be criminally punished.

In the course of investigating alleged book-making activities, police had secured a warrant and searched Stanley's house. They found little evidence of illegal gambling, but did uncover several reels of film, which upon later examination proved quite obscene. In the ensuing prosecution, both the state and the defense agreed that the films met the *Roth-Memoirs* definition of obscenity; the issue thus boiled down to whether the state had any justification in regulating what a person read or saw in the privacy of his or her own home. The state argued that just as it had an obligation to protect the physical well-being of its citizens, so it could protect their minds as well.

All nine members of the Court agreed on the reversal of Stanley's conviction. Stewart, Brennan, and White chose not to reach the First Amendment issues, believing that Stanley's Fourth Amendment rights had been violated. Justice Thurgood Marshall, who had replaced Tom Clark in 1967, finally did what the Court had failed to do earlier—examine what interests the state had in regulating obscene materials. Although he went to great trouble to claim that nothing in his opinion impaired the *Roth* holding that obscenity lay outside constitutional protection, the logic of *Stanley* did just that. If the state had no legitimate claim to interfere with what a person read or viewed privately, and if *Roth* remained intact, then a citizen of the United States had a constitutional right to possess obscene materials, but the person who provided those materials could be criminally prosecuted. The Court ignored this conundrum in *Stanley,* and as in so many other areas, the Warren Court left the hard cases to its successor.

The First Amendment: The Press Clause

Modern press clause jurisprudence begins with the landmark case of *Near v. Minnesota* in 1931, which reiterated the traditional views of free speech going back through Holmes and Blackstone to Milton, who had protested against the British system of licensing the press. The five-to-four decision might well have gone the other way had it been argued earlier, when William Howard Taft still occupied the center chair. But between the time the Court accepted the case and oral argument, Taft had died, and the new Chief Justice, Charles Evans Hughes, had greater sympathy toward the idea of a free press.

Minnesota had authorized abatement, as a public nuisance, of any "malicious, scandalous or defamatory" publication, a law aimed at *The Saturday Press*, a Minneapolis tabloid that, in addition to exploiting rumors, had also uncovered some embarrassing facts about local political and business figures. The state courts gladly "abated" the *Press*, which appealed to the Supreme Court, claiming that its First Amendment rights had been violated. The Court's decision extended the reach of the press clause to the states, and established as the key element of press protection freedom from prior restraint, that is, from having the government censor materials before their publication. Hughes quoted approvingly from Blackstone that the liberty of the press "consists in laying no *previous* restraints upon publication, and not in freedom from censure for criminal matter when published" (*Near v. Minnesota* [1931], 713). The chief justice conceded that the rule against prior restraint had some very narrow exceptions. No one would question, he asserted, "that a government might prevent actual obstruction to its recruiting service or the publication of the sailing days of transports or the number and location of troops" (*Near v. Minnesota* [1931], 716).

The early prior restraint cases following *Near* often dealt with censorship of motion pictures, which the Court did not equate with press publications. In 1961, for example, in *Times Film Corp. v. Chicago*, the Warren Court ruled against the notion that "the public exhibition of motion pictures must be allowed under any circumstances" (*Times Film Corp. v. Chicago* [1961], 49). In *Freedman v. Maryland* (1965), however, the Court struck down a Maryland censorship scheme and imposed such a high standard for procedural safeguards that it did, in effect, wipe out state film censorship.

Prior restraint, however, means only that the state cannot censor publications; it does not mean that the press is free to print anything it wants without fear of reprisal. In *Chaplinsky v. New Hampshire* (1942), the Court had placed criminal libel, along with obscenity and provocation, outside the protection of the First Amendment. Under the common law, three general rules had developed in regard to defamatory statements. First, such statements were presumed false, which placed the burden upon the alleged defamer to prove the truth of the comments. In many situations, "truth" might be difficult to establish, especially if it involved subjective judgments. Second, if the statement were false, it did not matter whether it had been printed through malice or negligence; one published at one's peril, and the common law presumed malice from the publication of false statements. Finally, the aggrieved party did not have to prove actual harm to reputation; the publication of false statements implied that general harm had occurred. Once a plaintiff proved that a libel had occurred, he or she was entitled to monetary damages; determination of these damages varied according to individual state law.

The Supreme Court first heard a libel case ten years after *Chaplinsky*. During World War II several state legislatures, in trying to prevent the rampant racism that marked Hitler's Germany, had enacted group libel statutes, which extended the rules of defamation against individuals to groups. Illinois passed such a law, and under it prosecuted the president of a "White Circle League" for remarks directed against Negroes. Shortly after the Supreme Court had struck down the validity of restrictive covenants in *Shelley v. Kraemer* (1948), Joseph Beauharnais published an ad urging city officials to prevent blacks from moving into white neighborhoods, because they would bring "rapes, robberies, knives, guns and marijuana" with them.

On appeal, the Supreme Court upheld the conviction by a five-to-four vote in *Beauharnais v. Illinois* (1952). Justice Frankfurter, writing for the majority, adopted the *Chaplinsky* comment that libel did not enjoy First Amendment protection, and reasoned that if the state could establish laws on individual libel, it could do the same for group libel. Among the dissenters, Justices Black and Douglas entered strong and prescient dissents. Black declared that the decision "degrades First Amendment freedoms," and warned that "the same kind of state law that makes Beauharnais a criminal for advocating segregation in Illinois can be utilized to send people to jail in other states for advocating equality and nonsegregation" (*Beauharnais v. Illinois* [1952], 274). Douglas labeled the majority opinion "a philosophy at war with the First Amendment," and warned that under group libel laws "tomorrow a Negro will be hauled before a court for denouncing lynch law in heated terms" (*Beauharnais v. Illinois* [1952], 286). In fact, the Warren Court first dealt with the libel issue in the context of the great civil rights revolution of the 1960s.

New York Times v. Sullivan (1964)

This case arose following publication of an advertisement in *The New York Times* paid for by veteran civil rights leaders A. Philip Randolph and Bayard Ruskin, as well as entertainer Harry Belafonte. "Heed Their Rising Voices" detailed the difficulties that Martin Luther King Jr. and his associates faced in the South and requested funds to aid in the civil rights struggle. The ad, a strong and effective attack on Southern intransigence, was signed by sixty-four civil rights activists. In addition, twenty others, mostly African American ministers in the South, signed a one-sentence statement of "warm endorsement," although it later turned out that several of them did not know how their names had been used.

Although L. B. Sullivan, the police commissioner of Montgomery, Alabama, had not been mentioned by name in the text, he sued the *Times* on the basis that the advertisement derogated his performance of his public duties. An Alabama court found the advertisement defamatory, and disallowed the defense of truth because of several minor inaccuracies in the text. The jury awarded general damages of $500,000 (a very large judgment in those days) and the Alabama Supreme Court affirmed the decision. Moreover, this was but the first of several libel suits against the paper.

No doubt the case involved more than a bit of malice on the part of Southerners directed against outside "interference" in the civil rights struggle. The *Times* had a minimal presence in the state. Only two reporters, both based elsewhere, had ever gone into the state to cover events, and out of a total national circulation of 650,000 only 394 copies came into Alabama on any given day. But in fact, Alabama had made no new law on this subject; rather the facts of the case merely showed how harsh the technical rules of criminal libel could be. When the Alabama trial court disallowed the defense of "fair comment" because of factual inaccuracies, it may have appeared vengeful, but in fact many other states had exactly the same rule. Nonetheless, the message was clear. If local judges and juries could impose staggering dollar damages on the nation's preeminent newspaper for failure to check the factual accuracy of an advertisement, then no newspaper would ever run the risk of publishing controversial material. The public debate on civil rights could be stifled, as news of Southern attacks on civil rights workers could be silenced. As the *Montgomery Advertiser* noted, "State and city authorities have found a formidable legal bludgeon to swing at out-of-state newspapers whose reporters cover incidents in Alabama" (Powe 2000, 306). When the newspaper appealed the judgment to the Supreme Court, Sullivan's lawyer declared "The only way the Court could decide against me was to change one hundred years or more of libel law" (Powe 2000, 307).

The Court, which in *Brown* had helped trigger the civil rights struggle, obviously, as one scholar noted, had "to rescue the *Times* and equally compelled by its role to seek high ground in justifying its result, arrived at some very high ground indeed" (Kalven 1988, 62). Unlike its decisions on seditious libel and obscenity, here the Court did indeed chart a new path, and in *New York Times v. Sullivan* (1964) wrote an important chapter in the history of freedom of expression.

Justice William Brennan, who in his more than thirty years on the Court helped shaped a large part of American constitutional doctrine, spoke in his opinion to more than the archaic common-law rules of libel. He addressed the larger issue of what limits constrain individuals and the press in a free society when they criticize the government or its officials. While Brennan had not been an absolutist on First Amendment rights (witness his opinions that obscenity remained outside constitutional protection), he had moved consistently to a Meiklejohnian view that political speech in any form must be completely protected. In this case he utilized what he termed "the central meaning of the First Amendment" to cut through centuries of accumulated restrictions on speech.

Because of some minor factual errors the defendant could not enter one of the traditional defenses against libel, that of "fair comment." Reporters may fairly comment on people or institutions that offer their work for public approval or in the public interest, provided that the criticism is fair, honest, and made without malice. By adhering strictly to the requirement of accuracy in the factual recital, the Alabama court cut off this defense. As a result, it had a chilling effect on criticism of public officials because newspapers would be very reluctant to offer any criticism, if—due to a minor and even irrelevant factual error—they would be denied their defense against libel suits.

Although Sullivan had sued in his private capacity, and the suit had been tried under the law of criminal libel that governed defamation of individuals, in a broader sense the case involved seditious libel, the criticism of the government itself. Sullivan claimed that the advertisement derogated the official performance of his department, and if government officials could sue every time their official conduct came under critical scrutiny, one would be back to the status of the 1798 Sedition Law. Brennan realized this, and in his opinion noted specifically that:

> Although the Sedition Act was never tested in this Court, the attack upon its validity has carried the day in the court of history. . . . The invalidity of the Act has also been assumed by Justices of this Court. . . . These views reflect a broad consensus that the Act, because of the restraint it imposed upon criticism of government and public officials, was inconsistent with the First Amendment. (*New York Times v. Sullivan* [1964], 276)

This marked the first time in history that a federal law, even one that had expired more than 160 years earlier, had been held to violate the First Amendment. The old notion of seditious libel, that criticism of the government even if factually in error, could no longer be tolerated in a free society. The central meaning of the First Amendment is that the concept of seditious libel in any form cannot be tolerated, and the Alabama rule, with its demand for strict accuracy, had the effect of making seditious libel an offense. The penalties faced under the Sedition Act and the Alabama law differed only in degree; they both had the same objective, to stifle "uninhibited, robust and wide-open" debate on public issues.

At one point in his opinion Brennan noted that in a 1959 case, *Barr v. Matteo*, the Court had ruled that high-ranking government officials enjoyed immunity from libel suits when acting in their public capacity. Certainly, the same privilege should be extended to citizens when they perform their duties, namely, to scrutinize closely public policies. In a democracy, as Meiklejohn claimed, the citizen is the ruler and therefore the most important official of the government.

Justice Brennan realized that at times criticism could be harsh, and might exceed the limits of good taste, perhaps even of truth, that it may, as he noted, "well include vehement, caustic, and sometimes unpleasantly sharp attacks on the government and public officials" (*New York Times v. Sullivan* [1964], 270). While this might not be comfortable for the officials under attack, it constituted a necessary part of the mechanism of democracy, protected in all its vigor by the First Amendment. To allow, as Alabama did, transmutation of such criticism into the basis for personal suit, would have a chilling effect on protected free expression, and that was constitutionally unacceptable.

There is no question that the decision marked a major step in broadening the level of free expression protected under the First Amendment, but it did not go far enough to assuage at least two members of the Court, Justices Black and Douglas, who entered a concurrence expressing their belief in an "absolute, unconditional constitutional right to publish" criticisms of public officials (*New York Times v. Sullivan* [1964], 293). Although the majority opinion did not speak of balancing competing interests, the decision did not, as Black and Douglas realized, affirm an unconditional protection of political criticism.

The normal criteria for evaluating First Amendment protection, which are explicitly balancing tests, are not mentioned in *Sullivan*. It is nonetheless balancing, although not of the ad hoc variety that marked the old seditious libel cases. In this case Brennan tried to define protected speech, and he did so far more successfully than in his efforts to define unprotected speech in the obscenity cases. Justice Lewis Powell later explained the need for such clear definitional rules. Case-by-case adjudication of competing interests—free speech versus reputational integrity—would produce "unpredictable results and uncertain expectations, and it would render our duty to supervise the lower courts unmanageable" (*Gertz v. Robert Welch, Inc.* [1974], 343). But definitions, as Black and Douglas well understood, invoke subjective judgments that always involve including and excluding certain types of speech, a result they believed incompatible with the First Amendment mandate against any restriction on speech. "The only sure way," Black later declared,

> to protect speech and press against these threats is to recognize that libel laws are abridgements of speech and press and therefore barred in both federal and state courts by the First and Fourteenth Amendments. I repeat what I said in the *New York Times* case that "An unconditional right to say what one pleases about public affairs is what I consider to be the minimum guarantee of the First Amendment." (*Rosenblatt v. Baer* [1966], 95)

New York Times v. Sullivan did not, as Justice Black recognized, do away with libel law in its entirety. Rather, it set up a dividing line between two types of allegedly defamatory speech, that directed against public officials and personalities, and that involving private persons. In general, criticism of public officials is now, with certain limited exceptions, protected under the First Amendment. The chief exception involves false information propagated with "actual malice," that is, the speaker knows the material to be untrue and prints or says it anyway in order to harm the official.

Refining the *Times* Test

The Court did not find actual malice in the inconsequential errors in the *Times* advertisement, but later in the year had the opportunity to develop this standard in *Garrison v. Louisiana*. James Garrison, the flamboyant district attorney of Orleans Parish, Louisiana, got into a public shouting match with eight justices of the Criminal District Court when they denied him access to state money to conduct an investigation of commercial vice. He called a press conference and claimed that the judges' decision "raises interesting questions about the racketeer influences on our eight vacation-minded judges" (Powe 2000, 318). They sued, and a Louisiana court tried and convicted Garrison of libel under the state Criminal Defamation Law. He appealed, and the Supreme Court unanimously reversed on the basis of the *New York Times* doctrine.

Honest though inaccurate statements always have the potential for furthering the search for truth, Justice Brennan exclaimed, and are to be protected:

> It does not follow that the lie, knowingly and deliberately published about a public official, should enjoy a like immunity. . . . For the use of the known lie as a tool is at once at odds with the premises of democratic government and with the orderly manner in which economic, social, or political change is to be effected. . . . Hence the knowingly false statement and the false statement made with reckless disregard of the truth do not enjoy constitutional protection. (*Garrison v. Louisiana* [1964], 75)

Garrison's charges may have been reckless, but there had been no showing made, nor even required under existing Louisiana law, that there had been actual malice against the officials.

Another refinement of the *Times* test came in two cases decided together in 1967, *Curtis Publishing Co. v. Butts* and *Associated Press v. Walker*. The first case came out of a *Saturday Evening Post* article alleging that Wally Butts, a former coach and then University of Georgia athletic director, had fixed a football game. In the second case Edwin Walker, a retired general, sued the Associated Press wire service following a story that he had led a violent crowd in opposing enforcement of a desegregation decree at the University of Mississippi.

Neither plaintiff held public office, and therefore did not come under the public official category of the *Times* test. But as Chief Justice Warren explained, "differentiation between 'public figures' and 'public officials' and adoption of separate standards of proof for each have no basis in law, logic, or First Amendment policy" (*Curtis Publishing Co. v. Butts* [1967], 163). Such public figures, by their reputation, have access to the press through which they may rebut allegations against them, a right enjoyed by public officials as well but denied to private citizens.

Although the Court did extend the *Times* doctrine, it also introduced the ideas of "reckless disregard" and "hot news" into the formula. In the *Butts* case, the magazine based its story on the questionable report of George Burnett, who allegedly overheard a telephone conversation because of an electronic error. As Justice Harlan explained in the five-to-four decision that upheld the libel award to Butts, the information provided by Burnett "was in no sense 'hot' news and the editors of the magazine recognized the need for a thorough investigation of the serious charges" (*Curtis Publishing Co. v. Butts* [1967], 157). They failed to do so, however, and this showed a reckless disregard for the facts and a gross failure to conform to normal standards for investigative journalism.

In the *Walker* case, however, a unanimous Court overturned the libel judgment because the news had been reported in the midst of riots on the Ole Miss campus. It was "hot" news that required immediate dissemination from a reporter on the scene who gave every indication of trustworthiness and reliability. Under the pressure of events, such errors must be considered innocent and not a reckless disregard of truth.

The *Butts* and *Walker* cases marked the limits to which the Warren Court was willing to expand the *Times* doctrine, and four members of the bench—Harlan, Clark, Stewart, and Fortas—opposed that extension. In fact, only three members of the Court actually supported the public figure doctrine (Warren, Brennan, and White), and they prevailed because Black and Douglas supported a broader immunity. The major innovation had been the *Times* decision, and although the Court had attempted to articulate manageable tests, such as actual malice and reckless disregard, the cases involved had been fairly easy ones.

The First Amendment: The Religion Clauses

Few decisions of the Warren Court engendered as much continuing controversy as its rulings on religious matters. The segregation cases caused a major social upheaval in the country, but within a relatively short period a majority of Americans acknowledged that legally sanctioned racial discrimination was constitutionally and morally wrong. The average person heard charges that the Court had been "soft on criminals" in cases affecting the rights of accused persons, but aside from the *Miranda* warnings seen on television police shows, few really understood what the Court had done in expanding Fourth, Fifth, and Sixth Amendment rights.

The religion decisions, however, affected millions of Americans personally, and in ways many did not like. They believed that because of the Court their children could no longer pray in school or read the Bible or receive religious training on school property. The fact that critics of the Court distorted the actual rulings certainly exacerbated the situation, but many people just could not agree that the framers of the Constitution had intended to excise religion from the public arena. Long after the furor had died down over *Brown* and *Miranda*, agitation—and misunderstanding—continued over the religion rulings. Conservatives demanded a constitutional amendment to allow prayer in schools, and in one of his weekly radio addresses to the nation, Ronald Reagan declared that "the good Lord who has given our country so much should never have been expelled from our nation's classrooms" (Urofsky 1991, 28). The fact that the president of the United States, more than two decades after the original school prayer decisions, publicly misinterpreted what the Court had said is but one sign of the continuing agitation on this issue.

The Establishment Clause before Warren

The First Amendment to the Constitution contains two clauses concerning religion: "Congress shall make no law respecting an establishment of religion, or prohibiting the free exercise thereof." For most of the first 150 years following the adoption of the Bill of Rights Congress obeyed this injunction, and not until 1947 did the Court rule that the religion clauses applied to the states. Mr. Justice Black, in his majority ruling in *Everson v. Board of Education*, expounded at length on the historical development of religious freedom in the United States, and concluded:

> The "establishment of religion" clause of the First Amendment means at least this: Neither a state nor the Federal Government can set up a church. Neither can pass laws which aid one religion, aid all religions, or prefer one religion over another. Neither can force nor influence a person to go to or remain away from church against his will or force him to profess a belief or disbelief in any religion. No person can be punished for entertaining or professing religious beliefs or disbeliefs, for church attendance or non-attendance. No tax in any amount, large or small, can be levied to support any religious activities or institutions, whatever they may be called, or whatever form they may adopt to teach or practice religion. Neither a state nor the Federal Government can openly or secretly, participate in the affairs of any religious organization or groups and vice versa. In the words of [Thomas] Jefferson, the clause against establishment of religion by law was intended to erect "a wall of separation between church and State." (*Everson v. Board of Education* [1947], 15–16)

In this paragraph we find the root rationale for nearly every religion case decided by the Court in the last fifty years, whether it involves the establishment clause (in which the government is forbidden from promoting a religious function) or the free exercise clause (in which the government is forbidden from restricting an individual from adhering to some practice).

Yet the *Everson* decision provided an interesting twist. A New Jersey statute authorized school districts to make rules providing transportation for students, "including the transportation of school children to and from school other than a public school, except such school as is operated for profit." One local board allowed reimbursement to parents of parochial school students for fares paid by their children on public buses when going to and from school, and a taxpayer in the district challenged the payments as a form of establishment.

After his lengthy review of the history of the clauses, and language that implied that no form of aid—direct or indirect—could be tolerated under the establishment clause, Justice Black concluded that the reimbursement plan did not violate the First Amendment, which only requires that

> the state be a neutral in its relations with groups of religious believers and non-believers; it does not require the state to be their adversary. . . . [The] legislation, as applied, does no more than provide a general program to help parents get their children, regardless of their religion, safely and expeditiously to and from accredited schools.
>
> The First Amendment has erected a wall between church and state. That wall must be kept high and impregnable. We could not approve the slightest breach. New Jersey has not breached it here. (*Everson v. Board of Education* [1947], 18)

The opinion evoked dissents from four members of the Court, and Justice Jackson noted that Black, after marshalling every argument in favor of a total separation of church from state, weakly allowed that no breach of the wall had occurred. "The case which irresistibly comes to mind as the most fitting precedent is that of Julia who, according to Byron's reports, 'whispering "I will ne'er consent,"—consented'" (*Everson v. Board of Education* [1947], 19). Justice Rutledge took the logic of Black's historical argument and reached the inevitable conclusion that if "the test remains undiluted as Jefferson and Madison made it, [then] money taken by taxation from one is not to be used or given to support another's religious training or belief, or indeed one's own. The prohibition is absolute" (*Everson v. Board of Education* [1947], 44–45).

In fact, by the time the Court heard its next religion cases, Justice Black had moved to the position Rutledge had suggested, that the prohibition had to be absolute. In a 1948 decision, *McCollum v. Board of Education*, the Court struck down a so-called released-time program in Illinois, in which classrooms in the public schools were turned over for one hour each week for religious instruction. Local churches and synagogues could send in instructors to teach the tenets of their religion to students whose families approved. To Justice Black, writing for the eight-to-one majority, the issue could not have been clearer. "Not only are the state's tax-supported public school buildings used for the dissemination of religious doctrines, the State also affords sectarian groups an invaluable aid in that it helps to provide pupils . . . through use of the state's compulsory public school machinery" (*McCollum v. Board of Education* [1948], 212).

Response to the decision varied. The attorney general of Virginia, Lindsay Almond, declared that programs, even those with shared public classrooms, might continue—a ruling applauded by both school officials and church leaders. In Northern states where the released-time program followed the Illinois model, with religious instruction taking place in school classrooms, there appears to have been general compliance with the Court's decision. But where local officials could differentiate between the Illinois model and their own, no matter how fine the distinction, the programs remained in operation.

Four years after *McCollum*, the Court issued what might be called its first "accommodationist" ruling on the establishment clause. To continue their released-time programs, a number of states had moved the religious instruction off school property; New York officials, for example, established times in which students left the school grounds and went to religious facilities for instruction. Taxpayers challenged the program on grounds that it still involved the state in promoting religion. The authority of the school supported participation in the program; public school teachers policed attendance; and normal classroom activities came to a halt so students in the program would not miss their secular instruction.

Justice Douglas's opinion for the six-member majority in *Zorach v. Clauson* indicated that the Court had heard the public outcry over the *McCollum* decision, and he went out of his way to assert that the Court was not antagonistic to religion. "We are," he intoned, "a religious people whose institutions presuppose a Supreme Being" (*Zorach v. Clauson* [1952], 313). Although the First Amendment prohibition against an establishment of religion was "absolute," this did not mean that "in every and all respects there shall be a separation of Church and State" (*Zorach v. Clauson* [1952], 312). He went on to argue that historically the amendment had been interpreted in a "common sense" manner, because a strict and literal view would lead to unacceptable conclusions; "municipalities would not be permitted to render police or fire protection to religious groups. Policemen who helped parishioners into their places of worship would violate the Constitution" (*Zorach v. Clauson* [1952], 312). Such a view would make the state hostile to religion, a condition also forbidden by the First Amendment.

Douglas distinguished between the Illinois and New York programs primarily on the basis that the former had taken place on school property (a direct aid forbidden by the Constitution) and the latter off the school grounds (indirect assistance not forbidden). Justices Black, Jackson, and Frankfurter dissented. Black put the issue in its bluntest form: New York "is manipulating its compulsory education laws to help religious sects get pupils. This is not separation but combination of Church and State" (*Zorach v. Clauson* [1952], 318). Justice Jackson, who sent his own children to private church schools, objected as strenuously. The schools did not close down during the released-time period, but suspended teaching so that students who did not choose to attend religious instruction would not get ahead of the "churchgoing absentees." The school, with all the power of the state behind it, thus "serves as a temporary jail for a pupil who will not go to Church" (*Zorach v. Clauson* [1952], 324).

The three opinions, *Everson, McCollum,* and *Zorach,* provided the context in which the Warren Court would hear its religion cases, and the conflicting opinions left very little clear, other than that the religion clauses now applied to the states as well as to the federal government. In all three cases the majority, as well as the dissenters, had seemingly subscribed to the "wall of separation" metaphor and to the absolute nature of the First Amendment prohibitions, but disagreed on how "absolute" the separation had to be. Justice Black, after fudging in *Everson,* moved to the absolutist view that characterized his interpretation of the First Amendment for the remaining two decades he sat on the high Court. Justice Douglas, who joined Black in that view, also abandoned the temporizing stance he uncharacteristically took in *Zorach.* Although the Warren Court heard no major establishment clause cases in its first terms, it appeared likely that a majority of the members would take a strict stand when the issue did arise.

School Prayer—The *Engel* Case

For many years, ritual marked the beginning of each school day all across America. Teachers led their charges through the "Pledge of Allegiance," a short prayer, the singing of "America" or the "Star-Spangled Banner," and possibly some readings from the Bible. The choice of ritual varied according to state law, local custom, and the preferences of individual teachers or principals. In New York the statewide Board of Regents had prepared a "nondenominational" prayer for use in the public schools. The brief invocation read: "Almighty God, we acknowledge our dependence upon Thee, and we beg Thy blessings upon us, our parents, our teachers and our Country." After one district had directed that the prayer be recited each day, a group of parents challenged the edict as "contrary to the beliefs, religions, or religious practices of both themselves and their children." The New York Court of Appeals, the state's highest tribunal, upheld the school board, providing that it did not force any student to join in the prayer over a parent's objection. The Supreme Court reversed in *Engel v. Vitale* (1962).

In his opinion for the six-to-one majority, Justice Black (who had taught Sunday school for more than twenty years) held the entire idea of a state-mandated prayer, no matter how religiously neutral, as "wholly inconsistent with the Establishment Clause" (*Engel v. Vitale* [1962], 424). A prayer, by any definition, constituted a religious activity, and the First Amendment "must at least mean that [it] is no part of the business of government to compose official prayers for any group of the American people to recite as part of a religious program carried on by government." Black went on to explain what he saw as the philosophy behind the Establishment Clause:

> [Although] these two clauses may in certain instances overlap, they forbid two quite different kinds of governmental encroachment upon religious freedom. The Establishment Clause, unlike the Free Exercise Clause, does not depend upon any showing of direct governmental compulsion and is violated by the enactment of laws which establish an official religion whether those laws operate directly to coerce nonobserving individuals or not. . . . When the power, prestige and financial support of government is placed behind a particular religious belief, the indirect coercive pressure upon religious minorities to conform to the prevailing officially approved religion is plain. But the purposes underlying the Establishment Clause go much further than that. [Its] most immediate purpose rested on the belief that a union of government and religion tends to destroy government and degrade religion. [Another] purpose [rested upon] an awareness of the historical fact that governmentally established religions and religious persecutions go hand in hand. (*Engel v. Vitale* [1962], 430–431)

For Black, the content of the prayer, its actual words, or the fact that its non-denominational nature allegedly made it religiously neutral, had no relevance to the case. The nature of prayer itself is religious, and by promoting prayer, the state violated the establishment clause by fostering a religious activity that it determined and sponsored.

Justice Douglas concurred with the decision, but his opinion shows how far he had traveled both from *Everson* and *Zorach*. He acknowledged that the former case seemed "in retrospect to be out of line with the First Amendment. Mr. Justice Rutledge stated in dissent what I think is desirable First Amendment philosophy" (*Engel v. Vitale* [1962], 443). The man who had approvingly noted the practice of starting sessions of the Court or of legislative bodies with prayers now argued that even those prayers ought to be ruled unconstitutional. Only Potter Stewart dissented, and he quoted Douglas's *Zorach* opinion that "we are a religious people whose institutions presuppose a Supreme Being." The practice in New York and elsewhere did no more than recognize "the deeply entrenched and highly cherished spiritual traditions of our Nation" as did the opening of Court and Congress with prayer (*Engel v. Vitale* [1962], 450).

The *Engel* decision unleashed a firestorm of conservative criticism against the Court that, while it abated from time to time, never died out. In the eyes of many the Court had struck at a traditional practice that served important social purposes, even if it occasionally penalized a few nonconformists or eccentrics. Taken in concert with the Court's other decisions, it appeared as if Earl Warren and his colleagues were hell-bent on overturning decades, even centuries, of cherished American values. One newspaper headline screamed "COURT OUTLAWS GOD." An outraged Billy Graham thundered "God pity our country when we can no longer appeal to God for help," while Francis Cardinal Spellman of New York denounced *Engel* as striking "at the very heart of the Godly tradition in which America's children have for so long been raised" (Urofsky 1991, 33).

The level of abuse heaped upon the Warren Court for the prayer decision reached its peak in Congress. "They put the Negroes in the schools," Representative George W. Andrews of Alabama complained, and "they have driven God out" (Murphy 1972, 392). Senator Sam Ervin of North Carolina charged that the Supreme Court "has made God unconstitutional" (Pfeffer 1967, 469), while Congressman Williams of Mississippi condemned the decision as "a deliberately and carefully planned conspiracy to substitute materialism for spiritual values and thus to communize America" (108 Cong. Record 11675 [1962]). In an obvious swipe at the Court, the House of Representatives voted the following September to place the motto, "In God We Trust," behind the Speaker's chair, and a number of congressmen and senators introduced constitutional amendments to reverse the ruling.

The Court had its champions as well. Liberal Protestant and Jewish agencies saw the decision as a significant move to divorce religion from meaningless public ritual and to protect its sincere practice. The National Council of Churches, a coalition of liberal and orthodox denominations, praised the *Engel* decision for protecting minority rights, while the Anti-Defamation League applauded it as a reaffirmation of basic American principles. President John F. Kennedy, who had been the target of vicious religious bigotry in the 1960 campaign (from many of the groups now attacking the Court), urged support of the decision, and told a news conference:

> We have, in this case, a very easy remedy. And that is, to pray ourselves. And I would think that it would be a welcome reminder to every American family that we can pray a good deal more at home, we can attend our churches with a good deal more fidelity, and we can make the true meaning of prayer much more important in the lives of all of our children. (*New York Times*, 28 June 1962)

The president's commonsense approach captured the Court's intent in *Engel*. The majority did not oppose either prayer or religion, but did believe that the Framers had gone to great lengths to protect individual freedoms in the Bill of Rights. To protect the individual's freedom of religion, the state could not impose any sort of religious requirement, even in an allegedly "neutral" prayer. As soon as the power and prestige of the government is placed behind any religious belief or practice, according to Justice Black, "the inherently coercive pressure upon religious minorities to conform to the prevailing officially approved religion is plain" (*Engel v. Vitale* [1962], 431).

Bible-reading in the Schools

One year after the prayer decision, the Court extended this reasoning in *Abington School District v. Schempp*. A Pennsylvania law required that:

> At least ten verses from the Holy Bible shall be read, without comment, at the opening of each public school on each school day. Any child shall be excused from such Bible reading, or attending such Bible reading, upon the written request of his parent or guardian.

In addition, the students were to recite the Lord's Prayer in unison. This time Justice Tom Clark, normally considered a conservative, spoke for the eight-to-one majority in striking down the required Bible reading. He built upon Black's comments in *Engel* that the neutrality commanded by the Constitution stemmed from the bitter lessons of history, which recognized that a fusion of church and state inevitably led to persecution of all but those who adhered to the official orthodoxy.

Recognizing that the Court would be confronted with additional establishment clause cases in the future, Clark attempted to set out rules by which lower courts could determine when the constitutional barrier had been breached. The test, he said, may be stated as follows:

> What are the purpose and the primary effect of the enactment? If either is the advancement or inhibition of religion then the enactment exceeds the scope of legislative power as circumscribed by the Constitution. That is to say that to withstand the strictures of the Establishment Clause there must be a secular legislative purpose and a primary effect that neither advances nor inhibits religion. (*Abington School District v. Schempp* [1963], 222)

In this last sentence Clark set out the first two prongs of what would later be known as the *Lemon* tripartite test, which the Court has used to evaluate all establishment clause challenges. To be valid under Clark's test, the legislation (1) had to have a secular purpose, and (2) must neither advance nor inhibit religion. (The third prong, added in *Lemon v. Kurtzman* [1971], prohibited "excessive entanglement" between the government and the religious agency.) Clark also sought some criteria for distinguishing between the two religion clauses. The establishment clause prohibited state sponsorship of religious activities, while the free exercise clause prohibited state compulsion. "The distinction between the two clauses is apparent—a violation of the Free Exercise Clause is predicated on coercion while the Establishment Clause violation need not be so attended" (*Abington School District v. Schempp* [1963], 223).

In this case there had been no formal coercion, as students could be excused from the exercises, but Clark correctly noted that nonparticipating students inevitably called attention to themselves by their absence and thus invited retribution in the form of peer ostracism. Justice William J. Brennan in his concurrence quoted from his teacher, Felix Frankfurter, that "non-conformity is not an outstanding characteristic of children. The result is an obvious pressure upon children to attend" (*Abington School District v. Schempp* [1963], 291). The Court thus apparently held that the coercion needed to trigger a free exercise claim might be indirect, one resulting from the situation created by the government's actions.

In response to Justice Stewart's criticism that in protecting the religious freedom of a few dissenters the Court violated the free exercise rights of the majority who wanted to read the Bible, Clark declared that the Court

> cannot accept that the concept of neutrality, which does not permit a State to require a religious exercise even with the consent of the majority of those affected, collides with the majority's right to free exercise of religion. While the Free Exercise Clause clearly prohibits the use of state action to deny the rights of free exercise to anyone, it has never meant that the majority could use the machinery of the State to practice its beliefs. (*Abington School District v. Schempp* [1963], 225–226)

Only Justice Stewart dissented, and he argued against either the necessity or the desirability of having a single constitutional standard. "Religion and government must interact in countless ways," most of which were harmless and should not be subject to a "doctrinaire reading of the Establishment Clause" (*Abington School District v. Schempp* [1963], 309). He chastised the majority for violating the free exercise claims of those who wished their children to start the school day with exposure to the Bible. He also objected to the majority's assumption that every involvement by the state necessarily led to coercion; such an assumption would cast suspicion on every type of activity in which one might find some religious component, and he wanted to shift the burden of proof from a presumption of coercion to an actual showing that it had occurred.

Although the *Schempp* case did not trigger quite the uproar that had followed *Engel*, Justice Stewart's dissent did reflect the feeling of many people that their rights had been restricted for the sake of a few kooks. Moreover, the Court seemed to say (despite Clark's specific assurances to the contrary) that the Bible could no longer be read in the schools. Americans had been reading the Bible ever since the Puritans had established schools in Massachusetts in the 1630s; generations of settlers had taught their children to read poring over the Bible by the light of oil lamps. Public officials from the president down often took the oath of office with one hand on the Bible. How could it be religious coercion to require schoolchildren to hear a few verses from the Good Book each day? One still finds many people who cannot understand why the Court should find the Bible so threatening.

The discussion might begin with the question, "Which Bible?" Most of the statutes or regulations called for the King James version of the Bible, which, without anything else, is anathema to Catholics. The King James also includes both the Old and New Testament, and Jews object not only to the New Testament, but also to the phrasing of certain passages in the Old Testament. Whatever the literary qualities of this seventeenth-century masterpiece, it is riddled with errors in its translations from the ancient Hebrew and Greek, and many of the resulting passages are unacceptable to current dogma in several Protestant sects. And given the patterns of recent immigration, one might well ask whether the Koran or any one of several Far Eastern texts might also be demanded in some schools.

Another consideration is that, whether one uses the King James or the Revised Standard or the Douay or the Jewish Publication Society or the Good News version, one is dealing with a book that is essentially a religious appliance. It is designed to promote belief and faith, and that is what every Jewish and Christian sect uses it for. It is the Good Book, the Holy Scriptures, and its official reading over the school public address system cannot fail but to remind of its reading from the pulpit as part of a religious service.

The fact that a majority—even a large majority—is not affronted by prayer in the school or Bible reading is, to a large extent, irrelevant in constitutional adjudication. The purpose of the Bill of Rights is not to protect the majority, but the minority. As Holmes once said of freedom of speech, it is not for the speech we agree with, but for the speech we detest. Freedom of religion, like freedom of speech, does of course protect the majority, but we need not invoke it when nearly everyone is Protestant and subscribes to middle-class values. The protection of the First Amendment is invoked when the majority, attempting to use the power of the state, tries to enforce conformity in speech or religious practice. Very often, to protect that one dissident, that one disbeliever, the majority may be discomfited; it is the price the Founding Fathers declared themselves willing to pay for religious freedom.

Civil libertarians also express concern about state agencies, especially schools, advocating particular religious doctrines or practices as society grows ever more heterogeneous. Those who do not accept the norms of the majority, as Justice Sandra Day O'Connor wrote in a later case, "are outsiders, not full members of the political community" (*Wallace v. Jaffree* [1985], 69). The dissenters are merely tolerated, because of their religion or lack of it, and they are made to feel as inferior members of the society, a situation the Framers of the Constitution wanted to avoid.

Finally, while fundamentalist religious groups attacked the Court's decision in *Engel* and *Schempp*, many of the mainstream religious bodies soon came to see that the Court had actually promoted religion rather than subverted it. The framers of the famed "Memorial and Remonstrance," which Virginia Baptists addressed to the General Assembly in 1785, believed that not only the state's antagonism, but its efforts at assistance, could damage religion and religious liberty. Their intellectual descendants have argued along similar lines, and believe that the state can never help religion, but only hinder it. To establish any form of state-sanctioned religious activity in the schools threatens to introduce denominational hostility. Moreover, the sincere believer does not need the state to do anything for him except leave him alone; those with confidence in their faith do not need Caesar's assistance to render what is due to God.

Evolution and Creation

One can describe the school prayer and Bible cases as instances in which a benign majority unthinkingly imposed its views, unaware that the results restricted the religious freedom of a minority. In the third major establishment clause case of the Warren Court, however, a local majority deliberately attempted to establish its views as official dogma in defiance of what the rest of the country believed.

One of the most famous battlegrounds of the 1920s between the forces of tradition and modernism had been the Scopes "Monkey Trial" in Dayton, Tennessee. The legislature had passed a bill outlawing the teaching of evolution in the state's schools. Civic boosters in Dayton had gotten a young teacher named John Scopes to test the law, and the American Civil Liberties Union then provided a lawyer for Scopes. To sleepy Dayton came William Jennings Bryan to thunder against science and uphold the literal interpretation of the Bible, and Clarence Darrow, the greatest trial lawyer of his time, who spoke for science, reason, and intellectual toleration. Darrow exposed Bryan as a narrow-minded bigot, but the local jury still convicted Scopes. The Tennessee Supreme Court reversed the conviction on a technicality, which forestalled Darrow's plan to appeal to the Supreme Court. The law remained on the Tennessee statute books, and similar laws could be found in other "Bible Belt" states, but following Dayton they remained essentially dead letters, unenforced and in many cases nearly forgotten.

In Arkansas, a statute forbade teachers in state schools from teaching the "theory or doctrine that mankind ascended or descended from a lower order of animals." An Arkansas biology teacher, Susan Epperson, sought a declaratory judgment on the constitutionality of the statute. The Arkansas Supreme Court, aware of anti-evolution sentiment within the state, evaded the constitutional issue entirely by expressing "no opinion" on "whether the Act prohibits any explanation of the theory of evolution or merely prohibits teaching that the theory is true" (*Arkansas v. Epperson* [1967]).

On either ground the law ran afoul of the Constitution. Without a dissenting vote the Warren Court struck down the Arkansas statute in *Epperson v. Arkansas* (1968) as a violation of the establishment clause. Justice Fortas concluded that the Arkansas law "selects from the body of knowledge a particular segment which it proscribes for the sole reason that it is deemed to conflict with a particular religious doctrine, that is, with a particular interpretation of the Book of Genesis by a particular religious group" (*Epperson v. Arkansas* [1968], 103). The Court, having found what it considered a sufficiently narrow ground on which to rule, ignored the larger issues of academic freedom.

Justices Black and Stewart concurred in the result, though they considered the statute void for vagueness. But Black raised some difficult questions in his opinion that foreshadowed some of the issues that would come back before the Court in later years. The majority, in his view, had raised several "troublesome" First Amendment questions. A state law, for example, that completely forbade all teaching of biology would be constitutionally different from one that compelled a teacher to teach that only a particular theory is true. Black also was not prepared to hold that a teacher had constitutional rights to teach theories—be they economic, political, sociological, or religious—that the school's elected and appointed managers did not want discussed.

Black's most interesting point, however, involved the question of whether the majority opinion actually achieved the constitutional desideratum of "religious neutrality." If the people of Arkansas considered evolutionary theory antireligious, did the Constitution nonetheless require the state to permit the teaching of such doctrine? Had the Court infringed "the religious freedom of those who consider evolution anti-religious doctrine?" (*Epperson v. Arkansas* [1968], 113). Because the record did not indicate whether Arkansas schools taught a literal reading of the Genesis creation story, could a state law prohibiting the teaching of evolution be considered a neutral statute if it removed a contentious issue from the classroom? He saw no reason "why a State is without power to withdraw from its curriculum any subject deemed too emotional and controversial for its public schools" (*Epperson v. Arkansas* [1968], 113).

Black's reasoning, or rather its obverse, proved the vehicle by which anti-evolutionists in Arkansas and elsewhere sought to bypass the *Epperson* ruling a generation later. Instead of removing biology and the evolutionary theory from the schools, they added so-called creation science, which advocated the Biblical narrative as supported by allegedly scientific evidence, and required that any school teaching evolution had to give "equal time" in the classroom to "creation science."

Louisiana's so-called Balanced Treatment Act of 1982 reached the Supreme Court in *Edwards v. Aguillard* (1987). Justice William Brennan spoke for a seven-to-two majority in striking down the statute as a violation of the establishment clause. The Court denounced the stated purpose of the law, to advance academic freedom, as a sham, because the sponsors of the bill had made it quite clear during the legislative debate that they wanted to inject religious teachings into the public schools. It is unlikely that the issue will go away; like prayer and Bible-reading, the true believers will keep seeking some way to get their views grafted onto the school curriculum.

Aid to Parochial Schools

At about the same time that the Court was expanding the reach of the establishment clause in regard to state laws, the federal government raised new problems through its greatly increased aid to education programs. In January 1965 Lyndon B. Johnson proposed $1.5 billion in grants to primary and secondary schools, both public and private, secular and parochial. With Johnson exerting all of his famed political arm twisting, the Elementary and Secondary Education Act passed both houses of Congress by wide margins, and the president signed it into law in April. By 1968 Congress was funneling more than $4 billion a year into elementary and secondary schools. Part of it went to church-related schools with high percentages of children from low-income families. That aid immediately drew criticism as a violation of the First Amendment, and opponents set about finding a way to challenge it in the courts.

The Supreme Court had first encountered the problem of federal aid to religious institutions in *Bradfield v. Roberts* (1899), in which it had sustained a federal appropriation for the construction of a public ward in a hospital owned and operated by a nursing order of the Roman Catholic Church. The Court did not at that time address the issue of whether aid to religious institutions is permissible, because it held the hospital did not constitute a religious body. In the 1947 *Everson* case, the Court had upheld a form of state aid because the primary purpose had been to benefit children, not religion. The Johnson administration hoped to prevent a challenge to the act from even coming before the Court, and it defeated an effort by Senator Sam Ervin of North Carolina to amend the measure so as to allow taxpayer suits to test its constitutionality. (Under the doctrine of *Frothingham v. Mellon* [1923], taxpayers lack standing to challenge the government's disposition of its tax revenues.)

In *Flast v. Cohen* (1968), however, Chief Justice Warren reversed a lower court ruling based on *Frothingham* and permitted a taxpayer to initiate a suit against the law. The policy considerations behind the earlier decision no longer applied, and in any event, the "barrier should be lowered when a taxpayer attacks a federal statute on the ground that it violates the Establishment and Free Exercise Clauses of the First Amendment" (*Flast v. Cohen* [1968], 85). By this decision, the chief justice ensured that the Supreme Court would have a significant voice in the debate over educational policies. Although most of those cases would not reach the Court until after Earl Warren retired, the late 1960s saw the enactment of dozens of state and federal programs to aid education, and many of them included parochial schools as beneficiaries. In the cases testing these laws, opponents would argue that they violated the establishment clause, while supporters would rely on the child benefit theory that had been enunciated in *Everson*.

The Free Exercise Clause

In some ways, but only some, free exercise cases are easier than establishment problems, because they involve the state restricting an individual's religious practices. There is, of course, much overlap between the two clauses, and often a governmental program that tries to help religion in general may in fact restrict the freedoms of individuals. School prayer and Bible reading in schools offended the Court not just on establishment grounds, but because they also limited the free exercise of those who disagreed with the prayer or whose worship was based on another book.

Free exercise claims also overlap with claims to freedom of expression; several important cases prior to 1953 involved Jehovah's Witnesses, who claimed a right to proselytize—without state regulation—as essential to the free exercise of their beliefs. In these cases, the Court's analysis concentrated almost solely on the criteria used to safeguard speech. In addition, some issues are unique to free exercise claims.

First is the belief/action dichotomy initially enunciated by Chief Justice Morrison Waite in the Mormon bigamy case, *Reynolds v. United States* (1879). While the First Amendment absolutely prohibits government efforts to restrict beliefs, it does not prevent the state from forbidding practices that threaten public order or safety. In the example Waite used, if a sect believed in human sacrifice, the government could do nothing to restrict that belief; but it could, without violating the free expression clause, bar the actual sacrifice. The Court soon recognized, however, that one could not divide belief and action so easily, and in the 1940s it modified Waite's rule; while action remained subject to regulation, it deserved some protection under free exercise claims.

A second problem involves limits placed by the establishment clause on the free exercise clause. The two clauses overlap in their protection, but there are also instances in which they conflict. A state's efforts to accommodate certain groups by exempting or immunizing them from general laws may also be seen as providing a preference to one sect.

Undoubtedly, the most famous of the early free exercise cases involved the Jehovah's Witnesses and their refusal to salute the American flag. The Witnesses took literally the Biblical command not to "bow down to graven images," and considered the flag as an icon. In the first case, *Minersville School District v. Gobitis* (1940), Justice Frankfurter sustained the school board requirement that all students participate in the morning ritual. He rejected the free exercise claim almost summarily: "The mere possession of religious convictions which contradict the relevant concerns of political society does not relieve the citizen from the discharge of political responsibilities" (*Minersville School District v. Gobitis* [1940]). Only Justice Stone dissented in that case, and argued that freedom of expression as well as religion had been violated.

One has to recall that the *Gobitis* decision came down with Europe already at war and the United States rearming. But the Witnesses refused to compromise their principles, and the Court soon realized that its decision had been interpreted as a green light to harass those who refused to conform. Moreover, as stories of Nazi atrocities seeped out of Europe, many Americans questioned the right of the state to impose its will on minorities in the name of patriotism.

In 1943 the Court reversed itself in *West Virginia State Board of Education v. Barnette.* Justice Jackson, writing for the majority, found the central issue to be less one of religious liberty than freedom of expression. In a passage often quoted in subsequent free exercise cases, he declared:

> The very purpose of the Bill of Rights was to withdraw certain subjects from the vicissitudes of political controversy, to place them beyond the reach of majorities and officials and to establish them as legal principles to be applied by the courts. . . . If there is any fixed star in our constitutional constellation, it is that no official, high or petty, can prescribe what shall be orthodox in politics, nationalism, religion or other matters of opinion or force citizens to confess by word or act their faith therein. (*West Virginia State Board of Education v. Barnette* [1943], 642)

Probably no other passage has so captured the modern meaning of religious freedom.

Sunday Closing Laws

The flag salute cases indicated how closely the free exercise of religion and freedom of expression clauses are intertwined; the Sunday Closing Laws cases show the interconnectedness of the two religion clauses. A number of states had, and some still do have, laws requiring the majority of businesses to close on Sunday. In 1961 the Court heard four cases challenging these laws as violations of the First Amendment, and in three of them the Court refused to consider free exercise claims. In *McGowan v. Maryland,* Chief Justice Warren conceded that "the original laws which dealt with Sunday labor were motivated by religious forces" (*McGowan v. Maryland* [1961], 431). He rejected, however, the argument that this constituted an establishment of religion, because in modern times the laws represented an effort by the state to enforce one day's rest in seven. "The fact that this day is Sunday, a day of particular significance for the dominant Christian sects, does not bar the State from achieving its secular [goals]. Sunday is a day apart from all others. The cause is irrelevant; the fact exists" (*McGowan v. Maryland* [1961], 452).

In the companion case of *Braunfeld v. Brown,* orthodox Jewish merchants attacked the Sunday laws on free exercise grounds. Their religious beliefs required them to close on Saturdays, and having their shops closed two days a week would seriously undermine their ability to earn a livelihood. Chief Justice Warren recited the accepted distinction between belief and action, and noted that nothing in the law forced the appellants to modify or deny their beliefs; at worst, they might have to change occupations or incur some economic disadvantages.

There is a striking insensitivity, almost callousness, in Warren's opinion to the problem raised by the Jewish merchants, especially when one considers the great sensitivity he showed to the plights of other minority groups. The opinion is mechanical in its recitation of previous cases setting forth the belief/action dichotomy, and then relief in finding that the law affected only action. Although it is true that nearly all laws have adverse affects on some groups, the Court had imposed a closer scrutiny on laws affecting First Amendment rights. To say that the law did not affect beliefs, but only made it economically difficult for adherents of Judaism to practice those beliefs, showed a complete misunderstanding of the spirit of the free exercise clause.

Justices Stewart and Douglas dissented, but Justice Brennan in his objections pointed the way toward future First Amendment jurisprudence. He had no doubt that the Sunday law imposed a great burden on the Jewish merchants, forcing them to choose between their businesses and their religion, and this, he believed, violated the free exercise clause. To impose such a burden, the state had to prove some compelling state interest to justify this restriction on freedom of religion, and the "mere convenience" of having everybody rest on the same day did not, in his eyes, constitute a compelling state interest.

Did Pennsylvania have any options by which the state's interest in fostering one day's rest in seven would not conflict with the appellants religious freedom? Of course it did. Of the thirty-four states with Sunday closing laws, twenty-one granted exemptions to those who in good faith observed another day of rest. The Court, he charged, had "exalted administrative convenience to a constitutional level high enough to justify making one religion economically disadvantageous" (*McGowan v. Maryland* [1961], 615–616).

Saturday Work

Brennan not only pointed out that a commonsense solution existed, but his opinion showed greater sensitivity to the problems economic hardship imposed on religious freedom, and the Brennan view triumphed fairly quickly. Two years after the Sunday closing law cases, the Court heard *Sherbert v. Verner* (1963), a case in which a Seventh-Day Adventist in South Carolina had been discharged from her job because she would not work on Saturday. Her refusal to work on her Sabbath prevented her from finding other employment, and then the state denied her unemployment compensation payments. South Carolina law barred benefits to workers who refused, without "good cause," to accept suitable work when offered.

In what we would now term the "modern" approach to First Amendment issues, Justice Brennan posed the same question he had in *Braunfeld:* Did the state have a compelling interest sufficient to warrant an abridgement of a constitutionally protected right? This is, of course, the same question the Court asks in regard to speech restrictions, because the analytical process in speech and free exercise claims are similar. Free expression of ideas is involved in religion just as in speech, press, assembly, or petition—namely, the right to say what one believes, whether it involves political, economic, social, or religious ideas. Justices Black and Douglas over the years argued for what they termed a "preferred position" for First Amendment rights, because the two men believed these rights to be at the core of a democratic society. Only the most compelling societal need can warrant any restrictions on these rights.

Justice Brennan found no compelling interest presented by the state, and in fact the state could do little more than suggest that some applicants might file fraudulent claims alleging that they could not find work for religious reasons. Brennan did recognize, however, the difficulties Potter Stewart raised in his concurrence, that in ruling that the state had to pay unemployment compensation benefits to Ms. Sherbert, South Carolina was favoring the adherents of one particular sect. Brennan went out of his way to indicate the very limited nature of the decision:

> In holding as we do, plainly we are not fostering the "establishment" of the Seventh-day Adventist religion in South Carolina. . . . [Nor] do we . . . declare the existence of a constitutional right to unemployment benefits on the part of all persons whose religious convictions are the cause of their unemployment. This is not a case in which an employee's religious convictions serve to make him a nonproductive member of society. [Our] holding today is only that South Carolina may not constitutionally apply the eligibility provisions so as to constrain a worker to abandon his religious convictions respecting the day of rest. (*Sherbert v. Verner* [1963], 409–410)

The *Sherbert* case raised the question of whether the Constitution can be read as totally "religion-neutral" or "religion-blind." Law professor Philip B. Kurland suggested that one can find a unifying principle in the two religion clauses, and that they ought to be "read as a single precept that government cannot utilize religion as a standard for action or inaction, because these clauses prohibit classification in terms of religion either to control a benefit or impose a burden" (Urofsky 1991, 43). The argument parallels the suggestion made by the first Justice Harlan in *Plessy v. Ferguson* that the Constitution is "color-blind," and like that argument, is manifestly incorrect.

Neither the Constitution nor the Court have been color-blind. Both the original Constitution and the Civil War Amendments recognized that blacks stood in a position of decided inferiority to whites; the original Constitution tended to sustain this arrangement, while the Amendments sought to erase the prevailing discrimination.

The Court that decided *Plessy* favored the post–Civil War South's efforts to recreate a dual society, while the Warren Court sought to erase the badges of discrimination.

Similarly, neutrality in religious matters is more of an ideal than a reality in constitutional adjudication, and for the same reason. Very few issues that reach the Court can be resolved in simple ways; if the cases had been easy, the Court would not have heard them. Religion, like race, is a tangled skein, and not amenable to simplistic solutions. The Court recognized this, and from the absolutist decisions of the early Warren era, the Court moved steadily toward a jurisprudence of balancing various considerations.

Conscientious Objectors

A final free exercise issue heard during the Warren years involved claims by those opposed to war in general, or specifically to American involvement in Vietnam. In this century Congress has shown a commendable sensitivity toward those with religious scruples against war, and in the World War I draft law had provided an exemption for conscientious objectors. The Supreme Court had summarily rejected First Amendment objections to this exemption, holding it to be an appropriate exercise of legislative discretion in *Selective Draft Law Cases* (1918).

Following World War II, Congress revised the draft in the Universal Military Training and Service Act of 1948. Section 6(j) exempted persons from military service who conscientiously opposed participation in war in any form because of their "religious training and belief." The statute defined this clause as a "belief in a relation to a Supreme Being involving duties superior to those arising from any human relation, but [not including] essentially political, sociological, or philosophical views or a merely personal moral code." Critics attacked Section 6(j) on establishment, free exercise, and due process grounds, arguing that it did not exempt nonreligious conscientious objectors and that it discriminated among various forms of religious expression.

A number of challenges reached the courts in the early 1960s as American involvement in Southeast Asia began to escalate, and in 1965 the Supreme Court heard three challenges decided together as *United States v. Seeger*. The Court evaded the constitutional challenges by the simple expedient of reading the statute so broadly as to provide exemptions for all of the petitioners. Justice Clark declared that Congress, by using the phrase "Supreme Being" rather than "God," meant to "embrace all religions," and exclude only nonreligious objections to military participation. Therefore, the proper test would not be adherence to a particular denomination, but "whether a given belief that is sincere and meaningful occupies a place in the life of its possessor parallel to that filled by the orthodox belief in God of one who clearly qualifies for the exemption" (*United States v. Seeger* [1965], 166).

Whether the Congress that had passed the 1948 statute really meant this is impossible to determine, but two years later Congress ratified, and in fact expanded, the scope of the exemption by deleting the phrase "belief in a relation to a Supreme Being." The Warren Court, for all that it read the statute broadly, nonetheless evaded the First Amendment questions, and also the more particular challenges of those opposed to the Vietnam war. In this, as in other areas, the Warren Court set out new interpretations in broad brush strokes, and left the harder problems to its successor.

The Burger Court continued this liberalizing trend. In *Welsh v. United States* (1970), the Court overruled a draft board that excluded agnostics, and reaffirmed the *Seeger* ruling that conscience, and not religion, dictated status. The Court did try to impose some rationale in *Clay v. United States* (1971) by imposing a tripartite test to see if conscientious objectors qualified, but it took a very broad view of just what constituted a "religious" claim. In *Gillete v. United States*, decided the same year, the Court did hold that the requirement that the person object to war in any form excluded those who objected only to specific wars.

The Rights of the Accused

Compared to England, the American colonies from the beginning had far more humane criminal laws with only a few capital crimes, but they highly valued the English idea of due process and the notion that an accused person should be considered innocent until proven guilty. Several grievances in the Declaration of Independence complained about the king's alleged infringements on due process, and the postwar state and federal constitutions established procedural safeguards to prevent arbitrary actions by the state as well as to ensure a fair trial.

The Fourth, Fifth, Sixth, and Eighth Amendments comprise the bundle of rights afforded to persons accused of crime. The Fourth Amendment protects the security of persons both personally and in their homes against search and seizure without proper authorization, and proscribes the issuance of warrants without probable cause.

The Fifth Amendment requires grand jury indictment and prohibits double jeopardy. Its most famous provision is a bar against forcing a person to testify against himself or herself. It also includes the guarantee that no one shall be deprived of life, liberty, or property without due process of law.

The Sixth Amendment guarantees a speedy and public local trial, thus preventing the state from keeping an accused person incarcerated indefinitely or trying him or her in secret or at a place where the accused would face a jury of strangers. In order to ensure a fair trial, the Amendment guarantees the accused the right to know the charges, to confront his or her accusers, to compel witnesses to appear to testify, and most important, to have the assistance of counsel.

The Eighth Amendment prohibits the infliction of cruel or unusual punishment, or the imposition of excessive bail or fines.

These four amendments, and the rights they encompass, are not only interrelated in their goal of protecting the rights of accused persons, but also in how they go about reaching that goal. The right to a fair trial often depends on whether the police act within their prescribed limits, or whether the accused has access to a lawyer at an appropriate stage in the proceedings.

The Framers of the Bill of Rights wrote in the context of the late eighteenth century, a simpler period than our own, with far simpler crimes, as well as a relatively limited system of criminal justice. Not until the twentieth century did the courts begin to deal with how and to whom these rights applied in the context of modern communications, an established police and court system, and a society whose criminals as well as statesmen functioned in national and global terms.

The Warren Court had in this area, as in its larger jurisprudence, two major aims. One involved a commitment to democracy, to making the guarantees of the Bill of Rights apply not only to the rich but to the poor as well. As Justice Douglas said in extending the right of counsel to appeals, "There can be no equal justice where the kind of appeal a man enjoys depends on the amount of money he has" (*Douglas v. California* [1963], 355). Clearly, the Court could not give every person in the United States the resources to match those of the wealthy in defending against criminal prosecution. But it could require the government to provide the basic ingredients to ensure fair procedures, and it could try to educate people so that they knew their rights.

Secondly, the Warren Court wanted to make eighteenth-century notions of rights relevant and applicable in the middle of the twentieth century, to make the Constitution a "living" document. To do this the justices had to look past the wording of the Bill of Rights to discern the spirit of the Framers. When wiretapping first came before the Court, Chief Justice Taft dismissed the Fourth Amendment claim by noting there had been no actual entry; in his dissent Justice Brandeis talked not about breaking and entering, but about what the Framers had intended—that people should be left alone by the government. This is the notion that Potter Stewart captured when he declared that the Fourth Amendment protects people, not places. It is also the spirit of the Framers that Justice Douglas invoked when he asked, "What did the Framers know about wiretapping? They didn't even have telephones!" But, he claimed, they knew, as Brandeis had taught, that the greatest of rights was the right to be let alone. How to make that, and other parts of the Bill of Rights, living rights for those accused of crimes consumed a great deal of the Warren Court's energy.

Criminal Procedure and Incorporation

Average, law-abiding citizens usually never have occasion to learn how the criminal justice system deals with offenders. But if, in 1960, those citizens were to consider what would happen if they were charged with a noncapital felony, they would probably have assumed that the Constitution required that they be accorded the assistance of counsel, a jury trial, confrontation of witnesses against them, and protection against double jeopardy—all guarantees listed in the Bill of Rights. They would have been wrong.

In *Barron v. Baltimore* (1833) the Supreme Court ruled that the Bill of Rights applied only against the federal government, and this remained the accepted interpretation until after the Civil War. In the *Slaughterhouse Cases* (1873), a bare majority of the Court read the Fourteenth Amendment's due process and equal protection clauses very narrowly. The minority, however, suggested that these clauses had been intended to change relations between the states and the federal government, and thus expand the constitutionally protected rights of individuals. When the Court adopted the doctrine of substantive due process in 1897, it extended the constitutional mantle to protect economic rights against arbitrary state interference, but failed to resolve whether this same doctrine affected noneconomic rights.

In *Hurtado v. California* (1884), the Court held that a state could indict through information rather than through the grand jury procedure called for in the Fifth Amendment, and nearly a quarter-century later ruled that the self-incrimination clause did not apply to the states in *Twining v. New Jersey* (1908). Not until 1932 did the Court apply any of the criminal procedure guarantees against the states; in that year, in the infamous Scottsboro case, *Powell v. Alabama* (1932), the Court found that denial of counsel in a capital case denied defendants the due process of law. (In that case the Court overturned the convictions of eight young black men who had been accused of raping two white women while riding the rails on a freight train. The attorneys appointed to represent them did nothing; they did not even speak with their clients until just before the trial.)

The incorporation of defendants' rights has proceeded in a more difficult and irregular pattern than have the protections of the First Amendment. Once the Court agreed that the Fourteenth Amendment incorporated freedom of speech, the debate ended; cases afterwards dealt with whether particular actions constituted an impermissible infringement of expression. Similarly, once the religion clauses applied to the states, subsequent cases took the fact of incorporation as a given, and the justices looked to see whether the state had violated the establishment clause or restricted free exercise.

But the Fourth, Fifth, Sixth, and Eighth Amendments cover a number of rights, and one of the major constitutional debates of this century has centered on which of those rights the Fourteenth Amendment applies to the states. The debate began with Justice Cardozo's opinion in *Palko v. Connecticut* (1937), upholding the right of a state to take an appeal from a "not guilty" verdict and secure a second trial. The majority held that granting the state the same right as the accused enjoyed did not violate the double jeopardy provision of the Fifth Amendment. Cardozo faced squarely the issue of whether the Fourteenth Amendment "absorbed" the entire Bill of Rights, and concluded that it did not. Only those guarantees "implicit in the concept of ordered liberty" applied to the states through the Fourteenth Amendment, and the stricture on double jeopardy did not meet that definition.

Ten years later, the question of self-incrimination came up again in *Adamson v. California*. Justice Frankfurter, writing for the majority, expanded upon Cardozo's *Palko* opinion, and urged a "selective incorporation" of the Bill of Rights. Not all rights are "implicit in the concept of ordered liberty," and the Court would be the arbiter of which rights met the test of "fundamental fairness" and which did not. Justice Black, who a decade earlier had agreed with Cardozo, had in the meantime grown increasingly uncomfortable with the idea that only some of the rights in the first eight amendments, but not others, applied to the states. In a dissent joined by Justice Douglas, Black set out the idea of "total incorporation" and argued that the Fourteenth Amendment prevented the states from denying their citizens any of the protections of the Bill of Rights. Black also objected to what he termed the "natural law" approach of *Palko*, which he claimed invited the Court to add rights not found in the Constitution if a majority thought such rights met the "fundamental fairness" standard.

The debate between the Cardozo/Frankfurter view of selective incorporation and the Black argument for total incorporation went on into the early 1960s. During the early years of Earl Warren's tenure, Frankfurter's jurisprudential view prevailed, and the Court, preoccupied with racial segregation, barely touched questions of criminal procedure. Beginning in the early 1960s, however, a significant change took place, caused only in part by Frankfurter's retirement from the bench in 1962. Justice Harlan developed his own ideas regarding what constituted fundamental fairness. One looked to the Bill of Rights for a start, he reasoned, but courts had to remember that due process is a flexible concept. If the right is in fact fundamental, then the states are bound by it; but states may choose a variety of ways to apply the right, provided the methods they choose are themselves fair. This approach allowed the establishment of national norms, but still permitted the states to experiment within certain boundaries. The Warren Court continued to use the language of "fundamental fairness," but incorporated more and more of the rights in the Fourth, Fifth, and Sixth Amendments. The Court also insisted that, once incorporated, the rights applied with equal vigor to the states as to the federal government.

The story of the Warren Court in this area is, therefore, quite revolutionary in some aspects, in that it took guarantees once applied only to the federal government and required the states to live up to the same standards. Beyond that, the Warren Court had to interpret what these eighteenth-century protections meant in the twentieth century. Its responses triggered some of the most vehement criticism of judicial activism in this century. Our survey of exactly what the Warren Court did will be easier if we look at the specific constitutional guarantees one at a time.

The Fourth Amendment: Search Warrants

The right of people to be secure in their home and persons is the heart of the Fourth Amendment. Simply stated, it prohibits the state from arbitrarily searching one's home, office, or person, or taking someone into custody without reason. For the police to search premises or arrest a suspect, they need—with certain exceptions—to convince a magistrate that they have reasonable suspicions that specific evidence can be found in a distinct place, or that a certain person did commit a particular crime.

The wording of the Fourth Amendment is ambiguous, however, and thus open to conflicting interpretations that can be used to expand or limit its protection. For example, the Amendment refers to the right of the *people*, not of individuals, and this has led some commentators to suggest that the courts ought to focus on general rules to regulate police conduct rather than on rectifying particular misdeeds. The Court did, in fact, deal with both the individual and the regulatory aspects of this language, and its most controversial decisions, concerning the exclusionary rule, addressed the regulatory problem.

The Amendment also includes words that are at best subjective and therefore open to a wide range of interpretation. What is an "unreasonable" search? What constitutes "probable" cause sufficient to secure a warrant? If a warrant issues, does that fact by itself make the search "reasonable"? The word "unreasonable" apparently modifies "search," but does it also provide a standard for the issuance of warrants? Furthermore, the language does not indicate against whom the right applies. It does not say the people shall be secure against police searches, but against searches, and the courts have interpreted this to mean all forms of governmental investigation. Finally, it should be noted that the Amendment appears to make no distinction between people and things, although the courts, applying common sense, have distinguished between the two. However, the language raises problems over nonintrusive techniques such as electronic eavesdropping. Is a wiretap a search, and if so, of persons or of objects?

The Warren Court in this area, as in so many others, did not write on a blank slate. The Cardozo/Frankfurter/Black debate had been underway for nearly two decades before Earl Warren joined the Court, and in that time the Court had handed down a number of Fourth Amendment decisions. Several of these had to do with the requirements police had to meet to secure a search warrant.

Prior to 1933, all a police officer had to do to get a warrant was intone a formula, "I have cause to suspect and I do believe that. . . ." While courts normally assume that a police officer is telling the truth, the Supreme Court in *Nathanson v. United States* (1933) held that the Fourth Amendment required some proof to secure a warrant, that the magistrate needed facts, not just opinion, to justify the search. In *Harris v. United States* (1947), the Vinson Court ruled five to four that when police had a valid arrest warrant, they did not need a separate search warrant to make a valid search. The following year the Court held invalid a warrantless search that preceded an arrest in *Johnson v. United States* (1948).

The Warren Court heard its first warrant case, *Giordenello v. United States*, in 1958 and in essence did little more than reaffirm the old rule. A federal agent had sworn to the magistrate that Vito Giordenello had received and concealed narcotics, but offered no facts to support this conclusion. The Court voided the conviction, and noted that a warrant could not issue unless the police could show some proof that the evidence sought would be in the place they wanted to search.

All of these cases involved the federal government, but in 1961 the Supreme Court extended Fourth Amendment guarantees to the states in *Mapp v. Ohio*. Three years later it heard its first major state warrant case, *Aguilar v. Texas*. In the application for a search warrant, local police had stated that they had received reliable information from credible persons that narcotics were being stored in a certain place, and they believed this information to be true. They offered no facts in support of their application, and the Court, relying on past cases, voided the conviction. The Warren Court made no new law in this case, but it did try to give police, magistrates, and lower courts some guidelines as to what the Constitution required. The police needed to provide: (1) facts to justify probable cause, and (2) reasons why the magistrate should believe that probable cause existed, such as the reliability of the source of the facts.

If this had been all, few people would have been upset by the course of developing Fourth Amendment jurisprudence. The Court really said little more than that the Constitution requires a warrant prior to a search; that although some searches are valid even without a warrant (such as search incident to arrest), it is always better for the police to get a warrant; and a valid warrant requires some factual proof, not just the officer's opinion, to support the magistrate's decision that probable cause exists. Only the most zealous law-and-order advocate could complain that this interpretation of the Fourth Amendment crippled police work; without these basic safeguards, the warrant clause would mean very little.

Then came two cases in the final term of the Warren Court that seemed to many people to be carrying the warrant requirements beyond reason. The FBI had been investigating the activities of William Spinelli, a known bookmaker, for suspected illegal gambling activities. Agent Robert L. Bender had followed Spinelli for several days and believed that Spinelli had a telephone bank operating out of an apartment rented by his girlfriend. The affidavit Bender filed to secure a warrant to search that apartment listed in detail the number of times Spinelli had been observed driving from his home in East St. Louis, Illinois, to his girlfriend's apartment in St. Louis, Missouri, and the quantity and numbers of the phones in that apartment. The final two paragraphs read as follows:

> William Spinelli is known to this affiant and to federal law enforcement agents and local law enforcement agents as a bookmaker, an associate of bookmakers, a gambler, and an associate of gamblers.
>
> The Federal Bureau of Investigation has been informed by a confidential reliable informant that William Spinelli is operating a handbook and accepting wagering information by means of the telephones [in the apartment]. (*Spinelli v. United States* [1969], 414)

The affidavit seemed to meet the *Aguilar* criteria, but the Court in *Spinelli v. United States*, speaking through Justice Harlan, said that it did not. Basically, the affidavit boiled down to assertions that Spinelli often drove back and forth from his own apartment to that of his girlfriend, that she had two phones in her apartment, and that an informant said that Spinelli operated a book out of that apartment. The facts did not support probable cause, because in and of themselves these facts could be quite innocent. The whole application rested on the assertion that Spinelli had a prior reputation, and that an unknown informant claimed Spinelli was engaged in illegal gambling. This constituted nothing more than hearsay, and the magistrate had to have real evidence, if not of actual gambling, then at least about the informant's reliability. The police need not disclose an informant's identity, but the magistrate at least had to know if there had been a prior relationship to support credibility.

Police screamed over the *Spinelli* decision, interpreting it to say that in order to get a warrant, they would have to present the type of evidence that would stand up in court, whereas they had always assumed that "probable cause" in an investigation required a lower level of evidence. As Justice Black noted in his dissent, the *Aguilar* and *Spinelli* decisions seemed to elevate the magistrate's hearing for a warrant to "a full-fledged trial" (*Spinelli v. United States* [1969], 414). The FBI had tailed Spinelli, had seem him engage in suspicious behavior that conformed to his reputation as a gambler, and had reliable information that Spinelli had been taking bets on the phones in his girlfriend's apartment. This had been good investigative work. What more could the Court want?

Part of the problem is Justice Harlan's opinion, for him an unusually poorly written one, that gave neither the police nor magistrates guidance as to what the Court expected. Yet the opinion contained a relatively simple two-prong test. First, the magistrate must evaluate the truthfulness of the source of information, whether it comes from a police officer or an informant; and second, the magistrate must evaluate the adequacy of the facts to support probable cause. The Court had not denied police the use of reputational evidence, but merely required them in some way to corroborate it so that the magistrate could believe its truthfulness. As a practical matter, *Spinelli* would force police to tighten up their procedures in securing a warrant.

On the day Earl Warren retired from the bench, the Court imposed a warrant requirement in situations previously considered legitimate warrantless searches incident to an arrest. California police went to the house of Ted Chimel, a coin dealer, with an arrest warrant relating to the burglary of a coin shop. After arresting him, they asked to look around, and when he objected, told him that on the basis of a lawful arrest, they had the right to conduct a search. Chimel's wife then accompanied the officers around the house, and they confiscated a number of coins and other items that they believed had been stolen.

In *Chimel v. California* (1969), Justice Stewart wrote for a six-to-two majority in holding that police had exceeded the limits of a search incident to arrest. Stewart examined the historic reasons for such a search, and held that they had been primarily for two reasons, to remove any weapons that the suspect might have on him or her or within his or her reach, and to seize evidence related to a crime that might be on a suspect, such as the proceeds of a robbery. Once police had satisfied themselves that the suspect had neither weapon nor evidence on his or her person or within immediate grasp, they needed a warrant to search further.

As former CBS legal correspondent Fred Graham noted, "under the best of circumstances, this ruling could be expected to run headlong into resistance in many states where search warrants have been oddities" (Graham 1970, 208). In this and in other cases, however, the Court had done little more than lay down certain rules for police procedure to bring some sense out of the ambiguities in the Fourth Amendment. To make the constitutional guarantees meaningful, the Court declared that a search warrant would always be the preferred means of police investigation of premises; that to secure a warrant, the police would have to present real facts, not just suspicions, and convince the magistrate of the truthfulness of their assertions; and that in terms of searching persons and places, the Court placed greater protection about persons.

These all appear to be fairly commonsensical, if one is to give any credence to the Fourth Amendment. The outcry that greeted these decisions must be seen in its historical context, namely, that state and local police had hardly bothered with warrants prior to the 1960s, and if they had (because required by some state constitutions to do so), they had been able to secure warrants from friendly magistrates with little more than an avowal of their suspicions. Earlier Courts had indeed taken a somewhat erratic course during the 1940s as to what the Fourth Amendment required, but those cases had for the most part been ignored at the state and local level. The Warren Court had not only attempted to determine consistent Fourth Amendment rules, but more importantly, to apply them to the states as well.

The above cases would seem to imply that all of the Warren Court's decisions tended to limit police, and that is far from true. In fact, some commentators believe that the Court, aware of the growing criticism about its opinions, took a harder line in its last few terms. Professor Yale Kamisar, one of the nation's leading authorities on criminal procedure, claims that in its final years, "the Warren Court was not the same Court that handed down *Mapp* and *Miranda*" (Blasi 1983, 67). As Kamisar notes, the mid-to-late sixties were marked by urban riots, college disorder, antiwar protests, rising crime rates, assassinations, and fear that public order would break down. Members of Congress as well as presidential candidate Richard Nixon blamed the Court for much of this turmoil, and the Omnibus Crime Law sent a clear message to the judiciary. All of this contributed "to an atmosphere that was unfavorable to the continued vitality of the Warren Court's mission in criminal cases" (Blasi 1983, 68).

In *McCray v. Illinois* (1967), for example, the Court ruled that police could withhold the identity of a confidential informant, so long as they could convince the magistrate that the information was reliable. That same year, Justice Brennan wrote the majority opinion in *Warden v. Hayden,* which allowed police wide discretion in the type of evidence they gathered in a search subsequent to a "hot pursuit." Both these cases took a hard and pragmatic look at what the police had to do in their line of work, and upheld standard police practice. One of the most "propolice" decisions of the Warren Court took this same approach, but is often overlooked by those who charge that the Court did nothing but coddle criminals.

Officer Martin McFadden, dressed in plain clothes, was patrolling a section of downtown Cleveland one afternoon when he noticed two men who "didn't look right to me at the time." The two men, John Terry and Richard Chilton, kept walking up and down past a certain store, and he suspected them of "casing" the store. When a third man joined the other two, McFadden decided to investigate further; he approached the three men, identified himself as a police officer, and asked their names. When Terry "mumbled something" in response, McFadden grabbed him, spun him around between himself and the other two men, and patted down his outer clothing. He felt a pistol on Terry, and later one on Chilton, seized their weapons, and arrested them.

The defendants tried to suppress evidence of the guns, because they claimed that Officer McFadden had not taken them in a search incident to an arrest, and that he had no probable cause to stop them. But the trial court and the Supreme Court in *Terry v. Ohio* (1968) both upheld McFadden's actions. He had been a policeman for thirty-nine years, a detective for thirty-five, and during that time he had built up instincts and habits based on experience. To deny the public the benefit of that experience would be foolish, declared the chief justice, and would hamper the police in their work.

The "stop and frisk" decision is a good indication of the Warren Court's philosophy. In situations involving private quarters or immobilized vehicles, where the evidence could not "walk away," the Court insisted that the police comply with regular warrant procedures. In on-the-street situations, or when the police were in hot pursuit of a suspect, rigid application of constitutional rules could not be expected. In the *Terry* case the Court adopted what might be called a "rule of reason" that allowed police wide discretion, provided they had some reasonable basis to support their action.

The Fourth Amendment and Wiretapping

In 1928 the Court began to deal with how modern technology affected the Fourth Amendment, when it ruled in *Olmstead v. United States* that wiretapping did not constitute an unauthorized search. In a highly formalistic opinion, Chief Justice Taft ignored the intent of the Amendment, and claimed that there had been no actual entry, merely the use by police of an enhanced sense of hearing. To pay too much attention to "nice ethical conduct by government officials," he said, "would make society suffer and give criminals greater immunity than has been known heretofore" *Olmstead v. United States* [1928], 468). The opinion brought dissents by Pierce Butler, Oliver Wendell Holmes Jr. (who called wiretapping "a dirty business"), and especially from Louis D. Brandeis. The Brandeis opinion not only set forth the idea of a constitutionally protected right to privacy, but also warned against "government law-breaking."

Taft had noted in his opinion that Congress could make wiretap evidence inadmissible in federal courts, and Congress did just that in § 605 of the 1934 Federal Communications Act. Early cases interpreted the statute to cover all federal officials, although as late as 1937 the Vinson Court in *Nardone v. United States* held that state officials could use such evidence in state courts. In *Goldman v. United States* (1942), the Court ruled that eavesdropping by placing a "detectaphone" (a primitive form of listening device) next to an office wall to hear conversations did not violate the Fourth Amendment because there had been no trespass, and a decade later upheld wiring an undercover agent to pick up what the defendant thought would be a private conversation in *On Lee v. United States* (1952).

One of the first decisions in this area by the Warren Court, *Benanti v. United States* (1957), barred the use in federal courts of state-gathered wiretap evidence. Then in 1961 the Court unanimously overruled *Olmstead* and vindicated Brandeis's view. In *Silverman v. United States*, federal agents had slipped a spike with a microphone under a baseboard and against a heating duct, so that they could hear conversations throughout the house. Justice Stewart dismissed as an irrelevant technicality the issue of whether an actual trespass had occurred; the decision "is based upon the reality of an intrusion into a constitutionally protected area" (*Silverman v. United States* [1961], 512).

In the 1960s the Court decided a number of cases dealing with undercover agents wired for sound or who had lured suspects into a location wired for sound. Justice Stewart labored with the problem of a "constitutionally protected area" as the technology for eavesdropping became ever more sophisticated. At least in the early part of the decade, a majority of the Court sustained the use of such devices by law enforcement agents, and often the deciding factor was the technicality of whether a trespass had taken place. A few of the justices raised the question of whether a warrant should have been secured, but the majority recognized that undercover work had very little connection to the type of investigation normally covered by warrants.

The justices, however, were becoming aware of the pervasiveness of electronic surveillance as well as the scientific advances in the devices used. In 1928 Brandeis's law clerk had objected to the justice suggesting that in the future it would be possible to listen to conversations through walls and from far off. Less than thirty years later, a leading authority on privacy, Alan Westin of Columbia University, warned that "modern technology has breached at vital points the physical limits that once guarded individual and group privacy" (Urofsky 1991, 151). Physical trespass no longer made any sense as a demarcation between permissible and impermissible electronic surveillance, and the Court acknowledged this in 1967.

A New York statute authorized warrants for wiretapping and eavesdropping, and as part of their investigation into alleged bribery of state liquor license officials, police had secured a warrant to place a recording device in the office of Ralph Berger. Within two weeks police had uncovered a conspiracy, and transcripts of recorded conversations helped secure Berger's conviction. The Court in *Berger v. New York* (1967), speaking through Justice Clark, found the statute defective, because it did not require that a particular crime be named to secure a warrant. This, in effect, made it a general warrant—the very thing proscribed by the Fourth Amendment. Clark admitted that it might be difficult to draft a statute that would be specific enough to meet the warrant criteria, yet flexible enough to permit the type of surveillance police wanted to use.

The opinion left obscure a number of issues, including the criteria that courts might apply to electronic surveillance. Part of the majority opinion would seem to indicate that police may only listen to particular conversations that relate to the suspected crime, obviously an impossibility. Justice Douglas's separate opinion hit the mark when he invoked historic precedent to argue that the Fourth Amendment barred all searches for mere evidence and limited the government to seizing contraband or fruits of crime. A wiretap is an open-ended type of general warrant, but the Court recognized that it could not deprive law enforcement officials of modern weapons while criminals availed themselves of the latest technological advances. So they left the issue to be resolved in future cases.

The next term the Court handed down its strongest decision yet in regard to wiretapping in *Katz v. United States* (1967). FBI agents had planted an electronic listening and recording device outside a public phone booth from which a known gambler normally placed his bets, and the evidence they obtained helped convict him of violating a federal statute prohibiting interstate transmission of wagering information. The lower court upheld the conviction, as there had been no physical intrusion into the phone booth. In a seven-to-one decision the Court voided the conviction, and Justice Stewart's opinion merged many of the Fourth Amendment ideas the Court had been developing for over a decade with its recently announced right to privacy in *Griswold v. Connecticut* (1965).

Stewart admitted that the phrase "constitutionally protected area" failed to define the meaning and reach of the Fourth Amendment. In a notable phrase, he declared that "the Fourth Amendment protects people, not places" (*Katz v. United States* [1967], 351). Where an action took place mattered less than whether a general expectation of privacy existed; if so, then the individual's privacy would be protected there.

The lone dissenter was Justice Black, who as he had grown older had become disillusioned with what he saw as a freewheeling interpretive style, especially by two men who had been his closest allies a decade earlier, William O. Douglas and William J. Brennan. As they and the chief justice labored to develop the idea of, and a jurisprudence for, a "living Constitution," Black clung tenaciously and ever more rigidly to his literalist approach to the Bill of Rights. His dissent in *Katz* echoes the formalism of Taft's opinion in *Olmstead:* "A conversation overheard by eavesdropping, whether by plain snooping or wiretapping, is not tangible and, under the normally accepted meanings of the words, can neither be searched nor seized" (*Katz v. United States* [1967], 351).

By the time the Court handed down *Katz*, the anti-Court forces had been gaining strength for nearly fifteen years, and much of the discontent generated by the desegregation, reapportionment, and First Amendment decisions seemed to focus on the alleged impact of the Court's criminal procedure decisions. When President Johnson called for progressive anticrime legislation, the law-and-order advocates in Congress went to work with a vengeance, and the Omnibus Crime Control and Safe Streets Act of 1968 had a decided animus against the judiciary. The law specifically attempted to overturn or modify several of the Court's major decisions, and Title III dealt with wiretapping and eavesdropping. The Crime Act authorized judge-approved taps that could monitor a wide range of activities, and allowed any law officer, or indeed any person obtaining information in conformity with the process, to disclose or use that information as appropriate. What impact, if any, that law would have on Fourth Amendment adjudication would be a question confronting the Burger Court.

The Exclusionary Rule

If the constitutional guarantee against unreasonable and unlawful searches is to have any significance, evidence seized in violation of the Fourth Amendment should be excluded from trial; otherwise it is a guarantee without meaning. Yet no criminal procedure decisions have been so bitterly complained about as the exclusionary rule that gives teeth to the Fourth Amendment. The complaints stem from the fact that the Amendment itself provides no clue as to what remedies are available when it is violated; the exclusionary rule has been, from the start, a judge-made rule, and critics condemn it as judicial activism at its worst, with judges making policy rather than interpreting the law.

For a century after the adoption of the Bill of Rights, victims of illegal searches had only civil remedies available to them, either suits in trespass for damages, or in replevin for return of the goods, and neither proved particularly effective. The Court first articulated the exclusionary rule in *Weeks v. United States* (1914), and Justice Day made as strong a case for the rule as one can find:

> If letters and private documents can thus be [illegally] seized and held and used in evidence against a citizen accused of an offense, the protection of the Fourth Amendment declaring his right to be secure against such searches and seizures is of no value, and, so far as those thus placed are concerned, might as well be stricken from the Constitution. The efforts of the courts and their officials to bring the guilty to punishment, praiseworthy as they are, are not to be aided by the sacrifice of those great principles established by years of endeavor and suffering which have resulted in their embodiment in the fundamental law of the land. (*Weeks v. United States* [1914], 393–394)

A few years later, the Court prohibited the use of copies of illegally seized documents as a basis to secure a warrant for the originals. Justice Holmes declared that the "essence" of the Fourth Amendment protection is not merely that "evidence so acquired shall not be used before the Court but that it shall not be used at all" (*Silverthorne Lumber Co. v. United States*, [1920], 392).

The Court had explicitly declared in *Weeks* that the rule did not apply to the states, so in the next thirty years state and federal authorities colluded in what came to be known as the "silver platter doctrine." Evidence obtained by state authorities in a manner that would be illegal if engaged in by federal agents could be admitted in federal court so long as there had been no federal participation in the search. In 1949 the Vinson Court took a small step toward reining in warrantless state searches in *Wolf v. Colorado*, where Justice Frankfurter spoke for the majority in holding that unreasonable state searches and seizures violated the Fourteenth Amendment's due process clause. Frankfurter, however, avoided the issue of remedies, and in fact allowed that evidence so seized could be used in a state trial for a state crime. As Justice Murphy wrote in dissent, "the conclusion is inescapable that but one remedy exists to deter violations of the search and seizure clause. That is the rule which excludes illegally obtained evidence" (*Wolf v. Colorado* [1949], 44).

In 1961 what initially appeared to be a First Amendment case came to the Court. Police officers attempted to gain entrance to the home of Dollree Mapp, because they had information that a person wanted in connection with a bombing was hiding there. She initially refused to allow them in without a warrant; three hours later they forced a door and waved a piece of paper they claimed was a warrant, but refused to let her read it. She grabbed the paper, and in the ensuing scuffle police manhandled and hand-cuffed her for, as Justice Clark noted in the Court's opinion, resisting the policemen's "official rescue of the 'warrant' from her person." After subduing her, police searched her house, found a cache of pornographic items in a trunk in the basement, and then arrested her for possession of obscene materials. The state courts conceded that there had probably never been a warrant, but the prosecution correctly claimed that under existing law, it could use evidence obtained by a warrantless, unreasonable search.

Although neither the state nor the appellant briefed or argued the exclusionary rule, the Court in *Mapp v. Ohio* overruled *Wolf* six to three, and held that the Four-teenth Amendment incorporated the Fourth Amendment and applied it to the states. It also applied the exclusionary rule remedy. Both the majority and minority in *Mapp* agreed that the police had acted egregiously, but the three dissenters—Harlan, Frank-furter, and Whittaker—objected to imposing a federal judge-made rule on the states. The majority argued, however, as had Justice Day a half-century earlier, that the only remedy to violation of the Fourth Amendment—the only way to ensure that police did not act as they did in Dollree Mapp's home—was to deprive them of the fruits of an illegal search.

General agreement prevails that for the Fourth Amendment to be effective, some remedy must exist for its violation. This seemingly obvious conclusion is clouded, however, by the public's failure to understand why evidence that clearly establishes guilt cannot be used, and, as Benjamin Cardozo once said, "the criminal is to go free because the constable has blundered" (*People v. Defore* [1926], 21).

The exclusionary rule rests on several considerations. In *Mapp* the Court spelled out one of them, namely that the only way to deter police from illegal searches is to deprive them of the evidence they obtain. Another was later described by Chief Justice Warren Burger as "the 'sporting contest' thesis that the government must 'play the game fairly' and cannot be a allowed to profit from its own illegal acts" (*Bivens v. Six Unknown Named Federal Agents* [1971], 414). Perhaps Justice Bran-deis said it best in his dissent in the original wiretapping case:

> Decency, security, and liberty alike demand that government officials shall be sub-ject to the same rules of conduct that are commands to the citizen. Our govern-ment is the potent, the omnipresent teacher. For good or ill, it teaches the whole people by its example. If the government becomes a lawbreaker, it breeds con-tempt for the law; it invites every man to become a law unto himself; it invites anarchy. (*Olmstead v. United States* [1928], 485)

The exclusionary rule does limit police investigations, and it may make it somewhat more difficult to obtain proof and convict criminals, although evidence on this claim is inconclusive. But as Justice Clark noted in *Mapp v. Ohio* [1961, 609], "nothing can destroy a government more quickly than its failure to observe its own laws, or worse, its disregard of the charter of its own existence."

The Sixth Amendment and the Right to Counsel

We will temporarily put aside the Fifth Amendment, because to understand the Warren Court's interpretation of the right against self-incrimination, we must first examine its views on the right to counsel embedded in the Sixth Amendment.

At the time of the American Revolution, English common law gave an accused person the right to counsel in misdemeanor but not felony cases; that right did not come until 1836. In practice, however, it appears that English courts, even in the absence of an acknowledged right, permitted counsel to appear and to argue points of law and assist in the defense. By the adoption of the Constitution, twelve of the original thirteen states had rejected the English practice, and established a right to counsel in all criminal cases. They applied this right to the federal government in the Sixth Amendment, which provides that "in all criminal prosecutions, the accused shall enjoy the right . . . to have the Assistance of Counsel for his defence."

Even before ratification of the Bill of Rights, Congress began to implement this right. Section 35 of the Judiciary Act of 1789 provided that in all federal courts "the parties may plead and manage their own causes personally or by the assistance of such counsel or attorneys at law." The wording indicates a privilege extended to the parties, and not a requirement that counsel be appointed. The following year, however, in the Federal Crimes Act of 1790, Congress imposed a duty on federal courts to assign counsel in capital cases, and over the years the custom developed in most federal courts to appoint counsel for indigents in all serious cases.

In *Johnson v. Zerbst* (1938) the Supreme Court held that the Sixth Amendment required counsel in all federal criminal proceedings, unless the defendant waived this right. Whether a right to counsel existed in state courts depended for the most part on state law, although as a result of the infamous Scottsboro trial, in 1932 in *Powell v. Alabama* the Court held that failure to provide effective counsel to indigents in capital cases violated their due process rights. By relying on due process, the Court avoided the question of whether the Fourteenth Amendment incorporated the Sixth.

The Court faced this question directly a decade later in *Betts v. Brady* (1942), and by a divided vote decided that counsel for indigents did not constitute a fundamental right "implicit in the concept of ordered liberty" nor an essential of a fair trial. The accused, according to the Court, "was not helpless, but was a man forty-three years old, of ordinary intelligence, and ability to take care of his own interests" at the trial (*Betts v. Brady* [1942], 472). The Court endorsed a case-by-case review with an emphasis on the totality of the circumstances. In situations involving illiterate defendants or complex legal questions, then due process required an attorney.

This approach proved enormously time-consuming, and despite hearing dozens of cases over the next two decades, the Court never established clear criteria to guide state judges in determining when counsel had to be provided. Moreover, it found special circumstances present in so many instances that by 1962 it had for all practical purposes eroded the *Betts* rule. Finally, the justices decided to review the situation, and accepted an appeal filed by an indigent, Clarence Earl Gideon, who had requested and been denied counsel in a Florida breaking-and-entering case. The Court named as his attorney an influential Washington lawyer and future member of the Court, Abe Fortas, and specifically requested both sides to argue whether *Betts* should be overruled.

Not only had the *Betts* rule come under increasing criticism over the years, but a number of states had voluntarily adopted the federal standard of providing counsel to indigents accused in felony trials. By 1962 forty-five states provided counsel for all, or nearly all, indigent felony defendants. Only five states—Alabama, Florida, Mississippi, North Carolina, and South Carolina—did not, and even there some cities and counties assigned attorneys to poor persons charged with serious crimes. As the Court prepared to hear Gideon's case, only two states backed the Florida position that the Court ought to leave the rule alone; twenty-two states filed amicus briefs condemning *Betts* as "an anachronism when handed down" and asking that it be overruled.

The Court agreed, and Justice Black, who twenty years earlier had dissented in *Betts*, spoke for a unanimous bench in *Gideon v. Wainwright* in declaring that *Betts* had been wrongly decided. Numerous cases in the intervening years had proved conclusively that one could not have a fair trial without assistance of counsel, and that it therefore was "implicit in the concept of ordered liberty." The importance of counsel meant that the Fourteenth Amendment's due process clause incorporated the Sixth Amendment right and applied it to the states. Moreover, the Court took the unusual step of applying *Gideon* retroactively, so that states that had originally not supplied counsel in felony cases now either had to retry the defendants properly, or, as it often happened, with witnesses dispersed and evidence grown cold, let them go.

Justice Black later said that "I never thought I'd live to see [*Betts*] overruled," but to get his colleagues to go along, Black had to moderate his view that the Fourteenth Amendment required total incorporation of all the provisions of the Bill of Rights (Newman 1994, 528). His opinion in *Gideon* calls the right to counsel "fundamental and essential to a fair trial," wording that echoes the Cardozo/Frankfurter notion of fundamental fairness. Although Black does not use the phrase "selective incorporation," he used the logic, with an assist from Justice Brennan. As he later admitted, if he could not get the Court to agree to total incorporation, he would get what he could.

In fact, he got nearly everything; the Warren Court, using the jurisprudence of selective incorporation, in the end applied nearly all of the Bill of Rights to the states.

Gideon was the Warren Court's most popular criminal justice decision, because it rested on an insight that most people could understand, namely, that without a lawyer a defendant in a criminal case cannot expect justice. Anthony Lewis immortalized the case in *Gideon's Trumpet* (1964), and then Henry Fonda starred as Gideon in a television movie. As Warren biographer Ed Cray wrote, "No tale so affirmed the American democracy. No story broadcast around the world so clearly proclaimed that not just the rich received justice in American courts" (Cray 1997, 405–406).

Behind *Gideon*, however, is a good example of how the Court controls its docket as well as its image. By the time the Court took the case, at least five of the justices had already joined an opinion in another case that would have effectively overruled *Betts*. In fact, even as the chief justice directed his clerks to look for a good case in which to overturn *Betts*, the Court issued two terse *per curiam* decisions regarding indigents' rights to counsel. Willard Carnley had been convicted of incest and indecent assault upon a minor in Florida. Florida did not provide Carnley with counsel, and like Gideon, Carnley filed an *in forma pauperis* petition from state prison. With an illiterate and poor defendant, *Carnley* would have been an ideal case except for the crime—incest—plus the fact that, unlike Gideon, there were eyewitnesses who testified to Carnley's guilt. So the justices reversed on the *Betts* "special circumstances" rule.

Another case involved two men, Bennie Meyes and William Douglas, convicted in California for robbery and assault with intent to commit murder. They had a lawyer, an overworked public defender; they claimed that he had done an inadequate job of defense, and that their two cases should have been separated because of an inherent conflict of interest. Here again the Court could have overruled *Betts* outright or reversed on special circumstances. At conference six of the eight justices voted to reverse but could not agree on a rationale. Then evidence appeared that the wrong man had appealed the conviction, and the justices voted, six to two, to dismiss the case on the rather rare grounds that certiorari had been improvidently granted.

Normally such a ruling carries little or no explanation, but in *Douglas v. California*, Justice William O. Douglas, joined by Justice Brennan, dissented, and he wrote such a powerful dissent that on circulation three more members of the Court joined, and Douglas's dissent had now become the opinion of the Court. In fact, *Douglas* determined what the opinion would be in *Gideon*, but again the unsavory nature of the defendants and of their crime led the Court to wait. In Clarence Earl Gideon, a drifter accused of a crime and convicted on primarily circumstantial evidence, the Court had the case it wanted. And when Abe Fortas agreed to represent Gideon, the justices now had the stage set for the drama as they wanted it played out. In the film, the assistant attorney general representing Florida appears to have had little chance of winning; in fact, he had none.

Gideon applied only to felony cases; not until 1972 did the Burger Court extend the right to misdemeanor cases as well in *Argersinger v. Hamlin.* The Warren Court, however, did expand the right to counsel in two 1967 cases. In response to growing criticism over shoddy and unreliable police identification methods, the Court extended the right to counsel back to the lineup, and applied this to the federal government in *United States v. Wade,* and on the same day to the states in *Gilbert v. California.* As Justice Brennan explained, the Sixth Amendment requires counsel from the time the police shift their investigation from a general sifting of facts to accusing a particular person. By this time Brennan could say that the Court had developed a set of precedents that agreed on the fact that the Sixth Amendment came into play at "critical" stages of criminal proceedings. In response to critics who claimed the Court had distorted the meaning of the right, he noted:

> When the Bill of Rights was adopted, there were no organized police forces as we know them today. The accused confronted the prosecutor and the witnesses against him, and the evidence was marshaled, largely at the trial itself. In contrast, today's law enforcement machinery involves critical confrontations of the accused by the prosecution at pretrial proceedings where the results might well settle the accused's fate and reduce the trial itself to a mere formality. . . . The plain wording of this guarantee [of counsel] thus encompasses counsel's assistance whenever necessary to assure a meaningful "defense." (*Gilbert v. California* [1967], 224)

In other words, the Court would apply the spirit of the Amendment to ensure a comparable level of protection intended by the Framers in differing circumstances. That same term the Court applied this reasoning to extend the right in the other direction, past the determination of guilt to the sentencing phase of a trial in *Mempa v. Rhay* (1967).

In the one case it heard dealing with the right of counsel on appeal, the Warren Court decided the matter on equal protection rather than Sixth Amendment grounds. In California convicted persons had one appeal as a matter of right, but the state did not provide counsel to indigents for appeal. The Court in *Douglas v. California* (1963) viewed denial of counsel on the basis of status, namely indigence, as discrimination violating the Fourteenth Amendment. This reasoning followed the Court's logic in an earlier case, *Griffin v. Illinois* (1956), in which it had ruled that the appeals process cannot be denied to convicted defendants because they have no money to purchase copies of the trial transcript. As Justice Douglas wrote in the California case, "There can be no equal justice where the kind of appeal a man enjoys depends on the amount of money he has" (*Douglas v. California* [1963], 355).

The Court, through *Gideon,* opened the eyes of the country to the great truth that absence of counsel means absence of justice. But what the Court understood, and which it would have a great deal of difficulty explaining in a manner that caught the popular imagination, was that the trial was not the only stage of the criminal justice process at which the accused needed the help of an attorney. Perhaps the greatest criticism of the Court in this area came, not when the Court extended the right of counsel to appeal, but took it back earlier to police confrontation with a suspect in custody. The Court's concern over providing accused persons with effective counsel at all critical stages of the proceedings carried over into its Fifth Amendment decisions.

The Sixth Amendment has provisions other than the right to counsel, and the Warren Court incorporated them as well, although with far less fanfare than that attached to *Gideon*. In *Pointer v. Texas* (1965) the Court unanimously applied the provision that in all criminal prosecutions "the accused shall enjoy the right . . . to be confronted with the witness against him" to the states, and in a companion case also incorporated the right to a speedy trial. In 1968 the missing Sixth Amendment piece—the right to a trial by jury—was incorporated in *Duncan v. Louisiana*.

The Fifth Amendment and the Great Privilege

The right against compulsory self-incrimination had been established as a tenet of English common law by the end of the seventeenth century. The origins of the privilege are somewhat murky, but in English common law, as historian Leonard Levy has explained, "the initially vague maxim that no man is bound to accuse himself had come to mean that he was not required to answer against himself in any criminal cause or to any interrogatories that might tend to expose him to persecution" (Levy 1968, 330). At about the same time a rule also developed that forced confessions could not be used against a defendant because of their unreliability.

The colonists prized this right greatly, and by 1652 Massachusetts, Connecticut, and Virginia had provisions against the use of torture to force confessions. Following the Revolution, George Mason wrote into Virginia's Declaration of Rights that a man cannot "be compelled to give evidence against himself." Eight other states followed suit, and the provision later found its way into the federal Bill of Rights. The provision that no person "shall be compelled in any criminal case to be a witness against himself" is lodged in a miscellany of rights in the Fifth Amendment that bar double jeopardy, guarantees due process, and require just compensation for the taking of land. There has thus been a controversy over the original intent of the Framers, whether the privilege extends to just the accused, or to witnesses as well, and to what portions of the criminal proceedings. As with so many other provisions of the Constitution and the Bill of Rights, the early records shed little light on precisely what the Framers intended. The few contemporary references seemed to view it as a shield against torture.

The Amendment came into some disrepute during congressional hearings in the 1950s, in which witnesses suspected of communist or criminal affiliations refused to answer and "took the Fifth." Aside from professional patriots who objected to people who might or might not be communists availing themselves of constitutional protection, serious commentators also questioned the propriety of the rule. Judge Henry Friendly, a former Brandeis law clerk and certainly no reactionary, noted that the theory of the privilege seemed to run against everything that we taught our children, namely, that a clean breast of a misdeed is the best policy. "Every hour of the day people are being asked to explain their conduct to parents, employers and teachers." He believed that nearly all of the reasons used to justify the right, such as protection of the innocent, deterrence of perjury and improper police conduct, and privacy, could not be supported by the privilege or could be managed in a more effective manner.

Despite such criticism, the Supreme Court from the beginning interpreted the privilege broadly. In *Boyd v. United States* (1886), the Court found the subpoenaing of business records to be equivalent to forcing a person to be a witness against himself or herself. (This, of course, is no longer the law; business records are routinely subpoenaed in criminal and civil investigations.) A few years later, the Court reaffirmed this broad view in *Counselman v. Hitchcock* (1892) by holding that the privilege extended to grand jury investigations.

The Fifth Amendment has never been interpreted to mean that the police have to make their case without any help from the accused. The defendant may not have to talk to police or to testify at his or her trial, but is required to give physical evidence, such as fingerprints or blood samples. Moreover, if a person wants to confess to a crime, or testify on his or her own behalf, he or she has a right to do so. The rule is that a person cannot be coerced into giving oral evidence.

Although there are a number of facets to Fifth Amendment cases, the question of confession caught the public's attention, and the Warren Court's most famous (or infamous) criminal procedure decisions came in this area. The essential issue in confession cases has always been whether confessions are truly voluntary—and therefore admissible as evidence—or if they have been coerced in violation of the defendant's rights.

From 1936 to 1964, the Court dealt with the issue of coercion on the basis of the due process clauses of the Fifth and Fourteenth Amendments. In its first major case, *Brown v. Mississippi* (1936), the Court summarily reversed convictions in a state court based on confessions obtained through whippings. The Court decided thirty-five confession cases between 1936 and 1964, and moved from the easy cases in which confessions had been induced through physical coercion to the much harder issue of psychological coercion. The justices attempted to define appropriate limits on police behavior through a case-by-case process. In some of its early cases, the Warren Court showed its sensitivity to such factors as illiteracy, limited education, mental retardation, incompetence, or unnecessary delay in bringing a suspect before a magistrate, all leading to a "totality of the circumstances" test to determine whether the confession had been voluntary and thus admissible.

Some members of the Court found the case-by-case approach as unsatisfactory in Fifth Amendment confession cases as they had in the post-*Betts* counsel cases, and they believed that the voluntariness standard did not give police and lower courts sufficient guidance. The "totality of the circumstances" standard appeared very subjective and caused confusion among trial and lower appellate court judges. In 1959 four members of the Warren Court pointed to the next phase of the evolving standard on confessions.

Vincent Spano had been arrested for murder, and although he repeatedly asked to see his attorney, who was in the police station, police refused his request and continued to interrogate him until he confessed. The Court unanimously threw out the confession as involuntary in *Spano v. New York* (1959), on the grounds that his will had been "overborne by official pressure." Justice Douglas, joined by Justices Black, Brennan, and Stewart, concurred in the result, but suggested that the real issue had been that Spano had been unable to see his attorney, and raised the question of whether any confession given without proper legal advice could be considered voluntary.

The question of counsel had been raised in a number of confession cases, mainly in relation to whether the accused knew or understood his rights. In *Crooker v. California* (1958), the Court sustained the conviction of a former law student, because he knew of his constitutional right to remain silent. Justice Douglas dissented, joined by Warren, Black, and Brennan, and claimed that:

> The mischief and abuse of the third degree will continue as long as an accused can be denied the right to counsel at this the most critical period of his ordeal. For what takes place in the secret confines of the police station may be more critical than what takes place at the trial. (*Crooker v. California* [1958] 444–445)

In 1964 the Court moved away from the due process, "totality of the circumstances" approach to confession, and emphasized in its place the Sixth Amendment right to counsel. The shift occurred in *Massiah v. United States*, a confusing case that some commentators believe to have been wrongly decided.

Winston Massiah, a merchant seaman, had been indicted along with Jesse Colson for attempting to smuggle cocaine into the United States. Massiah retained a lawyer and pleaded not guilty. Colson decided to cooperate with federal agents and agreed to have a radio transmitter placed in his car. He and Massiah subsequently had a long conversation in the car, which an agent monitored. The prosecution later used a number of incriminating statements made in that conversation against Massiah at his trial. Justice Stewart, for a six-to-three Court, held that use of the defendant's statements, obtained in a surreptitious manner after his indictment and retention of a lawyer, violated his Fifth Amendment rights against self-incrimination. Justice White, joined by Clark and Harlan, dissented, saying that the Court had no reason to scrap the voluntary/involuntary test, and had not substituted another test in its place.

Although nominally a Fifth Amendment case, *Massiah* is the intersection between the Court's development of Fifth and Sixth Amendment doctrines. Just as the various First Amendment guarantees cannot always be neatly differentiated, so the bundle of rights granted to accused persons are also closely interwoven. *Massiah* applied to the states as well as to the federal government, but what did it mean other than that the police could not utilize an accused person's statements "after indictment and in the absence of counsel"? Was the timing at all important? Why should it matter if police surveillance secured incriminating statements before or after indictment? The Court did not, in fact, indicate when it considered a defendant formally charged.

A little later in the term the Court decided a case that, unlike *Massiah*, clearly involved abusive and illegal behavior by the Chicago police. Danny Escobedo had been taken into custody and interrogated about the fatal shooting of his brother-in-law. He repeatedly asked to see his attorney, who was in the station house, and the attorney repeatedly asked to see his client. The police refused to allow the two to meet until after Escobedo had made statements incriminating himself in the shooting. The police charged him, and only then allowed him access to his attorney.

In *Massiah*, the Court had not given a clear indication of when a defendant is considered formally charged and in custody, and thus within the protective reach of the Fifth Amendment. In *Escobedo v. Illinois* (1964) the Court rejected the state's claim that a person must be formally charged before he or she can avail himself or herself of counsel. In this case, Justice Goldberg noted that when Escobedo "requested, and was denied, an opportunity to consult with his lawyer, the investigation had ceased to be a general investigation of an 'unsolved crime.' Petitioner had become the accused" (*Escobedo v. Illinois* [1964], 485). The fact that there had been no formal charge made no difference; once a suspect is treated as if accused, then he or she must have all the rights afforded to accused persons. Goldberg anticipated much of the criticism that the decision aroused, and his opinion indicates the emphasis the Warren Court placed on protection of rights and fairness in the criminal justice system:

> It is argued that if the right to counsel is afforded prior to indictment, the number of confessions obtained by the police will diminish significantly, because most confessions are obtained during the period between arrest and indictment, [and] "any lawyer worth his salt will tell the suspect in no uncertain terms to make no statement to police under any circumstances." . . . This argument, of course, cuts two ways. The fact that many confessions are obtained during this period points up its critical nature as a "stage when legal aid and advice" are surely needed. The right to counsel would indeed be hollow if it began at a period when few confessions were obtained. There is necessarily a direct relationship between the importance of a stage to the police in their quest for a confession and the criticalness of that stage to the accused in his need for legal advice. Our Constitution, unlike some others,

strikes the balance in favor of the right of the accused to be advised by his lawyer of his privilege against self-incrimination. (*Escobedo v. Illinois* [1964], 485)

Most of this rationale dealt with the right to counsel, a Sixth Amendment right, and only at the end did Justice Goldberg mention the Fifth Amendment right against self-incrimination. The Court had gradually come to see the close connection between the two, and realized that accused persons, often confused after police take them into custody, need legal advice in order to exercise their Fifth Amendment rights. Confessions need not be extracted by physical coercion to be involuntary; modern psychological methods could be just as effective in overbearing one's will.

Despite the sweeping language quoted above, the actual holding in *Escobedo* proved fairly narrow: When police take a person into custody for interrogation about a particular crime, and the suspect requests counsel, then counsel must be provided and given access to the client, or else statements taken in the interrogation may not be used against the suspect. But what if the suspect were illiterate, or did not know his or her rights, or had become confused by the stationhouse procedures, and failed to ask for counsel? These considerations did not appear to bother the dissenters in *Escobedo*, Justices Harlan, Stewart (author of the majority opinion in *Massiah*), Clark, and White. Their emphasis seemed to be that so long as the government did not use physical coercion and in the end allowed people to choose what to do, it could discourage people from exercising their rights. The majority of the Court took a different view, that the government had an obligation to nurture constitutional rights, and to encourage its citizens to exercise those rights.

Both the public and law enforcement officials reacted predictably to *Escobedo*. Danny Escobedo was no Clarence Gideon, a drifter accused of petit larceny, or a Winston Massiah, accused of smuggling; his crime was murder. Beyond that, Goldberg's opinion for the five liberals exhibited disdain not only for confessions but for how police operated generally. William Parker, the police chief of Los Angeles, charged that the Court was "handcuffing the police," and declared that "allegations that modern criminal investigation can compensate for the lack of a confession or admission in every criminal case is totally absurd!" Michael Murphy, the former New York City chief, complained that "what the Court is doing is akin to requiring one boxer to fight by the Marquis of Queensbury rules while permitting the other to butt, gouge and bite." Prosecutors, however, seemed far less alarmed. The Los Angeles district attorney said that the apparently "restrictive" decisions would actually make police more professional, efficient, and effective. As for charges that the Court decisions coddled criminals and encouraged crime, David C. Acheson, the assistant secretary of the treasury in charge of the Secret Service and Bureau of Narcotics, said that "changes in court decisions and prosecution procedure would have about the same effect on the crime rate as an aspirin would have on a tumor of the brain" (Powe 2000, 391).

The *Escobedo* decision also pulled the Court into presidential politics, a place it would occupy in the 1968 election as well. Republican candidate Barry Goldwater exclaimed "No wonder our law enforcement officers have been demoralized and rendered ineffective in their jobs" (Powe 2000, 391). "Impeach Earl Warren" bumper stickers were now joined by ones calling for citizens to "Support Your Local Police." At the Republican national convention, former president Eisenhower urged delegates "not to be guilty of maudlin sympathy for the criminal who, roaming the street with switchblade knife and illegal firearms seeking a prey, suddenly becomes upon apprehension a poor, underprivileged person who counts upon the compassion of our society and the weakness of many courts to forgive his offense" (Powe 2000, 391).

Given the reaction in the South against desegregation and in religious circles against the school prayer decisions, polls found that the public either did not understand or care about cases like *Escobedo* or the other ways in which the Court was expanding constitutional rights. In *Malloy v. Hogan* (1964) the Court ruled that the Fifth Amendment right against self-incrimination is applicable to the states through the Fourteenth Amendment. The Court had now moved from the due process concept of voluntariness as the standard for confessions to the belief that presence of counsel at the accusatory stage determined whether a confession had been properly obtained. All of these decisions, however, lacked precision; they lacked a bright-line test that would tell police, prosecutors, and trial and appellate judges whether constitutional standards had been violated or observed. What if police suspected a person, and bore down heavily in their preliminary questioning, eliciting incriminating statements that they then used as a basis for indictment? The police always had an advantage in such situations, and could deliberately confuse a person and trick him or her into confessing before the suspect realized or knew that a lawyer ought to be there. Where did one draw the line between good police investigation and improper procedures?

The Warren Court tried to answer these questions and provide a simple standard in its most vilified criminal procedure case, *Miranda v. Arizona* (1966). Although the final holding, expressed in the famous "Miranda warnings," was clear, Chief Justice Warren's majority opinion rambled all over the constitutional landscape, occasionally honing in on specifics, but for the most part getting lost in generalities. It made an all too easy target for critics, a "self-inflicted wound" in Fred Graham's phrase (Graham 1970, title).

In essence, the *Miranda* majority identified coercion in any form as the chief problem in determining the validity of confessions. Rather than proceed on a case-by-case basis attempting to evaluate the totality of the circumstances, the Court handed down definite rules to guide police and lower courts. If the rules had been obeyed and the suspect confessed, then that confession would be admissible as evidence. If police failed to obey the rules, then the confession would be thrown out.

The police had to inform a person in clear and unequivocal terms that he or she had a right to remain silent; that anything said could be used in court; that the accused had a right to a lawyer; and if he or she had no money, that the state would provide a lawyer. If the interrogation continued without the presence of an attorney after the accused had requested one, "a heavy burden rests on the Government to demonstrate that the defendant knowingly and intelligently waives his privilege against self-incrimination and the right to counsel" (*Miranda v. Arizona* [1966], 517).

Miranda, despite the objections of the four dissenting members, is a logical culmination of the Warren Court's journey in search of a workable method to deal with the issue of forced confessions. It started out with the premise of earlier courts, that physical coercion could not be allowed, and that an evaluation of the totality of the circumstances would determine whether due process had been violated. At the same time, the Court had been developing a broader interpretation of the Sixth Amendment right to counsel, and these doctrines coalesced in the *Massiah* and *Escobedo* rulings that if suspects asked for but had been denied counsel, then confessions under such circumstances had to be considered involuntary because coerced. In *Miranda* these various strands came together in the belief that for rights to be meaningful, a suspect must know about them before interrogation begins, a process in which the physical and psychological advantage resides with the police. As Warren explained, police custody and interrogation contain "inherently compelling pressures which work to undermine the individual's will to resist and to compel him to speak where he would not do so freely" (*Miranda v. Arizona* [1966], 467).

Because *Miranda* merged self-incrimination and confession law, and tied them to the right to counsel, it did depart from the due process analytical framework that had been the norm until the mid-1960s. Many critics, including the dissenters, characterized this as a radical departure from accepted doctrine. But the earlier due process "totality of the circumstances" rulings had never been all that clear, and one can certainly chart the seeds of *Miranda* in decisions reaching back nearly eight decades.

In *Miranda* the Court tried to do two separate things. First, it wanted to establish a prophylactic rule to aid judicial review. While it is still possible to have a tainted confession even if the warning is given, the failure to inform suspects of their rights is a clear indicator that the confession should not be admitted. Some state and local police departments, which had never paid scrupulous attention to constitutional protection, did run into methodological problems following the decision. Once they adopted the *Miranda* warning as part of their standard procedures, they discovered that it did not undermine their effectiveness; in many cases, those accused wanted to confess, and could hardly wait for the police to finish reading them their rights.

The second aspect of the decision reflected the Warren majority's view that in a democracy, with rights embedded in a written Constitution, all people had to be aware of those rights so that, if faced by police interrogation, they could make voluntary and intelligent choices. One should recall that few secondary school systems taught much in the way of law prior to 1966, and not many people knew what rights they had. This situation has changed considerably in the last two decades, with nearly all states adopting Constitution and law segments in their public school social studies guidelines.

The chief justice no doubt anticipated that the *Miranda* decision would evoke strong criticism, and he tried to point out that the states remained free to experiment with how they implemented the basic procedural safeguards the Court now required. "Our decision in no way creates a constitutional straightjacket," he declared. "We encourage Congress and the states to continue their laudable search for increasingly effective ways of protecting the rights of the individual while promoting efficient enforcement of our criminal law" (*Miranda v. Arizona* [1966], 467).

The level of response had been anticipated in Justice White's dissent that the new rule would have the effect of "returning a killer, a rapist, or other criminal to the streets to repeat his crime whenever it pleases him" (*Miranda v. Arizona* [1966], 542). Herman Talmadge of Georgia rose on the Senate floor to charge that the ruling virtually banned "effective police interrogation." In Senate hearings later in the year Sam Ervin declared that the Court had "stressed individual rights" at the expense of public safety, and he introduced a constitutional amendment to overrule the *Miranda* decision and to withdraw from Supreme Court review all rulings of trial judges, state or federal, admitting confessions into evidence. The executive director of the International Association of Chiefs of Police bitterly complained that "I guess now we'll have to supply all squad cars with lawyers" (Urofsky 1991, 164). Mayor Sam Yorty of Los Angeles denounced the decision as "another set of handcuffs on the police department" (Powe 2000, 399). The uproar over *Miranda* continued for the remainder of Earl Warren's tenure, affected provisions of the 1968 Omnibus Crime Control Act, and played a role in that year's presidential election.

Yet in many ways the public quickly internalized the *Miranda* decision. In 1967 the old police show *Dragnet* was brought back to the air, and Jack Webb as Joe Friday would give the requisite *Miranda* warning, although making it clear that he considered this a hindrance to good police work. In contrast, the star of the 1970s show, *Hawaii Five-O*, treated *Miranda* just as Earl Warren would have wanted, as a means of making the police more professional. Everyone in America who watched a police show on television soon became aware of the warnings; little children playing cops-and-robbers knew the words. Because giving the warning did not seem to interfere with good police work, before long all but the most fanatic conservatives stopped looking at *Miranda* as in any way "handcuffing" the police. Thanks in large measure to the media, one could argue that in this area Warren had been successful in achieving his goal of equalizing knowledge, so that poverty would not be a bar to exercising one's rights.

The Right to Privacy

The Court's expansion of enumerated liberties encouraged litigation by parties with special interests hoping that the mantle of constitutional protection might spread even further. In the spring of 1965, the Court decided one of a handful of cases that can truly be said to have established a new area of constitutional law. In *Griswold v. Connecticut*, the Court resurrected substantive due process to establish a constitutionally protected right of privacy.

Various privacy rights existed within the common law, but often they were attached to property, such as in the old adage that "a man's home is his castle." In the United States, the law of privacy remained poorly defined; commentators believed that a right existed, but there was practically no case law on the subject. In 1890 Louis Brandeis and his law partner, Samuel D. Warren Jr., had published a pioneering article on the subject in the *Harvard Law Review*, a piece later credited with launching American law on this subject.

Civil libertarians believed that privacy could be brought under constitutional protection through implied guarantees in the Bill of Rights and through implicit and explicit dicta in various Court rulings. The First Amendment, for example, protected various forms of freedom of expression; the Fourth limited government search and seizure of person or property; the Fifth barred self-incrimination; the Ninth provided a catchall for nonenumerated rights; and the Fourteenth applied all of them to the states. In addition, the Third forbade the quartering of soldiers; Justice Story had written in his *Commentary* on the Constitution that the Third had the "plain object . . . to secure the perfect enjoyment of that great right of the common law, that a man's house shall be his castle, privileged against all civil and military intrusions" (Story 1833, 709).

The Court had previously indicated the existence of nonenumerated rights that were embodied in so-called personal liberties. Over the years these had been held to include a right to educate one's child, decisions about marriage and procreation, travel, and choice of association. The most striking statement on privacy could be found in Brandeis's great dissent in the 1928 wiretap case, *Olmstead v. United States*, in which he declared that the Framers had "conferred, as against the government, the right to be let alone—the most comprehensive of rights and the right most valued by civilized men" (*Olmstead v. United States* [1928], 478).

The *Griswold* case involved an 1879 Connecticut statute prohibiting the use of any drug or device to prevent conception and penalizing any person who advised on or provided contraceptive materials. Civil libertarians had tried to get the Supreme Court to review this law twice before, most recently in *Poe v. Ullman* (1961). Justice Frankfurter had then written a plurality opinion denying review for lack of justiciability, noting that there had been only one prosecution in eighty years. With such a tacit understanding between the police and the public to leave people alone, the

Court need not interfere. Justices Douglas and Harlan entered strong protests: Douglas wanted to know what lawyer would advise clients to rely on a "tacit agreement" that police would not enforce a criminal statute, while Harlan suggested that a liberty interest (a personal right that came within the protection of the Fourteenth Amendment) existed that deserved protection.

Shortly after *Poe,* New Haven officials did prosecute Estelle Griswold, the executive director of the Connecticut Planned Parenthood League, along with one of the doctors in the League's clinic who had prescribed contraceptives to a married person. With Frankfurter's argument of nonjusticiability destroyed, the Court accepted the case, and Justice Douglas delivered one of the most creative and innovative opinions in his thirty-six years on the bench. Most of the references to privacy in earlier cases had relied on a liberty embodied in substantive due process, which in the mid-1960s still suffered from the bad odor of Lochnerism, the term for the use of substantive due process by conservative judges to strike down laws they did not like. Douglas did not want to invoke substantive due process, so he cobbled together justifications from various parts of the Bill of Rights. The amendments "have penumbras, formed by emanations from those guarantees that help give them life and substance" (*Griswold v. Connecticut* [1965], 484). These emanations together (joined in what one wit described as Amendment $3^1/_2$) form a constitutionally protected right of privacy; and no privacy could be more sacred, or more deserving of protection from intrusion, than that of the marital chamber. "We deal," Douglas wrote,

> with a right of privacy older than the Bill of Rights—older than our political parties, older than our school system. Marriage is a coming together for better or for worse, hopefully enduring, and intimate to the degree of being sacred. The association promotes a way of life, not causes; a harmony in living, not political faiths; a bilateral loyalty, not commercial or social projects. Yet is an association for as noble a purpose as any involved in our prior decisions. (*Griswold v. Connecticut* [1965], 486)

Justice Goldberg, joined by Brennan and the chief justice, concurred, relying on the rarely cited Ninth Amendment, which reserves to the people all nonenumerated rights. The right to privacy, Goldberg maintained, predated the Constitution, and the Framers intended that all such ancient liberties should also enjoy constitutional protection. Justice White concurred on due process grounds, while Justice Stewart dissented, claiming that the Court had exceeded the limits of judicial restraint. Stewart thought the statute "an uncommonly silly law," but he could find nothing in the Bill of Rights forbidding it.

The dissent by Justice Black and Justice Harlan's concurrence are of special interest because they illustrate two major theories of constitutional interpretation. Although Black advocated total incorporation of the Bill of Rights, he remained in many ways a strict constructionist; he would incorporate only those rights specified in the first eight amendments. He dismissed Goldberg's Ninth Amendment opinion scornfully, declaring that "[e]very student of history knows that it was intended to limit the federal government to the powers granted expressly or by necessary implication" (*Griswold v. Connecticut* [1965], 520).

Justice Harlan did not fear the idea of substantive due process and based his concurrence on that theme. Due process, he claimed, reflects fundamental principles of liberty and justice, but these change over time as society progresses. The Court has the responsibility of reinterpreting phrases such as "due process" and "equal protection" so that the Constitution itself may grow with the times. Harlan saw Black's view as too rigid; both the states and the federal government needed the flexibility to experiment in means to expand the protection of individual rights.

Douglas's result—the creation of a constitutionally protected right to privacy— and Harlan's substantive due process rationale established the basis for the expansion of autonomy rights in the 1970s. *Griswold* is the forebear of *Roe v. Wade* (the case that legalized abortion) and many other cases enlarging personal freedoms. *Griswold* became the launching pad for the new substantive due process and a progenitor of the fundamental interest interpretation of the due process clause.

The Warren Court decided one other noteworthy privacy case, and while it is also discussed above in the section on obscenity and the First Amendment, it bears a brief recapitulation here because it is so intimately involved with privacy. Police had searched Robert Stanley's home for book-making evidence, and discovered several pornographic films. Georgia then prosecuted Stanley under a statute prohibiting the "possession of obscene materials." The state claimed that if it could protect the physical well-being of its citizens, it could also protect their minds. The Court disagreed, and speaking through Justice Thurgood Marshall in *Stanley v. Georgia* (1969), declared that the right "to receive information and ideas, regardless of their social worth, is fundamental to our free society" (*Stanley v. Georgia* [1969], 564). The state conceded that Stanley did not sell the films, but merely owned them, presumably for his own viewing. Marshall dismissed the conviction with a ringing affirmation of the right to privacy: "If the First Amendment means anything, it means that a State has no business telling a man, sitting alone in his own home, what books he may read or what films he may watch" (*Stanley v. Georgia* [1969], 565).

A Final Lesson in Democracy

On June 16, 1969, Earl Warren delivered his final decision as chief justice in *Powell v. McCormack*. Adam Clayton Powell Jr., the flamboyant congressman from Harlem, had been reelected to the House in 1966. Although he met the age, citizenship, and residency requirements for membership detailed in Article I, Section 2, the House refused to let him take his seat. A select committee had reported that Powell had "wrongfully diverted House funds . . . and that he had made false reports on expenditures." Article I, Section 5 provides that "Each House [of Congress] shall be the Judge of the . . . Qualifications of its own Members" and may "expel a Member" with the concurrence of a two-thirds majority. The House did not vote to *expel* Powell, however; by a vote of 307 to 116, it *excluded* him from membership in the Ninetieth Congress.

Powell then sued the House, seeking his salary for the duration of the Ninetieth Congress and a declaratory judgment that the House had no constitutional power to deny him his seat. In circuit court, Judge Warren E. Burger ruled that Powell had no standing and the court no jurisdiction because the matter constituted a political question. Judicial intervention, according to Burger, would violate the doctrine of separated powers. Following Burger's ruling, Powell's district reelected him in 1968, and the House in the Ninety-first Congress permitted him to take his seat, thus mooting a major part of his suit.

A nearly unanimous Court (only Justice Stewart thought the case should have been dismissed for mootness) not only took the case, but ruled in Powell's favor. Although a "textually demonstrable constitutional commitment" gave each House the power to judge its members' qualifications in Article I, Section 5, this power, according to Chief Justice Warren, related only to the qualifications listed in Article I, Section 2, namely, age, citizenship, and residency. By this reading, the House had no power to expel for any reason other than failure to meet the three criteria. "The Constitution leaves the House without authority," Warren wrote, "to *exclude* any person duly elected by his constituents, who meets all the requirements for membership expressly prescribed in the Constitution" (*Powell v. McCormack* [1969], 547). Any other rule, he held, would deprive people of the right to elect their own representatives.

The political question boundary had been considerably narrowed in *Baker v. Carr*, and some commentators believed that it vanished completely in *Powell*. Warren took the old *Marbury v. Madison* syllogism and reasserted the Court's role as the ultimate arbiter of constitutional issues. Is there a constitutional question? If so, then the Court is the appropriate body to make constitutional interpretations, and the Supreme Court decides *all* constitutional questions. Even if another branch has authority under the Constitution to decide the merits of an issue, the Court has the power to determine if, in fact, that other branch does have the authority, and the ultimate appellate power to review the decision to see if that other branch got it right.

But the decision was more than a reassertion of the Court's authority; it was a lesson in democracy. Powell's behavior had been wrong, but so long as his constituents wanted him as their representative, then the House could not deny them their choice because they disapproved of him. Powell, an outspoken and flamboyant African American, had acted much as had senior white members of Congress, and the Court believed that there was more than a touch of racism in the House's exclusion decision. It was a fitting valedictory for the chief justice and for the Court he had led for sixteen years.

References

Blasi, Vincent, ed. 1983. *The Burger Court: The Constitutional Revolution That Wasn't*. New Haven, CT: Yale University Press.

Cahn, Edmund. 1955. "Jurisprudence." *New York University Law Review* 30: 150.

Chafee, Zechariah, Jr. 1941. *Free Speech in the United States*. Cambridge, MA: Harvard University Press.

Cray, Ed. 1997. *Chief Justice: A Biography of Earl Warren*. New York: Simon & Schuster.

Frank, John P. 1961. *Marble Palace: The Supreme Court in American Life*. Westport, CT: Greenwood.

Graham, Fred. 1970. *The Due Process Revolution: The Warren Court's Impact on Criminal Law*. New York: Hayden.

Kalven, Harry. 1988. *A Worthy Tradition: Freedom of Speech in America*. New York: Harper & Row.

Kluger, Richard. 1976. *Simple Justice*. New York: Knopf.

Levy, Leonard W. 1968. *Origins of the Fifth Amendment*. New York: Oxford University Press.

Meiklejohn, Alexander. 1960. *Political Freedom: The Constitutional Powers of the People*. New York: Oxford University Press.

Murphy, Paul L. 1972. *The Constitution in Crisis Times, 1919–1969*. New York: Harper & Row.

Newman, Roger. 1994. *Hugo Black: A Biography*. New York: Pantheon.

Pfeffer, Leo. 1967. *Church, State, and Freedom*. Boston, MA: Beacon Press.

Powe, Lucas A., Jr. 2000. *The Warren Court and American Politics*. Cambridge, MA: Harvard University Press.

Story, Joseph. 1833. *Commentaries on the Constitution of the United States*. Durham, NC: Carolina Academic Press.

Tushnet, Mark V. 1984. *The NAACP's Legal Strategy against Segregated Education, 1925–1950*. Chapel Hill: University of North Carolina Press.

Urofsky, Melvin I. 1991. *The Continuity of Change: The Supreme Court and Individual Liberties, 1953–1986*. Belmont, CA: Wadsworth.

Weaver, John D. 1967. *Warren: The Man, the Court, the Era.* Boston, MA: Little, Brown.

Wechsler, Herbert. 1959. "Toward Neutral Principles of Constitutional Law." *Harvard Law Review* 73: 1.

Wilkinson, J. Harvie, III. 1979. *From Brown to Bakke: The Supreme Court and School Integration.* New York: Oxford University Press.

Woodward, C. Vann. 1974. *The Strange Career of Jim Crow.* 3d ed. New York: Oxford University Press.

The Legacy

I n assessing the lasting impact of the Warren Court, one must keep several things in mind. First and foremost, the Warren Court did not spring full-blown on the day Earl Warren took over the center chair in 1953. Neither did it end when he stepped down as chief justice in 1969. The Supreme Court is an institution, and while some justices can certainly affect its direction, an institutional inertia exists that prevents radical shifts in any direction; one cannot make ninety-degree turns in an ocean liner. It is true that the Court, with only nine members, is easier to steer, and that as far as institutions go, it is more like a sleek yacht than a clumsy tanker. Sometimes the appointment of only one or two people can change a jurisprudential minority into a majority.

It had taken several years before Earl Warren had the majority he needed for his views. He began with Hugo Black and William O. Douglas, and soon picked up William Brennan. But not until Arthur Goldberg joined the Court in 1962 did the liberals have a majority. Similarly, after Warren retired, it took a number of years before conservative appointees gained control of the high Court; in fact, some scholars argue that the balance of power shifted not from liberal to arch-conservative, but from liberal to moderate-conservative. Moreover, the political skills of William Brennan, which had done so much to effectuate the liberal views of the Warren majority, remained potent during the entire period of the Burger Court and into the early years of the Rehnquist era. Brennan continued to put together majorities or pluralities up until the time of his retirement.

The Transformation of the Court

If we start with Warren himself, who left in 1969, his seat was taken by Warren E. Burger, whom Richard Nixon and many others considered a dyed-in-the-wool judicial conservative. But Burger either failed, or never tried very hard, to overturn the Warren legacy, and in many ways the Burger Court actually consolidated and extended the Warren legacy. Abe Fortas, tainted by scandal, was the first to leave after Warren, and Richard Nixon, after failing to put two Southerners on the Court, turned to Harry Blackmun. Although many observers at the time thought Blackmun to be an ideological appendage to Burger—pundits nicknamed them the "Minnesota twins"—in fact Blackmun proved to have one of the most flexible minds on the Court, and by the time he retired in 1994 he was arguably the most liberal member of the bench, someone who might have been right at home on a Court presided over by Earl Warren.

Hugo Black stepped down in 1971, to be replaced by the quintessential moderate, Lewis F. Powell Jr. The first really conservative appointee proved to be William H. Rehnquist, who took John Marshall Harlan's place in 1972, and who would later be elevated to the center chair in 1986. William O. Douglas, after serving longer than anyone else in the history of the Court, retired in 1975, and John Paul Stevens, another moderate, took his seat. When the moderate Potter Stewart retired in 1981, Ronald Reagan named the first woman to the high court, Sandra Day O'Connor. Although she has proved to be quite conservative on some issues, O'Connor picked and chose her issues, and by 1990 was a leader of the centrist bloc. William Brennan, appointed by Eisenhower in 1956, sent in his resignation to George Bush in 1990, and was replaced by David Hackett Souter, who quickly joined O'Connor as a centrist.

Perhaps the most dramatic change came when Thurgood Marshall, the last appointed member of the Warren Court and the architect of the NAACP's successful campaign against segregation, retired in 1991. George Bush named Clarence Thomas, an extreme conservative who won Senate confirmation primarily because the NAACP was afraid to challenge him. The organization's leaders were afraid that if they opposed him and he was defeated—as he surely would have been—then Bush would appoint a white man to the Court. It was a political blunder of monumental proportions, because Thomas stood ideologically opposed to nearly everything the NAACP and Thurgood Marshall represented.

The last remaining member of the Warren Court, Byron White, retired in 1993. Although liberal in race matters, White was as conservative in most other areas as Harlan, and he had no trouble adjusting, not only to the Burger Court, but to the bench headed by William Rehnquist. To take his place President Clinton named Ruth Bader Ginsburg who, although the chief litigator for women's rights issues in the 1970s, is also best described as a moderate—one who only appears liberal when compared to Clarence Thomas or Antonin Scalia (who took Rehnquist's seat in 1986 when the latter became chief justice).

Because of this relatively slow turnover, and because in many instances liberals and moderates gave way to other moderates, one does not find a radical shift in the Court's jurisprudence during the years that Warren Burger led the Court (1969–1986). Indeed, even in the years that Chief Justice Rehnquist presided, there were few dramatic turnarounds.

In this chapter we follow the fate of some of the doctrines we examined in Chapter Three, try to understand the persistence of the Warren legacy, and then say a few words about that legacy both on and off the bench.

The lasting impact of a Court can take several forms, of which the most obvious is the influence its decisions exert on future courts. For example, a relatively minor dispute between a frustrated office seeker and the Jefferson administration led to the decision in *Marbury v. Madison* (1803), which has been honored and relied upon by all subsequent courts. On the other hand, despite the great public controversy stirred up by the case of *Dred Scott v. Sanford* (1857), it had no lasting power at all, and succeeding courts ignored it as an embarrassment.

There is no question that Warren Court decisions such as *Brown, Griswold, Miranda, Sullivan,* and others quickly became landmarks, and later Courts built upon these cases as foundations, even if at times they tried to limit or refine their impact. At the end of the twentieth century, though, not a single major ruling of the Warren Court had been overturned or seriously restricted.

The Burger Court and Equal Protection

For whatever else it may be remembered, the bright star of Warren Court jurisprudence must be its decision in *Brown v. Board of Education* (1954), in which it declared racial segregation unconstitutional and began the process of tearing down apartheid in the South. There had been a few segregation cases during the Vinson Court years (1946–1953), but these had not confronted the "separate-but-equal" rationale of *Plessy v. Ferguson* (1896), and had merely ruled that particular circumstances did not meet the "equal" part of the formula. The Warren Court bit the bullet, and breathed new life into the equal protection clause.

Without taking anything away from the courage displayed by Earl Warren and his colleagues, in hindsight one can say that in this, as in other areas, from a jurisprudential basis they had the "easy" cases. Once they decided that laws requiring segregation by race violated the Fourteenth Amendment, then the entire sequence of school and nonschool desegregation decisions discussed in the previous chapter followed inevitably. Subsequent Courts had to confront far more complex questions of race relations and remedies, and if they did not come up with as clear answers as enunciated by their predecessor, that is because society as a whole had no easy answer. Where the Warren Court had dealt with overt de jure segregation (segregation mandated by law), the Burger Court grappled with three far more complex themes: (1) the desegregation of urban school districts, both North and South, where segregation resulted from longstanding residential patterns, rather than from law; (2) discriminatory effects in nonschool areas in the absence of a specific purpose to discriminate; and (3) affirmative action, the effort to remedy the effects of past discrimination through current preferential plans.

In the new chief justice's second term, the Court handed down its last unanimous school desegregation decision, *Swann v. Charlotte-Mecklenburg Board of Edu-*

cation (1971). Earlier cases had primarily involved rural school districts, where, even though blacks and whites lived in close proximity, they went to different schools. In such instances, the remedy had been simple; all students living in one part of the district went to the same school. But in cities with segregated residential patterns, if children went to the school nearest their home, they would in all likelihood be going to an all-white or all-black school. School officials argued that such segregation did not result from state law, and therefore should not be subject to forced desegregation. Their arguments, however, ignored the fact that these residential patterns had developed through decades of Jim Crow laws, and that often school boards had gerrymandered districts to make sure that they remained racially segregated.

Speaking for the Court, Chief Justice Burger charged that the current segregation had resulted from past misconduct and therefore had to be remedied. He affirmed the lower court's order that the school board redraw attendance zones and bus students in order to achieve a racial composition at each school approximating the racial mix of the entire district. The *Swann* case marked a significant departure for the Court aside from the fact that it had begun dealing with the problems of urban segregation. The majority of the Warren Court opinions had been aimed at desegregating schools by the stratagem of voiding those statutes that required or preserved racial separation. The underlying philosophy had been that if barriers to integrated schools could be removed, then within a short time the schools would be integrated. The *Swann* court recognized that simply removing old barriers would not be enough, because in addition to the actual laws, a variety of customs and extralegal sanctions still operated to keep blacks and whites separated. In the 1970s, therefore, the Burger Court shifted from simply striking down segregation statutes to requiring integration plans. In doing so it did not reverse the Warren Court legacy, but moved beyond it, taking positive steps to achieve what the earlier Court thought would happen once the overt barriers had been removed.

In its equal protection analysis, the Burger Court often focused on the difference between de jure and de facto segregation. The Court would not allow any type of discriminatory classification based on race, and if there had been de jure discrimination in the past, the justices permitted lower courts a greater leeway in fashioning an appropriate remedy. But if no evidence existed of legally established segregation in the past, then the Court gave local governmental units greater flexibility as to how or whether they would respond. Problems arose in the early seventies when the Court began hearing cases aimed at segregation in Northern school districts, and the unanimity that had marked the Warren era fell apart.

In *Keyes v. Denver School District No. 1* (1973), the Court heard its first challenge to a segregated Northern school system. Justice Brennan began his opinion by emphasizing that the legal difference between de jure and de facto segregation lay in whether there had been an intent to segregate. Although no formal laws required segregation in the Denver schools, the school board had used race as a determinant in drawing attendance zones and locating new schools, and that had the same effect and intent as passing a formal law requiring segregation.

The following year the Court addressed a more difficult issue: whether the remedy for segregation, even de jure segregation, could cut across jurisdictional lines. Following the *Brown* decision in 1954, many whites had begun moving to the surrounding, predominantly white counties, leaving the inner-city school population overwhelmingly black. Whether or not de jure segregation had ever existed, the fact remained that integration could not be achieved with an overwhelmingly black school population. Even if the suburbs had been historically white, the city constituted their reason for being. The city provided the jobs and the services that fueled the entire metropolitan economy. Moreover, the phenomenon known as "white flight," triggered by desegregation and busing orders, had sent tens of thousands of white families and their school-age children out of the cities, effectively resegregating the city systems.

A district judge had determined that Detroit's schools had been unconstitutionally segregated, and that desegregation of the city's 64 percent black schools would send whites fleeing to the suburbs. To prevent resegregation, he ordered the fifty-three surrounding school systems unified with that of Detroit. By a five-to-four vote in *Milliken v. Bradley* (1974), the Court held that federal judges could not order multidistrict remedies without proof that the district lines had originally been drawn in a discriminatory manner.

For some people, *Milliken v. Bradley* represented "the sad but inevitable culmination of a national anti-black strategy" (Jones 1975, 203). The case marked the first time since *Brown* that blacks had lost a school case, and Justice Marshall lamented that "after twenty years of small, often difficult steps toward that great end [of equal justice under law], the Court today takes a great step backwards" (*Milliken v. Bradley* [1974], 782). But for others, the decision came as a relief. Segregated Detroit schools were not the suburbs' creation and thus not their burden.

One wonders how the case might have been decided had it come up ten years earlier at the height of Warren Court activism. The four dissenters in *Milliken* were all members of that Court—Douglas, Brennan, Marshall, and White—and there is little doubt that had Warren, Goldberg, or Fortas still been sitting on the bench the decision would have gone the other way. But the case should not be seen as the Burger Court turning its back on African Americans. To look on *Milliken* in strictly racial terms would ignore considerations important to the majority, especially Lewis Powell and the chief justice. "No single tradition," Burger noted, "is more deeply rooted than local control over the operation of the schools; local autonomy has long been thought essential both to the maintenance of community concern and support for public schools and to the quality of the educational process" (*Milliken v. Bradley*

[1974], 241–242). The Court would not countenance legally sanctioned discrimination anymore than its predecessor, but in combatting de facto segregation, it would also look at other values involved. Because the states had had such a poor record in protecting civil rights in general and those of people of color in particular, the Warren Court tended to look at national standards and reliance upon the federal government. Since then the Court has rediscovered federalism and strengthened its values.

One might have expected that by the 1970s, given the strong civil rights legacy left by the Warren Court, even a supposedly "conservative" Court would strike down any facially discriminatory laws that deprived persons of basic rights—such as voting—simply on the basis of race. What is surprising is that the Burger Court went beyond this level, and struck down practices that, even if not adopted for discriminatory "intent," had a disproportionate "impact" on minority groups. The Court held that while the Constitution prohibits intentional discrimination, civil rights statutes went further, and barred discriminatory effects from neutral laws as well. As could be expected, the initial unanimity of the Court on this issue dissolved as the cases grew more complex.

The Court found clear evidence of discriminatory impact in *Griggs v. Duke Power Company* (1971), a case growing out of Title VII, the employment discrimination section of the 1964 Civil Rights Act. The chief justice spoke for a unanimous bench in interpreting the statute as prohibiting employers from imposing general intelligence tests or requiring a high school diploma when such tests had no relevance to job requirements and effectively disadvantaged black applicants. The law, he explained, "proscribes not only overt discrimination but also practices that are fair in form, but discriminatory in operation" *Griggs v. Duke Power Company* [1971], 431).

Although the Court's unanimity evaporated in subsequent cases, the basic principle of *Griggs* remained intact for more than two decades, not only in the courts, but also in regulations concerning federal hiring and funding. The decision validated statutory authority to attack facially neutral practices that had discriminatory impact; the Court, however, refused to expand the impact test to the constitutional level, and it made the distinction quite clear in another employment test case.

In *Washington v. Davis* (1976), black applicants challenged a verbal ability test that they claimed kept them off the District of Columbia police force. Because Title VII did not apply to the government, the black litigants asked the Court to make the impact criterion constitutional rather than just statutory. Justice White, speaking for a seven-to-two majority, refused to read *Griggs* as constitutional, that is, as a guarantee under the Fifth or Fourteenth Amendments. Title VII applied specifically to employment, while the expansive language of the equal protection clause could apply to any regulation or situation that disproportionately affected minorities. In his opinion, Justice White made it a point to state that racially disproportionate impact by itself did not violate the Constitution or civil rights statutes. The impact had to be in areas such as voting or employment specifically covered by the law. Moreover, unlike *Griggs*, in which the high school diploma requirement bore no relevance to the job, verbal skills for police officers met the Title VII standard.

Between the two cases one can pick out a strand that ran fairly consistently through the Burger years. If the plaintiffs could make out a case for intentional discrimination, then such action violated the constitutional promise of equal protection. If they could not show intent to discriminate, but could demonstrate a disproportionate impact of certain requirements on minorities, then they had a remedy under Title VII. Both cases reaffirmed the nation's commitment to merit and the idea that people ought to be able to compete for jobs on the basis of their ability. *Griggs* said that employment tests had to be fair and relevant to the jobs at issue and could not be a screen for discrimination. *Davis* upheld the validity of tests that were in fact relevant to the jobs sought. In such cases, the fact that a greater proportion of blacks than whites failed would not invalidate the tests.

The Burger Court's record disappointed some civil rights groups who wanted the Court to strike down any form of discrimination, whether de jure or de facto, and this far the Court would not go. The Court made it quite clear that it would not tolerate any form of de jure discrimination, and it gave Congress an extraordinarily broad reach of power under the Civil War Amendments to protect voting rights for both individuals and groups. Moreover, it also read Title VII quite extensively, and whether one wishes to read this as judicial deference to the legislature or commitment to equal rights, the result is the same. But not all discrimination is subject to legislative or constitutional remedy, nor is all "disproportionate impact" necessarily the result of discrimination. One might disagree with some of its distinctions, but in this area as in others, the Court under Warren Burger continued and expanded on the precedents set out under Earl Warren.

The Rehnquist Court and Equal Protection

In the opinion of some, the Rehnquist Court abandoned the high standards of equal protection established under Earl Warren and continued in the Burger years. Defenders of the Court believe that it has moved the nation toward what the civil rights movement had always declared to be its goal, a color-blind Constitution. Here again, the relatively straightforward questions confronting the Warren Court gave way to far more complex issues—ones that did not have the obvious answers that *Brown* or *Loving* did.

Where the Warren and Burger Courts had been heavily involved—critics said far too heavily involved—in the business of fashioning and implementing judicial remedies, the Rehnquist Court seemed to back off from judicial involvement in, and maintenance of, desegregation orders, possibly because by the 1990s it had become clear that as much desegregation had taken place that would occur without a major change in the nation's socioeconomic fabric. In *Missouri v. Jenkins* (1995), for example, the state of Missouri and the Kansas City school district were found to have operated a segregated school system within the district. A desegregation plan approved by the federal district court required expenditures of $450 million, but various state laws prevented the school district from raising taxes to finance its 25 percent of the costs. The district court judge thereupon ordered a significant increase in the local property taxes despite the state limitations.

Justice White found the district court's actions exceeded its authority, as well as the principles of federal-state comity. The judge, instead of raising taxes on his own authority, should have ordered the school board to do so. White held that the difference involved more than just form. Authorizing and even ordering the school board to act placed the responsibility for implementation on local authorities, where it belonged. Courts should only involve themselves directly as a last resort, and here other options existed.

The Rehnquist Court not only opposed excessive judicial intervention, but it also wanted to end long-term judicial involvement. In the 1950s and 1960s federal courts entered hundreds of decrees ordering local schools to desegregate. As years passed and overt resistance faded, should the decrees stay in force? What happened if the demographic profile of the school district changed? At what point could one say that a decree originally entered to remedy de jure segregation was no longer necessary?

The Court faced these questions in *Board of Education v. Dowell* (1991). At the time of *Brown*, Oklahoma City had operated a segregated school system. In 1971 the district court ordered systemwide busing as a remedy, and it seemed to work, producing significant integration. As a result, in 1977 the court entered an order terminating the case and its jurisdiction. Then in 1984, as a response to changing demographics, the school board introduced a plan for neighborhood schools for grades kindergarten through fourth, although allowing any student to transfer from a school in which he or she was in the majority to one in which he or she would be in the minority. A year later opponents challenged the plan, claiming it would reintroduce segregation, because very few students would avail themselves of the chance to transfer. The district court refused to reopen the case; the court of appeals reversed, holding that the 1972 decree remained in force and imposed a duty on the school system not to take any steps that might reintroduce segregation.

The Supreme Court disagreed. Chief Justice Rehnquist declared that orders entered in desegregation cases had never been intended to be permanent, and common sense dictated that such orders be dissolved after local authorities had operated in compliance for a reasonable period of time. If the board's new plan violated equal protection, then it should be evaluated under the proper criteria, but not under a decree issued in a different time and under different circumstances.

Justice Marshall, the last remaining member of the Warren Court, joined by Blackmun and Stevens, dissented, and complained that the majority had suggested that after sixty-five years of official segregation, thirteen years of desegregation was enough. But the dissenters seemed to ignore the fact that conditions in Oklahoma City had changed significantly between 1972 and 1984, as well as the fact that in many cities, civil rights groups had begun demanding a return to local schools with greater parental involvement and control. The majority had not said that outright discrimination would be ignored, but merely that a new situation had to be freshly reviewed, and if it violated established equal protection analysis, then a remedy could be imposed.

The following year, however, in a decision hailed by civil rights groups, the Court held that universities as well as primary and secondary schools had the same affirmative duty to dismantle dual school systems. Justice White relied heavily on statistics to find that Mississippi still operated a higher education system dominated by racially identifiable institutions. The state had argued that in higher education it had established a true freedom of choice, and therefore if whites went to predominantly white schools and blacks to predominantly black colleges, that represented individual choice and not de jure segregation. The entire Court rejected this argument, and mandated that the state had to take steps to do away with this racial separation in *United States v. Fordyce* (1992).

Looking at this record one can hardly claim that the Rehnquist Court had abandoned the legacy of *Brown*. Rather, four decades later the high Court would still move forcefully to strike down overt discrimination. But unlike the Warren Court, the justices of the 1990s felt less certain about the efficacy of judicial intervention, and more sensitive to the fact that de jure segregation could result from any number of demographic, economic, and social conditions that in and of themselves violated no constitutional mandate. The Rehnquist Court did not tolerate clear discrimination, but did not see it as the Court's business to resolve all of society's problems.

Affirmative Action

One of the thorniest inheritances of the Warren Court with which the Burger and Rehnquist Courts had to deal was the issue of affirmative action. We can look back now and see that it had always been a violation of equal protection to segregate schools and other public facilities by race; on reading *Brown* we are struck by the obviousness of its conclusion. Similarly, we can look at the early stages of the civil rights movements, and wonder why anyone ever questioned the rightness of demands for equal treatment without regard to skin color.

In the 1970s civil rights advocates, while still fighting overt discrimination, began to look at ways by which blacks could truly become equal members of society. The strategy they chose—affirmative action—became one of the most divisive issues in our society. The reasoning behind affirmative action is simple, perhaps even simplistic. Because society discriminated against blacks in so many ways for three hundred years, it is unrealistic to assume that mere removal of the old fetters made blacks suddenly equal and able to avail themselves of all opportunities. Rather, the analogy is of a runner kept in prison, without adequate food or exercise, and then expected to compete in the race. Just as no one would consider that a fair race, the argument went, then how could blacks, having been held down for so long, be expected to compete against whites on an equitable basis? Something had to be done to compensate for prior discrimination, so that in the future blacks could take full advantage of equal opportunities.

The answer would be programs granting some preference to blacks to help them overcome the effects of prior discrimination. Colleges would establish different admissions criteria for minority groups, and employers would make special efforts to recruit minority members and even hold a certain percentage of jobs aside for them. The most significant affirmative action step came in Executive Order 11246, promulgated by Lyndon Johnson and then greatly strengthened by Richard Nixon. It required federal contractors to take affirmative steps to hire more women and minorities, or run the risk of being barred from future government work.

On the surface affirmative action seemed an expeditious solution, but in fact it forced society to make some very difficult choices. In the analogy of the runner, one could either postpone the race until the runner regained strength, or handicap the other runners to compensate for the weakened condition of the one runner. Jobs, however, differ from races; if you give preferential treatment to one group, you penalize another. If giving a job to a black man that might have gone to a white person helped the black overcome a heritage of persecution, who paid for it? The white person denied a job may never have discriminated against blacks; his ancestors may not even have come to this country until after the end of slavery. One can talk about the collective guilt of white society, or the general disadvantaging of blacks, but in the end individuals pay the price. What some people called affirmative action others called reverse discrimination.

The issue first came before the Court in 1974, and the Court ducked. Marco DeFunis had been accepted by several law schools, but he wanted to live and practice in Seattle, and the University of Washington Law School had twice turned him down. The school had a separate admissions process for blacks, Chicanos, Indians, and Filipinos, and DeFunis learned that of the thirty-seven minority candidates accepted for fall 1971, thirty-six had combined test and grade scores below his. Believing federal courts too sympathetic to minorities, DeFunis sued in state court on claims of racial bias. He won, and the trial court ordered him admitted to the law school. By the time the case reached the Supreme Court, DeFunis had been attending law school, and would graduate regardless of the outcome. Five members of the Court declared the question moot in *DeFunis v. Odegaard*, and thus postponed having to decide the substantive issues surrounding affirmative action.

Four justices dissented, arguing that the constitutionality of special admissions programs ought to be resolved. However, only Justice Douglas reached the merits, and declared that even benign racial classifications violated the Constitution. The entire Douglas opinion, as law professor and later circuit court judge Harvie Wilkinson described it, "was a celebration of individualism, a Thoreauvian remonstrance against the powerful homogenizing forces of American life" (Wilkinson 1979, 258). If we want to guess how the Warren Court might have decided this case, then one needs to note that the most activist and arguably the most liberal member of the Warren Court—perhaps the most liberal justice of the twentieth century—opposed affirmative action on the grounds that it ignored individual rights in the name of group rights, a concept foreign to American traditions of law.

The issue, of course, would not go away, and even as the Court evaded it in *DeFunis*, another white male, upset at his rejection from the medical school at the University of California at Davis, began a similar law suit. Davis, a relatively new school, took in one hundred students in its medical school each year. It reserved sixteen slots under a special admissions program for minority students, mainly blacks, Chicanos, and Asian Americans. Allan Bakke, a Vietnam veteran and now an aerospace engineer, wanted to be a doctor, and had been turned down twice at Davis. He then learned about the special admissions program, and that most of those admitted in the sixteen slots had poorer records and backgrounds than his. Bakke sued in state court, claiming the racial preference shown to minorities under the special admissions program violated his rights as guaranteed under federal and state law. He lost his bid for admission in the trial court, but on appeal to the California Supreme Court, normally considered one of the most liberal in the nation, Bakke won, and the court ordered his admission. The University appealed and the Supreme Court granted certiorari.

The Court's opinion came from Lewis F. Powell and did not have the full support of any other member of the Court. Powell flatly rejected the use of quotas, and noted that the Court had upheld racial quotas in only a few instances in which they supplied a discrete remedy to specified prior discrimination, as determined by an appropriate judicial, legislative, or executive authority. At Davis there had been no record of prior discrimination, and it exceeded the medical faculty's competence or authority to establish a remedial program. But the faculty was within its competence as an educational body in seeking to diversify the student body along as many lines as possible—including racial ones. To use race flexibly, within the context of a comprehensive admissions policy with an educational, rather than a societal, goal would be permissible. Therefore, the Davis plan failed, and he ordered Bakke admitted to the medical school; but Davis, and other colleges and universities, would be able to take race into account in admissions policies.

Four members of the Court took a strict statutory approach, holding that the Davis program violated Title VI of the 1964 Civil Rights Act, which prohibited discrimination against any person—that is, an individual—because of race, color, or national origin in any institution or program receiving federal assistance. They supported Powell's conclusion that Bakke should be admitted, but refused to go along with his view that race could be a factor in admissions. Four other justices agreed that race could be a factor in admissions, and did not believe that the Davis program violated either Title VI or the Fourteenth Amendment; they dissented from ordering Bakke's admission.

The Burger Court never really resolved the question of affirmative action, and while it upheld some plans but not others, it failed to develop a useful test for when preferences would be acceptable. The Reagan administration opposed affirmative action except when actual harm to specific individuals could be shown, and by 1990 the Rehnquist Court had all but shut off any constitutional justification for preferential programs. (Private companies, it should be noted, continued to utilize affirmative action in the belief that a more diverse work force made more sense in the context of an increasingly diverse populace.)

It is difficult to gauge what the Warren Court would have done. Douglas, as noted, opposed affirmative action, as did White; it is a safe bet that had Black lived longer, he too would have been against preferential programs. Brennan and Marshall remained the chief proponents of affirmative action on the high Court, and theirs became increasingly lone voices. Unfortunately, no bright-line test such as the Warren Court was able to use in evaluating straight-out de jure segregation exists to apply to the affirmative action morass.

The Reagan appointees to the high Court opposed affirmative action, and the justices in the last years of Warren Burger's tenure had begun backing away from the strong statements made in 1970s cases. In the last affirmative action case heard by the Burger Court, *Wygant v. Jackson Board of Education* (1986), the justices began to dismantle the judicial basis for minority preference programs. The Jackson, Michigan, school board, in the face of considerable racial tension, had negotiated a contract with the teachers union that in the case of layoffs, seniority would be the guiding rule, but that the percentage of minority personnel (often the last hired) laid off would not exceed the percentage of minorities in the system. As a result of the agreement, during two layoffs in 1976–1977 and 1981–1982, the school administration retained minority teachers while letting go nonminority teachers with greater seniority. The white teachers sued, not only under Title VII but also under other civil rights statutes, as well as the equal protection clause of the Fourteenth Amendment, which established a high level of scrutiny for racial classification.

Justice Powell spoke for a fragmented Court. Only Chief Justice Burger and Justice Rehnquist joined his opinion fully, while Justices White and O'Connor concurred. Because the challenge relied in part on equal protection claims, the school board had to show a compelling state purpose and a means narrowly tailored to meet that goal. Because the school board itself had not caused discrimination, its broad purpose of providing role models for minority students failed the test. While race might be a factor in attempting to remedy past discrimination, the plan had to address discrimination that the agency had itself caused. A legitimate seniority system could not be trumped by an affirmative action program absent this showing of specific discrimination.

Very shortly the roof seemed to fall in on affirmative action. First the Court backtracked on two decades of precedent. Ever since the case of *Griggs v. Duke Power Co.* in 1971, the Court had permitted statistical evidence of racial imbalance to support a charge of discrimination under Title VII, even if the hiring practices appeared facially neutral. If an imbalance existed, the employer had the burden of proving that the disparity had been caused by the circumstances of the business and not by discrimination. But by a five-to-four vote in *Ward's Cove Packing Co. v. Antonio* (1989), the Court gave companies accused of discrimination an important procedural victory by shifting the burden of proof from the employer to the employee.

The Court then dealt two devastating blows against affirmative action plans. The first involved an archetypical consent decree in Birmingham, Alabama. In response to a discrimination suit by blacks against the city, a federal district court had approved two consent decrees in which the city agreed to hire more African American firefighters, and to arrange promotion goals for them. The court also ruled as untimely efforts by a white firefighters' union as well as some individual white firemen to intervene in the case. A group of other white firemen who had not been involved in the earlier suit then sued the city under Title VII, claiming they had been denied promotions in favor of less qualified blacks. The city admitted it had made race-conscious decisions, but that such decisions had been permitted—indeed required—under the consent decree and were therefore immune from this type of attack.

The Supreme Court disagreed in *Martin v. Wilks* (1989). Chief Justice Rehnquist rejected the idea that a court-approved consent decree cut off the constitutional rights of those who had not even been a party to the negotiations. The decision raised alarms all over the country in cities that had signed consent decrees in response to antidiscrimination suits. In nearly all of these situations some people had not been party to the agreement and might have been adversely affected by it. Under *Wilks* any such person could attack the decrees as impinging on his or her rights, and then tie up the municipal government for years in expensive and time-consuming litigation. Facing such a threat, local governments would be loath to enter into consent decrees that, instead of reducing their liability to lawsuit, might actually increase the risk.

That same year the Court voided a Richmond, Virginia, set-aside program for minority businesses that had been modeled on the federal program. Congress had established set-asides when it had determined the existence of long-term and widespread discrimination in the construction industry, and had required that prime contractors on federally financed construction projects subcontract 10 percent of the work to minority-owned businesses. The Burger Court had approved the set-asides in *Fullilove v. Klutznick* (1980), ruling that Congress had sufficient evidence of discrimination and ample power under the Fourteenth Amendment to enact such remedial legislation.

Following that decision, many state and local governments established similar programs. Richmond, which is 50 percent black, approved a local ordinance in 1983 calling for at least 30 percent of all city-financed prime contracts to go to minority businesses. The problem was that unlike Congress, which held investigatory hearings to establish the existence and extent of discrimination, the city council, which was dominated by minorities, developed no evidence of bias in the area construction industry other than noting that few blacks belonged to the local employer trade groups. The one bit of hard evidence showed that over the previous five years minority contractors had received less than 1 percent of the city's prime contracts. When the J. A. Croson Company could not find a minority business that met the city's bonding requirements, it had a contract for plumbing fixtures taken away for rebidding. Croson sued under Section 1983 of the Civil Rights Act, charging reverse discrimination.

In *Richmond v. J.A. Croson Co.* Justice O'Connor, for a six-to-three majority, held that the city had not proved a case of prior discrimination, and that its 30 percent quota bore no relation to any of the facts submitted in support of the set-aside. "An amorphous claim that there has been past discrimination in a particular industry cannot justify the use of an unyielding racial quota" *Richmond v. J.A. Croson Co.* [1989], 499). Unlike the federal government, which had specific power under the enforcement clause of the Fourteenth Amendment, racial preference programs undertaken by state and local governments are subject to a strict scrutiny standard, the highest criterion used by courts in racial classification cases.

A close reading of *Croson* indicates that it did not, as many opponents of affirmative action claimed, put an end to set-asides. Rather, Justice O'Connor made clear that in order for a set-aside to withstand judicial scrutiny, a solid factual basis must underlie a record of prior discrimination that the set-aside addressed. To highlight the difference between the national government and state and local programs, the following year the Court upheld the federal government's power under the Fifth and Fourteenth Amendments to authorize set-aside programs in allocating television and radio licenses in *Metro Broadcasting Inc. v. FCC* (1990).

Five years later, however, the Court reversed itself in *Adarand Constructors, Inc. v. Pena* (1995). Justice O'Connor, speaking for a highly splintered Court, held that under the Fifth and Fourteenth Amendments' due process clauses, any action involving racial classification, including set-asides, by *either* the states or the federal government would be judged by a standard of strict scrutiny. The greater leeway that the courts had hitherto allowed Congress in affirmative action programs no longer existed. Just as the courts frowned on measures that discriminated because of race, they would now frown with equal fervor on measures that favored on the basis of race. O'Connor again made it clear that this did not make all affirmative action programs automatically unconstitutional; rather the government—be it Congress, the state, or a municipality—would have to show a record of actual prior discrimination in order to justify a narrowly tailored plan.

Nearly five decades after the Court handed down its historic decision in *Brown v. Board of Education* and four decades after the Civil Rights and Voting Rights Acts became law, the mood of the country had shifted significantly. A poll around the time of the *Adarand* decision found that 77 percent of the people surveyed believed that affirmative action programs discriminated against whites; even 66 percent of the black respondents answered the same way.

The legal and political future of affirmative action seemed questionable. A ballot measure in California barred state universities from using race as a factor in admissions. In 1996 the Fifth Circuit Court of Appeals struck down the University of Texas affirmative action plan that favored black and Hispanic minorities. In *Hopwood v. Texas*, the appeals court told the University of Texas law school that it could not use admission standards for minority students different from those it used for white students, a ruling that appeared to run contrary to *Bakke*. The university then appealed to the Supreme Court, which refused to hear the case, thus leaving the Fifth Circuit decision in place. The immediate result of the California initiative and of *Hopwood* was a sharp decline in the number of minority students in the premier public universities in Texas and California. Both states found this situation unacceptable, and began seeking some other means to attract minorities. The Texas legislature changed the admissions procedure, providing that the top 10 percent of graduating high school seniors would be automatically admitted to the University of Texas. In California the number of blacks and Hispanics in higher education has stabilized, and while fewer may attend Berkeley or UCLA, many more are attending the second-tier schools.

Gender Discrimination

One final area of equal protection that we might note is that of gender, although here the influence of the Warren Court is, at best, indirect. The Warren Court, for all its expansive rulings on equal protection, ignored complaints against discrimination on the basis of sex. Through the Nineteenth Amendment, women had achieved the right to vote and nothing more; evidently the "persons" mentioned in the Fourteenth Amendment remained solely male. As late as 1961, a unanimous Warren Court in *Hoyt v. Florida* upheld a Florida statute excusing women from jury duty because the state could rationally find that it should spare women from this obligation in light of their place at "the center of home and family life" (*Hoyt v. Florida* [1961], 62).

The Burger Court, consisting of a majority supposedly appointed because of their devotion to judicial restraint and strict construction, attacked gender discrimination in a manner similar to its predecessor's assault on racial bias. While the Court did not always measure up to the demands of more militant feminists, the decisions it handed down on equal protection and reproductive choice completely transformed the legal landscape for women.

Until 1971 courts used a two-tiered analysis to evaluate equal protection claims. If the Court considered the rights involved as fundamental, or the legislation affected "suspect" classifications, then the courts applied strict scrutiny. (Suspect classifications are those usually immutable characteristics of people—such as race or national origin—that have engendered discrimination against them in the past.) To survive this rigorous review, the legislature had to have a compelling interest, the classification had to be necessary and relevant to accomplishing the objective, and the means had to be narrowly tailored to the goal. In all other equal protection cases, the legislation merely had to have a rational relationship to a permissible goal. Thus, in the Florida grand jury case, women were not a suspect group nor did the Court view a fully gender-representative grand jury as a fundamental right. Therefore, excusing women from grand jury service rationally served the state's permissible goal of fostering a wholesome family life.

The change began in 1971 when Chief Justice Burger spoke for a unanimous Court in *Reed v. Reed*, invalidating an Idaho law giving men preference over similarly situated women as administrators of decedent estates. While refusing to make gender a suspect classification akin to race, for the first time the Court had struck down a gender classification under the equal protection clause.

The early twentieth century comic character Mr. Dooley commented that the "Court follows the election returns," meaning that the justices are not totally oblivious nor immune to major social, political, and economic changes in our society. *Brown* may have struck the South as radical, but looking back one can see it as part of the broad attack on racial discrimination that emerged from the war against Hitler. The justices deciding the *Reed* case could hardly avoid news about the women's movement, either in their morning papers or evening telecasts. Moreover, Congress in 1963 had passed the Equal Pay Act, mandating equal pay for equal work, and the following year in Title VII of the Civil Rights Act had prohibited employment discrimination on the basis of race, religion, national origin, or sex.

Women looked to the civil rights experience and learned greatly from it. They quickly adopted various practices such as protest marches and boycotts to draw attention to inequities, and then utilized the NAACP Legal Defense Fund's strategy of going after specific forms of discrimination in the courts. The Warren Court, in reflecting and shaping the great drama of civil rights, had resurrected the Fourteenth Amendment's equal protection clause. The Burger Court responded to the women's movement, including its decision in the most controversial case of the twentieth century, *Roe v. Wade* (1973), upholding a woman's right to procure an abortion. If some advocates of women's rights thought that the Burger Court should have gone further, the fact remains that if we compare its decisions with the base it inherited from the Warren Court, the Burger Court rulings laid the foundation for a jurisprudence that looks at gender classification with a skeptical eye, and questions whether laws have a legitimate purpose or are merely furthering outmoded stereotypes and prejudice. The Rehnquist Court went even further; it did not hand down a single decision against equal protection for women, and beyond that, defined the jurisprudence on sexual harassment.

Women won their first battle before the Rehnquist Court in 1991 in *United Automobile Workers v. Johnson Controls*. The company operated thirteen factories making different types of batteries. Current medical knowledge recognizes that exposure to lead by women of child-bearing age may adversely affect a fetus should pregnancy occur. Men are evidently not similarly affected by lead exposure, and there appears no danger of their offspring becoming deformed. At the time of the case, there was no feasible technology to make batteries without lead, and so to avert potential lawsuits of the type initiated by asbestos workers in the 1980s, Johnson Controls adopted a policy of not employing women in jobs involving lead exposure. These jobs, however, were among the better paying in the plant, and women workers sued on the basis of alleged gender discrimination under Title VII of the 1964 Civil Rights Act. The Court unanimously struck down the company policy. Justice Blackmun, writing for the Court, declared women to be as capable of men in doing the jobs, and the decision about the welfare of future children should be left "to the parents who conceive, bear, support, and raise them rather than to the employers who hire those parents" (*United Automobile Workers v. Johnson Controls* [1991], 206).

The next issue to come before the Court involved peremptory challenges to women jurors solely on the basis of gender. In *Batson v. Kentucky* (1986), the Court had struck down peremptory challenges in jury selection when race had been the sole factor; people could not be dismissed arbitrarily solely because of their skin color. In *J.E.B. v. Alabama ex rel. T.B.* (1994), the Court extended that ban against gender challenges. Justice Blackmun wrote for the majority and condemned the stereotyping of women that lay behind the practice, and as Justice O'Connor pointed out in her concurrence, "We know that like race, gender matters. A plethora of studies make clear that in rape cases, for example, female jurors are somewhat more likely to convict than male jurors" (*J.E.B. v. Alabama ex rel. T.B.* [1994], 148–149).

The biggest victory women's rights activists won before the Rehnquist Court involved one of the icons of Southern culture, the Virginia Military Institute (VMI), which since its founding had been an all-male institution noted for its rigorous discipline. VMI is a state-supported school, and when women applied there, they were rejected. Moreover, Virginia offered no comparable military education to women. The school claimed that its goal of producing citizen-soldiers and its tough disciplinary methods were not suited to women; in particular, it pointed to the Spartan barracks, the "adversative model" of training in which indignities are heaped on "rats" or first-year students, and the lack of privacy. The state offered and in fact set up what it claimed was a comparable training program designed for women at another school, but none of these arguments influenced the Court.

Justice Ruth Bader Ginsburg, who had argued many of the gender discrimination cases before the Burger Court, delivered the Court's opinion in *United States v. Virginia* (1996), in which she ruled that the Commonwealth of Virginia had deprived women of equal educational opportunity, and ordered VMI to open its doors to women students. Ginsburg spent a fair amount of her opinion elaborating on the Court's criteria. Although gender did not constitute a suspect classification subject to strict scrutiny standards, it did merit a heightened scrutiny. For Virginia to support its men-only policy, it had to demonstrate an "exceedingly persuasive justification." Moreover, the burden of proof rests upon the state to meet this high standard. In the case of VMI, Virginia had failed.

Even though the Court has not elevated gender to a suspect category, decisions regarding women took on many of the aspects of the racial classification cases. Out-and-out discrimination affronted the Court no matter who the victim. The Court also recognized that some forms of invidious discrimination cannot be reached by either the equal protection clause or civil rights legislation, and for all their boldness in some areas, the Burger and Rehnquist Courts remained far more sensitive to the limits of judicial power than had the Warren Court. If one can find confusion in some of their equal protection decisions, one can find the same confusion in society over these issues.

The Legacy of Warren Court Equal Protection

Finally, one has to ask whether the Warren Court decisions actually made a difference in the status and condition of the one out of every eleven Americans who is black. The answer to this is far from simple.

Nearly a half-century after the Court handed down its historic decision in *Brown v. Board of Education*, it is unclear how much the decision accomplished in improving the education of African Americans. There is no question that legalized segregation has disappeared. Walk through any Southern town or city, even in the Deep South, and one sees blacks and whites intermingling, shopping in the same stores, seated side by side at lunch counters, and standing in line to vote. At schools that die-hard segregationists vowed would remain all white, students now gather at football and basketball games to cheer on black athletes. Where the face of Southern law and order had once been overwhelmingly white, today one finds black sheriffs, judges, city officials, and state legislators; in 1989 Virginia elected a black governor. The minuscule black middle class that existed at the time of *Brown* has now grown prodigiously, and approximates in terms of percentages that of whites.

But what about school desegregation? The greatest progress seemed to have taken place between 1968 and 1980, a direct result of both the Warren Court decisions and the decision by Congress to withhold federal funds from schools that refused to desegregate. The percentage of black students in public schools that were more than 90 percent minority declined from 62.9 percent in 1968 to 34.8 percent in 1980 and to 34.1 percent in 1992. The percentage of white students in schools 90 percent or more non-Hispanic white declined in the same period as well—77.8 percent in 1968, 60.9 percent in 1980, and 48.9 percent in 1992. Progress toward desegregation since then has been glacial.

The greatest change, of course, came in the South. In 1954 100 percent of black children in the South attended predominantly black schools; by 1968 this had dropped to 77.5 percent of black students, while 68.8 percent of white students still went to predominantly white institutions. These percentages fell sharply in the 1970s to 24.6 and 32.2 percent respectively, and then dipped only slightly afterwards. By contrast, the percentage of blacks in the Northeast who went to predominantly black schools rose these years from 42.7 percent in 1968 to 49.9 percent in 1992. In big cities like New York, Philadelphia, and Washington, most black children attend predominantly black schools.

In part the overwhelmingly black nature of public schools in big cities throughout the country is due to the growth of suburbs and so-called white flight, as financially able white parents either moved out of the cities or placed their children in private schools. In Summerton, South Carolina, where the Legal Defense Fund began its battles in the 1940s, the public schools in 1979—a quarter-century after *Brown*— were almost entirely black; one white student went to school with 2,029 blacks. The other white students went to the private Clarendon Academy or schools outside of town. When a reporter asked Harry Briggs, the plaintiff in *Briggs v. Elliot*, one of five cased decided jointly *as Brown v. Board of Education*, what he had accomplished, he replied, "Nothing!"

But the story is not all one-sided. Black teenagers are staying in school longer, and are almost as likely to complete high school as their white peers. This has led to a rapid rise in the number of blacks attending public colleges and universities, as well as the expansion of a black middle class. Nor should one discount the psychological value of an educational system that no longer systematically classifies blacks as second-class citizens.

The extent of change, especially in the South, has been phenomenal, but at the turn of the century the debate is not over legalized apartheid, but whether black children would be better off in primarily black schools. Many black intellectuals doubted the virtues of desegregated schools, despite the fact that the achievement scores of black students have risen far more significantly in integrated schools than in predominantly black schools. Black students in desegregated schools are more likely to stay out of trouble with the law, avoid out-of-wedlock pregnancy, and go on to college. Critics, however, claim that these achievements are class related. Most of the children attending desegregated schools come from middle-class homes, while poorer children go to predominantly black urban schools or small country schools.

Behind the debate over the effects of desegregation looms a larger question, and that is whether courts can, in fact, initiate social change. There is no question that the Warren Court's decisions in *Brown* and its progeny led to the end of legalized segregation, but the record is far from clear whether the end result will be the better education of black children, nominally the reason the NAACP went to court as well as the chief justification for the *Brown* decision. Much of the debate in the 1980s and 1990s over the efficacy of courts acting as agents of change grew out of the efforts to make, as the first Justice Harlan put, a Constitution that is truly color-blind.

It was perhaps inevitable that *Brown* raised hopes it could not fulfill. No one case—not even a series of cases—could overcome the deep-seated racism that has become institutionalized in American society. Jack Greenberg, who worked with Thurgood Marshall on *Brown* and who succeeded him as head of the Legal Defense Fund, wrote on the fortieth anniversary of the landmark decision that "altogether, school desegregation has been a story of conspicuous achievements, flawed by marked failures, the causes of which lie beyond the capacity of lawyers to correct. Lawyers can do right, they can do good, but they have their limits. The rest of the job is up to society." One can substitute "courts" for "lawyers," and the conclusion is still the same.

The Burger Court and Speech

The Warren Court, despite some notable decisions expanding freedom of expression, had never developed a comprehensive First Amendment jurisprudence. The Burger Court thus inherited a variety of precedents without the luxury, as it were, of a specific theory that it could either advance or reject. The noted First amendment scholar Thomas Emerson complained that at various times the Warren Court had used such diverse tests as bad tendency, clear and present danger, incitement, a variety of ad hoc balancings, vagueness, overbreadth, and prior restraint, but it had "totally failed to settle on any coherent approach" (Emerson 1970, 15–16). In analyzing the Warren Court's impact, especially in First Amendment areas, it must be understood that some issues, such as the intractable obscenity problem, may just not be amenable to simple formulas.

The major speech issue confronting the Warren Court had been sedition, and there the justices had a string of precedents dating back to 1919, as well as extensive academic commentary, upon which to rely. The Burger Court did not have to deal with sedition, because the Warren Court had settled that issue; but in other areas it did try to develop standards and rationales to guide lower courts. Its legacy is a mixed record of success and failure.

Some speculated following the Warren Court's ruling in *Stanley v. Georgia* (1969), that if a person could not be prosecuted for possession and viewing pornographic materials at home, then there could be no basis for any obscenity legislation. Although Justice Marshall had insisted that *Stanley* had not impaired *Roth v. United States*, some commentators and lower court judges assumed that *Stanley* had in fact brought obscenity within the ambit of First Amendment protection. After all, if one had a right to possess obscene materials, it seemed a logical corollary that someone else had a right to supply those items.

An opinion by Justice White for a six-to-three Court in *United States v. Reidel* (1971) reaffirmed the vitality of *Roth*. "To extrapolate from Stanley's right to have and peruse obscene material in the privacy of his own home a First Amendment right in Reidel to sell it to him would effectively scuttle *Roth*, the precise result that the *Stanley* opinion abjured" (*United States v. Reidel* [1971], 35). The Court had upheld First Amendment rights to read and think in one's own home; Reidel also had that right, but not the right to go out and sell the material. In case anyone missed the point, White reiterated that "*Roth* has squarely placed obscenity and its distribution outside the reach of the First Amendment and they remain there today. *Stanley* did not overrule *Roth*" (*United States v. Reidel* [1971], 356).

Reidel was a transitional case between the Warren and Burger Courts. Not only did the two new members (Burger and Blackmun) join Justice White's opinion, but so did Harlan, Stewart, and Brennan, while Marshall, the author of *Stanley*, concurred in the result. Only Black and Douglas dissented on their usual grounds of First Amendment absolutism. After fifteen years of obscenity cases, the Warren Court had reached the "threshold of the conclusion" that the First Amendment prohibited regulation of obscene materials for consenting adults. But as free speech scholar Harry Kalven noted, the Burger Court "was not quite ready to take the final step across that threshold" (Kalven 1988, 47–48). It never did take that step, as the two next appointees helped form a new majority on the bench. Lewis Powell and William Rehnquist, along with Burger and Blackmun, joined with Justice White, one of the dissenters in the *Memoirs* case. The five undertook what Chief Justice Burger called a reexamination of the issue in an effort to articulate a clearer definition of what constituted obscenity, and how far First Amendment protection went. They also wanted to settle the question as quickly as possible, so that the high Court could get out of the business of determining whether particular books or movies were pornographic.

There is no question but that all the members of the Court were, by this time, thoroughly tired of dealing with the issue. As Justice Brennan noted, "No other aspect of the First Amendment has, in recent years, demanded so substantial a commitment of our time, generated such disharmony of views, and remained so resistant to the formulation of stable and manageable standards" (*Miller v. California* [1973], 73). The Court had also read the "Report of the U.S. Commission on Obscenity and Pornography" (1970). The Commission had been established by Congress in 1967 to investigate the impact of obscene materials on behavior. The majority of its members had concluded that erotica did not substantially alter patterns of sexual behavior, and that existing studies had failed to establish any significant link between erotica and sex crimes or attitudes on sexuality and sexual morality. The majority also recommended repealing laws prohibiting the sale of sexually oriented materials to consenting adults, but retaining regulations regarding display of the materials and their sale to minors. The report came under immediate criticism from conservative groups for its conclusions, and a number of scholars questioned the scope and quality of the empirical studies that the Commission had used. The Court's response to the report, as well as its own frustration in dealing with obscenity cases, surfaced in two cases handed down the same day in 1973. In fact, the Court handed down eight obscenity decisions that day, each dealing with a different substantive or procedural aspect of regulation. The two most important, which are discussed here, involved the rationale for state regulation, and a new definition of obscenity. The Court's majority there set out its rationale of why obscene materials could be regulated, as well as a new definition of what constituted obscenity.

Paris Adult Theatre I v. Slayton (1973) involved a Georgia civil proceeding to stop the showing of allegedly obscene films at so-called adult theaters. The evidence at the trial consisted primarily of the films and photographs of the theater entrance. The former depicted simulations of various sexual practices, while the latter showed a rather nondescript building with a sign reading "Atlanta's Finest Mature Feature Films." Chief Justice Burger categorically rejected the rationale of both *Stanley* and the Obscenity Commission majority report that there should be no regulation in the case of consenting adults, or that obscene material acquired some sort of constitutional immunity when directed toward consenting adults. While people could read or do whatever they wanted in the privacy of their homes, the state had a right to protect the quality of life for the rest of its citizens. The fact that the Commission had been unable to find any link between erotica and social behavior did not mean that it did not exist.

Burger's opinion set out a two-fold rationale for regulation, namely, that the state had a right to protect the quality of life from the debasing influence of obscene material, and that such material did, as the Commission's minority claimed, have a direct relation to antisocial behavior. He also reaffirmed that obscenity per se is unprotected by the First Amendment.

That left the problem of defining what constituted obscenity, and the chief justice turned to that task in the companion case of *Miller v. California*. He believed the Court had gone astray in the *Memoirs* case when a majority had insisted that for the state to prove obscenity, it had to show that the material in question was "utterly" without redeeming social value, a "burden virtually impossible to discharge." Burger acknowledged the difficulty of articulating standards, and warned that states could not use obscenity laws in a fashion that would impinge upon legitimate works of art that dealt with sexual themes. The basic guidelines for the trier of fact are, he declared: "(a) whether the 'average person, applying contemporary community standards' would find the work, taken as a whole, appeals to the prurient interest, (b) whether the work depicts or describes, in a patently offensive way, sexual conduct specifically defined by the applicable state law, and (c) whether the work, taken as a whole, lacks serious literary, artistic, political or scientific value" (*Miller v. California* [1973], 24).

Miller thus reaffirmed the basic elements of the *Roth* test, first enunciated by the Warren Court sixteen years earlier, and in fact the first part of the new test came directly from *Roth*. The second prong was also not new, but reaffirmed the "patently offensive" standard of *Manual Enterprises* and *Jacobellis*, with the addition of a due process standard that the state had to be specific in its definitions. It also limited regulation to hard-core pornography, another reflection of earlier Warren Court decisions.

The major departure proved the definitional section, which rejected the *Memoirs* standard of "utterly without redeeming social value," a standard that had never had the support of more than three justices at any one time. As with all such tests, it is subjective and involves value judgments by the trier of fact, but it seemed to allow a wide scope for permissible regulation. Because local rather than national standards would apply, the danger existed of parochialism and of an administrative patchwork in which items deemed acceptable in one state might be found obscene in another. The Court tried to avert this problem by requiring very specific definitions in the state legislation, but obscenity is in the eye of the beholder, and it is difficult to define objective criteria in so subjective an area. As Justice Douglas noted in his *Miller* dissent, the justices "deal with highly emotional, not rational, questions. To many the Song of Solomon is obscene" (*Miller v. California* [1973], 46).

The dissent of Justice Brennan in these two cases is worth examining, because he had been the author of the *Roth* and *Memoirs* test. Unlike Douglas and Black, who had consistently opposed any and all censorship as violations of the First Amendment, Brennan had begun his intellectual odyssey committed to the idea that obscenity did not enjoy First Amendment protection. During the Warren years he had tried to fashion a workable test that would protect legitimate artistic expression while excluding pornographic materials, and in *Miller* he admitted his failure. "I am convinced," he said, "that the approach initiated 16 years ago in *Roth v. United States*, and culminating in the Court's decision today, cannot bring stability to this area of the law without jeopardizing fundamental First Amendment values, and I have concluded that the time has come to make a significant departure from that approach" (*Miller v. California* [1973], 73–74).

The majority opinion, Brennan argued, did not constitute a new approach, but merely continued down the futile trail of trying to establish a workable definition of obscene material that would then be subject to regulation. Every effort at definition he warned, would either be too vague for consistent application, or so broad as to include clearly protected expression as well. He recommended adopting the proposals of the Commission on Obscenity that would do away with all regulations with the exception of those dealing with minors and unwilling audiences, the two groups whose protection justified state intervention.

It should be noted that Brennan did not argue that obscenity enjoyed First Amendment protection, or that the state had only a trivial interest in its regulation. Rather, his experience had convinced him that no way could be found to regulate obscenity for consenting adults without violating the First Amendment or creating an administrative and judicial morass.

If the Warren Court had failed in its efforts to define obscenity, its successors fared no better. In fact, one gets the impression that the whole purpose of *Miller* was to get obscenity cases off the Supreme Court's dockets. The Warren Court had taken dozens of cases because a majority of its members felt constrained to protect freedom of expression in an area without any clear guidelines. The more conservative justices of the 1970s believed that the states were better at the job of gauging public values than the courts, and they also recognized their inability to fashion judicially manageable standards.

The net result is that although obscenity cases are no longer heard by the high Court, the states have no better standards by which to try to control pornography than they had under the Warren Court. The general loosening of social morals in the 1970s left many state officials wondering whether it was worth the effort to use scarce police resources in closing down dirty book shops. Even the rise of the religious and social conservatives in the 1980s and early 1990s made little difference; in the most publicized of these cases, the suit against an Ohio museum for showing the works of Robert Maplethorpe, a jury quickly acquitted when art experts testified in defense of the pictures. And in 1996 when Congress tried to pass the Communications Decency Act to restrict pornographic materials on the Internet, a unanimous Supreme Court struck the law down as an infringement on the First Amendment in *Reno v. ACLU* (1997).

The one area in which the justices did seem to agree is that states had ample powers to prevent pornographers from victimizing children. From the beginning, the Burger Court viewed protection of children as a legitimate exercise of the state's police power. In *New York v. Ferber* (1982), a unanimous bench rejected a First Amendment challenge to a New York law prohibiting the distribution of material depicting children engaged in sexual conduct, whether the material as a whole was considered legally obscene or not. Justice White's opinion was refreshing in that he eschewed a doctrinal approach, and instead delivered a careful and persuasive exposition of society's interest in this type of regulation. The state had always had a special obligation to safeguard the physical and psychological well-being of minors. Distribution of child pornography, he explained, related to the problem of sexual abuse of children; in fact, the use of children as actors constituted a form of sexual abuse to which the state could respond. Here New York had carefully defined what it wanted to prohibit; it had a clear interest in protecting children, and the law did not impinge on constitutionally protected expression.

The Burger Court did far more in areas of free speech than merely rid itself of the troublesome problem of obscenity. In no instance did it narrow the scope of free expression, and in a number of areas it took First Amendment jurisprudence beyond the boundaries established under the Warren Court. In this as in other areas, the Warren Court laid the foundation and its successors began building the house.

Obscenity, along with libel and offensive speech, had long been held outside the pale of constitutional protection. In *Chaplinsky v. New Hampshire* (1942), Justice Frank Murphy had spoken of words "which by their very utterance inflict injury," and whose suppression may be justified by society's interest in order and morality. Murphy included not only "fighting words" that might provoke a breach of the peace, but also speech that offended moral sensibilities. The question of offensive speech did not arise during the Warren years, but the Burger Court dealt with the issue in several cases. The justices carefully avoided the definitional approach it used in the obscenity cases, and instead followed the more traditional balancing evaluation, comparing the First Amendment values of free speech to state interests in restraint.

The first case to come before the Warren Court arose from the Vietnam protests, with the arrest and conviction of Paul Cohen for wearing a jacket with the slogan "Fuck the Draft" in the corridors of a Los Angeles courthouse. The California Court of Appeals upheld the conviction, on grounds that the state had a legitimate purpose in trying to prevent violence, and it was "reasonably foreseeable" that others might be provoked to such action by these words. The Supreme Court disagreed, and by a five-to-four vote reversed the conviction in *Cohen v. California* (1971). The opinion of

Justice Harlan (one of the more conservative members of the Warren Court) is a skilled and lawyerly piece of work, in which precedent is maintained while First Amendment coverage is expanded.

In the obscenity cases the Burger Court majority openly acknowledged the state's interest in preserving a moral and decent environment, and it appeared willing to allow "community standards" to determine those values. In the offensive speech cases, however, it recognized often competing values, and the issue became one of balancing the rights of the speaker against the sensitivities of the audience, some of whom might be offended by the speech. Here again one can see the bedrock principles enunciated by the Warren Court, that free expression must always be the rule and restraint the exception, and when an exception occurs, the state must have a compelling necessity for its actions. In the last three decades of the twentieth century, the Court has consistently followed this rule; it is one of the lasting legacies of the Warren Court.

In still another example of how the Burger Court expanded upon the Warren Court base, it proved very sympathetic to speech related to property, and expanded First Amendment coverage to areas previously considered unprotected, such as commercial speech, or advertising. Years earlier, the Court had, in what Justice Douglas later called a "casual, almost offhand" manner, stated that the First Amendment imposed no "restraint on government as respects purely commercial advertising" (*Valentine v. Chrestensen* [1942], 54). In *Valentine*, the Court viewed advertising as a function of business, rather than of speech, and thus subject only to the rational basis test applied to economic regulation. This ruling did not mean that First Amendment protection evaporated in the presence of a commercial motive; the Warren Court in the *New York Times* case had specifically rejected that claim. But the distinction between commercial and noncommercial remained significant for thirty years after *Valentine*.

Then in 1975 the Court dramatically changed direction. In *Bigelow v. Virginia* the Court struck down a state statute making it a misdemeanor to publicize how one could secure an abortion. The Court did not totally abandon the *Valentine* doctrine, but noted that the ads, while "simply propos[ing] a commercial transaction . . . contained factual material of clear 'public interest'." Thus one could infer that commercial information on important issues might be differentiated from advertisements for cars or personal deodorants. In 1977 the Court followed a similar rationale in *Carey v. Population Services International*, striking down a ban against advertising the mail-order sale of contraceptives. The Court rejected New York's argument that the ads were offensive or embarrassing to many people, and said that speech dealing with "the free flow of commercial information" that reflected "substantial individual and societal interests," could not be suppressed because it offended some people.

The following year, in the landmark case of *Virginia Pharmacy Board v. Virginia Consumer Council* (1976), the Court squarely faced the commercial speech issue. Virginia law held pharmacists guilty of unprofessional conduct if they adver-tised the prices of prescription drugs. Because only pharmacists could dispense these drugs, nearly all of which were prepared by the manufacturers rather than the phar-macists themselves, the ruling in effect prevented consumers from securing any price information prior to having a prescription actually filled. The challenge to the law came not from the pharmacists, but from a consumer advocacy group that claimed a First Amendment right to drug price information.

Justice Blackmun, speaking for everyone except Justice Rehnquist, held that First Amendment protection covered the communication, "to its source and to its recipient both" (*Virginia Pharmacy Board v. Virginia Consumer Council* [1976], 756). Plainly the content here was not of the type previously considered within con-stitutional protection. The state had justified the regulation on the need to maintain high standards within the pharmacy profession, and while a laudable goal, it had cho-sen the device of suppressing information. This brought it into conflict with the First Amendment, which prohibits states not only from hindering the flow of political mes-sages but also of commercial information. Commercial speech, therefore, with some exceptions (such as false or deceptive advertising) enjoys the same protection as do other varieties of speech.

The Burger Court and a Free Press

In terms of freedom of the press, there is one great decision by the Warren Court, *New York Times v. Sullivan* (1964), hailed by the press as a modern Magna Carta. In that case the Court abandoned the old rules about libel and greatly expanded press freedom. The most famous press case of the Burger era involved the so-called Penta-gon Papers, in which the Court also struck a blow for press freedom, but did little more than reaffirm the most basic rule of the press clause, that government shall impose no prior restraint on publications.

In 1967 Secretary of Defense Robert S. McNamara ordered a full-scale evalua-tion of how the United States became involved in the Vietnam war. The study team of thirty-six persons took more than a year to compile the report, which ran to forty-seven volumes with some 4,000 pages of documentary evidence and 3,000 pages of analysis. Dr. Daniel Ellsberg, a former Defense Department economist who had grown disillusioned with the war, copied major portions of the study, and then turned them over to the press.

On Sunday, June 13, 1971, the *New York Times* began publication of the papers with that part of the analysis dealing with clandestine South Vietnamese raids against North Vietnam in early 1964. The study concluded that these raids had been carried out with American knowledge and support, and with the goal of provoking a North

Vietnamese response that could then be used to justify greater American involvement. The *Times* announced that it would continue publication of the material in daily installments.

The government went into U.S. district court in New York and secured a temporary injunction to prevent further publication, pending a full hearing. Although the *Times* had already appeared with the third article, it obeyed the injunction and did not publish further documents. It refused, however, to turn over the actual documents to the government. On the day the *Times* hearing began in New York, the *Washington Post* began publishing articles based on the purloined documents. The administration managed to secure a restraining order, but the *Boston Globe* then became the third paper to begin publication, with other newspapers around the country announcing that they too would run selections. With restraining orders and appeals and contradictory rulings rapidly multiplying, the Supreme Court agreed to take the case on an expedited basis.

On June 30, seventeen days after the *Times* had begun publication of the Pentagon Papers, the Court handed down its decision. By a six-to-three vote, it upheld the newspapers' right to publish the materials, and the following day papers all across the nation carried excerpts from the documents. Although there was disagreement on the rationale and despite the dissenting justices' complaint about the haste of the proceedings, all of the justices believed that the general rule mitigated against prior restraint. In fact, in a speech to the American Bar Association a week later, Warren Burger described the opinions in the case as "actually unanimous" (Woodward and Armstrong 1979, 174).

In many ways, this was true. All of the justices did believe in the basic doctrine, and with the sole exception of Black and Douglas, who took an absolutist stance, they all believed that circumstances might exist in which the government could, in fact, suppress certain types of information, provided an appropriate procedural mechanism existed to meet constitutional requirements. Had the case been argued ten years earlier it might have had a larger majority, but the results would not have been different. The Warren Court believed in a robust press, and while it had only a few cases with which to express that view, its press clause jurisprudence definitely affected subsequent Courts.

The question of prior restraint came before the high Court again in the context of a so-called gag order, issued by a trial judge in an effort to secure a fair trial. In *Nebraska Press Association v. Stuart* (1976), we see a problem that often comes before the Court, a conflict between rights, in this case the First Amendment freedom of the press and the Sixth Amendment guarantee of a fair trial.

In the small town of Sutherland, Nebraska (pop. 850), an unemployed handyman had been charged with raping a ten-year-old child, murdering her and five members of her family, and then sexually assaulting some of the dead children. It would have been a sensational trial any place, but in the small town the trial judge decided that only a gag order prohibiting the press from printing reports about the crime would make it possible to get an unbiased jury.

In this case the Court did not deal with questions of power claimed by another branch of government, but with the traditional authority trial judges have always exercised in their courtrooms to ensure fair trials. The press objected to the total ban imposed, which they claimed made no sense; they could not even report on statements made in open court at the pretrial hearing. People in the audience could discuss what had been said, but the press could not report it. All the members of the Court except Justice Rehnquist believed the trial judge had gone too far, because alternative methods existed to prevent contamination of the jury process without resorting to prior restraint, methods that the trial judge had not utilized.

The real division came not on whether this particular ban had been ill advised, but on whether there should be a total prohibition against gag rules. Chief Justice Burger's majority opinion took a strong First Amendment stance, holding that "prior restraint on speech and publication are the most serious and least tolerable infringement on First Amendment rights" (*Nebraska Press Association v. Stuart* [1976], 174). But while striking down the Nebraska ban, Burger did not want to go further in the Court's first case in this area; the law, he believed, ought to develop slowly and incrementally. Moreover, only a minority of the brethren had ever held First Amendment rights absolute; there might be circumstances in which gag orders would be appropriate.

Although a majority of the Court had eschewed inferring a "right to know" from the press clause, the *Nebraska Press* decision may be seen as the first step on the road to recognizing a variation of that idea, a right of access. All the various speech theories utilized by the Warren Court to explicate the First Amendment agreed that political speech occupied the highest rung of the ladder. The people and the press could not be limited in their discussion and publication of political issues, as intelligent discussion by the body politic constituted the core of democratic government. But for the citizenry to carry on intelligent discussion, they had to be informed about the issues, and obviously 200 million people could not descend on a presidential press conference or research the small print in Pentagon contracts. Here the press served as the surrogate for the people, securing the information that made intelligent discussion possible. As the surrogate, the argument ran, the press had a constitutionally protected right of access to places and documents relevant to the news.

This view emerged victorious in a seven-to-one decision in the landmark case of *Richmond Newspapers, Inc. v. Virginia* (1980), which held that absent some overriding interest, the trial of a criminal case must always be open to the public. The case arose in regard to the trial of John Paul Stevenson for the stabbing death of a hotel manager in 1975. The first trial had been overturned by the Virginia Supreme Court because of the improper admission of certain evidence; the second trial ended in a mistrial, as did the third. When the fourth trial began, the defense requested that the courtroom be closed, so as to make sure this trial went properly. The judge, who had presided over two of the previous trials, asked the prosecution if it had any objections, and when the prosecutor agreed to abide by whatever decision the judge made, he ordered the court cleared of everyone except the parties and witnesses. In the audience were two reporters, and their motion for admittance initiated the series of appeals that led to the high Court.

Chief Justice Burger delivered the Court's opinion, and his historical enquiry concluded that at the time the Sixth Amendment had been adopted, it had been the practice both in this country and in England for criminal trials to be open. But while the Sixth Amendment provided the basis for an open trial, the right to attend a trial was rooted in the First Amendment. There were few things more important to the people than the proper conduct of criminal trials, and the First Amendment protects the right of everyone to attend trials. As for press attendance, it made little difference, the Chief Justice declared, if one spoke of a right to gather news or a right of access, "the explicit, guaranteed rights to speak and to publish concerning what takes place at a trial would lose much meaning if access to observe the trial could [be] foreclosed arbitrarily" (*Richmond Newspapers, Inc. v. Virginia* [1980], 576–577).

In neither case did the Court go as far as the press would have liked. Although a majority of the justices in *Richmond Newspapers* agreed on a principle, they could not agree on a clear rule to enunciate that principle. In many ways the Burger Court was following through on the line set out by the Warren Court, and like its predecessor, it refused to give the press a totally free hand. While *New York Times v. Sullivan* seemingly freed the press from the threat of libel, in fact it did not do so. The Court allowed for some instances, such as when the press acted maliciously in printing information it knew to be false, in which it would remain subject to libel suits. Similarly, in the three major press cases it decided, the Burger Court allowed the press much greater freedom in news gathering, but did not make it an absolute freedom. It could print all the material it gained, even if through illicit sources, but the government could still impose a prior restraint if it could show national security needs. Reporters could not be arbitrarily excluded from a trial, but in the end the judge would determine if that was the best means available to ensuring a fair trial.

Not everyone was happy with the Burger Court decisions. One view is that the Court abandoned the commitment to open and robust journalism espoused in the Warren years, and instead took what Justice Stewart called a "crabbed view" of the press clause. Others might claim that the press was not only no worse off in 1986 than in 1969, but in fact enjoyed greater constitutional privileges, especially in matters of access. There is no clear answer, and how one views the record is very dependent on one's personal philosophy.

As in other areas, one might suggest that the Warren Court had the easy case, that while *Sullivan* certainly is a landmark decision, it took the high ground and never dealt with the more complicated issues that it generated. The Burger Court had to face the question of whether all libel law should be proscribed by the First Amendment, and it decided against this proposition. That we tolerate a high level of often scurrilous comment, and grant it First Amendment protection, would seem to indicate that the press is far from cowed, as Burger Court critics would infer. Certainly one of the early decisions of the Rehnquist Court indicated that the First Amendment and the *Sullivan* decision were alive and well. How else to explain the unanimous decision reversing the libel judgment against *Hustler Magazine* for its parody of the Reverend Jerry Falwell.

The Rehnquist Court and Free Speech

Hustler ran a spoof about Falwell, a well-known conservative minister and founder of a political organization called the Moral Majority. The spoof portrayed Falwell as a drunkard whose first sexual encounter took place with his mother in an outhouse. Just in case anyone missed the point that this had been intended as humor, small print at the bottom of the page warned the reader "Ad parody—not to be taken seriously." Falwell took it seriously, sued the magazine for libel, invasion of privacy, and intentional infliction of emotional distress, and won on the latter count. The magazine's publisher, Larry Flynt, appealed to the Supreme Court, where he won in a unanimous decision.

Speaking for the Court, Chief Justice Rehnquist acknowledged the gross nature of the parody, but declared that for the courts to define and penalize the outrageous would require some very difficult line drawing, and would allow juries to award damages on the basis of their personal dislikes of particular forms of expression. Protecting offensive and vulgar parodies may not be a pleasant task, Rehnquist admitted, but it had to be done to give the First Amendment "breathing space." Using a strongly historical argument, Rehnquist compared the *Hustler* parody to political cartoons portraying George Washington as a jackass or Abraham Lincoln as an ape. The *Hustler* case raised no new constitutional issues, but followed and reaffirmed the basic holding of *New York Times v. Sullivan*, showing once again the long reach of the Warren Court's landmark decisions.

The Court, in another strong affirmation of the First Amendment, struck down an ordinance banning cross burnings and other hate crimes. A St. Paul teenager, Robert A. Viktora, had burned a cross on the front lawn of a black family, and was charged under a city ordinance that prohibited any action "which one knows . . . arouses anger, alarm, or resentment in others on the basis of race, color, creed, religion, or gender." The Minnesota Supreme Court held that states retain their authority to prohibit expressive conduct "likely to provoke imminent lawless conduct," citing the U.S. Supreme Court decision in *Chaplinsky v. New Hampshire* (1942) that sustained restrictions on fighting words.

In *R.A.V. v. City of St. Paul* (1992), Justice Scalia, along with four of his colleagues, disagreed and noted that in any and all instances content-based restrictions on speech are presumptively invalid. The Court had carved out certain exceptions, such as obscenity, defamation, and fighting words, but the lower court had misunderstood those exceptions. Those areas are not by themselves constitutionally invalid, but depend on how they are applied. "Thus, the government may proscribe libel; but it may not make the further content discrimination of proscribing *only* libel critical of the government" (*R.A.V. v. City of St. Paul* [1992], 384).

The high Court tried to make clear, however, that cities and states did not stand defenseless before this type of conduct. "Let there be no mistake," Scalia wrote, "about our belief that burning a cross in someone's front yard is reprehensible. But St. Paul has sufficient means at its disposal [such as trespass laws] to prevent such behavior without adding the First Amendment to the fire" (*R.A.V. v. City of St. Paul* [1992], 384). The very next term the Court drew a sharp distinction between expression and expressive conduct protected by the First Amendment and conduct it considered criminal.

On an evening in October 1989 a group of young black men had gathered in an apartment in Kenosha, Wisconsin. Several of them began discussing a scene from the movie *Mississippi Burning* in which a white man beat a young black boy who was praying. The group moved outside, and Todd Mitchell asked them: "Do you feel hyped up to move on some white people?" Soon afterwards they saw a young white man approaching them on the other side of the street. Mitchell said "There goes a white boy; go get him." On Mitchell's urging they ran after the youth, beat him severely and stole his tennis shoes. The boy remained in a coma for four days.

A jury found Mitchell guilty of aggravated battery, an offense that normally carries a maximum sentence of two years. But because the jury found that Mitchell had selected his victim because of his race, the maximum was increased to seven years imprisonment. The judge sentenced Mitchell to four years, but an appellate court, relying on *R.A.V.* held that the statute that increased penalties if race, religion, and other group characteristics were involved, violated the First Amendment by punishing what the legislature deemed offensive thought.

In *Wisconsin v. Mitchell* (1993) Chief Justice Rehnquist, speaking for the entire Court, reversed and held that a defendant's motives in committing a crime had traditionally been a factor taken into account in sentencing. The battery had been a criminal act, and by identifying antagonisms based on race, color, religion, or gender as aggravating factors, the state had not violated the First Amendment. The decision permitted the state to enhance punishment for a crime motivated by the victim's race;

the law had been passed in the first place to protect blacks against racially motivated attacks. The Court believed that such violence, be it for race, religion, or gender, has a greater terrorizing effect on society than ordinary violence.

What about indecent speech? The Court had avoided any obscenity cases since the early 1970s, and in any event, it had always drawn a line between the "indecent" and the "obscene." The latter enjoyed little or no constitutional protection, while the former might well fit under the First Amendment's umbrella. In 1988 Congress amended the Communications Act to target so-called dial-a-porn, in which one could, for a fee, dial numbers that played prerecorded sexually oriented messages. In *Sable Communications, Inc. v. FCC* (1989), the Court, speaking through Justice White, struck down the restrictive provisions, but intimated that obscene communications could be limited. Similarly, in *Denver Area Educational Telecommunications Consortium v. FCC* (1996), the Court voided provisions of the 1992 Cable Television Consumer Protection and Competition Act that required cable companies to block certain indecent programs, and authorized the FCC to promulgate regulatory definitions.

Perhaps the biggest surprise came when the Court struck down the Communications Decency Act of 1996, in which Congress had made it a crime to send or display sexually explicit material in a manner available to anyone under eighteen years of age. The bill had barely been signed into law by President Clinton when the American Civil Liberties Union (ACLU) filed a suit in federal court to enjoin enforcement, and a three-judge district court struck down the law on a variety of grounds. The Justice Department, which had in effect admitted that the law violated the First Amendment, nonetheless appealed to the Supreme Court, primarily to appease politically powerful conservative groups.

In *Reno v. American Civil Liberties Union* (1997), Justice Stevens spoke for a unanimous court in sustaining the district court's invalidation of the law. In an opinion that clearly showed a far more sophisticated understanding of the Internet than Congress had displayed, Justice Stevens explained the impossibility of setting such restrictions on a new medium that one of the district court judges had described as "a never-ending worldwide conversation" and a "far more speech-enhancing medium than print, the village green or the mails" (929 F. Supp 824, 882). Stevens described the worldwide web as "a vast library including millions of readily available and indexed publications and a sprawling mall offering goods and services" *Reno v. American Civil Liberties Union* [1997], 853). Granted, there are sexually explicit materials on the web, some quite crude, but devices exist that can block these sites. The Court asserted that it is for parents, and not the government, to take the necessary steps to protect their children if they choose to do so. The very chaos of the web—its freedom—makes it impossible to control, for there is no single organization controlling membership in the web, nor any centralized point from which individual websites or services could be blocked. The Communications Decency Act, in trying to do the impossible, violated several key points of constitutional jurisprudence, including vagueness and overbreadth.

Flag Burning

For the most part, the Rehnquist Court took a decidedly speech-protective stance, especially when it has involved pure speech; it has also been solicitous of so-called speech plus, speech tied to some act, of which the most well-known cases involve the burning of the American flag. Next to the abortion decision, no cases generated as much public controversy as those decided by the Court in 1989 and 1990, both by five-to-four votes.

Gregory Lee Johnson, a member of the Revolutionary Communist Youth Brigade, had burned an American flag as part of a political protest during the 1984 Republican national convention in Dallas. A Texas jury convicted him under a state statute prohibiting the intentional desecration of a state or national flag. The Texas Court of Criminal Appeals reversed on First Amendment grounds, and the Supreme Court affirmed.

Justice Brennan wrote for himself, Marshall, Blackmun, Scalia, and Kennedy, and he kept the decision as narrow in its scope as possible. Did the burning of the flag constitute expressive conduct? This was an easy question to answer because the state admitted that it did. If expressive conduct, was it of the type to fall under the First Amendment's protection of political expression? The majority found that it did, and that First Amendment values outweighed the state's argument that it needed to protect the symbol of national unity or that it deeply offended people nearby. "If there is a bedrock principle underlying the First Amendment," Brennan wrote, "it is that the Government may not prohibit the expression of an idea simply because society finds the idea itself offensive or disagreeable" (*Texas v. Johnson* [1989], 414). No one in the majority approved of the action, and as Justice Kennedy noted in a concurring opinion, "we sometimes must make decisions we do not like. We make them because they are right, right in the sense that law and the Constitution . . . compel the result" (*Texas v. Johnson* [1989], 420–421). Both the Brennan and Kennedy opinions could have been issued by the Warren Court.

The ensuing uproar spilled out over the airways and in hundreds of letters to newspapers and magazines. The Senate voted ninety-seven to three to express its "profound disappointment" in the decision, and President Bush called for a constitutional amendment, a proposal that appalled almost as many people as the decision itself. In looking over the controversy, constitutional scholar David O'Brien declared that "James Madison, who wrote the First Amendment, would have had his heart warmed by the decision, but he would have been appalled that it was a 5–4 vote." Eventually, many people, upon reflection, recognized that the majority had not condoned flag desecration, but, as Justice Brennan pointed out, jailing people for burning the flag or forcing them to recite the "Pledge of Allegiance" is not what patriotism in America is about.

Congress turned down Bush's request for a constitutional amendment, and instead passed the 1989 Flag Protection Act, an antidesecration law that critics claimed could not withstand judicial scrutiny. Within a few weeks of the law's enactment, four demonstrators—including Gregory Johnson—burned an American flag on the steps of the U.S. Capitol. In *United States v. Eichman* (1990), the same five-to-four majority held the federal statute unconstitutional as an interference with expressive conduct protected by the First Amendment. Justice Brennan rejected the government's argument that Congress could do what the states could not, namely, interfere with a form of political speech. Reiterating that the majority did not care for flag desecration any more than did other Americans, Brennan nonetheless pointed out that "punishing desecration of the flag dilutes the very freedom that makes it so revered" (*United States v. Eichman* [1990], 319).

This time the decision raised far less of an outcry, perhaps because people had had a chance to think about the majority's reasoning. Republicans tried to make an issue of the case, and called for a constitutional amendment to override the Court, an effort that immediately fell flat. A number of conservatives, such as Republican Senator Gordon Humphrey of New Hampshire, opposed the demand for an amendment. "I just don't like tampering with the First Amendment," he declared.

The Warren legacy in the area of free speech and press is not only alive and well, but it has flourished in the Burger and Rehnquist Courts. While we tend—and properly so—to trace modern First Amendment jurisprudence to the great dissents of Holmes and especially Brandeis in the 1920s and 1930s, not until the Warren Court did their ideas of the importance of free expression find constitutional embodiment. Although neither the Warren Court nor its successors ever formally adopted Hugo Black's notion of a "preferred position" for free speech, in fact all courts since the 1960s have given free expression, and especially political expression, the greatest constitutional protection imaginable. Even conservative justices such as William Rehnquist and Antonin Scalia, who normally pay deference to legislative policy, will not do so when speech is involved. They and their colleagues have fully adopted Brandeis's dictum that the cure for bad speech is more speech, and that free speech is at the heart of a democratic society.

The Burger Court and the Religion Clauses

The Warren Court dealt with the religion clauses almost as if they were a blank slate; as a result, its landmark cases on school prayer, Bible reading, evolution, and Sabbath observance captured public attention and struck many Americans, especially those who believed that religion belonged in schools, as wrong. Political and religious conservatives expected, indeed demanded, that the Burger and Rehnquist Courts reject these earlier rulings. Some members of the Court appeared quite willing to do so, and espoused an accommodationist view based on what came to be known as a jurisprudence of original intent. Debate over original intent, and what the religion clauses actually meant, occupied a central place in both popular and academic debate over the Court in the last three decades of the twentieth century.

Justice Black's opinion in *Everson v. Board of Education* (1947) had expounded at length on the historical development of the establishment clause, and had concluded that the clause against establishment of religion by law had been intended to erect "a wall of separation between church and State." Black's opinion set the basis for all establishment clause cases for the next fifty years, and also opened the door to the flourishing debate over the original intent of the Framers in drafting not only the First Amendment but the Constitution as a whole, and how justices today ought to interpret that document.

Edwin Meese, who served as attorney general in the second Reagan administration, led the campaign for a strict adherence to what he called a "jurisprudence of original intention," in which the courts would determine exactly what the Framers had meant, and interpret the Constitution accordingly. He believed that the founders had left a clear record of exactly what they meant when they had drafted the Constitution and the first ten amendments, and that the current court had to follow that intent in its interpretations. Meese and other conservatives also believed that this original intent had never been to establish a high wall of separation, but rather to foster cooperation between church and state on a nonpreferential basis; that is, the government would not give any one sect preferential treatment over another.

An argument can be made that the historic record is, at best, only a preliminary guide to interpreting what the Constitution means, and that the record is often confused and contradictory. At the core of the problem is one's view of the Constitution and its role in American government. Advocates of original intent believe that the vision of the Framers is as good today as two hundred years ago, and any deviation from that view is an abandonment of the ideals that have made this country free and great. Defenders of judicial activism agree that courts ought not to amend the Constitution, but believe that for the document to remain true to the intent of the Framers, it must be interpreted in the light of two lamps: the spirit of the Framers and the realities of modern society. They believe that the founding generation never intended to put a straight-jacket on succeeding generations; rather, they set out a series of ideals, expressed through powers and limitations, and deliberately left details vague so that those who came after could apply those ideals to the world they lived in. This debate framed the high Court's handling of religion clause cases in the years after Earl Warren retired.

If we ascribe to the Warren Court a jurisprudence of strict separation, then it has certainly been eroded. On the other hand, despite the presence on the bench of such strong accommodationists as Warren Burger, William Rehnquist, and Antonin Scalia, in many areas the legacy of the Warren Court remains fairly solid.

The conflict between these two schools of thought can easily be seen in the Burger Court's decisions on state aid to parochial education. Even as the Warren Court was broadening the reach of the establishment clause, the Johnson administration raised new problems through its education programs. In January 1965, Lyndon Johnson proposed a massive aid to education program as part of his Great Society initiative; the federal government would provide $1.5 billion in grants to the nation's schools—primary and secondary, public and private, secular and parochial. Recognizing that aid to religious schools would certainly be challenged in the courts, the administration attempted to immunize the provision from judicial scrutiny. This effort failed, and in one of the last decisions in his tenure, Warren ensured that the Court would have a significant voice in the national debate over educational policies. Most of these cases would not reach the Court until after Warren had retired, but there seemed little doubt that the issue would have to be adjudicated. Following the Elementary and Secondary Education Act of 1965, both Congress and the states passed dozens of educational aid programs that benefitted parochial schools.

The Warren Court had developed two tests for determining the validity of government programs under the establishment clause: The activity must have (1) a secular legislative purpose, and (2) a primary effect that neither advances nor inhibits religion. In *Lemon v. Kurtzman* (1971) the Burger Court formally announced a three-pronged standard: (1) the law must have a secular purpose; (2) its primary effect must neither advance nor inhibit religion; and (3) it must avoid excessive government entanglement with religion. The Court used the *Lemon* formula to test challenged legislation in practically every subsequent religion case, although it often claimed that it served as no more than a "helpful signpost." According to some critics both within and outside the Court, that signpost often pointed in different directions.

Purists call for a total wall of separation to forbid any form of governmental aid, even passive support such as tax exemptions. They claim that any aid leads to entanglement; the government is obliged to ensure that its money is spent lawfully and effectively, and that therefore it must be involved in church affairs whenever religiously affiliated agencies receive state or federal aid. At the other end of the spectrum are those who insist that the First Amendment never meant that the government could not aid churches; they see the establishment clause as no more than a prohibition against the government favoring one denomination over the others. The wall of separation, they claim, is no more than Jefferson's personal belief, which the Framers did not adopt. (The phrase appears nowhere in the Constitution or Bill of Rights.) By this view, all state aid to parochial schools is legitimate, provided that it is available on an equal basis to all denominations.

The Burger Court's decisions on state aid to parochial education proved so contradictory that no one—on or off the bench—seemed to know with any certainty what the Constitution permitted or forbade. A quick survey of the decisions highlights the confusion.

The Court held that states cannot lend maps, tape recorders, and other instructional materials to parochial school students in *Wollman v. Walter* (1977), although it did not overrule the Warren Court's 1968 decision in *Board of Education v. Allen* that lending books is permissible. In 1973 the Court held that states may not reimburse parochial schools for the costs of administering state-mandated but teacher-prepared tests in *Levitt v. Committee for Public Education,* but seven years later it said that states may subsidize the cost of giving state-prepared tests in *Committee for Public Education and Religious Liberty v. Regan* (1980). The Court upheld a Minnesota law allowing taxpayers to deduct some of the costs for parochial education from state taxes in *Mueller v. Allen* (1983), although it had earlier struck down a similar New York plan of tuition rebates and tax deductions in *Committee for Public Education v. Nyquist* (1973). The Court also ruled that restrictions that apply to elementary and secondary schools do not necessarily apply to colleges in *Tilton v. Richardson* (1971) and *Hunt v. McNair* (1972). Because several of these cases had been reached by five-to-four votes, hopes and fears abounded that the Court would soon take a more "accommodationist" view toward aid to parochial education. But in June 1985 the Court reaffirmed the wall of separation, although again by only a five-to-four vote. In *Grand Rapids School District v. Ball* and *Aguilar v. Felton,* the justices invalidated both state and federal shared-time programs, in which full-time public school teachers taught classes, usually of a remedial nature, in the parochial schools.

Some thought the wall had been breached in *Widmar v. Vincent* (1981), when the Court held that a state university that made its facilities available for the activities of registered student organizations could not bar a student group from using rooms for religious worship and discussion. The University of Missouri in Kansas City had a general policy of prohibiting religious meetings in its facilities, but the Court found that the mandate of free speech outweighed that of the establishment clause. Justice Powell noted that the university had created a forum that was generally open for student use; by excluding religious discussion, the school had imposed a content regulation that violated the First Amendment. Powell indicated that an "equal access" policy would be compatible with the Constitution. In 1985 Congress passed the Equal Access Act, which extended the *Widmar* holding to secondary schools receiving federal aid. Some of the law's provisions, such as the requirement that a school official be present in "a nonparticipatory capacity" and that nonschool persons may not direct or attend such meetings, may well lead to constitutional challenges.

The Court's "accommodationist" side also came through in *Marsh v. Chambers* (1983), in which it upheld the Nebraska assembly's practice of beginning every legislative day with a prayer by a paid chaplain. Chief Justice Burger's majority opinion concentrated on the historical prevalence of the practice, which he believed outweighed the minor breach of the establishment clause. Then in *Lynch v. Donnelly* (1984), the chief justice delivered a five-to-four opinion approving the display of a municipally owned creche in a Pawtucket, Rhode Island, public park at Christmastime. Burger managed to offend both First Amendment purists as well as some Christian groups, the former by his characterization of the wall of separation as little more than a useful metaphor, and the latter by describing the creche, which depicted the biblical story of the birth of Jesus, as only a secular image.

The *Lynch* decision triggered serious criticism of the Court in academic circles, and some scholars charged the chief justice with undermining the establishment clause by his willingness to accommodate religious interests. Yet the Court disappointed those who hoped that with the addition of the Nixon appointees it would reverse the *Engel* decision barring school prayer. In fact, the Burger Court's first pronouncement in this area struck down a Kentucky statute requiring the posting of the Ten Commandments, purchased with private funds, in all public school classrooms. The *per curiam* opinion in *Stone v. Graham* (1980) characterized the law as "plainly religious."

The Burger Court's record on the free exercise clause proved far more consistent than on establishment. The Court reaffirmed the basic holding of *Sherbert v. Verner*—that a person may not be denied government benefits due to religious belief—when it reversed by an eight-to-one vote Indiana's denial of unemployment compensation benefits to a Jehovah's Witness who had left his job in a munitions factory because of religious objections to war in *Thomas v. Review Board* (1981). But although the free exercise clause requires exemption from government regulation under certain circumstances, these are not unlimited. In *United States v. Lee* (1982), the Court refused to exempt the Old Order Amish from paying Social Security taxes on religious grounds, and in *Tony and Susan Alamo Foundation v. Secretary of Labor* (1985) it rejected fundamentalist Christian claims that religious scruples prevented compliance with the minimum wage and other provisions of the Fair Labor Standards Act. The Court also sustained an Internal Revenue Service ruling denying tax-exempt charitable status to schools that practiced racial discrimination. In *Bob Jones University v. United States* (1983), Chief Justice Burger rejected the free exercise claim and found a compelling governmental interest in promoting racial equality.

A state's claim that compulsory education for all children constituted a compelling interest would be approved by most Americans, yet it failed to convince the Court in *Wisconsin v. Yoder* (1972). The Amish objected to provisions of state law requiring attendance past the eighth grade. They believed, and the state did not challenge the sincerity of their belief, that sending adolescent children to high school would endanger their salvation. Although the Court recognized that the Amish marched completely out of step with contemporary society, Chief Justice Burger affirmed their constitutional right to do so. Enforcement of the law would raise "a very real threat of undermining the Amish community and religious practices as they exist today; they must either abandon belief and be assimilated into society at large, or be forced to migrate to some other and more tolerant region." Given the relatively small number of children involved, the state's interest in educating its citizens would not suffer if it allowed the Amish an exception.

What the *Yoder* majority did not anticipate is that the ruling would provide an impetus for the home-schooling movement. While there have always been parents who have taught their children at home, growing dissatisfaction with the nation's public school system, a rising urban crime rate, and the phenomenal growth of the religious right with its suspicion of all things secular led to tens of thousands of parents deciding to keep their children out of the public schools. While home schooling is not limited to social and religious conservatives, they have been the backbone of the movement, and their publications have hailed the *Yoder* decision for giving their movement a constitutional imprimatur. It is doubtful if the Burger Court even considered home schooling in its deliberations, because at the time the numbers involved were truly insignificant. One might well point to *Yoder* and the home-school movement as a good example of the law of unanticipated consequences.

The mixed record of the Burger Court led to much speculation about the future of the two religion clauses, as a change of only one or two votes might give the accommodationists a majority. Whether the Jeffersonian wall of separation could stand with large sections removed or whether it would just collapse remained a question that the post-Burger Court would have to consider.

The Rehnquist Court and the Religion Clauses

One goal of conservatives in the 1980s was to get judges on the nation's courts who would reverse what the conservatives considered to be the godlessness of decisions from the Warren *and* Burger eras, and who would tear down the wall of separation between church and state. For these groups, a nation without religion could not survive and prosper, and they read history as "proving" that the Framers had always intended there to be a close relation between religion and the state. In their view, all the establishment clause meant was that no one church would receive preferential treatment at the expense of others, and that all religions could receive aid from the state. While the Rehnquist Court in some areas proved receptive to this view, a majority of the Court refused to abandon the notion of separation enunciated by the Warren Court. To the dismay of strict separationists the Court allowed some accommodation, but far from what those on the right demanded.

In *Lamb's Chapel v. Center Moriches Union Free Schools District* (1993), a local evangelical society had been denied use of school facilities to show a six-part film featuring a psychologist who would argue in favor of "Christian family values instilled at an early age." The school board routinely allowed its facilities to be used after school hours by social, civic, and even political groups, but claimed that by allowing Lamb's Chapel access it would be sponsoring a church-related activity. The sect claimed that the school district had opened its buildings to such a wide group of activities that it had become a de facto public forum.

Speaking for a unanimous Court, Justice White rejected the claim that the school had become a public forum, since the school district had not been required to open its buildings for any after-school outside activities. Once it did, however, denying Lamb's Chapel equal access amounted to content discrimination. The Court held that denial of access had to be "viewpoint neutral," and the school district had failed this test. While the Warren Court had never had to decide a case like this, its First Amendment jurisprudence would certainly have supported this notion of content neutrality.

Similarly, in *Capitol Square Review Board v. Pinette* (1995), the Court struck down the denial of permission to the Ku Klux Klan to erect a large Latin cross on Capitol Square in Columbus, Ohio. The state had designated the square as a public forum, and the Court assumed that permission had been denied because of the religious symbolism of the cross. The plurality opinion by Justice Scalia rejected the state's contention that permitting the sign would have been a form of establishment. He went on to put the issue in speech terms as well, noting that the activity should be considered private religious expression, fully protected by the First Amendment.

Perhaps the most accommodationist decision of the Court involved funding of a Christian-oriented magazine at a state-sponsored university. Wide Awake Publications sought funding from the University of Virginia, claiming that as a student organization it should not be denied student activity funds merely because it wished to focus on religious rather than secular matters. The university denied the application, arguing that to support a proselytizing club would violate the establishment clause. In *Rosenberger v. Rector and Visitors* (1995), the Court by a five-to-four vote held that the university could not discriminate against Wide Awake. Justice Kennedy, relying on *Lamb's Chapel*, declared that the case rested more on the speech than the establishment clause, and he held that denying funds to a publication because of its orientation amounted to content discrimination.

But the opinion held more than its share of establishment clause comments. In dismissing the university's argument, Kennedy found that the program involved—funding of student activities through student fees—did not require the state in the form of the university to favor or disfavor religion. The program was facially neutral, and the object of student funding was to open a forum for speech and other enterprises. The university's argument also suffered from the fact that while denying funding to Wide Awake, it had given monies to other clearly religious groups, such as the Hillel Society and a Muslim student organization.

One could find other examples of accommodation in the Court's decisions both before and after *Rosenberger.* In *Bowen v. Kendrick* (1988) the Court upheld those provisions of the Adolescent Family Life Act of 1982 that authorized federal funds to a variety of public and nonpublic organizations, including those with religious affiliation, for counseling services "in the area of premarital adolescent sexual relations and pregnancy." Opponents labeled the law the "Chastity Act" and claimed that the statute violated the establishment clause by providing public funds to promote particular religious views. Speaking for the Court the chief justice ignored the fact that one of the purposes of the act had been to fund religious groups opposed to abortion and premarital sex and to support their efforts to utilize religious-oriented counseling to attack the problem of teenage pregnancy. He rejected the claim that the law violated the *Lemon* test, and that any effect of advancing religion was merely "incidental and remote." To make their case, Rehnquist said, challengers of the law would have to show that federal funds went to organizations that were "pervasively sectarian" and not merely religiously affiliated or inspired.

In *Zobrest v. Catalina Foothills School District* (1993), the Court held that providing a publicly funded sign-language interpreter to a deaf student in a parochial school classroom did not violate the establishment clause. The case relied in large measure on an 1986 case, *Witters v. Washington Department of Services for the Blind,* that held that no violation of the First Amendment occurred when a visually handicapped person used state vocational rehabilitation money to pay tuition to a Christian college in order to prepare himself for a career in the ministry. The two decisions, especially *Zobrest,* indicated that the Court might reconsider its opinion in two closely divided 1985 cases, *Grand Rapids School District v. Ball* and *Aguilar v. Felton,* in which the Court had invalidated a popular after-school program of publicly funded remedial sessions that took place in parochial schools.

In *Agostini v. Felton* (1997) the Court by a five-to-four vote declared that the earlier decisions no longer could be squared with intervening establishment clause cases that gave a greater flexibility to using public funds in parochial settings. Of the original justices who had decided the case, O'Connor and Rehnquist had been in the minority, but now prevailed with the addition of Scalia, Kennedy, and Thomas. Justice Stevens, the sole remnant of the 1985 majority, now joined in dissent with Souter, Ginsburg, and Breyer.

In her opinion, Justice O'Connor ticked off the assumptions that the earlier Court had made to reach its conclusion that the after-school program had the impermissible effect of advancing religion. First, any public employee who works on the premises of a religious school is presumed to inculcate religion. Second, the presence of public employees on private school premises creates a symbolic union between church and state. Third, any and all public money that directly aids the educational function of religious schools impermissibly finances religious indoctrination.

In the twelve years since *Ball* and *Aguilar*, the Court had abandoned the first presumption; it no longer assumed that if a public employee set foot in a parochial school he or she automatically inculcated religion. It also no longer presumed that aid to any educational function somehow also served to foster religious indoctrination. With these two assumptions gone, then even using the standard *Lemon* test the after-school program did not violate the establishment clause. The four dissenters, Souter, Stevens, Ginsburg, and Breyer denied that the cases since 1986 meant that the Court's tests for violation had changed. The program had transgressed the First Amendment then, and it still did.

Those who demanded that the Court allow some accommodation could look at this series of cases with some satisfaction, but in two areas where religious conservatives wanted change, the court sorely disappointed them.

Although the famous Scopes trial in the 1920s had seemed to discredit those who rejected evolution outright, the belief in a literal reading of the account of creation in the book of Genesis had never died among religious fundamentalists. In the 1960s they had tried to outlaw the teaching of evolution again, only to be slapped down by the Warren Court in *Epperson v. Arkansas* (1968). A more sophisticated religious bloc hit upon a new tack and labeled the Genesis version "creationism" or "creation science," and in Louisiana passed a so-called balanced treatment act. Schools did not have to teach either creation science or evolution, but if either one was taught, then the other had to be taught as well.

Nearly all reputable scientists dismiss creationism—which accepts the story of Genesis uncritically—as a fraud, bearing no relation to real science, which questions the validity of everything. With only Justice Scalia and the chief justice dissenting, Justice Brennan spoke for a seven-to-two majority in *Edwards v. Aguillard* (1987) striking down the balanced treatment act. While the Court always defers to legislative purpose in secular matters, the debate and legislative record in this instance left no doubt as to the religious purposes behind the statute. The act's primary purpose—to advance a particular religious belief—could not pass the *Lemon* test.

Opposition to the Warren Court's most famous religion clause case, the original school prayer decision in *Engel v. Vitale* (1962) had not faded, and with a more accommodationist majority on the Court advocates of school prayer hoped to see the case overruled. But in *Lee v. Weisman* (1992), the Court, albeit by a slim majority, reaffirmed the vitality of the wall of separation.

The case arose in Providence, Rhode Island, where the school system had for many years invited clergy from various denominations to offer prayers at graduation and promotion ceremonies. When their eldest daughter graduated from middle school in 1986, Daniel and Vivien Weisman (who are Jewish) were offended by the prayer of a Baptist minister, and they protested to school officials. Although they never received an answer to their letter, when their younger daughter was to graduate from the same school, the Weismans learned that a rabbi had been invited to give the blessing, apparently in an effort to appease them. The Weismans, however, had not objected just to the particular prayer, but believed that under *Engel* there should be no prayer in public school.

By a five-to-four vote, the Court refused to abandon precedent and adopt a new test in lieu of *Lemon* for establishment clause cases. The new centrist majority, including Justices O'Connor, Souter, and Kennedy, indicated it saw no need for a new test. Justice Kennedy's opinion reaffirmed previous rulings and held that prayers at public school graduations, no matter how nonsectarian in nature, violate the Constitution.

A few years later the Court reinforced its ban on prayers in school by an even wider margin. Advocates of school prayer hit upon the tactic of voluntarism in an attempt to bypass the strong line of precedents that ran from *Engel* to *Weisman*. If the student voluntarily chose to pray, then there could not be any objection regarding the state imposing prayer. The Santa Fe school district allowed its students to choose one student who would lead prayers before each football game. The Court by a six-to-three majority ruled in *Santa Fe Independent School District v. Doe* (2000) that this still amounted to an unconstitutional establishment of religion. While some of the spectators may have been there voluntarily, the team, the cheerleaders, the band, and other students were there because they had to be in attendance, and requiring them to be in an audience with this type of prayer, according to Justice Stevens, had the same effect as *Weisman*—creating a barrier between the accepted and those outside.

In the area of free exercise, the Rehnquist Court will probably be remembered for its marked insensitivity to Indian beliefs, most notably in *Employment Division v. Smith* (1990). By a five-to-four vote, the Court held that the First Amendment does not bar a state from applying its general criminal prohibition of peyote to individuals who claim to use it for sacramental purposes. In addition, the majority announced that the test balancing governmental action burdening religious practices against a compelling governmental interest, first enunciated in *Sherbert v. Verner* (1963), would no longer apply in cases involving criminal laws of general applicability.

While many western states and the federal government provided exemptions for peyote when used in religious ceremonies, Oregon did not. Two employees in a drug rehabilitation program, Alfred Smith and Galen Black, were fired from their positions because they ingested peyote at a religious ceremony of the Native American Church. The two were then denied unemployment compensation because they had been dismissed for misconduct—the use of a criminally proscribed substance. In a line of cases going back to *Sherbert v. Verner* (1963), the Supreme Court had ruled that state unemployment insurance could not be conditioned on an individual's willingness to forego conduct required by his or her religion, when that conduct was otherwise legal. Smith and Black argued that the same rule should apply to them, even though the Oregon law made ingestion of peyote illegal, because the Oregon law itself was unconstitutional.

Justice Scalia, writing for a bare majority of the Court, took an extremely narrow view of the free exercise clause. Going all the way back to the 1879 case of *Reynolds v. United States*, he argued that religion could never be used as an excuse for violating "an otherwise valid law regulating conduct that the state is free to regulate" (*Employment Division, Department of Human Resources v. Smith* [1990], 879). Justice O'Connor, joined in part by Brennan, Marshall, and Blackmun, sharply criticized the Court for abandoning the balancing test. Moreover, by denying the applicants the opportunity to challenge a general criminal law on free exercise grounds, the majority had cut out "the essence of a free exercise claim." Just because this was a criminal statute did not mean that it did not burden religious freedom. Nonetheless, O'Connor joined in the result because she believed the state had a compelling interest under the balancing test, namely its effort to wage a war on drugs.

The general criticism of the *Smith* decision led a broad coalition of religious groups to petition Congress for redress, and they asked for a federal law that would restore a number of exemptions for religious activities. The coalition garnered strong bipartisan support, and in 1993 Congress overwhelmingly passed and President Clinton signed into law the Religious Freedom Restoration Act (RFRA). The statute contained a number of formal findings that "laws 'neutral' toward religion may burden religious exercise without compelling justification." The law and its accompanying legislative history could not have been blunter in its statement that the Supreme Court had been wrong in *Smith* for eliminating the requirement that government justify burdens on religious exercise imposed by facially neutral laws and that the better interpretation had been the compelling interest test of *Sherbert*. Although popular, RFRA was a sweeping law purporting to bind all government action at all levels—federal, state, and local. In practical terms, it attempted to overrule a Supreme Court decision by creating a broad federal guarantee of religious freedom greater than that created by the First Amendment.

But where did Congress get its authority to pass RFRA? While Congress can always "overrule" a court's interpretation of a statute by legislating more precise language, what provision of the Constitution allowed the Congress to override the Court's interpretation of the First Amendment? Congress claimed that it was not actually overturning *Smith*, but merely passing civil rights legislation, in this case religious civil rights. In the past Congress has passed laws creating greater rights than embodied in the Constitution, and it claimed the authority to do so from Section 5 of the Fourteenth Amendment: "Congress shall have the power to enforce, by appropriate legislation, the provisions of this article." Since 1803, however, the Court had held itself to be the definitive interpreter of the Constitution. The test case to determine who would prevail arose in the small Texas city of Boerne, located some twenty-eight miles northwest of San Antonio.

The city council had authorized the Historic Landmark Commission to prepare a preservation plan for the downtown area, and in order to maintain the historic look of the area, required anyone seeking to change landmarks or buildings in that area to get preapproval. St. Peter's Catholic Church dated from 1923 and had been built in the mission style of the area's earlier history. The parish was growing, but the sanctuary could hold only 230 worshippers, and on any given Sunday between forty and sixty people could not be accommodated at some masses. The church sought permission to expand, but the city denied the application on the grounds that the altered structure would damage the integrity of the historic district. The archbishop brought suit, claiming that the denial of the permit violated the RFRA. *City of Boerne v. Flores* (1997) could hardly have been a better test case to demonstrate the weaknesses of the law.

The decision had less to do with religious free exercise than with federalism and the separation of powers. The Court denied that Congress had the power under Section 5 to impose upon the courts a particular constitutional interpretation, and Justice Kennedy in essence read a civics lessons to the Congress. The Court would decide what the Constitution meant.

Had the Court sustained RFRA, it would have opened a Pandora's box of litigation and problems. In *Boerne* the church was asking for something no one else in the downtown area could get—approval to expand and alter a historic building. Had the church been successful, what would have stopped the hardware store across the street from demanding approval for its plans to expand, and arguing under an equal protection claim that it should be treated at least the same as the church? (Justice Stevens in his concurring opinion made this point, and claimed that RFRA violated the establishment clause by granting preferences for religious groups.) The Court had been insensitive in *Smith,* and for reasons that are unclear abandoned a perfectly usable balancing test that had been in effect for more than three decades. In their separate opinions, Justices O'Connor, Souter, and Breyer indicated that they heard the message, and argued that the *Smith* doctrine should be reconsidered.

If the Court would not give religious groups exemptions from general laws, at the same time it would not countenance laws aimed specifically at inhibiting particular practices. The Santeria sect, which originated when the Yoruba people were brought to Cuba as slaves, involved an amalgam of West African religion intermixed with Roman Catholicism. Animal sacrifice (after which the animals were cooked and eaten) constituted an essential part of the group's practices. The animals were not tortured, but killed by a clean cutting of the carotid artery in the neck.

When the Santeria announced plans to open a church in Hialeah, many residents objected, and the city council quickly passed a series of ordinances effectively preventing animal sacrifice within the city limits and punishing violations with fines not to exceed $500 and/or imprisonment of up to sixty days. Although masquerading as health regulations, the taped sessions of the city council clearly indicated the hostility of officials toward the Santeria as well as the fact that the ordinances had been passed specifically to keep the Santeria out of Hialeah.

In *Church of the Lukumi Babalu Aye v. City of Hialeah* (1993), the Court unanimously invalidated the regulations as a violation of the free exercise clause, although the justices differed in their reasoning. Justice Kennedy, in his opinion for the Court, called the Hialeah law "religious gerrymandering"—"an impermissible attempt to target petitioners and their religious practices" (*Church of the Lukumi Babalu Aye v. City of Hialeah* [1993], 535). The law ran afoul not only of the First Amendment but of the Fourteenth as well, in that it violated the equal protection clause by singling out one group's practices.

The Warren Court actually had only a few religion clauses cases, but each of them set up an important constitutional principle, and while there has been some erosion of those ideas, their basic tenets are still intact. It is not the job of the state to foster religion, and every effort to do so, either by financial assistance or requiring some sort of religious exercise, violates the establishment clause. While the Burger decisions in this area are totally lacking in consistency, the Rehnquist Court exceptions are based on common sense and, although they may offend some purists, do not undermine the principle of separation. The fact is that there are a number of areas of close contact between church and state, and the question is not whether there is contact—which is the basic test for the purists—but whether such contacts discriminate against religious minorities, whether, in Justice O'Connor's view, the practice tends to exclude certain groups. Allowing a sign-language interpreter or letting a student use public funds for which he or she qualifies to attend a religious school do not exclude, and do not seem to undermine the wall of separation.

In overtly religious efforts to install religious practices the Burger and Rehnquist Courts proved determined to maintain religious neutrality. While some of the justices would have been willing to be more accommodationist, the majority has consistently ruled against state-sponsored religious practices. It proved less willing to sustain the liberal approach that the Warren Court had established for religious accommodation, and while many states continue to follow the rule of *Sherbert v. Verner*, it is questionable whether that is still good constitutional law.

The Burger Court and Rights of the Accused

If conservatives expected anything from the Burger Court, they thought it would reject its predecessor's alleged "softness" on criminals and, in Richard Nixon's words, redress the balance in favor of the "peace forces." However, despite the uproar over cases like *Miranda*, the Warren Court had never attempted to alter significantly American criminal justice. In most of its criminal procedure cases, it had either endorsed police tactics or imposed minor modifications. Even the holdings in some "great" cases like *Gideon* (entitling indigents to counsel) and *Katz* (requiring a search warrant for a wiretap) had already been accepted in principle. The allegedly radical decisions came early; by the mid-1960s, the Warren Court had begun to reexamine and consolidate its earlier rulings.

At first the Burger Court seemed intent on restricting the rights of the accused, but over the course of the seventeen terms that Warren Burger sat in the center chair, the word that best describes his Court's decisions on criminal procedure is "fluid." The initial effort to cut back on Warren Court decisions passed after a few years, and in the late 1970s a less police-oriented bench emerged that breathed new life into the substantive and procedural safeguards accorded accused persons. Then in the 1980s a "tougher" Court began handing down more progovernment decisions, especially in the area of drug enforcement. Perhaps most important, the Burger Court backed away from the absolute prophylactic standards of the Warren Court, and in their place erected a "totality of the circumstances" approach that gave courts much greater leeway in evaluating police procedures.

In one of its first Fourth Amendment cases, the Burger Court rolled back some of the strict standards necessary to secure a search warrant. The Burger Court did not at first abandon the old two-prong test—the reliability of the information and the credibility of its source—but allowed the magistrate to take greater account of the police officer's knowledge of an informant in *United States v. Harris* (1971). It finally abandoned the test in 1983, replacing it with a "totality of circumstances" approach. According to Justice Rehnquist, who wrote the six-to-three majority opinion in *Illinois v. Gates*, reliability and credibility still mattered, but only as factors in a commonsense, practical inquiry into whether evidence or contraband probably could be found in a particular location. Rehnquist emphasized that the new approach was not standardless; the Court had deliberately not spelled out too many details, because it wanted to leave local magistrates with as much flexibility as possible. The Court reaffirmed the "totality of the circumstances" approach the following year in *Massachusetts v. Upton*.

Critics complained that the Burger Court showed less concern with privacy under the Fourth Amendment than did its predecessor. In several cases, the majority ruled that the police could cast a broad net in their searches and even confiscate some items without a warrant. The Court allowed police who were searching a lawyer's office with a warrant directed to a specific item to take away files, search them at the station, and then return nonrelevant materials in *Andreson v. Maryland* (1976). A bank depositor, according to Justice Powell writing in *United States v. Miller* (1975), had no reasonable expectation of privacy in his accounts, and therefore a bank could deliver subpoenaed records of transactions without notifying the customer. The Court also ruled in *Smith v. Maryland* (1979) that police could install a pen register, which recorded the numbers dialed on a telephone, without a warrant. Although a person could expect the contents of a telephone conversation to be private, dialing a number left a record with the telephone company. Therefore, using a pen register to record which numbers a person called did not constitute a search and did not require a warrant.

The Court, much to the distress of civil libertarians, expanded the doctrine of "consent." No warrant is needed if someone agrees to have a person or premises searched. In *Schneckloth v. Bustamonte* (1973), the majority ruled that police do not have to recite a *Miranda*-type formula informing a person that he or she might refuse police access until they procure a warrant. Police need only demonstrate that consent "was in fact voluntarily given, and not the result of duress or coercion" *Schneckloth v. Bustamonte* [1973], 248). The Court ignored arguments that some people would agree to an otherwise impermissible search because they did not know their rights.

Although the Burger Court modified (and in the eyes of some downplayed) Fourth Amendment protection in certain areas, it did not retreat fully, as conservatives had hoped. In fact, the Court expanded some Fourth Amendment rights. In *Gerstein v. Pugh* (1975), for example, the Court dealt with a long-festering problem of detention under warrantless arrest. The Fourth Amendment calls for a warrant before officials may seize a person, but customarily police may arrest persons who are suspected of a felony or caught committing a misdemeanor. Police, however, could often detain suspects several hours or even several days for questioning without formally charging them with any crime. Under *Gerstein*, a person once arrested must be brought before a magistrate within a reasonable time (a few hours); if police cannot make out probable cause for arrest, the person must be released.

The Court did show a strong attachment to privacy of home and person, striking down in *Payton v. New York* (1980) the widespread practice in many states of allowing police to enter a home and make a warrantless arrest for suspicion of a felony. The Court also ruled in *Ybarra v. Illinois* (1980) that a valid warrant to search a tavern and the person of the bartender for drugs gave police no authority to search the patrons. "Mere propinquity to [those] suspected of criminal activity does not, without more, give rise to probable cause to search that person" (*Ybarra v. Illinois* [1980]), 91). And in *United States v. United States District Court* (1972), a unanimous bench held that neither the 1968 federal electronic surveillance law nor the president's inherent powers to protect against domestic subversion "justify departure

[from] the customary Fourth Amendment requirement of judicial approval prior to the initiation of a search or surveillance" (*United States v. United States District Court* [1972], 321). In a number of other cases, the Burger Court consistently required the procurement of a search warrant in circumstances in which it had not previously been thought necessary, and it declined the opportunity to draw back on some of the Warren Court precedents.

The Burger Court did, however, respond to the public outcry against drug abuse and gave its endorsement to the war against drugs. To some observers it seemed that however protective the Court might be in other areas of Fourth Amendment rights, it seemed willing to permit law officers great leeway in drug-related cases. In *New Jersey v. T.L.O.* (1985), the justices permitted school officials, on reasonable suspicion, to conduct warrantless searches of student belongings for drugs or other proscribed articles. And in one of the last opinions handed down before Burger's retirement, a five-to-four majority ruled that aerial surveillance of a person's backyard did not constitute a search, even if police in the airplane photographed marijuana under cultivation and then secured a warrant for an on-ground search. In *California v. Ciraolo* (1986), the facts made clear that the the yard was within the curtilage of the house, that a fence shielded the yard from observation from the street and that the occupant had a subjective expectation of privacy. The majority, however, found this expectation of privacy "unreasonable and not an expectation that society is prepared to honor" (*California v. Ciraolo* [1986], 214), although Chief Justice Burger's opinion could provide neither empirical or constitutional reasons why society was not prepared to honor the privacy of a person who put up a high fence around his yard.

Perhaps the best intimation of the Burger Court's reluctance to assume a strictly law-and-order orientation could be found in its handling of the exclusionary rule, the judge-made ban on using illegally seized evidence. Burger and Rehnquist pushed for a "good-faith" exception, that is, for admitting evidence obtained by "inadvertent" violations, or when police believed in good faith that they had a valid warrant. In 1982 in *Taylor v. Alabama* the Court dismissed an argument for such an exception by noting that "to date we have not recognized such an exception, and we decline to do so here" (*Taylor v. Alabama* [1982], 693). The following term, the Court asked counsel to reargue *Illinois v. Gates* and address the issue of whether changes should be made in the exclusionary rule. When the decision came down in the late spring of 1983, however, Justice Rehnquist apologized for bringing up the good-faith issue and simply noted that the Court was not ready to change the rule.

The Court finally did adopt a very limited good-faith exception in *United States v. Leon* (1984). Police, following up a report by an unproven informer, staked out a house and observed activity indicative of drug trafficking. On this basis, they secured a warrant and arrested a number of persons while seizing a quantity of drugs. Both the district and circuit courts ruled that the warrant had been faulty; it had been issued with less than probable cause, mainly due to reliance on "stale" information and because the police had failed to establish the reliability of the informer. Both lower courts also declined to rule on a good-faith exception in light of *Gates*. But Justice White, speaking for a six-to-three majority, used a cost-benefit analysis to uphold the government's claim for a good-faith exception.

The exclusionary rule, he explained, deterred official misconduct and provided a remedy for egregious mistakes. Here the police had followed appropriate procedures; the fault, if any, lay with the magistrate, who possibly misjudged the validity of police information. "When law enforcement officials have acted in good faith or their transgressions have been minor," White explained, "the magnitude of the benefit conferred on such guilty defendants offends basic concepts of the criminal justice system" (*United States v. Leon* [1984], 908). In a companion case, *Massachusetts v. Sheppard*, the Court applied a good-faith exception when police relied on a warrant that failed to describe specifically the objects to be seized. The police had submitted a sufficiently detailed affidavit, but had used an inappropriate form; both they and the magistrate, however, knew exactly what they wanted. The magistrate had said he would edit the form to make it proper, but then had failed to do so. The police and society should not be penalized, White declared, because the magistrate had made a clerical error.

The two cases provided a relatively narrow exception carved out of the exclusionary rule, and it will take many more decisions to determine how far—if at all—subsequent Courts will widen that exception. The bench is certainly aware of recent studies showing that the exclusionary rule has had little impact on prosecutions. Evidence is excluded as a result of Fourth Amendment violations in only 1.3 percent of cases, and prosecutions have been dropped in less than 0.5 percent of cases because of search and seizure problems. One legacy of the Warren Court is that a strict adherence to constitutional safeguards has made for better police work. Procuring a proper warrant at the start avoids problems later on, and the Burger Court, even in the good-faith cases, emphasized that it would not lower constitutional standards to accommodate sloppy police procedures.

A pattern somewhat similar to that indicated in the good-faith cases appeared in the Burger Court's handling of the most controversial criminal procedure ruling of the Warren Court: the *Miranda* decision, which required police to advise suspects of their rights and then to desist from questioning if the suspects asserted those rights. In a series of rulings in the first half of the 1970s, the Court seemed determined to limit *Miranda*, if not do away with it entirely. In *Harris v. New York* (1971), over a bitter dissent by Justices Brennan, Douglas, and Marshall, the Court held that although statements obtained after a defective *Miranda* warning could not be used by the prosecution to show guilt, they could be used to impeach the defendant's credibility, which would be just as damaging. Later rulings allowed impeachment use of statements obtained by continued police interrogation even after the defendant had asserted his or her right to remain silent (*Oregon v. Haas* [1975]), and permitted police to come back and requestion a suspect repeatedly, so long as they recited the *Miranda* warning each time. (*Michigan v. Mosely* [1975]) The doctrine appeared doomed in 1974 when Justice Rehnquist, in *Michigan v. Tucker*, described the *Miranda* warnings as "not themselves rights protected by the Constitution," but only "prophylactic standards" designed to "safeguard" or to "provide practical reinforcement" for the privilege against self-incrimination (*Michigan v. Tucker* [1974], 444).

Nevertheless a few years later, in the controversial case of *Brewer v. Williams* (1977), the Burger Court indicated that the doctrine remained alive and well. Robert Williams, an escaped mental patient, had allegedly abducted and then murdered a ten-year-old girl on Christmas eve in Des Moines, Iowa. Two days later, he called his attorney from Davenport, and upon the lawyer's advice, surrendered to the police there. The attorney also advised Williams not to talk to the police until he arrived back in Des Moines, where the lawyer would be present. The police there promised the attorney they would not interrogate Williams after they picked him up to bring him back to Des Moines. At the start of the 160-mile trip from Davenport to Des Moines, Williams expressed his intent to remain silent. The two police officers, however, aware of his religious beliefs, engaged him in discussions about religious questions and addressed him as "Reverend." It had started to snow, and the police pointed out it would be difficult to find the little girl's body and give her "a Christian burial," a point they made several times. Williams eventually led them to the body.

By a five-to-four vote, the Court upheld a lower court ruling that the evidence had been obtained improperly, because the two police officers had in fact interrogated a suspect in custody without benefit of counsel. They also pointed out that the defendant had insisted on his right to have counsel present and that the police had agreed to that request. The Court remanded for a second trial, in which a jury again found Williams guilty. He appealed, but the Court in *Nix v. Williams* (1984) ruled that the tainted evidence had not prejudiced the defense because the body inevitably would have been discovered.

Rhode Island v. Innis (1980) dealt with a similar situation. Innis had been arrested for murder. After he stated in response to a *Miranda* warning that he wanted to see a lawyer, the police captain told the three patrolmen who took Innis to the stationhouse not to question him. As the car passed a school for handicapped children, one officer expressed concern that a child might find the missing murder weapon, a shotgun, and be injured. Innis then offered to lead them to the gun; they returned to the scene of the arrest, where the captain again read Innis a *Miranda* warning. Innis said he understood his rights, but wanted to retrieve the shotgun because of the children, and showed the police its location. The Rhode Island Supreme Court ruled that the gun, as well as the testimony of the officers, had to be excluded because it constituted "custodial interrogation" in violation of *Miranda*.

The Supreme Court reversed, but did so without damaging *Miranda*. Unlike Williams, Innis had not yet been charged with a crime, he had no mental problems, he had received and understood the *Miranda* warnings, and he had voluntarily agreed to show police the location of the weapon. The Court thus distinguished between "casual questioning," which is allowed, and "custodial interrogation," which is not. The chief justice entered a concurrence in which he declared that he "would neither overrule *Miranda*, disparage it, nor extend it at this late date" *Rhode Island v. Innis* [1980], 304).

The following year, in *Estelle v. Smith* (1981), the Court gave *Miranda* a generous reading when it ruled that the privilege against self-incrimination applied at the penalty stage of the trial as well as at guilt determination. That same term, in *Edwards v. Arizona*, a unanimous Court held that when a suspect invokes the right to counsel as opposed to the right to remain silent, the police may not "try again."

In its last terms, the Burger Court continued to uphold *Miranda*, although it permitted an exception in a unique emergency situation. In *New York v. Quarles* (1984), police apprehended a reportedly armed rape suspect in a supermarket, and before reading him his rights, asked the whereabouts of the gun, to which Quarles replied, "It is over there." The officers retrieved a loaded 0.38 caliber revolver from an empty carton, formally arrested Quarles, and read him the *Miranda* warning. The defendant then said he would answer questions without an attorney and identified the gun as belonging to him. The high Court, through Justice Rehnquist, agreed by a split vote with the lower court ruling that the questioning constituted custodial interrogation. But the circumstances could not be ignored. There had been a concealed weapon; there might have been an accomplice; and reading the *Miranda* warning might have led the suspect to remain silent and thus endanger both the police and the public. The police had an obligation to control the situation, and retrieving a loaded weapon constituted their highest priority. The Court thus carved out a minor exception in *Quarles*, one far more limited than it might have been had the case been decided a decade earlier.

The Burger Court began the process not of repealing Warren Court decisions, but of tempering the rules and replacing absolute standards with a "totality of the circumstances" test. This trend continued and accelerated in the Rehnquist years, and in the eyes of some observers went so far as to constitute a "revolution on the right."

The Rehnquist Court and Rights of the Accused

Miranda v. Arizona remains the most controversial of the Warren-era decisions, and the Rehnquist majority has modified but not abandoned it. In a 1986 case, *Moran v. Burbine*, a six-to-three majority that included both Sandra Day O'Connor and William

Rehnquist in effect reaffirmed the *Miranda* rule, while giving police somewhat greater latitude. The following year Justice Stevens spoke for a six-to-two Court in *Arizona v. Robertson*, holding that the general rule against interrogating an in-custody defendant after that person had requested counsel covered all crimes of which the defendant might be suspected. In 1990 the Rehnquist Court reaffirmed an earlier interpretation and expansion of *Miranda*. The 1981 case of *Edwards v. Arizona* held that when a suspect effectively asserts a right to a lawyer (as opposed to a right to remain silent), the suspect cannot be subjected to further police questioning until a lawyer arrives. In 1990 a seven-to-two majority of the Rehnquist Court (with the chief justice and Justice Scalia dissenting) upheld and even expanded the *Edwards* rule—with reasoning strikingly similar to the rationale behind *Miranda*. The Court wanted a prophylactic rule to determine the voluntariness of a confession. By adhering strictly to the *Edwards* rule, judicial resources could be conserved. In essence, *Miranda* and *Edwards* serve to make the job of the courts, as well as the police, easier by ensuring that confessions are properly made and can therefore be admitted into evidence. In *Withrow v. Williams* (1993), Justice Souter went out of his way to point out that while a prophylactic rule, "in protecting a defendant's Fifth Amendment privilege against self-incrimination, *Miranda* safeguards a fundamental trial right" (*Withrow v. Williams* [1993], 691).

Then in 2000 Chief Justice Rehnquist himself spoke for a seven-to-two majority in *Dickerson v. United States*, and reaffirmed the constitutional importance of the *Miranda* ruling. In 1968 Congress had attempted to reverse the Warren Court in Section 3501 of the Omnibus Crime Control Act by giving a very broad definition to "voluntary" confessions. Every administration since then, including that of Nixon and Reagan, has considered that section unconstitutional, and has never defended it in court. But a conservative advocacy group managed to win friend-of-the-court status in the Fourth Circuit, and convinced a panel that Section 3501 and not *Miranda* ought to govern the admissibility of confessions. The Supreme Court reversed, and with little margin as to doubt. One of the most criticized of all Warren Court rulings had now received sanction from the Court's conservative descendants.

But if the Court has not been willing to abandon *Miranda*, it has nonetheless been far stricter than its predecessors in rebuffing appeals, and has been vigilant against what it views as abuse of habeas corpus. In 1991 the majority lectured lower federal courts against entertaining constitutional claims not raised in accordance with state rules, a decision that can be seen both as part of its push for a stronger federalism as well as a tightening up of habeas corpus procedures. The majority enunciated a general rule that unless the prisoner could both show cause as to why the normal appeal procedures had been flouted as well as prejudice from alleged constitutional violations, the claim should not be heard. This two-pronged test had first been enunciated in *Wainwright v. Sykes* (1977), but lower courts had tended to follow an earlier and more lenient rule propounded by the Warren Court in *Fay v. Noia*

(1963). In *Keeney v. Tamayo-Reyes* (1992), the high Court indicated that it expected the federal judiciary to toughen up its habeas procedures.

The following year, in *Brecht v. Abrahamson* (1993), the Court made it harder for persons convicted in state courts to obtain habeas relief on the basis of constitutional errors regarding trial type. If deemed harmless error, even a constitutional violation would not provide grounds for habeas. Again, the determination of whether there had been harmless error, like the determination whether an exception to the two-pronged rule was justified, would belong to state courts. Rehnquist himself actively lobbied Congress to tighten up habeas procedures, and in 1996 the legislature passed the Antiterrorism and Effective Death Penalty Act, which set up hurdles for state prisoners seeking to obtain relief through a second or successive petition for federal habeas. When prisoners challenged this rule on the grounds that it impermissibly infringed on the Court's appellate jurisdiction, all of the justices united in upholding the new rules in *Felker v. Turpin* (1996).

In the area of search and seizure, the Court has been less sympathetic to the exclusionary rule than it has to the *Miranda* warning, but it has not rejected it outright. Rather, as in earlier warrant cases, the Court has adopted a "totality of the circumstances" approach in place of the strict and inflexible rules of the Warren-era decisions. A good example is *Arizona v. Evans* (1995), in which a seven-to-two majority held that errors caused by a court's clerical employees that result in an unconstitutional arrest do not trigger a Fourth Amendment exclusionary rule. Evans had been pulled over on the basis of a computer error showing an outstanding misdemeanor warrant; in fact the warrant had been quashed seventeen days earlier, but the computer records had not been updated. While being handcuffed, Evans dropped a marijuana cigarette, and a subsequent search of the car turned up a bag of the illicit substance. The state court said that the arrest had been illegal, and therefore the search had been illegal, and declined to draw a line between police error and judicial error. But the purpose of the exclusionary rule had always been to limit police behavior. In this instance the police, relying on the information they had, had acted appropriately; the conduct of the officer had been reasonable, and therefore the evidence could be admitted. In a companion case, *Wilson v. Arkansas*, Justice Thomas spoke for a unanimous court holding that the requirement that the police knock and announce their presence is part of the Fourth Amendment's command that searches and seizures be reasonable.

The Right to Privacy—Abortion and the Right to Die

Griswold v. Connecticut (1965) is in many ways one of the Warren Court's greatest decisions, what some have called a "living landmark." It has had a lasting impact for a number of reasons, aside from constitutionalizing the right to privacy. Because of the latent distrust of substantive due process going back to the Court fight of the 1930s, Justice Douglas had to do what amounted to a jurisprudential pretzel twist to find some home for privacy among the rights listed in the Constitution. Justice Harlan, however, recognized the core issue as substantive due process, and his view won the day.

In *Roe v. Wade* (1973), Justice Blackmun boldly ventured to do what Douglas had avoided in *Griswold*—he identified a new substantive due process as the basis of noneconomic individual rights. The right of privacy, he asserted, "is broad enough to encompass a woman's decision whether or not to terminate her pregnancy," and the choice is best left to the woman and her physician.

The *Roe* decision touched off a public uproar as great as the segregation decision, and one that may yet prove more enduring. When Earl Warren left the Court fifteen years after *Brown*, the principle that racial segregation was wrong and immoral had been accepted by a vast majority of the American people. The reaction to *Roe*, far from quieting down, has remained vehement. "Right to Life" groups continue to picket abortion clinics, petition legislatures and Congress for a constitutional amendment to forbid abortions, and seek state and federal laws defining when life begins so as to undercut *Roe*. Some individuals have resorted to violence by bombing clinics, murdering doctors who perform abortions, and physically intimidating women who seek abortions.

Following *Roe*, anti-abortion groups managed to get various state legislatures to enact laws limiting abortions, and in some cases the limits had the practical effect of outlawing the procedure. Although the Burger and Rehnquist Courts both allowed some limits to stand, they continually—albeit often by a five-to-four margin—reaffirmed the basic right. A quick review of these cases shows how the issue continues to incite people, and the divisions on the Court reflect those in the larger society.

In the first major post-*Roe* case, *Planned Parenthood of Missouri v. Danforth* (1976), the Court by a six-to-three vote invalidated a state law barring a woman from seeking an abortion during the first trimester without spousal consent. According to Justice Blackmun, the state did not have the power to forbid the abortion and therefore could not delegate it to the husband, despite his proper concern and interest in his wife's pregnancy.

The question of parental authority over pregnant minors came before the court several times. In *Bellotti v. Baird* (1976), a companion case to *Danforth*, the Court struck down a requirement for written parental permission on similar grounds; the state could not delegate power it did not have itself. But Justice Blackmun's opinion intimated that in the case of a minor, some restrictions might be permissible if they did not "unduly burden" the right to seek an abortion. Three years later, in *Bellotti v. Baird II* the Court again struck down a law limiting minors' access to abortion, this time by an eight-to-one vote. The Massachusetts law in question required an unmarried minor to obtain the consent of both her parents; if they refused, a state judge could authorize the abortion if he or she believed that the young woman was mature enough to make her own decision in regard to terminating her pregnancy. Justice Powell's opinion set out guidelines for the states: (1) minors had to have alternatives to parental consent available to them; (2) if they feared their parents or did not want to inform them of their pregnancy, they must be allowed to go directly to an appropriate judicial or nonjudicial authority; (3) if the young woman demonstrated her maturity and that she was well informed about the nature of the choices open to her, the third party had to give the permission she sought. But, Powell made clear, while the state may intervene in cases in which the minor is immature or there is evidence that she is incapable of acting responsibly, the presumption is on the side of the woman.

In 1981 the Court narrowly approved a parental notice requirement in *H.L. v. Matheson,* in which physicians had to "notify if possible" the parent or guardian of a minor seeking an abortion if she lived at home, was economically dependent, or otherwise not legally emancipated. In subsequent decisions on this issue, the Court failed to develop a clear policy and evaluated each case on its particular circumstances.

In its last term, the Burger Court struck down in *Thornburgh v. American College of Obstetricians and Gynecologists* (1986) a highly restrictive Pennsylvania statute, whose provisions on informed consent, public disclosure of information, and regulation of medical care—according to Justice Blackmun—disguised the obvious policy of discouraging abortions. The five-to-four vote led some anti-abortion groups to cheer that the Court had changed its mind and had begun to retreat away from *Roe,* and that one or two new appointments would lead to a complete overturn of that case. A closer reading of the opinions did not justify that view; seven members of the Court still stood by the *Roe* decision, but obviously they differed over where they would draw the line between the women's right to an abortion and the state's legitimate interests in medical supervision and protection of the fetus in the third trimester.

More than anything else, conservatives wanted the Rehnquist Court to reverse *Roe* and either return control over abortion to state legislatures or ban the procedure altogether on a theory that life begins at conception and thus the Fourteenth Amendment protects the civil rights of a fetus. Opposition to abortion became the litmus test imposed by the Reagan administration in selecting men and women for the federal bench, and the strategy seemed to be working. In 1987 the court of appeals for the Eighth Circuit, by a vote of seven to three, upheld a Minnesota law requiring women under eighteen to notify both parents or secure approval from a judge before getting an abortion. Of the seven judges in the majority, Reagan had appointed six of them. Just four days later a three-judge panel in the Sixth Circuit struck down a similar Ohio statute as unconstitutional. Both cases would reach the high Court on appeal.

The Rehnquist Court handed down its first major abortion decision on the last day of the October 1988 term. Although some people had anticipated—indeed prayed—that the Court would overturn *Roe,* the decision did not go that far, thus pleasing neither the supporters nor the opponents of abortion rights. The issue came before the high Court in a challenge to a Missouri statute that banned the use of public facilities and public employees to perform abortions, required physicians to perform viability tests on any fetus believed to be at least twenty weeks old, and declared that life begins at conception. Just a few weeks before the court handed down its decision, more than 300,000 abortion rights supporters marched in Washington, the largest demonstration there since the antiwar gatherings of the early 1970s.

The chief justice spoke for a highly splintered court in *Webster v. Reproductive Health Services* (1989). Joined by Justices White, O'Connor, Scalia, and Kennedy, he ruled that the statute's preamble declaring that life started at conception amounted to no more than a value judgment by the legislature and could not by itself regulate abortion. The same majority upheld the state's ban on the use of public facilities and employees as consistent with earlier decisions regarding the power of a state to specify its employees' duties and restrictions. Although an individual woman may have a right to an abortion, the state was not obligated to provide either funds or facilities to help her realize that right.

On the fetal viability section, only White and Kennedy joined Rehnquist in construing the provision to leave its application up to the judgment of the individual doctor. The chief justice used this section, however, to attack the trimester framework of the original *Roe* decision as "unworkable." In a bitter dissent, Justice Blackmun, joined by Brennan and Marshall, defended the trimester scheme and accused the majority of cowardice, deception, and disingenuousness in failing to come to grips with the basic issues involved in the abortion debate. Justice Stevens dissented separately, noting that he would have invalidated the testing provision and the preamble, which he claimed violated the establishment clause by endorsing particularistic Christian beliefs.

The next term the Court heard the cases from the Sixth and Eighth Circuits on parental notification. In *Ohio v. Akron Center for Reproductive Health,* a six-to-three majority upheld the Ohio law requiring notice to one parent or a judicial bypass alternative. In contrast, different five-to-four majorities struck down Minnesota's two-parent notification requirement when it did not provide for judicial bypass, but then upheld the same provision when coupled with a bypass in *Hodgson v. Minnesota.* Neither case broke new ground, but many observers noted that it had been Justice O'Connor who provided the critical fifth vote in the Minnesota case, and that for the first time she found that a state restriction unduly burdened a woman's reproductive freedom. The dissenters, led by Justice Marshall, would have found the law, even with the bypass provision, too restrictive. Marshall pointed to the dilemma of a pregnant young woman "in an already dire situation [forced] to choose between two fundamentally unacceptable alternatives: notifying a possibly dictatorial or even abusive parent or justifying her profoundly personal decision in an intimidating judicial proceeding to a black-robed stranger" (*Hodgson v. Minnesota* [1990], 479).

Anti-abortion activists took heart from these decisions, and they looked forward confidently to the time in the near future when *Roe* would be overturned. They hoped that time had come when the Court heard arguments in *Planned Parenthood of Southeastern Pennsylvania v. Casey,* decided in 1992. The law seemed to include nearly every restriction that abortion opponents could think of to burden the procedure to the point of making it impossible for a woman to elect an abortion. The Pennsylvania law required minors to get parental consent and wives to notify their husbands before getting an abortion; doctors had to inform women about potential medical complications; women had to wait twenty-four hours after requesting an abortion before the procedure could be performed; and doctors had to adhere to strict and onerous reporting requirements. A district court had struck the law down, but on appeal the Third Circuit had upheld all of the provisions except spousal notification. The appeals court also declared that abortion could no longer be considered a fundamental right and as a result restrictions on abortion need not be subject to strict scrutiny. The circuit court in effect said that it would accept any restriction the legislature thought necessary.

The Supreme Court on the surface upheld the court of appeals, insofar as it sustained the restrictions, but in its reasoning the majority reaffirmed the "essential holding" of *Roe.* Justices O'Connor, Kennedy, and Souter took the unusual step of coauthoring an opinion in which Justices Blackmun and Stevens joined in part. The majority opinion reaffirmed three components of *Roe:* (1) the right of a woman to choose to have an abortion before viability and to obtain it without undue interference from the state; (2) the state's power to restrict abortion after viability, providing the law contains exceptions for pregnancies that endanger the woman's life; and (3) the state's legitimate interests "from the outset of pregnancy in protecting the health of the woman and the life of the fetus that may become a child." According to the three coauthors, "These principles do not contradict one another, and we adhere to each" (*Planned Parenthood of Southeastern Pennsylvania v. Casey* [1992], 846). The opinions did not, however, reaffirm the strict scrutiny standard that *Roe* had called for in evaluating restrictions. Unlike some earlier decisions, which had grounded the right to an abortion in privacy, the majority placed it within the liberty interest of the Fourteenth Amendment's due process clause. Under this reasoning, a "realm of personal liberty" exists that the government may not enter, and this realm protects personal decisions related to marriage, procreation, conception, family relationships, and abortion.

While the majority underscored the Court's obligation to *stare decisis* (legal precedent) and the need to make "legally principled decisions," O'Connor, Kennedy, and Souter rejected what they considered *Roe's* "elaborate but rigid" trimester framework, and also rejected the notion that a woman has an unfettered right to choose abortion without interference from the state. Rather, states are free to enact a reasonable framework in which a woman can "make a decision that has such profound and lasting meaning" (*Planned Parenthood of Southeastern Pennsylvania v. Casey* [1992], 873). Only when these laws "unduly burden" a woman's decision do they violate her personal liberty. By this standard, the Court upheld four of the five Pennsylvania restrictions. The minority of the chief justice, joined by White, Scalia, and Thomas, concurred in the judgment, but dissented from the reaffirmation of *Roe*, which they would have abandoned.

Concurring only in the parts that reaffirmed a woman's basic right to an abortion, Justice Blackmun took the unusual step of praising his colleagues for what he termed "an act of personal courage and constitutional principle" (*Planned Parenthood of Southeastern Pennsylvania v. Casey* [1992], 923). Yet he worried that four members of the Court stood waiting for a fifth vote to overturn *Roe*, and in another unusual statement noted that "I am 83 years old. I cannot remain on this Court forever, and when I do step down, the confirmation process for my successor may well focus on the issue before us today" (*Planned Parenthood of Southeastern Pennsylvania v. Casey* [1992], 943). When Blackmun did retire two years later, however, the dynamic had changed. Byron White, who had voted against *Roe* in 1973, had retired and Bill Clinton, a supporter of choice, had nominated Ruth Bader Ginsburg to replace him. At her confirmation hearings Ginsburg repeated criticism she had made earlier that *Roe* had short-circuited the debate about abortion in the states at a time when many legislatures had begun reforming their abortion statutes. But she made clear that she herself believed in a woman's right to choose. The following year Clinton named Steven Breyer to replace Blackmun, and it no doubt gave Blackmun great pleasure that his successor also supported choice.

Yet in the next abortion case heard by the Rehnquist Court, a Nebraska law banning so-called partial-birth abortions fell by a bare five-to-four vote. The procedure is only used in late-term abortions, and critics charge that in effect it takes a viable fetus and kills it by inhumane means; opponents claim that "partial-birth" is a total misnomer, that the procedure is used extremely rarely, and then only to save the life of the mother. In *Stenberg v. Carhart* (2000) the majority ruled that because the procedure may be the most medically appropriate, it cannot be constitutionally banned. Moreover, the wording of the law, according to Justice Breyer, could be interpreted to ban most abortions, a step the state could not legitimately take.

In 1990 the Supreme Court confronted an issue it had never heard before, a claim for a right to die, which its proponents based on the right to privacy. In fact, it was a relatively new issue for the nation as a whole, arising from the amazing explosion of medical technology in the previous three decades. People who up until the 1960s would have been expected to die from severe accidents or illnesses could now be helped, although there were significant limits on this technology as well as some unexpected negative effects.

In January 1983 Nancy Cruzan's car swerved on a patch of ice, skidded off the road, and turned over. The twenty-five-year-old woman was thrown from the vehicle and landed face down in a ditch. A medical team arrived in time to save her life, but not fast enough to get oxygen to her brain. She never regained consciousness, and for the next seven years lay in what is known as a permanent vegetative state, awake but totally unaware of anyone or anything. Her autonomous functions, such as heartbeat and breathing, continued without the help of machines, but she received nourishment and water through a tube into her stomach.

Her parents, Joyce and Joe Cruzan, finally gave up hope that their daughter would regain consciousness, and went into court to ask that the feeding tube be removed and that Nancy be allowed to die with dignity. Although a local judge granted permission, the Missouri Supreme Court reversed, holding that the state had an important interest in preserving life. In this case, the state's interest had to prevail because Nancy had left no "living will" or other clear and convincing evidence that in such circumstances she would want to have the feeding tube removed. Without this type of evidence, the state court concluded, "we prefer to err on the side of life."

When Chief Justice Rehnquist announced the high Court's decision in *Cruzan v. Director, Missouri Department of Health* (1990), he indicated his clear sympathy with the plight of Nancy Cruzan and her parents. He described them as "loving and caring," and if the state of Missouri had to let anyone decide to end medical treatment for their daughter, "the Cruzans would surely qualify." But by a five-to-four vote, the Court upheld the state's interest, and found its demand for clear and convincing evidence of Nancy's wishes to be reasonable.

The vote is misleading, however. Rehnquist, widely recognized as an ardent advocate of judicial restraint and an opponent of court-created rights, carefully declared that there is a right to die. It derives not from any alleged constitutional right of privacy, but rather from the guarantees of personal autonomy embedded in the Fourteenth Amendment's due process clause. A long line of decisions, he held, supports the principle "that a competent person has a constitutionally protected liberty interest in refusing unwanted medical treatment" (*Cruzan v. Director, Missouri Department of Health* [1990], 278). The four dissenters, led by Justice Brennan, agreed that a person has the right to die, but believed that as a federally protected liberty interest it should trump the state's demand for a higher level of evidence.

Had Nancy Cruzan left a living will or other evidence of her desires, there would have been no controversy. But a state also has interests, and the majority did not find a violation of personal autonomy for the state to set a reasonable evidentiary demand. In many ways, this case can also be seen as part of the Rehnquist Court's effort to revive federalism and to shift authority and responsibility away from the federal courts back to the states. Justice Scalia, the only member of the Court opposed to recognizing a right to die, bluntly declared that the federal courts "have no business in this field" (*Cruzan v. Director, Missouri Department of Health* [1990], 293).

Following the decision, the Cruzans went back to local court, this time with additional evidence of their daughter's intent in the form of three new witnesses who testified about specific conversations in which Nancy had said she would not like to live "like a vegetable." The state of Missouri, having made its point, did not contest the evidence, and on December 5, 1990, the Cruzans received the court order they wanted, directing the Missouri Rehabilitation Center to disconnect the feeding tubes. Twelve days later, Nancy Cruzan died.

Within a few years, the so-called right to die had become statutorily and judicially embedded in the laws of all fifty states, and Congress had passed a patients' rights bill that required hospitals receiving federal funds to obey patient directives in regard to refusal of treatment. But a new problem arose when on June 4, 1990—just three weeks before the Court handed down its decision in *Cruzan*—Dr. Jack Kevorkian hooked up what he called his "mercy machine" to fifty-four-year-old Janet Adkins, a schoolteacher suffering from the early stages of Alzheimer's disease. With that single act, the issue of physician-assisted suicide hit the front pages and became a burning issue in public policy debate thereafter.

Although suicide had at one time been considered a felony, all states had wiped that crime off their books. But many states still made assisting in a suicide a crime, and this nominally prevented doctors from helping patients who suffered greatly and wanted to die. *Cruzan* had established the right of a competent person, or a surrogate for an incompetent, to turn off life support and thus hasten death. Both law and ethics reasoned that this did not constitute suicide; death resulted from the underlying illness. Many people, however, could not see why a suffering person on life support could legally elect death, while a suffering person not on life support could not.

Within a few years courts heard challenges to state proscriptions on assisting suicide. On the West Coast, the Ninth Circuit Court of Appeals struck down Washington state's ban on assisted suicide. The judges read dicta in the *Casey* decision broadly, and found that electing death, like the decision to terminate pregnancy, was one of those acts "too intimate and personal" to brook interference from the state. Such a right, the court reasoned, constituted a liberty interest protected by the due process clause. On the East Coast the Second Circuit Court of Appeals voided New York's law, but based its decision on the equal protection clause, arguing that the law discriminated between people on life support and others.

The justices, had they agreed with the results of the two appeals courts, could have let the decisions stand, even if the two tribunals disagreed on the constitutional rationale. When the high Court announced it would hear the cases, most commentators believed that the conservatives—especially Rehnquist, Scalia, and Thomas, who opposed creating new rights—had granted certiorari for the sole purpose of reversing the appeals courts. The decisions in *Washington v. Glucksberg* and *Vacco v. Quill* came down on the last day of the term in 1997, and while the results may have been what most people expected, the divisions on the Court and the multiple opinions seemed to indicate something else.

The chief justice wrote the opinion for the court in which Justices O'Connor, Scalia, Kennedy, and Thomas joined, and in which all of the justices concurred in the result. But O'Connor, Stevens, Souter, Ginsburg, and Breyer filed concurring opinions that differed significantly with Rehnquist's reasoning and conclusions. Following what was for him now a familiar pattern, Rehnquist asked whether the right claimed—a right to physician-assisted suicide—had existed either at the time of the framing of the Constitution or of the ratification of the Fourteenth Amendment. Because it had not, and given the longstanding legal and moral antipathy to suicide, then there was no historical justification for including it in the liberty interests subsumed under the due process clause. The chief justice also claimed that the lower courts had misread *Casey*, and the reference to "intimate and personal" decisions had never been intended to apply to suicide. The opinion was straightforward and simplistic, and ignored nearly all of the complex issues that the lower courts had discussed, such as individual autonomy and the lack of distinction between suffering patients on life support and those who were not. Rehnquist was consistent though, and the opinion is characteristic of his opposition to the creation of new rights and the desire to leave as much authority in the states as possible.

The fact that a majority of the Court filed concurrences is somewhat unusual, and a close reading indicates that while these five justices might be prepared to accept the results at this time, each indicated that should the states make end-of-life choices too narrow, they would be prepared to revisit the matter. The most elegant and sophisticated of the opinions is that of Justice Souter, who not only indicated his awareness of the human suffering involved, but went into an extended discussion of how new liberty interests may develop under the due process clause. Souter's judicial hero was the second Justice Harlan, and Souter quoted extensively from Harlan's dissent in *Poe v. Ullman* (1961), the predecessor case to *Griswold v. Connecticut* (1965). In *Poe*, Justice Harlan laid the basis for a right to privacy grounded in due process rather than in the penumbras and emanations of the Bill of Rights relied upon by Justice Douglas. Taking a similar reasoning, Souter showed how one might reach the conclusion that the right to die included a right to assisted suicide. Like the others, he preferred to wait and see what the states would do, a lesson he and the others had learned from *Roe v. Wade*. The state of Oregon had recently passed an initiative allowing physician-assisted suicide, and the Court would wait to see how this state's experiment fared. Like Rehnquist, Souter believed it would be best if the states could resolve the issue satisfactorily and in a way that promoted individual autonomy. If not, the Supreme Court had left the door open to revisit this issue.

One final area where we can see the legacy of the Warren Court on the issue of privacy is the nomination of Robert Bork to the Supreme Court. In June 1987, after the Court had handed down its last decisions of the term, Justice Lewis F. Powell Jr. stunned the nation by announcing his resignation from the bench after fifteen years of service. News of the resignation elicited widespread praise for Powell from both liberals and conservatives, who extolled his integrity and adherence to principle while at the same time remaining open to new ideas. He had been the "man in the middle," the leader of the Court's center bloc who was rarely on the minority side of a five-to-four decision. Given the growing tensions in the nation's political climate, many people urged President Ronald Reagan to appoint a moderate to replace Powell.

Although the White House went through the motions of issuing a list of people supposedly under consideration, in fact the president and his close aides had already chosen their man—Judge Robert Bork of the U.S. Court of Appeals for the District of Columbia. A former law professor at Yale and solicitor general in the Nixon administration, Bork hardly fit Reagan's description of him as a moderate conservative. In his academic writings, his circuit court opinions, and his speeches, Bork had denounced some of the most important decisions of both the Warren and Burger Courts. He questioned the wisdom of many of the civil rights decisions, declared that the Constitution did not embody any right to privacy, and condemned *Roe v. Wade*, the 1973 decision granting women the right to secure abortions.

Opposition to the nomination gathered quickly, and involved many civil rights and minority groups, the American Civil Liberties Union, labor organizations, and ad hoc committees created to prevent confirmation. Conservative groups, on the other hand, including many fundamentalist religious organizations, praised the president's selection. The conservative agenda, in their view, would never be complete until the Court had been converted away from liberalism through the appointment of people who shared their ideas on how the Constitution should be interpreted.

The Senate Judiciary Committee held lengthy hearings, with Bork appearing to defend and explain his views. To many observers, the attack on Bork by his critics did not do him half the harm that his own testimony did—the more he talked, the more he convinced people that he was in fact far to the right of what had been the mainstream in American constitutionalism for the previous half-century.

Discussing the landmark case of *Griswold v. Connecticut* (1965), which had established a constitutional right to privacy, Bork declared that privacy "was a free-floating right that was not derived in a principled fashion from constitutional materials." The nominee also criticized *Shelley v. Kraemer* (1948), which had outlawed state enforcement of racially restrictive covenants, as opening up too much private discriminatory action to possible constitutional litigation. In addition, he had condemned the antitrust laws as economic nonsense. Other scholars besides Bork had raised some of the same issues he did, but he had attacked not one but a great many of the major constitutional decisions expanding individual rights and liberties.

Politically, the Reagan administration appeared completely inept in its handling of the nomination. White House spokesmen called upon the Senate to ratify the appointment because the Constitution gives the nominating power to the president; they totally ignored the upper house's very important role of reviewing judicial selections and, on occasion, withholding their assent. The administration claimed that so long as the nominee met the basic criteria, the Senate had no right to look at anything else, and because the Senate had already approved Bork for the circuit court he had met the criteria for the bench and that should be the end of the inquiry. But as former senator Harry F. Byrd Jr. of Virginia, himself a conservative, noted: "[T]he Senate may look at anything it pleases to look at. That is the meaning of 'advice and consent.'"

The administration had counted heavily on Southern support for Bork, but that failed to materialize, thanks in large measure to Warren Court decisions. The Court's validation of the Voting Rights Act of 1965 made African Americans a major force in Southern politics. Many senators from below the Mason-Dixon line owed their seats to black support, and just about every civil rights organization opposed Bork. Like any politicians, these senators were not about to antagonize their constituents. In addition, numerous polls showed Southern businessmen and Southern women against the nomination. As one Richmond, Virginia, business leader put it, "We have finally got the segregation issue behind us, and black and white groups are working together to build up this city. If Bork goes on the Court, I am afraid it will open up all the old wounds." Bork's views on privacy—namely, that privacy did not enjoy any constitutional protection—upset many women, and not only those who supported abortion. Privacy is a cherished value in the South, and rightly or wrongly, Southern women—among the most conservative in the nation—believed that Bork on the Court would destroy that value.

Conclusion: The Warren Court's Legacy

Some Courts exert relatively little influence on the overall course of constitutional history; their decisions have little or no precedential value. One thinks of the Chase Court in the nineteenth century or the Vinson Court in the middle of the twentieth. The Warren Court, on the other hand, decided a number of important constitutional issues, and the rulings in those cases continue to influence the course of American constitutional law in the twenty-first century. Enter any course in constitutional history or law in college, graduate school, or law school, and one will study *Brown v. Board of Education, Cooper v. Aaron, Engel v. Vitale, Sherbert v. Verner, Gideon v. Wainwright, Griswold v. Connecticut, Miranda v. Arizona, Baker v. Carr, Reynolds v. Sims, Brandenburg v. Ohio, New York Times v. Sullivan,* and others decided between 1953 and 1969. Moreover, they provide the standard against which the decisions of subsequent Courts are measured. If presidents in the second half of the twentieth century had to labor in the shadow of Franklin Roosevelt, subsequent Courts have and will continue to function in the shadow of the Warren Court legacy.

Why have these cases proved so influential? First, they deal with big themes that are of great importance to modern society—racial equality, religious liberty, democracy, and freedom of expression. Some advocates of judicial restraint argue that courts should avoid these big issues, and leave their resolution to the elected representatives of the people. Yet, at least in the Warren era, one can make the case that without the activism of the Court, without its commitment to a living Constitution, these matters would not have been resolved, they would have festered and poisoned the body politic.

Does anyone really believe that left alone, Southern state legislatures would have willingly ended Jim Crow? Does anyone seriously think that state legislatures dominated by rural minorities would have voluntarily ended this system and given urban and suburban voters their right to equal representation? Should anyone forget that it is the legislatures, and not the courts, that have attempted to limit free speech, restrict the ability of the press to report on unpleasant facts, and impose religious practices on unwilling schoolchildren?

Second, in each and every one of these areas the Court "got it right." If one looks at *Brown* or *Gideon* or *Sullivan* or *Reynolds*, is it not clear that the answer given by the Warren Court in each and every one of these cases is the right one: People should not be discriminated against and segregated because of the color of their skin. People accused of crimes need a lawyer in the criminal justice system. Newspapers ought not to be afraid to publish the truth because of libel laws. Voters in cities ought to have their votes count the same as voters in the countryside. For all that the Warren Court rulings in these and other areas triggered wide-spread hostility, within a fairly short time the American people came to recognize the wisdom and the justice of those decisions.

Members of the Burger and Rehnquist Courts may have disagreed with some of the particulars, and especially in the areas of the rights of accused persons and the separation of church and state have carved out minor exceptions. These have been accepted not because people are hell-bent on overturning Warren Court decisions, but because they make sense. In some areas the Warren Court, trying to establish clear rules, went further than necessary, and the pendulum has swung back a little closer to the center.

One should also note that in some ways the Warren Court had the "easy" cases. By this I do not mean that it took no courage to decide *Brown* or *Reynolds*, but rather that once the question was framed—Should skin color determine caste? Should city residents be second-class voters?—then the answer was clear. The Burger and Rehnquist Courts built upon these basic truths, but in areas such as affirmative action and majority-minority districting, the answers were not as clear because the issues were so much more complex.

One other aspect of the Warren Court legacy needs mentioning, and that is the model it established for aspiring lawyers. The young men and women who graduated from law school starting in the sixties have seen the Warren Court as the embodiment of what justice under law means. They have also been taught by the very brightest products of American law schools in the 1950s and 1960s, mainly young men and a few women who went to Washington to clerk on the high Court and then went on to take teaching positions at the nation's top law schools. As a result, Warren Court activism, so despised by conservatives, is seen as the norm in most American law schools. The men and women clerks who came out of the Burger years had no similar unifying vision, and the presence of Black and Douglas, and Brennan and Marshall, led many of them to adopt the same world view of the law as their predecessors in the Warren years. Whether the clerks who come out of the Rehnquist Court will have a different view is difficult to tell, and even if they do, will they be able to inspire students with that view? The Rehnquist Court's emphasis on federalism is very important in terms of American constitutional structure, but it cannot compare in appeal to cases involving equality and justice.

That perhaps is one of the Warren Court's greatest legacies. It taught the American people that the law mattered, that justice could be secured in the courts rather than on the streets, and that as the nation develops, the rights embodied in the Constitution are capable of change and growth as well.

References

Emerson, Thomas. 1970. *The System of Freedom of Expression.* New York: Vintage.

Jones, Nathanial R. 1975. "An Anti-Black Strategy and the Supreme Court." *Journal of Law and Education* 4: 203.

Kalven, Harry. 1988. *A Worthy Tradition: Freedom of Speech in America.* New York: Harper & Row.

Wilkinson, J. Harvie, III. 1979. *From Brown to Bakke: The Supreme Court and School Integration.* New York: Oxford University Press.

Woodward, Bob, and Scott Armstrong. 1979. *The Brethren.* New York: Simon & Schuster.

PART TWO

Reference Materials

Key People,
Laws, and Events

Accommodationist

An accommodationist is one who believes that the First Amendment's establishment clause does not require a strict separation of church and state. The accommodationist view is that some contact between church and state is permissible so long as government does not prefer or endorse one religion over another. The Supreme Court said in *Everson v. Board of Education* (1947) that government must remain "neutral" toward religion. Neutrality does not prohibit all contact between church and state, but only those actions that might either aid or inhibit religion. The Warren Court's school prayer (*Engel v. Vitale* [1962]) and Bible-reading (*Abington School District v. Schempp* [1963]) decisions in the early 1960s were highly controversial. The Court was criticized in many quarters for the separationist position taken in those cases. Many felt that the Court was more adversarial than neutral toward religion. The year before Warren ended his tenure as chief justice, the Court decided *Board of Education v. Allen* (1968). *Allen* held that public school districts could loan textbooks to nonpublic school students as long as the books were suitable for use in public schools—that is, that the content of these books was wholly secular. The basis of *Allen* was the "child benefit" concept, which was introduced in *Everson*. Under the child benefit concept, government is prohibited only from providing direct aid to institutional religion. Government benefits that primarily aid individuals are permissible, even if the church is aided indirectly. In *Allen* and *Everson*, students were seen as the principal beneficiaries of the government aid. The number of cases involving aid to education became more frequent during the Burger and Rehnquist periods, and a majority of justices on both Courts typically opted for accommodation of government and religion.

Agricultural Adjustment Acts of 1933 and 1938 (AAA)

The first Agricultural Adjustment Act (1933) was part of Franklin D. Roosevelt's New Deal program and was enacted to deal with the problems of low farm prices and overproduction. The key principle was "parity," the notion that the market could be regulated so as to assure farmers the same purchasing power for their crops they had received in the base period of 1909–1914. Farmers would voluntarily agree to restrictions on production, and in return would receive price supports for the crops they grew within their allotments—the program created incentives for farmers to reduce or eliminate the planting of potentially surplus crops. The scheme was to be paid for by a tax on the first processor, such as the millers who ground wheat to flour. The Supreme Court struck down the act in *United States v. Butler* (1936). The Court acknowledged that Congress could subsidize farmers on the basis of its power to tax and spend, but concluded that the program unlawfully encroached on the sovereign powers of the states over agriculture.

Congress sought to address the defects identified by the Court in *Butler* by reenacting parts of the initial act in several statutes, but the key measure was the 1938 act. In the second act, Congress declared a national goal of an "ever-normal granary," by which surplus crops from bumper harvest years would be stored against the possible shortages in years of draught or failed harvests. Again there would be a voluntary cap on production, but the plan would be paid for out of general tax revenues rather than by a specific tax. The Supreme Court upheld this law in *Mulford v. Smith* (1939). From a constitutional standpoint, the principal difference between *Mulford* and *Butler* was the Court's recognition that agricultural production affected the national economy, and, thus, was subject to regulation through the interstate commerce power. This change in viewpoint, sometimes referred to as the constitutional "revolution" of 1939, governed the Court's rulings on federal power thereafter and was manifest in the decisionmaking of the Warren Court.

Blackmun, Harry Andrew (1908–1999)

Appointed associate justice by Richard Nixon in April 1970, Harry Blackmun replaced Abe Fortas and served from 1970 to 1994. Although considered a conservative when first appointed, Blackmun was more of a moderate, and by the time he resigned was counted as among the more liberal members of the court. Blackmun was raised in Minnesota and was, from grade school, a close friend of Warren Burger. Following graduation from Harvard Law School and a clerkship with a federal judge, Blackmun joined a large law firm in Minneapolis where he specialized in estate and tax law and civil litigation. In 1950 he became in-house counsel for the Mayo Clinic, a position he held until he was appointed to the U.S. Court of Appeals for the Eighth Circuit nine years later. His record on the Eighth Circuit was conservative and reflected a commitment to judicial self-restraint. It was expected when Blackmun joined the Court that he would mirror Burger's vote. Indeed, the two were referred to as the "Minnesota Twins" at the outset of his tenure. This expectation was generally met, but Blackmun began to distance himself from Burger and the other conservatives, at least on such issues religious establishment, equal protection, and abortion rights. It was on the abortion issue that Blackmun was most outspoken had perhaps his greatest impact. He wrote the Burger Court's opinion in the landmark *Roe v. Wade* (1973) ruling, and was an emphatic critic of attempts to diminish abortion rights until he left the Court in 1994.

Brandeis, Louis Dembitz (1856–1941)

Brandeis was a successful attorney and reformer during the Progressive Era. He introduced an innovation later called the "Brandeis brief" as he argued in support of a state law limiting the number of hours women could work in a day. The "brief" featured the socioeconomic justifications for such regulation. Brandeis was nominated to the Supreme Court in 1916 by Woodrow Wilson and confirmed by the Senate, notwithstanding concerns about his "radical" inclinations. During the 1920s he and Oliver Wendell Holmes Jr. opposed the conservatives on the Taft Court by arguing for a more speech-protective interpretation of the First Amendment and for judicial restraint in regard to economic regulation. Many of Brandeis's dissents on issues such as wiretapping, privacy, and speech were later embraced by the Warren Court. Brandeis was a strong advocate of judicial self-restraint. He believed that the judiciary should play a minimal role in policy making. Brandeis saw it as both unwise and undemocratic for appointed judges to substitute their policy preferences for those of elected legislators. A representative statement of his views on the limits of judicial power can be found in *Ashwander v. Tennessee Valley Authority* (1936).

Breyer, Stephen G. (1938–)

Appointed associate justice by William Clinton in 1994, Breyer is considered a liberal moderate on the Rehnquist Court. He graduated with honors from Harvard Law School in 1964, clerked for Associate Justice Arthur J. Goldberg, and spent two years with the Justice Department before joining the law faculty at Harvard. He returned to Washington three years later as a member of the staff of special Watergate prosecutor Archibald Cox, a faculty colleague at Harvard. Breyer rejoined the Harvard faculty in 1976, following two years as special counsel for the Senate Judiciary Committee. After briefly serving with the Senate Judiciary Committee a second time, Breyer was appointed to the U.S. Court of Appeals for the First Circuit in 1980 by President Jimmy Carter, where he served for fourteen years. Breyer's record since joining the Supreme Court is moderately liberal and reflects a general inclination to defer to federal legislative power. At the same time, he is willing carefully to scrutinize governmental actions that affect First Amendment rights or that may have discriminatory effects.

Burger, Warren Earl (1907–1995)

Warren Burger was chief justice of the United States from 1969 to 1986, when he resigned to head the Bicentennial Commission. A conservative by nature, Burger never had a well-articulated jurisprudence, and is generally considered a mediocre judge. Burger was the first Supreme Court nominee of President Richard Nixon. He was born, raised, and educated in St. Paul, Minnesota. He was active in Republican politics in Minnesota, and, among other things, managed Harold Stassen's attempts to secure the presidential nomination at the 1948 and 1952 Republican conventions. Burger shifted his support to Dwight Eisenhower at the 1952 convention, which was instrumental in Eisenhower securing the nomination. Burger joined the Eisenhower Justice Department and eventually headed the civil division. Burger was appointed to the U.S. Court of Appeals for the District of Columbia in 1955, where he remained until his elevation to the Supreme Court. Burger was a conservative justice by any measure, but the Court under Burger was not able to establish a consistently conservative record. Rather, the Burger Court appeared to some as "rudderless," and possessing no clear direction. His Court disappointed conservatives by not reversing the jurisprudence of the Warren Court; he presided over the "counterrevolution that wasn't." Indeed, a notable part of the Burger Court record is its recognition of a woman's right to abortion and expansion of the scope of the equal protection clause, among others.

Cardozo, Benjamin Nathan (1870–1938)

Cardozo gained national renown as chief judge of New York's Court of Appeals (the highest court in that state), and was widely considered the greatest common-law judge of the twentieth century. Appointed to the Supreme Court in 1932 to take Justice Holmes's place, he did not serve long enough to make as great a mark as he had in New York. But he did articulate the idea of incorporation, by which the various guarantees of the Bill of Rights might be applied to the states as well as the national government. One of the key debates during the Warren years involved the method by which incorporation should take place, and it used the "selective incorporation" approach fashioned by Cardozo in *Palko v. Connecticut* (1937). Cardozo was a liberal, but believed in judicial restraint, which led him to defer to legislative judgments in most instances. As a result, he typically voted in favor of Roosevelt's New Deal programs as enacted by Congress.

Civil Rights Act of 1964

The most comprehensive federal civil rights law since the Reconstruction period, the Civil Rights Act of 1964 contains a number of sections, including Title II, the public accommodations title, and Title VII, the job discrimination title. Title II prohibits discrimination in motels, hotels, restaurants, and other public halls and arenas. Title VII prohibits discrimination in the workplace and established the Equal Employment Opportunities Commission (EEOC) to enforce it. The 1964 law was enacted by Congress pursuant to its authority to regulate interstate commerce and all that affects it. The Warren Court unanimously upheld the constitutionality of this approach in *Heart of Atlanta Motel v. United States* and *Katzenbach v. McClung* (1964). Title VII has provided the basis for much litigation in recent years, including suits alleging sexual harassment or other discriminatory conduct that creates a hostile or abusive working environment. Other provisions of the act include Title III, which authorizes the Justice Department to take legal action to desegregate noneducational public facilities; Title IV, which targets school segregation; and Title VI, which authorizes the withholding of federal funds from any discriminatory state or local program. Title IX, which prohibits gender discrimination in any activity receiving federal funding, was added to the act by amendment in 1972.

Clear and Present Danger Test

First articulated by Oliver Wendell Holmes Jr. in *Schenck v. United States* (1919), the test held that government could regulate and even forbid speech if it posed a "clear and present danger" to social peace and security. Schenck was convicted of violating the Espionage Act of 1917 by obstructing the draft. The Court upheld Schenck's conviction, concluding that the right to free speech is a conditional right that must be assessed in a situational context. Each situation, said Holmes, must be examined to determine whether expression is "of such nature as to create a clear and present danger that will bring about the substantive evil which legislatures are empowered to prevent." The test was designed to allow government to restrict speech that creates substantial and immediate danger. The test is clearly influenced by context; Holmes himself allowed that under different circumstances—perhaps in peacetime Schenck's expression would not have created a clear and present danger. In the hands of the conservative majority of the 1920s, the test was used in a speech-restrictive manner, and Holmes, but especially Brandeis, called for it to be applied to protect speech. During the Warren years the Court gradually moved away from this test to a more speech-protective stance.

Common Law

Common law is law made by judges when deciding cases, as opposed to statutory law made by legislatures in enacting laws. Common law is a body of principles that come from court judgments when prevailing customs and usages of the community are used to decide disputes. Once a decision is made, its root principles are used as guides or referents in subsequent cases involving the same issues. Common law must yield to statutory law when the two are incompatible, although statutes are typically grounded on common law principles. The common law is one of the great legacies of Anglo-American law, allowing the courts to respond to new problems and situations in a flexible manner.

Congress of Racial Equality (CORE)

A civil rights organization founded in Chicago in 1942, CORE pioneered the "sit-in" demonstration in 1943. The sit-in became a major tool of civil rights activists in the 1960s. CORE embraced the tactic of nonviolent civil disobedience as its primary means of confronting racial segregation. During the 1950s, CORE sought to address job discrimination. It frequently picketed discriminatory businesses and occasionally used economic boycotts in selected cases. CORE was one of the sponsoring organizations of the Freedom Rides in the early 1960s. The rides were intended to protest segregation on interstate buses by having people sit in seats barred to black riders. CORE was also heavily engaged in drives to register minority voters.

Eisenhower, Dwight David (1890–1969)

A career army officer, Eisenhower won national and international fame as commander in chief of the Allied forces in Europe during World War II. He left the army in 1948 and became president of Columbia University. He was courted by both major political parties as a possible presidential candidate. He chose to pursue the Republican nomination and prevailed after a protracted struggle with Senator Robert Taft of Ohio. Elected president in 1952, he named several members of the Warren Court including Chief Justice Earl Warren. Eisenhower would later call the appointment of Warren "the biggest damn-fool mistake I ever made." He repeated the "mistake" of appointing a liberal activist to the Court three years later with his nomination of William Brennan. Eisenhower proved a weak supporter of civil rights and failed to use effectively his immense moral influence to back up the Court's demand that blacks be treated equally under the law. When pushed far enough, however, as he was in the Little Rock school desegregation situation, he sent in troops to secure compliance with the Warren Court's decision in *Cooper v. Aaron* (1958).

Fair Employment Practices Commission

In 1941 Franklin Roosevelt, in response to demands from African American groups, issued an executive order barring discrimination in the awarding of government contracts. This commission was set up to enforce the order by investigating alleged discriminatory practices, but it had little power other than moral suasion to do so, despite a 1943 executive order intended to strengthen it. Fair employment practice statutes were enacted in some states following the war, and they remained the principal means of dealing with job discrimination until Congress enacted the Civil Rights Act of 1964, which included a specific title aimed at discrimination in the workplace. The Warren Court's contact with the Fair Employment Practices Commission was limited, but its involvement with the EEOC was influenced by the earlier experiences of the Commission.

Ginsburg, Ruth Joan Bader (1933–)

Appointed associate justice by William Clinton in 1993, Ginsburg had won renown as the chief architect of the American Civil Liberties Union (ACLU) cases establishing equal protection rights for women in the 1970s. Ginsburg completed her law degree at Columbia and served as law clerk for a federal judge for two years following graduation. She joined the law faculty at Rutgers in 1963 and remained there for seventeen years. While at Rutgers, Ginsburg continued to practice and represented a number of women with gender discrimination claims of various kinds. In 1971 Ginsburg organized the Women's Rights Project for the ACLU and then served as the Project's director and general counsel. It was during this period that she earned her reputation as an unusually effective advocate on women's rights issues. President Jimmy Carter appointed Ginsburg to the U.S. Court of Appeals for the District of Columbia in 1980. Ginsburg is a moderate liberal, but her deference to legislative judgments and prior judicial decisions sometimes subordinates ideological preferences. She believes that constitutional protections must be given full effect, a view particularly evident in cases involving procedural due process and equal protection of the laws.

Holmes, Oliver Wendell, Jr. (1841–1935)

A well-known legal scholar and Massachusetts state court judge before his appointment to the Supreme Court in 1902, Holmes is best remembered for his pithy opinions and defense of individual liberties. He and Justice Louis Brandeis defended the notion of free speech in the 1920s, as well as demanded that judges not impose their views on legislative policy making. Educated at Harvard, Holmes was admitted to the bar in 1867 and began a successful practice in Boston. During this period, Holmes taught at Harvard and received international recognition with a volume entitled *Common Law*. The volume established his scholarly credentials, and he was offered a faculty position endowed by Brandeis at Harvard. Holmes accepted the position with the proviso that he would be free to accept a judicial appointment should that opportunity present itself. Less than a year later, he was appointed to the Massachusetts Supreme Court where he served for twenty-three years. Holmes was appointed by President Theodore Roosevelt to the U.S. Supreme Court in 1902. He served on the Court until 1932 when he retired at the age of ninety-one. He is commonly acknowledged as one of the two or three greatest justices in the Court's history. He was an ideological conservative, but he separated his personal political orientation from his judicial philosophy. Holmes was fully committed to democratic principles, which led him to defer to the judgments of elected legislatures. It was his strongly held view that elected representatives could make whatever policy decisions they felt their constituents would tolerate. If, however, government action interfered with a person's constitutional rights, judicial intervention was justified. He developed a standard known as the "clear and present danger" test to use in cases in which free speech interests were involved. Holmes thought all views must be exchanged in the "market place of ideas," and that the Court must be "eternally vigilant against attempts to check the expression of opinions we loathe unless they so imminently threaten the society" that judicial intervention is required (*Abrams v. United States* [1919], 630). The Warren Court's free speech jurisprudence was significantly influenced by Holmes's thinking.

House Committee on Un-American Activities (HUAC)

The U.S. House of Representatives created the HUAC in 1938 to look into suspected threats to the United States from the Axis powers. Instead, under the chairmanship of Martin Dies and his successors, it became a communist-hunting and red-baiting organization that smeared the reputations of many people and never uncovered any threats to the national security. Congress first investigated so-called un-American activities during World War I, but undertook a broader and more earnest inquiry into subversion during World War II. The committee of the early 1940s, known as the Dies Committee after its chairman, set the tone for the standing Committee on Un-American Activities created in 1945. The committee's tactics were often arbitrary and self-serving. Those accused of being communist sympathizers were afforded little or no opportunity to defend themselves, and the contempt power was used to leverage information from uncooperative witnesses. When witnesses invoked the privilege against self-incrimination, they were often labeled "Fifth Amendment communists." Chief Justice Warren acknowledged in *Watkins v. United States* (1957) that congressional committees may conduct investigations pertinent to a valid legislative objective, but HUAC investigations tended to "expose for the sake of exposure" (*Watkins* [1957], 199). HUAC was renamed the House Internal Security Committee in 1969 and its charge was narrowed to communism in the United States. The committee was abolished altogether in 1975.

Incorporation

The Bill of Rights originally applied only to the national government, while the Four-teenth Amendment applied to the states. The question is whether the due process clause of the Fourteenth Amendment applies or incorporates the original eight amendments and extends them to the states as well. The Court under Chief Justice Marshall rejected any connection between the Bill of Rights and the states in *Barron v. Baltimore* (1833). The Fourteenth Amendment was ratified thirty-five years after *Barron*, and the issue of incorporation was reconsidered. Several schools of thought emerged in what turned out to be a century-long debate. One view, for example, was that the Fourteenth Amendment totally incorporated the Bill of Rights, making all its provisions applicable at the state level. While some justices, such as Hugo Black, sub-scribed to this view, it never achieved the support of a majority of any Court. Instead, the Court adopted a "selective incorporation" approach in *Palko v. Connecticut* (1937) in which those Bill of Rights provisions that are "implicit in the concept of ordered liberty" are applied to the states.

Internal Security (McCarron) Act of 1950

A law enacted by Congress intended to prevent Communist subversion. The act, named after its principal sponsor, Senator Patrick McCarron of Nevada, created the Subversive Activities Control Board (SACB), which had the authority to require organizations deemed threats to American internal security to register with the gov-ernment and submit information about their membership and activities. The act made criminal any conduct that might further the establishment of a totalitarian govern-ment in the United States. The government had limited success in implementing the act, and in *Albertson v. Subversive Activities Control Board* (1965), the Warren Court unanimously held that the privilege against self-incrimination protected indi-vidual members of the Communist Party from compulsory registration. In 1968 Con-gress chose not to appropriate funds for SACB operations, and it ceased to function.

Judicial Activism

Judicial Activism is the belief that courts may involve themselves in contemporary social problems by deciding cases rather than waiting for the legislature to act. It also refers to the attitude of some judges that they may impose their own views of proper policy in reviewing legislative action. A judicial activist is less inclined to defer to the policy judgments of the elective branches of government. As a result, an activist is more likely to find more issues appropriate for judicial response, and more likely to conclude that legislative or executive actions exceed constitutional limits and invali-date those actions. Judicial activism does not necessarily coincide with a liberal policy orientation. The Hughes Court of the 1930s vetoed many New Deal initiatives in an effort to preserve conservative, laissez-faire economic doctrine. The Warren Court is generally regarded as an activist Court because it frequently intervened in cases where claims of unlawful governmental conduct were asserted. This was particularly likely in cases involving government attempts to regulate expression and political actions. The Warren Court's activism was also evident on the issue of legislative districting, among others.

Judicial Restraint

The philosophy put forth first by Louis Brandeis and Oliver Wendell Holmes and later championed in the Warren Court by Felix Frankfurter that judges should defer to the legislature in matters of policy making. Judicial restraint is a role perception that limits the exercise of judicial power because the elective or political branches are seen as the more appropriate places to resolve policy issues. The restraintist approach is urged, particularly for appointed judges, because it is consistent with democratic principles; the best deterrent for legislative excess is the electorate, not the courts. Louis Brandeis offered some operational guidelines for the self-restraint approach in *Ashwander v. Tennessee Valley Authority* (1936). Known as the Ashwander Rules, Brandeis counseled that appellate judges should not "anticipate" constitutional questions or formulate constitutional rules more broadly than necessary to address the precise facts of particular cases.

Kennedy, Anthony McLeod (1936–)

Appointed associate justice by Ronald Reagan in 1987, Kennedy is generally conservative but has occasionally aligned himself with the centrist bloc of the Rehnquist Court along with O'Connor and Souter. Kennedy took over his father's legal practice in Sacramento soon after his graduation from Harvard Law School and served on the faculty of the McGeorge School of Law at the University of the Pacific. During Reagan's tenure as governor of California, Kennedy provided counsel to several members of his administration. Reagan later recommended Kennedy to President Gerald Ford for nomination to the U.S. Court of Appeals for the Ninth Circuit. He was confirmed by the Senate in 1975. Twelve years later, President Reagan nominated Kennedy for the Supreme Court after an unsuccessful attempt to put Robert Bork on the Court. While his judicial record is conservative, Kennedy is not doctrinaire and is reluctant to draw bright doctrinal lines in his opinions. He prefers that states make policy decisions for themselves and often votes to limit federal power to clear the way for the exercise of power at the state level.

Legal Realism

The judicial philosophy developed at the Columbia and Yale Law Schools in the 1920s that held that all sorts of nonlegal issues impinged on judicial decision making, and that courts as well as the legal profession had to take these prejudices into mind is known as Legal Realism. Legal Realists believe that law is the product of social forces, as well as the behavior of those in the legal process. Realists reject abstract legal principles as the basis for judicial decisions. Rather, Legal Realists see judicial decisions as stemming from a judge's notion of what is "right." As a result, Realists favor an adaptive approach to interpretation of the Constitution and statutes. The realist view drove, at least in part, the judicial activism of the Warren Court. Among the Warren Court proponents of legal realism were Justices William O. Douglas and William J. Brennan.

Living Constitution

The belief that the Constitution needs to be interpreted in the light of contemporary conditions is often referred to as the "living Constitution" theory, as opposed to the notion of original intent, by which the document must be narrowly interpreted according to the intent of the Framers. Those subscribing to this view see the Constitution as evolving with its provisions adapted to the particular needs of particular times and contexts. Justice William Brennan was a strong proponent of the living Constitution viewpoint.

Marbury v. Madison (1803)

The case of *Marbury v. Madison* (1803) marked that first time that the Supreme Court declared an act of Congress (in this case a portion of the Judiciary Act of 1789) unconstitutional. That decision laid the basis for the Court's power to review and void both state and federal laws when, in its opinion, the laws violate the Constitution. It was Chief Justice John Marshall's view that the Constitution is the supreme law, with everything else subordinate to it. In order to protect the integrity of the Constitution as the supreme law of the land, it is the function of the Supreme Court to act as its "guardian" by striking down any statutory provisions that conflict with it.

McCarthyism

McCarthyism is the name given to the unfounded charges of disloyalty and smear tactics employed by Senator Joseph McCarthy of Wisconsin during the late 1940s and early 1950s. McCarthy earned a law degree from Marquette in 1935 and almost immediately was elected judge of a state trial court. He interrupted his judicial career to serve in the military during World War II. He returned to Wisconsin after the war to successfully challenge the three-term incumbent U.S. Senator Robert LaFollette Jr. During his first term, he lost a valued committee assignment for his abrasive conduct. Early in 1950 McCarthy made a speech in which he claimed that there were many communists in President Truman's State Department. The allegations, which played into troublesome events such as the fall of China to the communists and the Cold War tensions with the Soviet Union, garnered McCarthy all the media attention he sought. Following his reelection in 1952, he was named chair of the Senate Committee on Government Operations and its Investigations Subcommittee. From this position, McCarthy intensified his hunt for communists. In late 1953 he began a series of hearings on communist infiltration into the U.S. Army. The highly controversial Army-McCarthy hearings were televised nationally and revealed to the American public McCarthy's cruel and self-serving tactics. In December 1954, the Senate voted to censure McCarthy for dishonoring the Senate. He died in 1957 before he completed his second term in the Senate. The Warren Court did not review specific tactics used by Senator McCarthy, but attempted to counteract the hysteria he provoked with such decisions as *Pennsylvania v. Nelson* (1956), *Watkins v. United States* (1957), and *Yates v. United States* (1957).

National Association for the Advancement of Colored People (NAACP)

The National Association for the Advancement of Colored People (NAACP) is the nation's leading civil rights organization. The NAACP was founded in 1909 and was an outgrowth of the Niagara Movement, a more militant civil rights organization led by W. E. B. DuBois. The NAACP has chosen from the outset to pursue its objectives through litigation and lobbying rather than engaging in direct confrontation. Its Legal Defense Fund was responsible for challenges that led to a number of early Supreme Court rulings on civil rights issues. These included *Guinn v. United States* (1915), which struck down the use of the grandfather clause (exempting people from new regulations such as literacy tests or property requirements because ancestors were not so regulated), and *Smith v. Allwright* (1944), which invalidated the so-called "white primary" (racially exclusive primary elections conducted a political party) as unlawful interferences with the right to vote. The Fund also led the attack against the "separate but equal" doctrine that was first announced in *Plessy v. Ferguson* (1896) and litigated nearly all of the major civil rights cases during the Warren Court era including *Brown v. Board of Education* (1954).

New Deal

The New Deal was the reform program associated with Franklin Roosevelt's first two terms as president (1933–1941), in which the national government took the lead in attempting to solve numerous social and economic problems caused by the Great

Depression. The term "New Deal" was first used by Roosevelt when he accepted the Democratic Party's nomination for president in 1932. Following his inauguration in March 1933, Roosevelt called Congress into special session and began what became known as the Hundred Days, a period in which a large number of significant proposals were enacted into law. Among the measures included in the New Deal package were the Emergency Banking Act, the Agricultural Adjustment Act, the Federal Emergency Relief Act, and the National Industrial Recovery Act. Another period of intensive legislative activity took place in mid-1935, when Congress enacted a number of Roosevelt initiatives known as the Second New Deal. Among the proposals adopted during this period were the National Labor Relations Act and the Social Security Act. The New Deal proposals were based on a view of expansive federal power to regulate the national economy. After a great deal of conflict, the Supreme Court embraced the New Deal position on federal power beginning in 1937, and the Warren Court regularly reaffirmed this position. Similarly, the Warren Court saw the federal government as the primary guardian of individual rights.

Nixon, Richard Milhous (1913–1994)

Nixon had been Eisenhower's vice president from 1953 to 1961. He lost the race for the presidency to John Kennedy in the 1960 election, and then returned to political life by winning the 1968 and 1972 presidential elections. Nixon earned a law degree at Duke and practiced law in Whittier, California, until 1942 when he moved to Washington D.C. to work for the Office of Price Administration. Soon thereafter Nixon was commissioned an officer in the navy, where he served until 1946. Following the war, he returned to California to begin his political life. He won election to the U.S. House of Representatives in 1946 and to the Senate in 1950. He took full advantage of the Cold War and fears about communism by representing his political opponents as communist sympathizers. Nixon gained national notoriety as a member of the House Committee on Un-American Activities, which sought to expose subversives. He won the vice presidential nomination in 1952 and served two terms in that position before his failed presidential campaign in 1960. He lost in his 1962 bid to become governor of California, and spent the next several years writing and rebuilding his political base. Nixon was the Republican presidential nominee in 1968. During the campaign, Nixon attacked the Warren Court, suggesting that it was too liberal and too soft on criminals. He pledged to make appointments to the Court that would decide cases more favorable to the "peace forces" rather than the accused. Before the end of his first term, he was presented with the opportunity to replace four of the Warren Court justices including Warren himself. Nixon's nominees to the Court were Warren Burger, Harry Blackmun, Lewis Powell, and William Rehnquist. All four nominations occurred during a 30-month period in Nixon's first term (May 1969 and October 1971).

In June 1972 the Democratic National Committee headquarters at the Watergate complex in Washington was broken into by people associated with Nixon's reelection campaign. The illegal actions stemming from the break-in grew in number, and Nixon was eventually forced to resign the presidency in 1974.

O'Connor, Sandra Day (1930–)

Appointed associate justice by Ronald Reagan in 1981, Sandra Day O'Connor was the first woman named to the high Court. Although many believed her an arch conservative, O'Connor from the start tended to seek the middle and has been a leader of the centrist bloc during the Rehnquist years. O'Connor received her law degree from Stanford in 1950 and divided the next fifteen years between practicing law and raising her children. She resumed her legal career in 1965, when she was appointed assistant attorney general in Arizona. Four years later she was appointed to complete an unexpired state senate term. Elected to a full term the following year, she was elected majority leader of the Arizona Senate in 1972. She ended her legislative career in 1974 when she successfully sought a superior court judgeship. She was appointed to the Arizona Court of Appeals in 1979, the position she held when nominated to replace Justice Potter Stewart on the U.S. Supreme Court. O'Connor blended easily into the conservative majorities on the Burger and Rehnquist Courts. When she splits with the conservative bloc, it typically is on abortion or equal protection issues, particularly gender discrimination in the workplace. Even when she votes with the conservatives, she occasionally separates herself from its conclusions through more moderate concurring opinions, which she has done on establishment of religion issues, for example.

Original Intent

Original intent refers to the jurisprudential philosophy, pushed by conservatives in the 1980s, that the Constitution must be interpreted in a narrow manner that faithfully reflects the intentions of its drafters in 1787. Originalists contend that judges must carefully search history to determine what the Framers intended by the particular provisions they included in the Constitution. Originalists oppose the theory of a living Constitution, whose advocates believe the Constitution should be interpreted in the light of present conditions. The originalist approach is rationalized as a way to minimize or subordinate the influence of personal values when interpreting the Constitution. There were no originalists on the Warren Court, at least during the decade of the 1960s. Rather, there were several proponents, Justices Douglas and Brennan for example, of a "living constitution" theory. These justices believed the Constitution should be interpreted in the light of present conditions.

Powell, Lewis Franklin, Jr. (1907–1998)

Appointed associate justice by Richard Nixon in 1972, Lewis Powell served until his retirement in 1987. Powell became the "man in the middle" on the high Court. His was the centrist voice, and during his fifteen years on the bench he was rarely on the losing side of a five-to-four decision. Powell earned law degrees from both Washington and Lee and Harvard. He returned to Virginia in 1931, where he began a successful private practice with a prominent Richmond law firm. Powell was active with the American Bar Association, serving as its president in 1964–1965. He was also heavily involved in public education, serving as president of the Richmond Board of Education from 1952 to 1961 and the Virginia State Board of Education from 1961 to 1969. Though nominally a Democrat, Powell was highly regarded within the legal profession as conservative enough to satisfy Nixon's selection criteria. Powell believed in judicial restraint and favored legislative solutions for major policy issues. He also believed in a limited role for the federal judiciary. Though conservative, Powell did not pursue an ideological agenda. He favored a balancing approach to resolving cases and sought to do so on the narrowest basis possible.

Rehnquist, William Hubbs (1924–)

Appointed an associate justice by Richard Nixon in 1972, William Rehnquist was elevated by Ronald Reagan to chief justice in 1986. A clear conservative, Rehnquist has not been able to bend the Court as far as he wants in a number of key areas, including abortion and establishment clause issues. He graduated first in his class at Stanford Law School and served as law clerk for Justice Robert Jackson. He began a successful private practice in Phoenix, Arizona, while at the same time involving himself in Republican politics in the state. He played a substantial role in the presidential bid of Arizona Senator Barry Goldwater in 1964. The political contacts he made during that campaign led to his appointment to the Nixon Justice Department in 1969. Rehnquist was one of four justices appointed to the Court during Richard Nixon's first presidential term; Rehnquist was nominated on October 12, 1971. It was expected that the Court would quickly reverse the Warren Court's liberal activist rulings. While that did not occur, Rehnquist was the Burger Court's conservative anchor and chief spokesman. When Rehnquist was elevated to chief justice, he relinquished that role to Justice Antonin Scalia. He remains, however, a dependable conservative vote.

Roosevelt, Franklin Delano (1882–1945)

The only man elected four times to the White House (1933–1945), Roosevelt led the nation first through the Great Depression and then through World War II. His New Deal transformed the way people thought about government; instead of being a neutral distant party, government was now expected to involve itself in solving social and economic problems. Roosevelt took office at the time the country was mired in a deep economic depression, and he responded with a number of recovery measures known collectively as the New Deal. Roosevelt won reelection three times and had just begun his fourth term when he died. Roosevelt's initiatives permanently expanded the role the federal government and influenced the thinking of many of the liberal activist justices of the Warren Court. Most of these justices subscribed to the view that the federal government could extensively regulate the national economy on behalf of the public interest. Roosevelt also believed that government could facilitate the achievement of political and social equality, a view shared by many of the Warren Court justices.

Scalia, Antonin (1936–)

Appointed associate justice by Ronald Reagan in 1986, Scalia's has been the most consistently conservative voice on the Rehnquist Court. Scalia graduated magna cum laude from Harvard Law School. After six years of private practice, he joined the law faculty at the University of Virginia. In 1971 he became general counsel for the Office of Telecommunications Policy in the Nixon administration. Three years later, he became assistant attorney general for the Office of Legal Counsel. He returned to the academic world in 1977, where he remained until 1982 when he was appointed to the U.S. Court of Appeals for the District of Columbia. In 1986 President Ronald Reagan nominated him for the Supreme Court. Scalia is a judicial conservative, and is an advocate the of the "textualist" approach to judicial interpretation; he views the actual text of the Constitution (or a statute under review) as the only appropriate basis for making interpretations of law. Scalia is commonly regarded as the leader of the conservative bloc, a position he assumed when William Rehnquist became chief justice. Scalia is comfortable revisiting previous judicial decisions, but has yet to reverse some of the Warren Court's precedents with which he most strongly disagrees. Indeed, he has disappointed expectations that he along with Rehnquist would be able to forge a new conservative majority, because, like William O. Douglas, he seems more intent on advocating his own view rather than forging coalitions.

Smith Act (Alien Registration Act) of 1940

The pre–World War II scare over aliens prompted Congress to criminalize attempting to undermine the morale of the armed forces or advocating the overthrow of the government. The act was initially justified as a means of countering Nazis and Nazi sympathizers, but was subsequently used against communists in the 1940s and 1950s. The act required aliens living in the United States to register with the federal government. Any alien found to be associated with a subversive organization was subject to deportation. The Vinson Court upheld the Smith Act against First Amendment claims in *Dennis v. United States* (1951). Chief Justice Vinson said in *Dennis* that the government is obligated to act when it is "aware that a group aiming at its overthrow is attempting to indoctrinate its members and to commit them to a course whereby they will strike when the leaders feel the circumstances permit." An attempt to forcibly overthrow the government, even if doomed from the outset, is a "sufficient evil for Congress to prevent it." (Dennis [1951], 509–510).

Souter, David Hackett (1939–)

Named to the court by George Bush in 1990, Souter had trouble his first few terms adjusting to the court's procedures and workloads. Since then he has become a leader of the centrist bloc and has written a number of thoughtful and influential opinions. Souter graduated from Harvard Law School in 1966 and joined a prominent law firm in Concord, New Hampshire. He left private practice to join the staff of the New Hampshire attorney general soon thereafter. He became chief deputy attorney general in 1971 and attorney general five years later. In 1978 Souter was appointed to New Hampshire's superior court, and in 1983 he was elevated to the state supreme court. President George Bush appointed Souter to the U.S. Court of Appeals for the First Circuit in 1990, followed shortly thereafter with the Supreme Court nomination. Souter's record is generally conservative, especially on criminal rights issues. At the same time, Souter has distanced himself from the conservative bloc on issues involving the First Amendment, equal protection, and abortion rights. He is also less inclined to favor state sovereignty over federal power than the other conservative justices and is often aligned with Justices Stevens, Ginsburg, and Breyer, the moderate-liberal bloc of the Rehnquist Court.

State Action

"State action" refers to the jurisprudential notion that any activity in which the state is an actor, or by its laws causes certain actions to take place, makes the state liable to challenges under the Fourteenth Amendment's equal protection clause. The state action requirement limits the reach of the clause to situations in which discriminatory conduct occurs "under color of law." The state action requirement was first applied by the Court in the *Civil Rights Cases* (1883), which placed private acts outside the scope of the Fourteenth Amendment. The Court of the latter half of the twentieth century, particularly the Warren Court, looked more carefully for instances of private discrimination that might be furthered by state involvement. If such a connection could be established, even privately initiated discriminatory conduct falls within the reach of the Fourteenth Amendment.

Stevens, John Paul (1920–   )

Appointed associate justice by Gerald Ford in 1975, Stevens has for the most part pursued a centrist philosophy. He has not developed a particular area or theory that would make him a leader of the court. Stevens graduated at the top of his class at Northwestern University Law School and then served as law clerk to Justice Wiley Rutledge for almost two years. Stevens returned to Chicago in 1948 and joined a prestigious law firm, where he developed an expertise in antitrust law. While maintaining his private practice, Stevens served as a part-time faculty member of the law faculties at Northwestern and the University of Chicago. Stevens was appointed to the U.S. Court of Appeals for the Seventh Circuit by President Richard Nixon in 1970. He was elevated to the Supreme Court five years later. Stevens is a moderate and is one of the justices least inclined to pursue an ideological agenda. He attempts to avoid taking "bright line" positions, preferring instead to resolve issues on narrow, case-specific grounds. He seldom aligns himself with the Rehnquist Court's conservative bloc, especially on issues of federalism and civil liberties. Indeed, Stevens was often found voting with Justices Brennan and Marshall, two liberal-activist justices, before they left the Court in the early 1990s. Since then, Stevens is typically found as a member of the moderate minority of the Rehnquist Court.

Stone, Harlan Fiske (1872–1946)

Associate justice (1925–1941) and the chief justice of the U.S. Supreme Court (1941–1946), Stone was one of the liberal dissenters against the conservative bloc in the 1920s and 1930s. Stone completed his law degree at Columbia in 1898. While he was engaged in private practice in New York, he joined the faculty of Columbia Law School and later became its dean for thirteen years. Stone left Columbia in 1924 at the request of President Calvin Coolidge, with whom he had attended Amherst, to become attorney general. The following year, Coolidge nominated Stone for the Supreme Court. Although a Republican at the time he joined the Court, Stone joined Justices Brandeis and Cardozo in supporting most of the New Deal measures struck down by the Hughes Court in the 1930s. His greatest contribution to jurisprudence may have been his famous Footnote 4 in *United States v. Carolene Products Inc.* (1938), in which he suggested that while the courts should in general defer to the legislature in reviewing economic regulation, they should adopt a higher standard of scrutiny in cases involving individual rights or discreet minorities. This notion became the basis for the Warren Court's defense of equal protection of individual liberties.

Thomas, Clarence (1948–)

His nomination hearings marked by accusations of sexual harassment, Clarence Thomas narrowly won confirmation by a vote of fifty-two to forty-eight in the Senate in 1991. Since then he has been a twin vote to Scalia's, and is considered not only conservative but in some areas reactionary. Thomas was the second nominee of President George Bush. He graduated from Yale Law School in 1974 and joined the staff of Missouri attorney general John Danforth. In 1976 Danforth was elected to the U.S. Senate, and Thomas joined the Monsanto Chemical Company as a staff counsel. Thomas rejoined Danforth in 1979, becoming his legislative assistant. He was appointed assistant secretary for civil rights in the Department of Education soon after Ronald Reagan became president. Less than a year later, he was made director of the Equal Employment Opportunity Commission, a position he held for eight years. Bush appointed Thomas to the U.S. Court of Appeals for the District of Columbia in 1990, and nominated him as a replacement for Justice Thurgood Marshall on the Supreme Court a year later. Thomas subscribes to the same judicial philosophy as Justice Antonin Scalia, and the two vote together in more than 90 percent of the Court's cases. Thomas uses historical practice as the basis for interpreting the Constitution by looking at what was standard practice at the time the Constitution was written.

Thomas typically supports the exercise of state authority as against federal power, and his most outspoken opinions have come in cases in which federal power and equal protection considerations converge. He categorically rejects, for example, federal affirmative action initiatives, and the use of federal voting rights laws as the basis for so-called racial gerrymandering.

Truman, Harry S. (1884–1972)

At first derided as an "accidental president," Truman became one of the most respected presidents in the twentieth century. He succeeded to the office on the death of Franklin Roosevelt in April 1945, and won reelection in his own right in 1948. He helped to consolidate many of the gains of the New Deal, and also was the first president to forthrightly defend equal rights for African Americans. Truman was a product of the Pendergast political machine in Kansas City. After a period of time in local politics, Truman twice won election to the U.S. Senate from Missouri. When Franklin Roosevelt was nominated to run for a fourth term, his third-term vice president, Henry Wallace, was replaced by Truman. Less than three months after his inauguration as vice president, Truman succeeded to the presidency on the death of Roosevelt. He presided over the conclusion of World War II and established himself as an advocate of a strong United Nations. The Republicans took control of the U.S. House of Representatives in 1946 and limited Truman's capacity to pursue his Fair

Deal domestic agenda. He sought to contain the spread of communism through a foreign policy known as the Truman Doctrine. American involvement in the Korean War was ultimately his political undoing, and he announced in early 1952 that he would not seek reelection. Although he was a New Deal Democrat, Truman's nominees to the Supreme Court—Frederick Vinson, Harold Burton, Sherman Minton, and Tom Clark—did not share the liberal activist views frequently associated with the Warren Court. With the exception of *Brown v. Board of Education* (1954), Truman's nominees delayed the liberal activist bloc of the Warren Court from becoming a numerical majority and delivering some of its most important rulings.

Vinson, Frederick Moore (1890–1953)

Chief justice from 1946 to 1953, Vinson proved an ineffectual leader of the Court. He was a conservative whose First Amendment opinions are quite speech restrictive. Although initially it was believed that he opposed civil rights, in fact he was moving the Court in the direction that culminated in the 1954 decision in *Brown v. Board of Education*. Vinson served six terms in Congress and was a key supporter of New Deal legislation. In 1937 Roosevelt nominated him for the U.S. Court of Appeals for the District of Columbia. He resigned the judgeship in 1943 to become Roosevelt's director of economic stabilization and later Truman's treasury secretary. Vinson came to the Supreme Court as something of a compromise nominee. President Truman needed to fill the vacancy created by the death of Chief Justice Harlan Stone, but the Court was badly divided and two possible chief justices, Hugo Black and Robert Jackson were engaged in a bitter feud. Truman selected Vinson because, under the circumstances, he could choose neither Black nor Jackson. Truman hoped that Vinson could unify the badly divided Court, but he was unable to do so, and the Court remained divided throughout his seven-year tenure as chief justice. As an old New Dealer, he supported expansion of federal regulatory power, and he was inclined to subordinate individual rights claims to government authority. Vinson authored the Court's opinions in *Dennis v. United States* (1951) as the Court upheld Smith Act convictions of leaders of the Communist Party. At the same time, Vinson wrote for a unanimous Court in *Sweatt v. Painter* (1950), forcefully indicating that the Texas law school for minority students was not comparable to the law school for white students. *Sweatt v. Painter* was the beginning of the end for the "separate but equal" doctrine in race relations.

Voting Rights Act of 1965

A federal law first enacted in 1965 (and renewed in 1970, 1975, and 1982), the Voting Rights Act was an effort to eliminate discriminatory voting practices. The act as reenacted is the most comprehensive federal voting rights law. It authorized the federal government to register voters in counties where less than half of voting age persons were already registered voters. The act also prohibited the use of literacy tests, accumulated poll taxes, and other practices that had been used as ways of furthering discriminatory objectives. The Warren Court upheld the Act in *South Carolina v. Katzenbach* (1966). The 1970 extension of the act attempted to lower the national voting age to eighteen, but the Supreme Court ruled in *Oregon v. Mitchell* (1970) that Congress could not lower the voting age for state and local elections. The Twenty-Sixth Amendment was ratified in 1971 to lower the voting age for all elections.

Chronology

1952

November — Dwight D. Eisenhower elected president

1953

April — Eisenhower issues Executive Order 10450 establishing loyalty and security program for federal employees

June — School desegregation cases set for reargument in fall

Ethel and Julius Rosenberg executed as spies

July — Korean War ends with cease-fire

CIA-led coup in Iran puts Reza Shah Pahlevi on throne

September — Chief Justice Fred Vinson dies of heart attack

October — Eisenhower nominates Earl Warren as chief justice

December — Playboy commences publication

1954

March — Hydrogen bomb tests on Bikini atoll

Edward R. Murrow's "See It Now" begins exposé of McCarthy

April — Army-McCarthy hearings

May — *Brown v. Board of Education*

Bolling v. Sharpe

French forces fall at Dienbenphu

Geneva accords on Vietnam

June — CIA-led coup in Guatemala

September — SEATO formed

December — Senate condemns Joseph McCarthy

1955

March — John Marshall Harlan replaces Robert Jackson

April — Salk polio vaccine announced

1955 cont.

May	*Brown v. Board of Education II*
July	Geneva summit between Eisenhower and Krushchev
December	Montgomery, Alabama, bus boycott

1956

February	Nikita Krushchev denounces Stalin
	Authorine Lucy turned away from University of Alabama
	Butler v. Michigan
March	Southern Manifesto against desegregation
April	*Pennsylvania v. Nelson*
June	Interstate Highway Act
October	William J. Brennan replaces Sherman Minton
	Suez Crisis
November	Hungarian revolt put down by Soviet Union
	Eisenhower reelected to second term
December	Montgomery, Alabama, boycott ends with black victory

1957

March	Charles Whittaker replaces Stanley Reed
June	*Watkins v. United States*
	Roth v. United States
	Sweezy v. New Hampshire
	Yates v. United States
September	First Civil Rights Act since Reconstruction
	Arkansas National Guard blocks Little Rock, Arkansas, desegregation; Eisenhower sends federal troops to Little Rock
October	Soviet Union launches satellite "Sputnik"

1958

June	*NAACP v. Alabama*
September	*Cooper v. Aaron*
October	Potter Stewart replaces Harold Burton

1959

June	*Kingsley International Pictures Corp. v. Board of Regents*
September	Prince Edward County, Virginia, closes schools
October	TV quiz shows scandal

1960

February	First "sit-in" in Greensboro, North Carolina
May	Francis Gary Powers shot down in U-2 spy plane over Russia
	FDA approves Enovid, first birth control pill
October	First televised presidential debates between Kennedy and Nixon
November	John F. Kennedy elected president
	Gomillion v. Lightfoot

1961

April	Yuri Gagarin orbits the earth
	Bay of Pigs invasion of Cuba fails
May	Freedom Rides begin
	McGowan v. Maryland
	Braunfeld v. Brown
June	*Communist Party v. Subversive Activities Control Board*
	Noto v. United States
	Poe v. Ullman
	Mapp v. Ohio
	Scales v. United States
August	Berlin Wall erected
November	*Hoyt v. Florida*

1962

February	John Glenn orbits earth
March	*Baker v. Carr*
April	Byron White replaces Charles Whittaker
June	*Engel v. Vitale*
September	Antidesegregation riots at Ole Miss
October	Arthur Goldberg replaces Felix Frankfurter
	Vatican II convenes
	Cuban missile crisis

1963

January	Kennedy proposes first Keynesian tax cuts
March	*Gideon v. Wainwright*
	Douglas v. California
	Gray v. Sanders
	Fay v. Noia
	Gibson v. Florida Legislative Investigating Committee
	Peace Corps established

1963 *cont.*

April	Good Friday march in Birmingham, Alabama
June	Medgar Evars assassinated in Mississippi
	Abingdon School District v. Schempp
	Sherbert v. Verner
	Goss v. Board of Education
August	March on Washington
	Peter, Paul & Mary's "Blowin' in the Wind" number one song
September	Church bombing kills four black children in Birmingham
	Atmospheric nuclear test ban treaty ratified
November	Ngo Dinh Diem killed in South Vietnam coup
	President Kennedy assassinated
	Lyndon Johnson becomes president

1964

January	Surgeon General warns against hazards of cigarette smoking
	Johnson declares war on poverty
	"Beatles" rock group arrives in United States
March	*New York Times v. Sullivan*
May	*Massiah v. United States*
	Griffin v. Prince Edward County School Board
	President Johnson calls for a "Great Society"
June	Freedom Summer starts
	Reynolds v. Sims
	Lucas v. Forty-fourth General Assembly of Colorado
	Malloy v. Hogan
	Jacobellis v. Ohio
	Bell v. Maryland
	Escobedo v. Illinois
	Aptheker v. Secretary of State
	Senate passes Civil Rights Act
	Goodman, Chaney, and Schwerner killed in Mississippi
July	Civil Rights Act signed into law
	Four days of rioting in Harlem
August	Gulf of Tonkin resolution
September	Warren Commission issues report on Kennedy assassination
October	Free Speech movement in Berkeley
	Nikita Krushchev deposed
November	Lyndon Johnson elected president
December	Berkeley administration building occupied by protesting students

Heart of Atlanta Motel v. United States
Katzenbach v. McClung

1965
January	*Cox v. Louisiana*
February	Malcolm X assassinated
	Operation "Rolling Thunder" in Vietnam
March	*United States v. Seeger*
	First official U.S. combat troops land in Vietnam
June	*Griswold v. Connecticut*
July	Medicare created
August	Voting Rights Act
	Six days of rioting in Watts
October	Abe Fortas replaces Arthur Goldberg
November	*Albertson v. Subversive Activities Control Board*

1966
January	Senate opens investigation into Vietnam war
February	*Brown v. Louisiana*
March	*South Carolina v. Katzenbach*
	Memoirs v. Massachusetts
	Ginzburg v. United States
	Mishkin v. New York
	Harper v. Virginia Board of Elections
June	*Miranda v. Arizona*
	Stokely Carmichael of SNCC calls for "Black Power"
November	Ronald Reagan elected governor of California
	Adderley v. Florida

1967
January	*Keyishian v. Board of Regents*
March	Martin Luther King leads his first antiwar march
May	*Redrup v. New York*
June	"Long Hot Summer" of urban rioting begins
	Six Days War in Middle East
	Loving v. Virginia
	United States v. Wade
July	Five days of rioting in Newark
	Four days of rioting in Detroit
	Federal troops sent to Detroit

1967 *cont.*

October	Thurgood Marshall replaces Tom Clarke
December	*Katz v. United States*

1968

January	Tet offensive
March	Lyndon Johnson announces he will not seek reelection
April	Martin Luther King Jr. assassinated
	Students take over Columbia University
	Ginsberg v. New York
	Duncan v. Louisiana
June	Robert Kennedy assassinated
	Terry v. Ohio
	Flast v. Cohen
	Board of Education v. Allen
	Earl Warren announces retirement
	Johnson nominates Abe Fortas to be chief justice, and Homer Thornberry as associate justice
July	Senate hearings on Fortas and Thornberry
August	Warsaw Pact troops invade Czechoslovakia
	Democratic National Convention in Chicago
October	Fortas withdraws as nominee for chief justice
November	Richard Nixon elected president
	Epperson v. Arkansas
December	Apollo 8 circles the moon

1969

January	U.S. troop strength in Vietnam reaches 542,000
April	*Stanley v. Georgia*
May	Abe Fortas resigns from court
June	*Brandenburg v. Ohio*
	Powell v. McCormack
	Chimel v. California
	Warren Burger replaces Earl Warren

Table of Cases

287

Benanti v. United States, 355 U.S. 96 (1957)

Berger v. New York, 388 U.S. 41 (1967)

Betts v. Brady, 316 U.S. 455 (1942)

Bigelow v. Virginia, 421 U.S. 809 (1975)

Bivens v. Six Unknown Named Federal Agents, 403 U.S. 388 (1971)

Board of Education of Oklahoma City v. Dowell, 498 U.S. 237 (1991)

Board of Education v. Allen, 392 U.S. 236 (1968)

Bob Jones University v. United States, 461 U.S. 574 (1983)

Bolling v. Sharpe, 347 U.S. 497 (1954)

Bowen v. Kendrick, 487 U.S. 589 (1988)

Boyd v. United States, 116 U.S. 616 (1886)

Bradfield v. Roberts, 175 U.S. 292 (1899)

Brandenburg v. Ohio, 395 U.S. 444 (1969)

Braunfeld v. Brown, 366 U.S. 599 (1961)

Brecht v. Abrahamson, 507 U.S. 619 (1993)

Brewer v. Williams, 430 U.S. 387 (1977)

Brown v. Board of Education, 337 U.S. 483 (1954)

Brown v. Board of Education II, 349 U.S. 294 (1955)

Brown v. Mississippi, 297 U.S. 278 (1936)

Buchanan v. Warley, 245 U.S. 600 (1917)

Buck v. Bell, 274 U.S. 200 (1927)

Butler v. Michigan, 352 U.S. 380 (1956)

California v. Ciraolo, 476 U.S. 207 (1986)

Camara v. Municipal Court, 387 U.S. 523 (1967)

Capitol Square Review Board v. Pinette, 515 U.S. 753 (1995)

Carey v. Population Services International, 431 U.S. 678 (1977)

Carter v. Carter Coal Co., 298 U.S. 238 (1936)

Chaplinsky v. New Hampshire, 315 U.S. 568 (1942)

Chimel v. California, 395 U.S. 752 (1969)

Church of the Lukumi Babalu Aye v. City of Hialeah, 508 U.S. 520 (1993)

City of Boerne v. Flores, 521 U.S. 507 (1997)

Civil Rights Cases, 109 U.S. 1 (1883)

Clay v. United States, 403 U.S. 698 (1971)

Cohen v. California, 403 U.S. 15 (1971)

Colgrove v. Green, 328 U.S. 549 (1946)

Committee for Public Education v. Nyquist, 413 U.S. 756 (1973)

Committee for Public Education and Religious Liberty v. Regan, 444 U.S. 646 (1980)

Communist Party v. Subversive Activities Control Board, 367 U.S. 1 (1961)

Cooper v. Aaron, 358 U.S. 1 (1958)

Giordenello v. United States, 357 U.S. 480 (1958)

Goldman v. United States, 316 U.S. 129 (1942)

Gomillion v. Lightfoot, 364 U.S. 339 (1960)

Goss v. Board of Education, 373 U.S. 683 (1963)

Grand Rapids School District v. Ball, 473 U.S. 373 (1985)

Gray v. Sanders, 372 U.S. 368 (1963)

Green v. County School Board, 391 U.S. 431 (1968)

Griffin v. Illinois, 351 U.S. 12 (1956)

Griffin v. Prince Edward County School Board, 377 U.S. 218 (1964)

Griggs v. Duke Power Co., 401 U.S. 424 (1971)

Griswold v. Connecticut, 381 U.S. 419 (1965)

Guinn v. United States, 238 U.S. 347 (1915)

H. L. v. Matheson, 450 U.S. 398 (1981)

Harper v. Virginia Board of Elections, 383 U.S. 663 (1966)

Harris v. New York, 401 U.S. 222 (1971)

Harris v. United States, 331 U.S. 145 (1947)

Heart of Atlanta Motel v. United States, 379 U.S. 241 (1964)

Hodgson v. Minnesota, 497 U.S. 417 (1990)

Hopwood v. Texas, 78 F.3d 932, cert. denied, 518 U.S. 1033 (1996)

Hoyt v. Florida, 368 U.S. 57 (1961)

Hunt v. McNair, 413 U.S. 734 (1972)

Hurtado v. California, 110 U.S. 516 (1884)

Hustler Magazine v. Falwell, 485 U.S. 46 (1988)

Illinois v. Gates, 452 U.S. 213 (1983)

J.E.B. v. Alabama ex rel. T.B., 511 U.S. 127 (1994)

Jacobellis v. Ohio, 378 U.S. 184 (1964)

Johnson v. United States, 333 U.S. 10 (1948)

Johnson v. Virginia, 373 U.S. 61 (1963)

Johnson v. Zerbst, 304 U.S. 458 (1938)

Katz v. United States, 389 U.S. 347 (1967)

Katzenbach v. McClung, 379 U.S. 294 (1964)

Keeney v. Tamayo-Reyes, 504 U.S. 1 (1992)

Keyes v. Denver School District No. 1, 413 U.S. 189 (1973)

Keyishian v. Board of Regents, 385 U.S. 589 (1967)

Kingsley International Pictures Corp. v. Regents, 360 U.S. 684 (1959)

Lamb's Chapel v. Center Moriches Union Free School Dist., 508 U.S. 384 (1993)

Lee v. Washington, 390 U.S. 333 (1968)

Lee v. Weisman, 505 U.S. 577 (1992)

Lemon v. Kurtzman, 403 U.S. 602 (1971)

Levitt v. Committee for Public Education and Religious Liberty, 413 U.S. 472 (1972)

Near v. Minnesota, 283 U.S. 697 (1931)

Nebraska Press Association v. Stuart, 427 U.S. 539 (1976)

New Jersey v. T.L.O., 469 U.S. 325 (1985)

New York v. Ferber, 458 U.S. 747 (1982)

New York v. Quarles, 467 U.S. 649 (1984)

New York Times Co. v. United States, 403 U.S. 713 (1971)

New York Times v. Sullivan, 376 U.S. 254 (1964)

Nix v. Williams, 467 U.S. 431 (1984)

Noto v. United States, 367 U.S. 290 (1961)

Ohio v. Akron Center for Reproductive Health, 497 U.S. 502 (1990)

Olmstead v. United States, 277 U.S. 438 (1928)

On Lee v. United States, 343 U.S. 747 (1952)

Oregon v. Haas, 420 U.S. 714 (1975)

Oregon v. Mitchell, 400 U.S. 112 (1970)

Pace v. Alabama, 106 U.S. 583 (1883)

Palko v. Connecticut, 302 U.S. 319 (1937)

Paris Adult Theatre I v. Slayton, 413 U.S. 49 (1973)

Payton v. New York, 445 U.S. 573 (1980)

Pennsylvania v. Nelson, 350 U.S. 497 (1956)

People v. Defore, 242 N.Y. 13 (1926)

Planned Parenthood of Missouri v. Danforth, 428 U.S. 52 (1976)

Planned Parenthood of Southeastern Pennsylvania v. Casey, 508 U.S. 833 (1992)

Plessy v. Ferguson, 163 U.S. 537 (1896)

Poe v. Ullman, 367 U.S. 497 (1961)

Pointer v. Texas, 380 U.S. 400 (1965)

Powell v. Alabama, 287 U.S. 45 (1932)

Powell v. McCormack, 395 U.S. 486 (1969)

Quinn v. United States, 349 U.S. 155 (1955)

R.A.V. v. City of St. Paul, 505 U.S. 377 (1992)

Redrup v. New York, 386 U.S. 767 (1967)

Reed v. Reed, 404 U.S. 71 (1971)

Regents of the University of California v. Bakke, 438 U.S. 265 (1978)

Regina v. Hicklin, L.R. 3 Q.B. 360 (1868)

Reno v. American Civil Liberties Union, 521 U.S. 844 (1997)

Reynolds v. Sims, 377 U.S. 533 (1964)

Reynolds v. United States, 98 U.S. 145 (1879)

Rhode Island v. Innes, 446 U.S. 291 (1980)

Richmond Newspapers, Inc. v. Virginia, 448 U.S. 555 (1980)

Richmond v. J.A. Croson Co., 488 U.S. 469 (1989)

Rochin v. California, 342 U.S. 165 (1952)

Times Film Corp. v. Chicago, 365 U.S. 43 (1961)

Tony and Susan Alamo Foundation v. Secretary of Labor, 471 U.S. 290 (1985)

Twining v. New Jersey, 211 U.S. 78 (1908)

United Automobile Workers v. Johnson Controls, 499 U.S. 187 (1991)

United States v. Butler, 297 U.S. 1 (1936)

United States v. Carolene Products Co., 304 U.S. 144 (1938)

United States v. Eichman, 496 U.S. 310 (1990)

United States v. Fordyce, 505 U.S. 717 (1992)

United States v. Harris, 403 U.S. 573 (1971)

United States v. Lee, 455 U.S. 252 (1982)

United States v. Leon, 468 U.S. 897 (1984)

United States v. Miller, 425 U.S. 435 (1975)

United States v. Reidel, 402 U.S. 351 (1971)

United States v. Seeger, 380 U.S. 163 (1965)

United States v. United States District Court, 407 U.S. 297 (1972)

United States v. Virginia, 518 U.S. 515 (1996)

United States v. Wade, 388 U.S. 218 (1967)

Uveges v. Pennsylvania, 335 U.S. 437 (1948)

Vacco v. Quill, 521 U.S. 793 (1997)

Valentine v. Chrestensen, 316 U.S. 52 (1942)

Virginia Pharmacy Board v. Virginia Consumer Council, 425 U.S. 748 (1976)

Virginia Railway v. System Federation No. 40, 300 U.S. 313 (1937)

Wainwright v. Sykes, 433 U.S. 72 (1977)

Wallace v. Jaffree, 472 U.S. 38 (1985)

Warden v. Hayden, 387 U.S. 294 (1967)

Ward's Cove Packing Co. v. Antonio, 490 U.S. 642 (1989)

Washington v. Davis, 426 U.S. 229 (1976)

Washington v. Glucksberg, 521 U.S. 702 (1997)

Watkins v. United States, 354 U.S. 178 (1957)

Webster v. Reproductive Health Services, 492 U.S. 490 (1989)

Weeks v. United States, 232 U.S. 383 (1914)

Welsh v. United States, 398 U.S. 333 (1970)

West Coast Hotel Co. v. Parrish, 300 U.S. 379 (1937)

West Virginia State Board of Education v. Barnette, 319 U.S. 624 (1943)

Whitney v. California, 274 U.S. 357 (1927)

Wickard v. Filburn, 317 U.S. 111 (1942)

Widmar v. Vincent, 454 U.S. 263 (1981)

Wilson v. Arkansas, 514 U.S. 927 (1995)

Wisconsin v. Mitchell, 508 U.S. 476 (1993)

Wisconsin v. Yoder, 406 U.S. 205 (1972)

Glossary

abortion   The medical termination of a pregnancy prior to term.

absolutism, First Amendment   The theory, advocated particularly by Justice Hugo L. Black but never fully accepted by the Court, that the rights of the First Amendment are absolutely protected from any governmental interference.

affirm   An appellate court ruling that upholds the judgment of a lower court, in effect holding that the judgment of the lower court is correct and should stand.

affirmative action   Programs under which minorities and women are given some degree of preference in job applications, university admissions, and other competitive contexts. While some affirmative action initiatives were sustained through the 1980s, Rehnquist Court rulings in the 1990s have made it very difficult for government to meet the required level of justification.

amicus curiae   Latin meaning "friend of the court." A person or group, not a party to a case, that submits a brief detailing its views on a case. The purpose of an *amicus* brief is to direct a court's attention to an issue or argument that might not be developed in the same way by the parties themselves.

antimiscegenation laws   Statutes common throughout the Southern states forbidding cohabitation or marriage between members of different races. The Warren Court declared in *Loving v. Virginia* (1967) that such laws violate the Equal Protection Clause.

appeal   A process by which a final judgment of a lower court ruling is reviewed by a higher court.

appellant   The party who seeks review of a lower court ruling before a higher court; the party dissatisfied with a lower court ruling who appeals the case to a superior court for review.

appellate jurisdiction   Authority of a superior court to review decisions of inferior courts. Appellate jurisdiction empowers a higher court to conduct such a review and affirm, modify, or reverse the lower court decision. Appellate jurisdiction is conveyed through constitutional or statutory mandate. Federal appellate jurisdiction is granted by Article III of the Constitution, which states that the Supreme Court possesses such jurisdiction "both as to law and fact, with such exceptions and under such regulations as the Congress shall make."

appellee   The party who prevails in a lower court and against whom an appeal of the judgment is sought; in some situations called a "respondent."

apportionment   The distribution of legislative representatives and the drawing of electoral district lines.

assembly, right to   A fundamental right provided by the First Amendment that the people are entitled to gather peaceably and petition the government for "redress of grievances." It includes the right to protest governmental policies as well as to advocate particular, even distasteful, views. The government can impose regulations on the time, place, and manner of assembly, provided that substantial interests, such as preventing threats to public order, can be shown.

assistance of counsel, right to   Sixth Amendment provision that assures that a person can utilize a lawyer in a criminal proceeding. The protection has been expanded to include that a state must provide legal counsel to indigent criminal defendants for all felony-level charges and those misdemeanor prosecutions that might result in detention.

association, right of   The right of a group of people to act together to advance a mutual interest or achieve a common objective. The right of association is not expressly protected by the First Amendment, but is derived the First Amendment protection of speech and assembly.

balancing test   A judicial decision-making approach whereby interests on one side of an issue are weighed or balanced against interests on another. This approach is used most frequently when courts are reviewing individual rights issues. An individual's free speech interests, for example, may be balanced against a societal interest in protecting national security to determine whether the latter interest prevails and the speech may be regulated. The test is based on the traditional idea that individual freedoms and governmental authority must be kept in equilibrium.

brief   A document containing arguments on a matter under consideration by a court. A brief submitted to a court by an attorney typically contains, among other things, points of law from previous rulings.

case or controversy   A constitutional requirement that disputes or controversies be definite and concrete, and involve parties whose legal interests are truly adverse. This requirement is contained in Article III of the U.S. Constitution, establishing a bona fide controversy as a precondition for adjudication by federal courts.

certification   A process by which judges in one court state uncertainty about the rule of law to apply in a case and request instructions from a higher court.

certiorari   Latin word meaning "to be informed of, to be made certain in regard to." A writ or order to a court whose decision is being challenged on appeal to send up the records of the case to enable a higher court to review the case. The writ of certiorari is the primary means by which the U.S. Supreme Court reviews cases from lower courts.

chilling effect   The notion that vague or overly broad laws may inhibit, or "chill," the exercise of protected expression because speakers will be unclear as to just what type of expression is illegal and hence will be afraid to speak for fear of punishment. Laws that entail this chilling effect are usually declared unconstitutional.

civil liberties   Those liberties spelled out in a bill of rights or a constitution that guarantee the protection of persons, opinions, and property from the arbitrary interference of government officials. Civil liberties create immunities from certain governmental actions that interfere with an individual's protected rights.

civil rights   Acts of government designed to further the achievement of political or social equality as well as protect persons against arbitrary and discriminatory treatment by government or individuals. Civil rights guarantees may be found in constitutions, but more frequently take the form of statutes such as the Civil Rights Act of 1964.

class action   A legal action in which one or more persons represent both themselves and others who are similarly situated with regard to the subject of the lawsuit. All members of a class must share a common legal interest and meet particular requirements in order to proceed as a class or collective action.

classification, suspect   The categorization of people by the state on the basis of race, color, or national origin. Using these categories to subject individuals to different treatment under the law is considered inherently "suspect" because it may be motivated by impermissible discrimination. Therefore, courts subject such laws to the high test of "strict scrutiny" to determine their constitutionality.

clear and present danger test   The First Amendment test by which courts allow speech to be regulated only if the speaker's words are likely, in a particular context, to incite lawless action.

commerce clause   Provision found in Article I, Section 8 of the U.S. Constitution. The Clause empowers Congress to "regulate commerce with foreign nations, and among the several states, and with the Indian tribes." Since the 1930s, the commerce power has been the basis for extensive federal regulation of the economy and, to a limited extent, federal criminal law. It also provided the basis for the Civil Rights Act of 1964.

common law   A body of principles deriving their authority from court judgments that are grounded in traditional customs and usages. Common law consists of principles that do not have their origin in statute and, as such, is distinct from law created by legislative enactments.

compelling interest test   The standard that the state must prove exists in order to justify laws that interfere with certain individual liberties. The compelling interest test typically comes into play when a governmental action impinges on a constitutionally protected right. The compelling interest test is also used in equal protection cases that involve a "suspect classification" such as race. Most claims of discrimination are resolved using a less demanding rational basis test which requires that the government only show that a policy reasonably pursues a legitimate as opposed to a compelling governmental interest.

compulsory process, right to   The Sixth Amendment right that a person accused of a crime can subpoena witnesses to appear in his or her favor.

concurring opinion   An opinion by a judge that agrees with the decision of the majority, but disagrees with the majority's rationale. In other words, a judge who presents a concurring opinion has arrived at the same conclusion as the court's majority, but for different reasons.

conference   The regular meeting in which Supreme Court justices conduct all business associated with deciding cases, including determining which cases will be reviewed, discussing the merits of cases after oral argument, and voting on which party in a case will prevail. Conferences are closed to all but the justices.

confrontation of adverse witnesses, right to   The Sixth Amendment entitlement that an accused person may confront adverse witnesses, most commonly through cross-examination of those witnesses.

cruel and unusual punishment, right against   The Eighth Amendment provision prohibiting the imposition of a penalty which is excessive to the crime or is incompatible with society's current standards of decency.

de facto   Latin for "in fact;" actual.

de jure   Latin for "by right." A de jure action occurs as a result of law or official government action.

decree   A judgment or order of a court.

defendant   The party who is sued in a civil action or charged in a criminal case; the party responding to a civil complaint. The defendant in a criminal case is the person formally accused of criminal conduct.

dissenting opinion   The opinion of a judge who disagrees with the result reached by the majority.

double jeopardy, right against   The Fifth Amendment provision that prohibits the government from successively subjecting a citizen to criminal prosecution for the same offense.

due process, procedural   The concept that the Constitution's due process clauses require government to follow fundamentally fair procedures when interfering with a person's life, liberty, or property. Such procedurally protected rights are enumerated, for example, in the Fourth, Fifth, and Sixth Amendments.

due process, substantive   The notion that due process also forbids laws that unreasonably interfere with a person's life, liberty, or property, as well as unenumerated rights.

Eighth Amendment   The Amendment is divided into two clauses. The first prohibits the requirement of "excessive bail" or the imposition or "excessive fines." The second bars the use of "cruel and unusual punishments."

en banc   French for "in the bench." A proceeding in which all the judges of an appellate court participate, as distinguished from a proceeding heard by a panel of three judges.

equity   A system of remedial justice administered by certain courts empowered to order remedies based on principles, and precedents developed by courts.

establishment of religion, right against   The Establishment Clause bars, at minimum, government initiatives that formally establish a official or state church. A more rigorous construction of the clause would prohibit those government actions that would advance or endorse religious doctrine in some manner.

ex parte   Latin for "only one side." Done for, on behalf of, or on the application of one party only.

excessive bail, right against   The Eighth Amendment protection against conditioning pre-trial release in criminal cases on bail amounts that are greater than what is reasonably expected to assure an accused's presence at trial.

excessive fines, right against   The Eighth Amendment protection against fines in criminal cases which are inordinately high in relation to the offense.

exclusionary rule   The court-made rule that evidence seized in violation of the Fourth Amendment may not be introduced at a trial.

executive order   A regulation issued by the president, a state governor, or some other executive authority for the purpose of giving effect to a constitutional or statutory provision. An executive order has the force of law and is one means by which the executive branch implements laws.

federal question   An issue arising out of provisions of the U.S. Constitution, federal statutes, or treaties. A federal court has authority to hear federal questions under powers conferred by Article III of the U.S. Constitution.

federalism   A political system in which a number of sovereign political units join together to form a larger political unit that has authority to act on behalf of the whole. A federal system, or federation, preserves the political integrity of all the entities comprised by the federation. Federal systems are regarded as "weak" if the central government has control over very few policy questions. A "strong" system is one in which the central government possesses authority over most significant policy issues. Authority that is not exclusively assigned may be shared by the two levels and exercised concurrently. The supremacy clause of the U.S. Constitution requires that conflicts arising from the exercise of federal and state power are resolved in favor of the central government. Powers not assigned to the national government are "reserved" for the states by the Tenth Amendment.

Fifteenth Amendment   A post–Civil War amendment ratified in 1870 that provides that citizens of the United States cannot be denied the right to vote "on account of race, color, or previous condition of servitude."

Fifth Amendment   The Fifth Amendment contains a number of somewhat diverse provisions. It mandates that no federal criminal defendant shall be accused of a serious crime except by action of a grand jury. It also contains provisions that bar the government from prosecuting an individual for the same crime twice and from compelling a person to provide incriminating evidence against him or herself. There is also language that provides that no person shall be "deprived or life, liberty, or property, without due process of law: nor shall private property be taken for public use, without just compensation."

First Amendment   The First Amendment is aimed generally at protecting religious and expressive rights. It provides that Congress shall "make no law respecting an establishment of religion, or prohibiting the free exercise thereof." The Amendment also prohibits the government from abridging the freedom of speech, assembly, press, and the petitioning of government for redress of grievances.

Fourth Amendment   The Fourth Amendment limits the government's power to search and seizure to only those occasions where such action is "reasonable." The Amendment conditions reasonableness on securing a warrant, which requires that before the government can search or seize, reliable evidence must exist in support of the any action taken by a governmental agent.

free exercise of religion, right to The First Amendment right to engage in religious exercise—to engage in actions in pursuit of religious beliefs.

free press, right to The First Amendment right that generally protects the press from governmental censorship or other regulation of press functions.

free speech, right to The First Amendment protection from unreasonable governmental interference with individual or group expression.

gerrymandering The drawing of election district lines in such a way as to favor one party or another, or to exclude particular groups of voters.

good faith exception An exception to the exclusionary rule arising when police seize evidence while acting in the reasonable belief that the search warrant they have is valid, even though later examination reveals that the warrant was in fact defective.

grand jury A panel of twelve to twenty-three citizens who review prosecutorial evidence to determine if there are sufficient grounds to formally accuse an individual of criminal conduct. The charges a grand jury issues are contained in a document called an indictment.

habeas corpus Latin for "you have the body." Habeas corpus was a procedure in English law designed to prevent the improper detention of prisoners. The habeas process forced jailers to bring a detained person before a judge who would examine the justification for his or her detention. If the court found the person was being improperly held, it could order the prisoner's release by issuing a writ of habeas corpus.

implied power Authority that is possessed by inference from expressed provisions of a constitution or statute. Implied power is not conveyed by explicit language, but rather by implication or necessary deduction from circumstances, general language, or the conduct of parties.

incorporation The extension of the protections of the first eight amendments of the U.S. Constitution to apply to the states as well as the federal government through the due process clause of the Fourteenth Amendment.

indictment A written accusation presented by a grand jury to a court, charging that a person has done some act or omission that by law is a punishable offense.

injunction An order prohibiting a party from acting in a particular way or requiring a specific action by a party. An injunction allows a court to minimize injury to a person or group until the matter can otherwise be resolved, or it may prevent injury altogether. Failure to comply with an injunction constitutes a contempt of court. Once issued, an injunction may be annulled or quashed. An injunction may be temporary or permanent. Temporary injunctions, known as interlocutory injunctions, are used to preserve a situation until the issue is resolved through normal processes of litigation. A permanent injunction may be issued upon completion of full legal proceedings.

judgment of the court   The final conclusion reached by a court—the outcome as distinguished from the legal reasoning supporting the conclusion.

judicial activism   An interventionist approach or role orientation for appellate decision making that has the appellate courts playing an affirmative policy role. Judicial activists are inclined to find more constitutional violations than those who see a more restrained role for courts; activists are more likely to invalidate legislative and executive policy initiatives. Judicial activism is seen by its critics as legislating by justices to achieve policy outcomes compatible with their own social priorities.

judicial review   The power of a court to examine the actions of the legislative and executive branches with the possibility that those actions could be declared unconstitutional. The power of judicial review was discussed extensively at the Constitutional Convention of 1787, but it was not included in the Constitution as an expressly delegated judicial function. The Supreme Court first asserted the power of judicial review in *Marbury v. Madison*, 5 U.S. 137 (1803).

judicial self-restraint   A role view of appellate court decision making that minimizes the extent to which judges apply their personal views to the legal judgments they render. Judicial self-restraint holds that courts should defer to the policy judgments made by the elected branches of government.

jurisdiction   Jurisdiction defines the boundaries within which a particular court may exercise judicial power; it defines the power of a court to hear and decide cases. The jurisdiction of federal courts is provided for in Article III of the Constitution in the case of the Supreme Court, and in acts of Congress in the case of the lower federal courts. Federal judicial power may extend to classes of cases defined in terms of substance and parties as well as to cases in law and equity stemming directly from the federal Constitution, federal statutes, treaties, or those cases falling into the admiralty and maritime category. Federal judicial power also extends to cases involving specified parties. Regardless of the substance of the case, federal jurisdiction includes actions in which the federal government itself is a party, or controversies between two or more states, between a state and a citizen of another state, between citizens of different states, between a state and an alien, between a citizen of a state and an alien, and when foreign ambassadors are involved. State constitutions and statutes define the jurisdiction of state courts.

jurisprudence   A legal philosophy or the science of law. A term used to refer to the course or direction of judicial rulings. Jurisprudence draws upon philosophical thought, historical and political analysis, sociological and behavioral evidence, and legal experience. It is grounded on the view that ideas about law evolve from critical thinking in a number of disciplines. Jurisprudence enables people to understand how law has ordered both social institutions and individual conduct.

jury, right to impartial jury   The Sixth Amendment right to have criminal charges heard by a group of impartial citizens.

justiciable   A matter is "justiciable" if it is appropriate for a court to hear and decide.

libel laws   Statutes that prevent people or news organizations from saying allegedly defamatory things about other individuals.

liberty of contract   A laissez-faire type doctrine used to free private agreements from governmental regulation. The liberty of contract concept holds that individuals have a right to assume contractual obligations affecting their personal affairs. This includes the right of employers and employees to agree about wages, hours, and conditions of work without government interference. The concept was a central element of substantive due process in which the courts closely examined the reasonableness of governmental regulations. The liberty of contract concept was used to strike down laws establishing minimum wages and maximum hours of work.

litigant   A party to a lawsuit.

living Constitution   The belief that the Constitution was intended to endure for the ages and thus can be adapted by courts to changing social and economic conditions, as well as altered perceptions of liberty and justice.

***Miranda* warnings**   The warnings police must give to suspects prior to in-custody questioning informing them of their right to remain silent, their right to an attorney, their right to have an attorney appointed and paid for at public expense if they have no money, and that anything they say can and may be used against them in court. The rule that these warnings must be given was first announced by the Supreme Court in the case of *Miranda v. Arizona* (1966).

mootness   A question presented in a lawsuit that cannot be answered by a court either because the issue has resolved itself or conditions have so changed that the court is unable to grant the requested relief.

motion   A request made to a court for a certain ruling or action.

Ninth Amendment   The amendment provides that the enumeration of rights in the Constitution should "not be construed to deny or disparage others retained by the people." Many contend that this language was intended to allow courts to identify and protect rights not enumerated in the Bill of Rights.

obiter dictum   Latin for "a remark by the way." *Dicta* are statements contained in a court's opinion that are incidental to the disposition of the case. Obiter dicta often are directed to issues upon which no formal arguments have been heard, thus the positions represented in dicta are not binding on later cases.

opinion of the court   The statement of a court that expresses the reasoning, or *ratio decidendi*, upon which a decision is based. The opinion summarizes the principles of law that apply in a given case and represents the views of the majority of a court's members. Occasionally, the opinion of a court may reflect the views of less than a majority of its members and is then called a plurality opinion.

oral argument   The arguments presented by counsel before the court, usually limited to thirty minutes a side before the Supreme Court.

original jurisdiction   The authority of a court to hear and decide a legal question before any other court. Original jurisdiction typically is vested with trial courts rather than appellate courts, although Article III of the Constitution extends very limited original jurisdiction to the United States Supreme Court. Trial courts are assigned specific original jurisdiction defined in terms of subject matter or parties.

penumbra doctrine   The theory that rights enumerated in the Constitution imply or suggest related rights that are in the shadow or "penumbra" of the listed right, and also are entitled to constitutional protection. For example, Justice William O. Douglas found a right to privacy in the "penumbras" of numerous rights specified in the Bill of Rights when he wrote the opinion in *Griswold v. Connecticut* (1965).

***per curiam* opinion**   Latin for "by the court." An unsigned written opinion issued by a court.

petitioner   A party seeking relief in court.

plaintiff   The party who brings a legal action to court for resolution or remedy.

plurality opinion   An opinion announcing a court's judgment and supporting reasoning in a case, but that is not endorsed by a majority of the justices hearing the case. Such an opinion arises when a majority of justices support the court's ruling in the case, but do not support the majority's reasoning behind it.

police power   Authority that empowers government to regulate private behavior in the interest of public health, safety, and general welfare. In the American constitutional system, police power resides with the state and not the federal government. The police power enables states and their respective local units of government to enact and enforce policies deemed appropriate to serve the public good. It is a comprehensive power, and substantial discretion is possessed by the states for its exercise. Police power is limited by various provisions of the U.S. Constitution and state constitutions, however, and must conform to the requirements of due process.

political question An issue that is not justiciable or that is not appropriate for judicial determination. A political question is one in which the substance of an issue is primarily political or involves a matter directed toward either the legislative or executive branch by constitutional language. The political question doctrine is sometimes invoked by the Supreme Court, not because the Court is without power or jurisdiction, but because the Court adjudges the question inappropriate for judicial response. In the Court's view, to intervene or respond would be to encroach upon the functions and prerogatives of one of the other two branches of government.

precedent The theory that decisions reached in earlier cases with similar fact patterns should determine the judgment in subsequent cases.

preferred position doctrine Holds that legislative enactments that affect First Amendment rights must be scrutinized more carefully than legislation that does not. The preferred position doctrine says that certain legislative activity deserves priority consideration because it affects fundamental rights such as free speech. The burden is clearly on the state to demonstrate justification for limiting a preferred position freedom. The preferred position doctrine is attributed to Justice Harlan Fiske Stone, who said in Footnote 4 to his opinion in *United States v. Carolene Products Co.*, 304 U.S. 144, (1938) that a lesser presumption of constitutionality exists when legislation "appears on its face to be within a specific prohibition such as those of those of the first ten amendments."

prior restraint A restriction placed on a publication before it can be published or circulated. Prior restraint typically occurs through a licensure or censorship process or by a full prohibition on publication. Censorship requirements involve a review of materials by the state for objectionable content. Prior restraint poses a greater threat to free expression than after-the-fact prosecution because government restrictions are imposed in a manner that precludes public scrutiny, and the First Amendment prohibits prior restraint in most instances. Prior restraint may be justified, however, if the publication threatens national security, incites overthrow of the government, is obscene, or interferes with the private rights of others, but is otherwise heavily suspect.

privacy The sense that individuals are entitled to have certain areas of their lives totally secure from governmental surveillance or interference.

public accommodation A hotel, restaurant, or other facility that caters to the public.

public forum An area normally considered a place where people have traditionally exercised their right of free speech, such as a street corner or park, and where government may only regulate the time, manner, and place of such speech.

public trial, right to   The Sixth Amendment requirement that criminal trials occur in public or in the "open."

remand   To send a case back to an inferior court for additional action. Appellate courts send cases back to lower courts with instructions to correct specified errors.

republicanism (guaranty clause)   Government by representatives chosen by the people. A republic is distinguished from a pure democracy in which the people make policy decisions themselves, rather than through an elected representative. Article IV, Section 4 of the Constitution provides that the national government shall guarantee to each state a "republican form of government."

respondent   The party against whom a legal action is filed.

reversal   An action by an appellate court setting aside or changing a decision of a lower court. The opposite of affirmation.

right   A power or privilege to which a person is entitled. A right is legally conveyed by a constitution, statutes, or common law. A right may be absolute, such as one's right to believe, or it may be conditional so that the acting out of one's beliefs will not injure other members of a political community.

search and seizure, right to reasonable   The Fourth Amendment requirement that no person may be arrested or any location be searched unless such action is "reasonable," that is, based on objective evidence that a person or location is related to a crime.

Second Amendment   The Amendment provides that because a "well regulated militia" is necessary to the security of a "free State," the right of the people to "keep and bear arms shall not be infringed."

segregation   The separation of people, usually on the basis of race, in public schools and accommodations.

self-incrimination, right against   The Fifth Amendment provides that the government cannot be compelled to disclose incriminating information against him or herself. This provision requires the state to demonstrate guilt without coerced assistance from the accused.

separation of powers   The principle of dividing the powers of government among several coordinate branches to prevent excessive concentration of power. The principle of separation of powers is designed to limit abusive exercise of governmental authority by partitioning power and then assigning that power to several locations. The distribution of powers embodied in the U.S. Constitution functionally distinguishes between government and people, and between legislative, executive, and judicial branches. While the Constitution creates three separate branches, it also assigns overlapping responsibilities that makes the branches interdependent through the operation of a system of checks and balances.

Seventh Amendment   The Amendment protects a civil litigant's access to a jury in federal courts. The Amendment also provides that judgments of civil juries are to be reviewed in federal courts according to existing principles of common law.

Sixth Amendment   The Amendment is generally intended to ensure fair criminal trials. The Amendment requires that criminal trials occur in a timely fashion and in public, that defendants have cases heard by a jury of impartial citizens and that trials occur in the district where the alleged offense was committed. In addition, the Sixth Amendment requires that the accused be informed of the charges against him or her, that the accused be able to confront (cross-examine) adverse witnesses, compel the appearance of witnesses in his or her favor, and be able to be represented by a lawyer during the proceedings.

sovereignty   The supreme power of a state or independent nation free from external interference. Sovereignty is exercised by government, which has exclusive and absolute jurisdiction within its geographical boundaries.

speedy trial   The Sixth Amendment right to have a trial occur without unreasonable delay following accusation or arrest.

standing   The requirement that a real dispute exist between the prospective parties in a lawsuit before it can be heard by a court. As a result, courts typically are unable to respond to hypothetical questions. If a party does not have standing to sue, the matter is not justiciable.

stare decisis   Latin for "let the decision stand." Stare decisis holds that once a principle of law is established for a particular fact situation, courts should adhere to that principle in similar cases in the future. The case in which the rule of law is established is called a precedent. Stare decisis creates and maintains stability and predictability in the law. Precedents may be modified or abandoned if circumstances require, but the expectation is that rules from previously adjudicated cases will prevail.

state action   An action taken by an agency or official of government. The state action concept is used to determine whether an action complained of has its source in state authority or policy. The concept is critically important in cases presenting allegations of discrimination. The equal protection clause typically cannot be applied to prevent private acts of discrimination. Rather, it requires conduct that occurs "under color" of governmental authority.

strict constructionism   The belief that the Constitution must be interpreted as written and that judges do not have the power to interfere with the Framers' intent by adjusting the meaning of the words to modern conditions.

summary judgment A decision by a trial court made without a full hearing or without receiving briefs or oral arguments. A summary judgment may be granted on motion to a party in a civil action when the accumulated evidence shows that there is no issue as to any underlying facts or as a matter of law. Summary judgments may be made in cases asserting equal protection or First Amendment violations, for example.

taxing power Article I, Section 8 of the U.S. Constitution permits Congress to "lay and collect taxes, duties, imposts and excises" and to provide for the "common defense and general welfare" of the United States. The scope of federal power to tax and spend has depended, at least in part, on the Court's interpretation of the "general welfare" phrase.

Tenth Amendment Provision added to the U.S. Constitution in 1791 that retains or "reserves" for the states powers not assigned to the federal government. The Tenth Amendment has frequently been used to limit the actions of the federal government.

Third Amendment A prohibition against the government forcing homeowners from housing soldiers during peacetime.

Thirteenth Amendment A post–Civil War amendment ratified in 1865 abolishing slavery or involuntary servitude.

vacate To void, rescind, annul, or render void.

vested right A right that so completely applies to a person that it cannot be impaired by the act of another person. Such rights must be recognized and protected by the government.

Selected Bibliography

Chapter 1

On the Struggle between Roosevelt and the Court

Ackerman, Bruce. 1998. *We the People: Transformations.* Cambridge: Harvard University Press.

Baker, Leonard. 1967. *Back to Back: The Duel between FDR and the Supreme Court.* New York: Macmillan.

Buhite, Russell, and David Levy. 1992. *FDR's Fireside Chats.* Norman: University of Oklahoma Press.

Corwin, Edward S. 1938. *Court over Constitution.* Princeton: Princeton University Press.

Cushman, Barry. 1998. *Rethinking the New Deal Court: The Structure of a Constitutional Revolution.* New York: Oxford University Press.

Irons, Peter. 1982. *The New Deal Lawyers.* Princeton, NJ: Princeton University Press.

Jackson, Robert H. 1941. *The Struggle for Judicial Supremacy.* New York: Knopf.

Leuchtenburg, William E. 1963. *Franklin D. Roosevelt and the New Deal.* New York: Harper & Row.

———. 1995. *The Supreme Court Reborn: The Constitutional Revolution in the Age of Roosevelt.* New York: Oxford University Press.

On the Changing Agenda of the Court

Currie, David P. 1990. *The Constitution in the Supreme Court: The Second Century, 1888–1986.* Chicago: University of Chicago Press.

Fine, Sidney. 1984. *Frank Murphy: The Washington Years.* Ann Arbor: University of Michigan Press.

Murphy, Paul L. 1972. *The Constitution in Crisis Times, 1918–1969.* New York: Harper & Row.

Newman, Roger K. 1994. *Hugo Black: A Biography.* New York: Pantheon.

Pritchett, C. Herman. 1948. *The Roosevelt Court: A Study in Judicial Politics and Values, 1937–1947.* New York: Macmillan.

Urofsky, Melvin I. 1991. *Felix Frankfurter: Judicial Restraint and Individual Liberties.* Boston, MA: Twayne.

———. 1997. *Division and Discord: The Supreme Court under Stone and Vinson, 1941–1953.* Columbia, SC: University of South Carolina Press.

Wiecek, William M. 1998. *The Lost World of Classical Legal Thought: Law and Ideology in America, 1886–1937.* New York: Oxford University Press.

On the Postwar Struggle for Civil Rights

Berman, William C. 1970. *The Politics of Civil Rights in the Truman Administration.* Columbus: Ohio State University Press.

Kluger, Richard. 1976. *Simple Justice.* New York: Knopf.

Lawson, Steven F. 1976. *Black Ballots: Voting Rights in the South, 1944–1969.* New York: Columbia University Press.

Lemann, Nicholas. 1991. *The Promised Land: The Great Black Migration and How It Changed America.* New York: Knopf.

Morris, Aldon. 1984. *The Origins of the Civil Rights Movement: Black Communities Organizing for Change.* New York: Free Press.

President's Commission on Civil Rights. 1947. *To Secure These Rights.* Washington, DC: Government Printing Office.

Tushnet, Mark V. 1987. *The NAACP's Legal Strategy against Segregated Education, 1925–1950.* Chapel Hill: University of North Carolina Press.

On the Cold War and the Red Scare

Belknap, Michal R. 1977. *Cold War Political Justice: The Smith Act, the Communist Party, and American Civil Liberties.* Westport, CT: Greenwood Press.

Caute, David. 1978. *The Great Fear: The Anti-Communist Purge under Truman and Eisenhower.* New York: Simon & Schuster.

Fried, Richard M. 1990. *Nightmare in Red: The McCarthy Era in Perspective.* New York: Oxford University Press.

Kutler, Stanley I. 1982. *The American Inquisition: Justice and Injustice in the Cold War.* New York: Hill & Wang.

Schrecker, Ellen. 1998. *Many Are the Crimes: McCarthyism in America.* Boston, MA: Little, Brown & Co.

On the Debate over Incorporation

Cortner, Richard C. 1981. *The Supreme Court and the Second Bill of Rights.* Madison: University of Wisconsin Press.

Hockett, Jeffrey D. 1996. *New Deal Justice: The Constitutional Jurisprudence of Hugo L. Black, Felix Frankfurter, and Robert H. Jackson.* Lanham, MD: Rowman & Littlefield.

Silverstein, Mark. 1984. *Constitutional Faiths: Felix Frankfurter, Hugo Black, and the Process of Judicial Decision Making.* Ithaca, NY: Cornell University Press.

Simon, James F. 1989. *The Antagonists: Hugo Black, Felix Frankfurter, and Civil Liberties in Modern America.* New York: Simon & Schuster.

Yarbrough, Tinsley E. 1988. *Mr. Justice Black and His Critics.* Durham, NC: Duke University Press.

Chapter 2

Hugo Lafayette Black

Dunne, Gerald T. 1971. *Hugo Black and the Judicial Revolution.* New York: Simon & Schuster.

Freyer, Tony. 1990. *Hugo L. Black and the Dilemma of American Liberalism.* Glencoe, MA: Scott Foresman/Little, Brown.

Magee, James J. 1980. *Mr. Justice Black: Absolutist on the Court.* Charlottesville: University of Virginia Press.

Newman, Roger K. 1994. *Hugo Black: A Biography.* New York: Pantheon.

Simon, James F. 1989. *The Antagonists: Hugo Black, Felix Frankfurter, and Civil Liberties in Modern America.* New York: Simon & Schuster.

Yarbrough, Tinsley E. 1988. *Mr. Justice Black and His Critics.* Durham, NC: Duke University Press.

William Joseph Brennan, Jr.

Clark, Hunter R. 1995. *Justice Brennan: The Great Conciliator.* New York: Carol Publishing Group.

Eiser, Kim Isaac. 1993. *A Justice for All: William J. Brennan, Jr., and the Decisions That Transformed America.* New York: Simon & Schuster.

Marion, David E. 1997. *The Jurisprudence of Justice William J. Brennan, Jr.: The Law and Politics of "Libertarian Dignity."* Lanham, MD: Rowman & Littlefield.

Michelman, Frank I. 1999. *Brennan and Democracy.* Princeton, NJ: Princeton University Press.

Rosenkranz, E. Joshua, and Bernard Schwartz, eds. 1997. *Reason and Passion: Justice Brennan's Enduring Legacy.* New York: Norton.

Harold Burton

Berry, Mary Frances. 1978. *Stability, Security, and Continuity: Mr. Justice Burton and Decision-Making in the Supreme Court, 1945–1958.* Westport, CT: Greenwood Press.

Thomas Campbell Clark

Beeman, Mary Purser. 1993. *New Deal Justice: Tom Clark and the Warren Court, 1953–1967.* Ann Arbor: University of Michigan Press.

William Orville Douglas

Ball, Howard. 1992. *Of Power and Right: Hugo Black, William O. Douglas, and America's Constitutional Revolution.* New York: Oxford University Press.

Douglas, William O. 1974. *Go East, Young Man.* New York: Random House.

———. 1981. *The Court Years: The Autobiography of William O. Douglas.* New York: Random House.

Simon, James F. 1980. *Independent Journey: The Life of William O. Douglas.* New York: Harper & Row.

Urofsky, Melvin I. 1991. "William O. Douglas as a Common Law Judge." *Duke Law Journal* 41: 133.

Wasby, Stephen L., ed. 1990. *"He Shall Not Pass This Way Again": The Legacy of Justice William O. Douglas.* Pittsburgh, PA: University of Pittsburgh Press, 1990.

White, G. Edward. 1988. "The Anti-Judge: William O. Douglas and the Ambiguities of Individuality." *Virginia Law Review* 74: 17.

Abe Fortas

Kalman, Laura. 1990. *Abe Fortas: A Biography.* New Haven, CT: Yale University Press.

Felix Frankfurter

Hirsch, Harry. 1981. *The Enigma of Felix Frankfurter.* New York: Basic Books.

Kurland, Philip B. 1971. *Mr. Justice Frankfurter and the Constitution.* Chicago: University of Chicago Press.

Parrish, Michael E. 1982. *Felix Frankfurter and His Time: The Reform Years.* New York: Free Press.

Silverstein, Mark. 1984. *Constitutional Faiths: Felix Frankfurter, Hugo Black, and the Process of Judicial Decision Making.* Ithaca, NY: Cornell University Press.

Urofsky, Melvin I. 1991. *Felix Frankfurter: Judicial Restraint and Individual Liberties.* Boston, MA: Twayne.

Arthur Joseph Goldberg

Stebenne, David. 1996. *Arthur J. Goldberg: New Deal Liberal.* New York: Oxford University Press.

John Marshall Harlan

Symposium. 1991. "John Marshall Harlan Centennial." *New York Law Review* 36: 1.

Yarbrough, Tinsley E. 1992. *John Marshall Harlan: Great Dissenter of the Warren Court.* New York: Oxford University Press.

Robert Houghwout Jackson

Gerhart, Eugene. 1958. *America's Advocate: Robert H. Jackson.* Indianapolis, IN: Bobbs-Merrill.

Hockett, Jeffrey D. 1996. *New Deal Justice: The Constitutional Jurisprudence of Hugo L. Black, Felix Frankfurter, and Robert H. Jackson.* Lanham, MD: Rowman & Littlefield.

Schubert, Glendon. 1969. *Dispassionate Justice: A Synthesis of the Judicial Opinions of Robert H. Jackson.* Indianapolis, IN: Bobbs-Merrill.

Thurgood Marshall

Tushnet, Mark V. 1997. *Making Constitutional Law: Thurgood Marshall and the Supreme Court, 1961–1991.* New York: Oxford University Press.

Williams, Juan. 1998. *Thurgood Marshall: American Revolutionary.* New York: Times Books.

Sherman Minton

Gugin, Linda C., and James E. St. Clair. 1997. *Sherman Minton: New Deal Senator, Cold War Justice.* Indianapolis: Indiana Historical Society.

Stanley Reed

Fassett, John D. 1994. *New Deal Justice: The Life of Stanley Reed of Kentucky.* New York: Vantage.

O'Brien, William. 1958. *Justice Reed and the First Amendment: The Religion Clauses.* Washington, DC: Georgetown University Press.

Potter Stewart

Binion, Gayle. 1979. "Justice Potter Stewart on Racial Equality: What It Means to Be a Moderate."*Hastings Constitutional Law Quarterly* 6: 853.

White, Ethel S. 1985. "The Protection of the Individual and the Free Exchange of Ideas: Justice Potter Stewart's Role in First and Fourth Amendment Cases." *University of Cincinnati Law Review* 54: 87.

Earl Warren

Cray, Ed. 1997. *Chief Justice: A Biography of Earl Warren.* New York: Simon & Schuster.

Schwartz, Bernard. 1983. *Super Chief: Earl Warren and His Supreme Court.* New York: New York University Press.

Warren, Earl. 1977. *The Memoirs of Earl Warren*. Garden City, NJ: Doubleday.

White, G. Edward. 1982. *Earl Warren: A Public Life*. New York: Oxford University Press.

Byron Raymond White

Hutchinson, Dennis J. 1998. *The Man Who Once Was Whizzer White: A Portrait of Justice Byron R. White*. New York: Free Press.

Charles Evans Whittaker

Berman, D. M. 1959. "Mr. Justice Whittaker: A Preliminary Appraisal." *Missouri Law Review* 24: 1.

Chapter 3

On the Warren Court in General

Bickel, Alexander M. 1965. *Politics and the Warren Court*. New York: Harper & Row.

——. 1978. *The Supreme Court and the Idea of Progress*. New Haven, CT: Yale University Press.

Cox, Archibald. 1968. *The Warren Court: Constitutional Decision as an Instrument of Reform*. Cambridge, MA: Harvard University Press.

Cray, Ed. 1997. *Chief Justice: A Biography of Earl Warren*. New York: Simon & Schuster.

Horwitz, Morton J. 1998. *The Warren Court and the Pursuit of Justice*. New York: Hill & Wang.

Lewis, Frederick P. 1999. *The Context of Judicial Activism: The Endurance of the Warren Court Legacy in a Conservative Age*. Lanham, MD: Rowman & Littlefield.

Powe, Lucas A., Jr. 2000. *The Warren Court and American Politics*. Cambridge, MA: Harvard University Press.

Schwartz, Bernard, ed. 1996. *The Warren Court: A Retrospective*. New York: Oxford University Press.

Tushnet, Mark V., ed. 1993. *The Warren Court in Historical and Political Perspective*. Charlottesville: University of Virginia Press.

Urofsky, Melvin I. 1991. *The Continuity of Change: The Supreme Court and Individual Liberties, 1953–1986*. Belmont, CA: Wadsworth.

On Equal Protection

Abraham, Henry J. 1994. *Freedom and the Court: Civil Rights and Liberties in the United States*. 6th ed. New York: Oxford University Press.

Bickel, Alexander M. 1955. "The Original Understanding and the Segregation Decision." *Harvard Law Review* 69: 1.

Branch, Taylor. 1988. *Parting the Waters: America in the King Years, 1954–1963.* New York: Simon & Schuster.

Cahn, Edmund. 1955. "Jurisprudence." *New York University Law Review* 30: 150.

Freyer, Tony. 1984. *The Little Rock Crisis.* Westport, CT: Greenwood Press.

Greenberg, Jack. 1994. *Crusaders in the Courts.* New York: Basic Books.

Kluger, Richard. 1976. *Simple Justice.* New York: Knopf.

Lawson, Steven F. 1976. *Black Ballots: Voting Rights in the South, 1944–1969.* New York: Columbia University Press.

Sitkoff, Harvard. 1993. *The Struggle for Black Equality, 1954–1992.* 2d ed. New York: Hill & Wang.

Tushnet, Mark V. 1984. *The NAACP's Legal Strategy against Segregated Education, 1925–1950.* Chapel Hill: University of North Carolina Press.

———. 1994. *Making Civil Rights Law: Thurgood Marshall and the Supreme Court, 1936–1961.* New York: Oxford University Press.

Tushnet, Mark V., and Katya Lezin. 1991. "What Really Happened in *Brown v. Board of Education.*" *Columbia Law Review* 91: 1867.

Weaver, John D. 1967. *Warren: The Man, the Court, the Era.* Boston, MA: Little, Brown.

Wechsler, Herbert. 1959. "Toward Neutral Principles of Constitutional Law." *Harvard Law Review* 73: 1.

Woodward, C. Vann. 1974. *The Strange Career of Jim Crow.* 3d ed. New York: Oxford University Press.

On Freedom of Speech and Press

Belknap, Michal R. 1977. *Cold War Political Justice: The Smith Act, the Communist Party, and American Civil Liberties.* Westport, CT: Greenwood Press.

Brennan, William J., Jr. 1965. "The Supreme Court and the Meiklejohn Interpretation of the First Amendment." *Harvard Law Review* 79: 1.

Chafee, Zechariah, Jr. 1941. *Free Speech in the United States.* Cambridge, MA: Harvard University Press.

Clor, Harry M. 1969. *Obscenity and Public Morality: Censorship in a Liberal Society.* Chicago: University of Chicago Press.

Frank, John P. 1961. *Marble Palace: The Supreme Court in American Life.* Westport, CT: Greenwood.

Fried, Richard M. 1990. *Nightmare in Red: The McCarthy Era in Perspective.* New York: Oxford University Press.

Kalven, Harry. 1988. *A Worthy Tradition: Freedom of Speech in America.* New York: Harper & Row.

Lewis, Anthony. 1991. *Make No Law: The Sullivan Case and the First Amendment.* New York: Random House.

Meiklejohn, Alexander. 1960. *Political Freedom: The Constitutional Powers of the People.* New York: Oxford University Press.

Murphy, Paul L. 1972. *The Constitution in Crisis Times, 1919–1969.* New York: Harper & Row.

Rabban, David M. 1983. "The Emergence of Modern First Amendment Doctrine." *University of Chicago Law Review* 50: 1205.

Schwartz, Bernard. 1992. *Freedom of the Press.* New York: Facts on File.

On Reapportionment

Cortner, Richard C., Jr. 1970. *The Apportionment Cases.* Knoxville: University of Tennessee Press.

Dixon, Robert G., Jr. 1968. *Democratic Representation: Reapportionment in Law and Politics.* New York: Oxford University Press.

McKay, Robert B. 1965. *Reapportionment: The Law and Politics of Equal Representation.* New York: The Twentieth Century Fund.

On the Religion Clauses

Laubach, John H. 1969. *School Prayers: Congress, the Court, and the Public.* Washington, DC: Public Affairs Press.

Levy, Leonard. 1994. *The Establishment Clause: Religion and the First Amendment.* 2d ed. Chapel Hill: University of North Carolina Press.

Morgan, Richard E. 1972. *The Supreme Court and Religion.* New York: Free Press.

Newman, Roger. 1994. *Hugo Black: A Biography.* New York: Pantheon.

Noonan, John T., Jr. 1998. *The Lustre of Our Country: The American Experience of Religious Freedom.* Berkeley: University of California Press.

Pfeffer, Leo. 1967. *Church, State, and Freedom.* Boston, MA: Beacon Press.

Sorauf, Frank J. 1976. *The Wall of Separation: The Constitutional Politics of Church and State.* Princeton, NJ: Princeton University Press.

On the Rights of Accused Persons

Baker, Liva. 1983. *Miranda, Crime, Law, and Order.* New York: Atheneum.

Becker, Theodore L., and Malcolm M. Feeley, eds. 1973. *The Impact of Supreme Court Decisions.* 2d ed. New York: Oxford University Press.

Blasi, Vincent, ed. 1983. *The Burger Court: The Constitutional Revolution That Wasn't.* New Haven, CT: Yale University Press.

Graham, Fred. 1970. *The Due Process Revolution: The Warren Court's Impact on Criminal Law.* New York: Hayden.

Howard, A. E. Dick, ed. 1965. *Criminal Justice in Our Time.* Charlottesville: University of Virginia Press.

Kamisar, Yale. 1980. *Police Interrogation and Confessions.* Ann Arbor: University of Michigan Press.

Leonard, A. V. 1975. *The Police, the Judiciary, and the Criminal.* 2d ed. Springfield, IL: Thomas.

Levy, Leonard W. 1968. *Origins of the Fifth Amendment.* New York: Oxford University Press.

Lewis, Anthony. 1964. *Gideon's Trumpet.* New York: Random House.

Stephens, Otis H. 1973. *The Supreme Court and Confessions of Guilt.* Knoxville: University of Tennessee Press.

On Privacy

Garrow, David J. 1994. *Liberty and Sexuality.* New York: Macmillan.

Story, Joseph. 1833. *Commentaries on the Constitution of the United States.* Durham, NC: Carolina Academic Press.

Westin, Alan F. 1967. *Privacy and Freedom.* New York: Atheneum.

On Adam Clayton Powell Jr.

Weeks, Kent M. 1971. *Adam Clayton Powell and the Supreme Court.* New York: Dunellen.

Chapter 4

On the Burger Court in General

Blasi, Vincent, ed. 1983. *The Burger Court: The Counter-Revolution That Wasn't.* New Haven, CT: Yale University Press.

Lamb, Charles M., and Stephen C. Halpern, eds. 1991. *The Burger Court: Political and Judicial Profiles.* Champaign: University of Illinois Press.

Schwartz, Bernard. 1990. *The Ascent of Pragmatism: The Burger Court in Action.* Reading, MA: Addison-Wesley.

Schwartz, Bernard, ed. 1998. *The Burger Court: Counter-Revolution or Confirmation?* New York: Oxford University Press.

Schwarz, Herman, ed. 1987. *The Burger Years: Rights and Wrongs in the Supreme Court, 1969–1986.* New York: Viking.

Urofsky, Melvin I. 1991. *The Continuity of Change: The Supreme Court and Individual Liberties, 1953–1986.* Belmont, CA: Wadsworth Press.

Woodward, Bob, and Scott Armstrong. 1979. *The Brethren.* New York: Simon & Schuster.

On the Rehnquist Court in General

Friedelbaum, Stanley H. 1994. *The Rehnquist Court: In Pursuit of Judicial Conservatism*. Westport, CT; Greenwood Press.

Irons, Peter. 1994. *Brennan vs. Rehnquist: The Battle for the Constitution*. New York: Knopf.

Savage, David G. 1992. *Turning Right: The Making of the Rehnquist Supreme Court*. New York: Wiley.

Simon, James F. 1995. *The Center Holds: The Power Struggle Inside the Rehnquist Court*. New York: Simon & Schuster.

Yarbrough, Tinsley E. 2000. *The Rehnquist Court and the Constitution*. New York: Oxford University Press.

The Burger Court and Equal Protection

Belz, Herman. 1991. *Equality Transformed: A Quarter-Century of Affirmative Action*. New Brunswick, NJ: Transformation Publishers.

Fiscus, Ronald J. 1992. *The Constitutional Logic of Affirmative Action*. Durham, NC: Duke University Press.

Jones, Nathanial R. 1975. "An Anti-Black Strategy and the Supreme Court." *Journal of Law and Education* 4: 203.

Karst, Kenneth L. 1989. *Belonging to America: Equal Citizenship and the Constitution*. New Haven, CT: Yale University Press.

Moreno, Paul D. 1997. *From Direct Action to Affirmative Action: Fair Employment Law and Policy in America, 1933–1972*. Baton Rouge: Louisiana State University Press.

Patterson, James T. 2000. *Race, Courts, and Schools: Ironies of* Brown v. Board of Education *since 1954*. New York: Oxford University Press.

Schwarz, Bernard. 1986. *Swann's Way: The School Busing Case and the Supreme Court*. New York: Oxford University Press.

Wilkinson, J. Harvie, III. 1979. *From Brown to Bakke: The Supreme Court and School Integration*. New York: Oxford University Press.

The Rehnquist Court and Equal Protection

Issacharoff, Samuel. 1995. "The Constitutional Contours of Race and Politics." *Supreme Court Review* 1995: 45.

Karlan, Pamela S. 1995. "Still Hazy after All These Years: Voting Rights in the Post-Shaw Era." *Cumberland Law Review* 26: 287.

Post, Robert, and Michael Rogin, eds. 1998. *Race and Representation: Affirmative Action*. New York: Zone Books.

Tucker, D. F. B. 1995. *The Rehnquist Court and Civil Rights*. Brookfield, NH: Dartmouth Publishing Co.

Urofsky, Melvin I. 1997. *A Conflict of Rights: The Supreme Court and Affirmative Action.* Lawrence: University Press of Kansas.

The Burger Court and Free Expression

Daniels, Stephen. 1980. "The Supreme Court and Obscenity: An Exercise in Empirical Constitutional Policy-Making." *San Diego Law Review* 17: 757.

Emerson, Thomas. 1970. *The System of Freedom of Expression.* New York: Vintage.

Henkin, Louis. 1971. "The Right to Know and the Duty to Withhold: The Case of the Pentagon Papers." *University of Pennsylvania Law Review* 120: 271.

Schauer, Frederick. 1982. *Free Speech: A Philosophical Enquiry.* New York: Cambridge University Press.

Strossen, Nadine. 1995. *Defending Pornography: Free Speech, Sex, and the Fight for Women's Rights.* New York: Scribner's.

The Rehnquist Court and Free Expression

Michelson, Frank I. 1990. "Saving Old Glory: On Constitutional Iconography." *Stanford Law Review* 42: 1337.

Smolla, Rodney A. 1988. *Jerry Falwell v. Larry Flint—The First Amendment on Trial.* New York: St. Martin's Press.

The Burger Court and the Religion Clauses

Bryson, Joseph E., and Samuel H. Houston. 1990. *The Supreme Court and Public Funds for Religious Schools: The Burger Years, 1969–1986.* Jefferson, MO: McFarland Press.

Levy, Leonard W. 1994. *The Establishment Clause: Religion and the First Amendment.* 2d ed. Chapel Hill: University of North Carolina Press.

Miller, William Lee. 1986. *The First Liberty: Religion and the American Republic.* New York: Knopf.

Pfeffer, Leo. 1984. *Religion, State, and the Burger Court.* Buffalo, NY: Prometheus Books.

Redlich, Norman. 1985. "The Separation of Church and State: The Burger Court's Tortuous Journey." *Notre Dame Law Review* 60: 1094.

The Rehnquist Court and the Religion Clauses

Davis, Derek. 1991. *Original Intent: Chief Justice Rehnquist and the Course of Church/State Relations.* Buffalo, NY: Prometheus Books.

Ivers, Gregg. 1991. *Lowering the Wall: Religion and the Supreme Court in the 1980s.* New York : Anti-Defamation League.

McConnell, Michael. 1990. "The Origins and Historical Understanding of Free Exercise of Religion." *Harvard Law Review* 103: 1409.

The Burger Court and Rights of the Accused

Levy, Leonard. 1974. *Against the Law: The Nixon Court and Criminal Justice.* New York: Harper & Row.

Saltzburg, Stephen A. 1980. "Foreword: The Flow and Ebb of Constitutional Criminal Procedure in the Warren and Burger Courts." *Georgetown Law Journal* 69: 488.

Symposium. 1984. "The Good Faith Exception to the Exclusionary Rule." *Whittier Law Review* 6: 979.

The Rehnquist Court and Rights of the Accused

Decker, John F. 1992. *Revolution to the Right: Criminal Procedure during the Burger-Rehnquist Era.* New York: Garland.

Kamisar, Yale. 1999. "Confessions, Search and Seizure, and the Rehnquist Court." *Tulsa Law Journal* 34: 465.

Smith, Christopher E. 1997. *The Rehnquist Court and Criminal Punishment.* New York: Garland.

On the Warren Court Legacy in General

Kalman, Laura. 1996. *The Strange Career of Legal Liberalism.* New Haven, CT: Yale University Press.

Lewis, Frederick P. 1999. *The Context of Judicial Activism: The Endurance of the Warren Court Legacy in a Conservative Age.* Lanham, MD: Rowman & Littlefield, 1999.

Internet Sources

New Internet sites are introduced frequently. Readers who use the sites listed below are encouraged to explore the countless number of links to other sites that are provided in virtually every site you visit.

There are a number of excellent sites with information about the U.S. Supreme Court, some of which are listed below. The full text of Court of decisions is available from some of these sites, but generally is limited to cases decided since approximately 1900.

Emory University School of Law (2 sites)

http://www.law.emory.edu/LAW/refdesk/toc.html

The electronic reference desk initial menu offers several useful categories of information including federal and state laws in the United States, and selected representation of laws from over seventy other countries. This site contains a reference option as well as sections on law by subject, law schools, legal periodicals, legal career information, and selected law firms.

http://www.law.emory.edu/FEDCTS

This U.S. federal courts finder site links the user to all federal appellate courts. Supreme Court links connects the user to the LII site. Excellent source for U.S. Court of Appeals decisions. Click any of the circuits on the U.S. maps to access rulings covering the last several years.

Federal Judicial Center

http://www.fjc.gov/

Home page for the Federal Judicial Center, the research and education agency of the federal judicial system. Contains links to other courts, including the new Supreme Court site, and the newly added link to the History of the Federal Judiciary site, which contains a biographical database of all federal judges since 1789, histories of the federal courts and other historical materials related to the federal judicial branch.

Federal Judiciary Homepage

http://www.uscourts.gov/

This page is maintained by the Administrative Office of the U.S. Courts and is a good source of information on the federal courts. The site contains a number of links to other valuable court/law-related sites. There is also a link that features recent developments regarding the federal courts, including the latest on the status of federal judicial vacancies.

Federal Legal Information Through Electronics (FLITE)

wysiwyg://14/http://www.fedworld.gov/supcourt/index.htm

Site contains the full text of about 7,500 U.S. Supreme Court decisions from 1937 to 1975. Cases can be retrieved by case name or keyword. Links are provided to other sites such as the Cornell University site.

Findlaw

http://www.findlaw.com/

Extraordinarily valuable and comprehensive site. Among other things, the site has federal and state cases and codes, U.S. and state resources, news and references, a legal subject index, links to bar associations, lawyers, and law firms. Decisions of the U.S. Supreme Court back to 1893 can be accessed, as can federal courts of appeals rulings.

Jurist: The Legal Education Network

http://jurist.law.pitt.edu/supremecourt.htm

Pittsburgh University Law School guide to the U.S. Supreme Court as an online introduction to the "jurisprudence, structure, history and Justices of America's highest court." Links the user to sites that contain Supreme Court decisions (e.g., Cornell, Findlaw), news about the Court, biographies of the justices, the Court's procedures, and the latest media coverage of the Court.

Legal Information Institute (LII)

http://www.law.cornell.edu/index.html

> Cornell Law School site containing Supreme Court decisions since 1990, U.S. and state constitutions and codes, law by source or jurisdiction (including international law), and "law about" pages providing summaries of various legal topics. The site has a "current awareness" page that contains news about the Court. LII provides a free e-mail service that distributes syllabi of Supreme Court decisions within hours of their release.

Lexis-Nexis Academic Universe

http://web.lexis-nexis.com/universe/

> Lexis-Nexis is a subscription database that covers a wide range of news, business, and reference information. Free access can be obtained to Lexis-Nexis through Academic Universe, which is available through most educational institutions.

National Center for State Courts

http://www.ncsc.dni.us

> A comprehensive site with extensive information on state courts, state judges, and state court caseloads. Links are provided for information about federal courts and international courts.

Oyez Project

http://oyez.nwu.edu/

> Northwestern University multimedia database that allows users to hear oral arguments from selected cases, obtain summaries of more than 1,000 Court opinions, biographical information on all the justices who have served on the Court, and a virtual-reality tour of the Supreme Court building.

Supreme Court

http://supremecourtus.gov/

> A newly accessible site that overviews the Supreme Court as an institution, its functions, traditions, procedures, court rules, docket, and calendar. Also, information is available on the justices and the Supreme Court building. "Plug in" capability is required to access information from this site.

Westlaw

http://westlaw.com/

> Westlaw is one of the largest and most comprehensive legal and business databases available on the Internet. Subscription is required for access, but prospective subscribers are able to fully explore the site on a "trial" basis.

Yahoo Law

http://dir.yahoo.com/Government/Law/

> Yahoo is a search engine with a separate and extensive listing of law-related sites. An easy-to-use and comprehensive searching device.

A number of newspapers provide good coverage of the U.S. Supreme Court. Among the best are the *New York Times* (http://www/nytimes.com) and the *Washington Post* (http://www.washpostco.com).

Index

Melvin I. Urofsky is director of the doctoral program in public policy and professor of history at the Virginia Commonwealth University in Richmond. He has written or edited more than 30 books, including *Division and Discord: The Supreme Court under Stone and Vinson, 1941–1953*.